DICKENS AND THE ART OF ANALOGY

DICKENS
and the Art of Analogy

by

H. M. DALESKI

SCHOCKEN BOOKS · NEW YORK

Published in U.S.A. in 1970
by Schocken Books Inc.
67 *Park Avenue*
New York, N.Y. 10016

Copyright © 1970 *by H. M. Daleski*
Library of Congress Catalog Card No. 75=122330

Printed in Great Britain

to

RUTH NEVO

'My wink, at all events, would have been nothing for any question between us, as I've just said, without yours. That's what I call your responsibility. It was, as we put the matter, the torch of your analogy——'

'Oh, the torch of my analogy! . . .'

'It was your making me, as I told you this morning, think over what you had said about Brissenden and his wife: it was *that*——'

'That made you think over'—I took him straight up—'what you yourself had said about our troubled lady? Yes, precisely. That *was* the torch of my analogy. What I showed you in the one case seemed to tell you what to look for in the other. . . .'

HENRY JAMES: The Sacred Fount

The most important thing in a work of art is that it should have a kind of focus, i.e., there should be some place where all the rays meet or from which they issue. And this focus must not be able to be completely explained in words. This indeed is one of the significant facts about a true work of art—that its content in its entirety can be expressed only by itself.

LEO TOLSTOY: Talks with Tolstoy

NOTE ON TEXTS

Page references to Dickens's novels are, with one exception, to *The New Oxford Illustrated Dickens* (London, 1948–58). References to *Oliver Twist* are to the Clarendon edition of the novel, ed. Kathleen Tillotson (Oxford, 1966).

CONTENTS

NOTE ON TEXTS   *page* 10

PREFACE   13

1. PICKWICK PAPERS   17

2. OLIVER TWIST   49

3. MARTIN CHUZZLEWIT   79

4. DOMBEY AND SON   116

5. BLEAK HOUSE   156

6. LITTLE DORRIT   191

7. GREAT EXPECTATIONS   237

8. OUR MUTUAL FRIEND   270

INDEX   337

PREFACE

In this study I have set out to trace Dickens's development as a novelist. Given the scope of a single volume of criticism, and wishing to attempt a detailed analysis of the works I discuss, I have reluctantly had to exclude a substantial number of Dickens's novels. In making my selection of texts I have been guided by two considerations. I have chosen to discuss novels which seemed to me to be representative of stages in Dickens's development and at the same time rewarding in their own right, thus trying to reconcile the need to establish a line of development with the desire to include a preponderance of good work. Accordingly I have chosen *Pickwick Papers* and *Oliver Twist* as representative of the period of Dickens's apprenticeship as a novelist; *Martin Chuzzlewit* and *Dombey and Son* as representative of his journeyman work, of the work, that is, of his early maturity in which he is not yet a master; and *Bleak House, Little Dorrit, Great Expectations* and *Our Mutual Friend* as representative of his work as a finished craftsman, these four novels constituting one of the supreme achievements in the English novel of the nineteenth century.

In analysing the novels chosen I have tried in each case to discover what Tolstoy calls the 'focus' of a work, the point from which 'all the rays' issue. In undertaking this kind of analysis in relation to the swarming multifariousness of the worlds Dickens creates in his novels, I have been greatly indebted to an observation of Steven Marcus, who (in *Dickens: from Pickwick to Dombey*) says that Dickens has an 'analogical imagination'. Taking a lead from Marcus, I have tried to show how our perception of the play of analogy in Dickens both directs us to the focus of a given work and makes manifest its structure. In

13

tracing Dickens's development, therefore, I have been concerned to demonstrate both the increasing complexity of the cluster of ideas that is at the thematic centre of the novels, and the increasing comprehensiveness of vision that results from his more and more skilful use of analogy as a structural principle.

What this study reveals, I believe, is the rich resourcefulness of Dickens's art. It also reveals the existence of a Dickens who has tended to disappear from sight amid the subtleties of much modern criticism. It discloses, that is, a traditional Dickens who is pre-eminently concerned with money and love.[1] Dickens's major theme from *Martin Chuzzlewit* onwards is the corrupting power of wealth, and this theme is constantly developed and amplified until its conclusive statement in *Our Mutual Friend*. At the same time, tentatively and uncertainly in the work before *Great Expectations* but with great imaginative force in that novel and in *Our Mutual Friend*, Dickens affirms the transforming and regenerative power of love, finally seeing in love the only ever-fixéd mark in a shifty commercial world.

I should like to record my indebtedness to the critics who are referred to in the text and notes of this book. I often refer to them by way of registering disagreement with their views, but I am strongly and gratefully aware of how much I owe to the stimulus of their work. I should like to make special mention of Edmund Wilson's justly famous essay, 'Dickens: The Two Scrooges', which is the source of so much of what one now takes for granted about Dickens; and also of Edgar Johnson's biography, *Charles Dickens: His Tragedy and Triumph*, which provides so fine a portrait of the man behind the artist.

I am also personally indebted to Professor A. A. Mendilow of the Hebrew University, who enabled me to work on the final chapters of this book by reducing my teaching load, and who made many helpful comments on Chapters 1 and 8; to Professor Ada Nisbet of the University of California, Los Angeles, who suggested numerous improvements in Sections I and II of Chapter 8; to members of a graduate seminar on Dickens at both the Hebrew University and Tel-Aviv University, whose challenges led me to a greater precision of formulation; to my wife, Aviva, who constantly pointed out lapses in style;

---

[1] It is heartening to find that two recent critics have also returned to a more straightforward view of Dickens. See Ross H. Dabney, *Love and Property in the Novels of Dickens* (London, 1967); and Grahame Smith, *Dickens, Money, and Society* (Berkeley and Los Angeles 1968).

Preface

and to Mrs. Bubbles Sachs, who efficiently prepared the typescript with unfailing good humour. But above all I am immeasurably indebted to Professor Ruth Nevo, the friend and colleague to whom this book is dedicated. She was good enough to read my work as it was being written, chapter by chapter, and the marks of her astute, penetrating criticism are evident to me throughout.

The Hebrew University   H.M.D.
Jerusalem

I

PICKWICK PAPERS

I

The story of how Dickens's first novel came to be commissioned is too well known to need repeating, but we cannot help being struck afresh by the debonair confidence with which he undertook the project: 'My views being deferred to, I thought of Mr. Pickwick, and wrote the first number . . .'[1] Whether he thought at the same time of subsequent numbers is another matter. Certainly the evidence which Kathleen Tillotson provides would seem to support her conclusion that he initially regarded *Pickwick Papers* as only 'one of several journalistic sidelines', and that he began the novel without a plan.[2] It seems reasonable to assume, therefore, that when he started writing he had projected nothing more specific than a series of comic misadventures in which Pickwick was to figure as a comic victim, and to be attended by his friends, the lover, the poet, and the sportsman.

The bedroom scene at the Great White Horse Inn at Ipswich is a representative instance of the kind of comic predicament in which Pickwick is placed. Going by mistake into the room of Miss Witherfield, he draws the bed-curtains 'on the outside' and is proceeding to undress when someone comes into the room. Peeping between the curtains, he 'almost [faints] with horror and dismay' when he sees that the intruder is 'a middle-aged lady, in yellow curl-papers', who is busy brushing her hair. The 'self-possession' of the lady makes it clear to him that it is he who has 'come into the wrong room'. Since he is 'one of the most modest and delicate-minded of mortals', he is appalled at

---

[1] Preface, p. xi.
[2] See John Butt and Kathleen Tillotson, *Dickens at Work* (London, 1957), pp. 65–6. The chapter on *Pickwick Papers* is by Kathleen Tillotson.

'the very idea of exhibiting his night-cap to a lady'; and, shrinking behind the curtains, he calls out loudly (pp. 308–9):

'Gracious Heaven!' said the middle-aged lady, 'what's that?'

'It's—it's—only a gentleman, Ma'am,' said Mr. Pickwick from behind the curtains.

'A gentleman!' said the lady with a terrific scream.

'It's all over!' thought Mr. Pickwick.

'A strange man!' shrieked the lady. Another instant and the house would be alarmed. Her garments rustled as she rushed towards the door.

'Ma'am,' said Mr. Pickwick, thrusting out his head, in the extremity of his desperation, 'Ma'am!'

... the sudden apparition of Mr. Pickwick's night-cap [drove the lady] back into the remotest corner of the apartment, where she stood staring wildly at Mr. Pickwick, while Mr. Pickwick in his turn stared wildly at her.

'Wretch,' said the lady, covering her eyes with her hands, 'what do you want here?'

'Nothing, Ma'am; nothing, whatever, Ma'am;' said Mr. Pickwick earnestly.

'Nothing!' said the lady, looking up.

'Nothing, Ma'am, upon my honour,' said Mr. Pickwick . . . 'I am almost ready to sink, Ma'am, beneath the confusion of addressing a lady in my night-cap . . . but I can't get it off, Ma'am . . . It is evident to me, Ma'am, now, that I have mistaken this bed-room for my own. I had not been here five minutes, Ma'am, when you suddenly entered it.'

'If this improbable story be really true, sir,' said the lady, sobbing violently, 'you will leave it instantly.'

'I will, Ma'am, with the greatest pleasure,' replied Mr. Pickwick.

'Instantly, sir,' said the lady.

'Certainly, Ma'am,' interposed Mr. Pickwick very quickly. 'Certainly, Ma'am. I—I—am very sorry, Ma'am,' said Mr. Pickwick, making his appearance at the bottom of the bed, 'to have been the innocent occasion of this alarm and emotion; deeply sorry, Ma'am.'

The lady pointed to the door. . . .

'I trust, Ma'am,' resumed Mr. Pickwick, gathering up his

shoes, and turning round to bow again: 'I trust, Ma'am, that my unblemished character, and the devoted respect I entertain for your sex, will plead as some slight excuse for this'—But before Mr. Pickwick could conclude the sentence the lady had thrust him into the passage, and locked and bolted the door behind him. (pp. 310–11)

If this is traditional bedroom comedy, Pickwick is presented as a particular kind of comic victim. Having made the initial mistake that creates the predicament, he is thereafter exhibited as a victim of the misunderstanding of the lady; and it is his exposure to the misunderstanding of others that constitutes the principal comic formula of the novel. There are, of course, other formulas, most notably the comedy of physical discomfiture—of simple slapstick—as when Pickwick essays the ice-slide only to end by disappearing into the water together with 'a large mass of ice', leaving hat, gloves and handkerchief 'floating on the surface' (pp. 413–14); and the comedy of the victim's own misapprehension of things, as when Pickwick, like Don Quixote, allows his presuppositions to transform the 'evidence' that is presented to his 'senses' in the case of the 'curious inscription of unquestionable antiquity' that is Bill Stumps's mark (pp. 137–8, 148). Such misapprehension on Pickwick's part, however, is more often than not merely the prelude to the comic exploitation of the further misunderstanding to which it gives rise. In the scene at the inn Pickwick soon realizes that he has 'come into the wrong room', and the delicious humour of the passage is rooted in the spectacle of the chaste and virtuous Pickwick being regarded by an apprehensive and outraged Miss Witherfield as a designing 'wretch', the shameless purveyor of an 'improbable story'.

That this is the essence of Dickens's comic technique is suggested by the way in which he at once proceeds to extend the misunderstanding to which Pickwick is subjected. On the day following the scene in the bedroom, Mr. Peter Magnus, whom Pickwick has previously informed of his having come to Ipswich 'to expose the treachery and falsehood of an individual, upon whose truth and honour [he has placed] implicit reliance' (p. 305), insists on introducing Pickwick to Miss Witherfield, to whom he has just proposed. When they meet, 'the lady [screams], and Mr. Pickwick [starts]', but they both refuse to reveal to Magnus where they have made acquaintance. Magnus's worst suspicions are aroused, words follow, and the lady, foolishly convinced that Pickwick and Magnus intend to fight a duel, requests Nupkins, the magistrate, 'to secure the [person] of Mr. Pickwick' (pp. 324–8).

It is to this comic pattern that the central comic predicament of the novel (or, at any rate, what starts as a comic predicament) conforms: the culmination of Pickwick's momentous announcement to Mrs. Bardell is that his friends find her in his arms:

> 'I cannot conceive—' said Mr. Pickwick, when his friend returned—'I cannot conceive what has been the matter with the woman. I had merely announced to her my intention of keeping a man-servant, when she fell into the extraordinary paroxysm in which you found her. Very extraordinary thing.'
>
> 'Very,' said his three friends.
>
> 'Placed me in such an extremely awkward situation,' continued Mr. Pickwick.
>
> 'Very,' was the reply of his followers, as they coughed slightly, and looked dubiously at each other. (pp. 153–4)

Pickwick at the inn, Pickwick and Nupkins, Pickwick and Mrs. Bardell, Pickwick at the girls' school—the pattern is repeated again and again. Indeed, Pickwick's brush with the cabman at the start of his travels can be regarded as the comic paradigm of his misadventures: diligently entering every tall word of the cabman's in his note-book, 'as a singular instance of the tenacity of life in horses, under trying circumstances' (p. 7); he finds himself accused of being an 'informer' who goes about 'in a man's cab, not only takin' down his number, but ev'ry word he says into the bargain'—and, before he is rescued by Jingle, is severely knocked about by the cabman (pp. 8–9).

Two further characteristic features of Pickwick's comic predicaments are revealed in the bedroom scene at the inn. Because Pickwick has acted in good faith and in all innocence but is faced by the misunderstanding of the lady, the predicament presents itself to him as above all a need to put himself right, to make her believe in his innocence. Hence he characteristically insists that he has been no more than 'the innocent occasion of this alarm and emotion', bravely maintaining that he is 'only a gentleman' and declaring 'upon [his] honour' that he wants 'nothing, whatever' in her room; and by way of final extenuation he 'pleads' both his 'unblemished character' and 'the devoted respect' he entertains for the female sex. Second, Pickwick feels

20

the predicament acutely because his own sense of propriety is substantially the same as that of the outraged lady—he is himself 'one of the most modest and delicate-minded of mortals'—and consequently his characteristic feeling is one of great embarrassment:[1] he 'almost [faints] with horror and dismay' when he first sees the lady; the 'cold perspiration [starts] in drops upon his night-cap' (p. 309); he is 'overpowered' by the mere idea of showing himself in his night-cap, and admits to being 'almost ready to sink beneath the confusion' of addressing a lady in that article of attire.

If these, then, are the typical components of the most distinctive comic pattern in the novel, it would seem that Pickwick is not quite 'the Quixote of Londoners', as John Forster maintains he is;[2] and that *Pickwick Papers* is not exactly the 'quixotic work' that Welsh (in a continuing critical tradition) believes it to be.[3] Though Don Quixote is exposed to the misunderstanding of others, the comic emphasis in Cervantes's novel falls on the Don's own misunderstanding of what he sees, on the ludicrous discrepancy between the reality and his apprehension of it. As a comic victim, moreover, Don Quixote rarely feels called on, as Pickwick characteristically does, to extenuate or explain his conduct; and, as Welsh himself points out, the knight is 'seldom embarrassed' (p. 23). Welsh admirably defines 'a true quixotic hero' as 'the ridiculous exponent of ideals that we must sincerely admire'; and he goes on to say that, since 'quixotism raises questions about ideals', a quixotic work is 'typically disturbing' (p. 21). But Pickwick, even at his most quixotic (as in the incident of the Bill Stumps inscription), and though a perfect gentleman, can by no means be thought of as the exponent of an ideal; and this is true, I think, of the way in which he is presented in most of the novel. Nor is the Bill Stumps incident disturbing—unless to researchers in the Pickwickian image. Where Pickwick can be regarded as the exponent of an ideal, he is not ridiculous; and where *Pickwick Papers* is disturbing, this quality, I shall argue, is not a function of the *Don Quixote* mode of comedy.

[1] I am indebted here to Alexander Welsh, who says that 'embarrassment . . . is the key to the comic situations in *Pickwick*'. 'Waverley, Pickwick, and Don Quixote', *Nineteenth-Century Fiction*, 22 (June, 1967), 23.
[2] *The Life of Charles Dickens* (London, 1872), I, 111.
[3] 'Waverley, Pickwick, and Don Quixote', *loc. cit.*, p. 21. Ada Nisbet has pointed out how pervasive this view of the novel has been: 'Ever since Sam Weller's appearance in the fourth number of *Pickwick* readers have hailed him as a Dickensian Sancho Panza. Early reviewers and almost all biographers and critics since Taine, as well as Dostoyevsky . . . have linked *Don Quixote* and *Pickwick*, and yet no clear lines of inheritance have been established.' 'Charles Dickens', *Victorian Fiction: A Guide to Research*, ed. Lionel Stevenson (Cambridge, Massachusetts, 1964), p. 124.

I believe that the influence of Cervantes on Dickens is mediated, as it were, by that of the eighteenth-century English novelist who set out consciously to follow in the Spaniard's footsteps, and acknowledged as much on the title page of his first novel.[1] So far as I know, it has not been recognized that Dickens's immediate debt in *Pickwick Papers* is to the Fielding of *Joseph Andrews*.[2] I would suggest, indeed, that Dickens took over a whole comic technique from Fielding.

The correspondence between the comic procedures of the two writers is made strikingly apparent if we compare the bedroom scene at the end of *Joseph Andrews* with that at the inn in *Pickwick Papers*. Beau Didapper, it will be recalled, steals at night into Mrs. Slipslop's bed under the impression that it is Fanny's. Parson Adams, hearing cries of alarm ('Murther! murther! rape! robbery! ruin!'), at once rushes into the bedroom:

> He made directly to the bed in the dark, where laying hold of the beau's skin (for Slipslop had tore his shirt almost off) and finding his skin extremely soft, and hearing him in a low voice begging Slipslop to let him go, he no longer doubted but this was the young woman in danger of ravishing, and immediately falling on the bed, and laying hold on Slipslop's chin, where he found a rough beard, his belief was confirmed; he therefore rescued the beau, who presently made his escape, and then turning towards Slipslop, received such a cuff on his chops, that his wrath kindling instantly, he offered to return the favour . . . stoutly . . . She then cried she was a woman; but Adams answered she was rather the devil, and if she was, he would grapple with him . . . Adams then seizing her by the hair . . . pinned her head down to the bolster, and then both called for lights together. The Lady Booby . . . had been alarmed from the beginning; and, being a woman of a bold spirit . . . she walked undauntedly to Slipslop's room; where she entered just at the instant as Adams had discovered, by the two mountains which Slipslop carried before her, that he was

---

[1] The original, full title of Fielding's first novel was: *The History of the Adventures of Joseph Andrews and his Friend Mr. Abraham Adams: Written in Imitation of the Manner of Cervantes, Author of Don Quixote.*

[2] In *Charles Dickens: His Tragedy and Triumph* (London, 1953), Edgar Johnson describes the passage in *David Copperfield* (pp. 55–6) in which Dickens refers to David's favourite childhood reading as 'literally autobiographical' (I, 20). *Joseph Andrews* is not specifically referred to in this passage, but *Tom Jones* is; and it seems reasonable to assume that Dickens knew the earlier novel too, especially since the correspondences between it and *Pickwick Papers* are so close. I am indebted to my colleague, Professor A. A. Mendilow, for the suggestion that it would be worth considering Parson Adams as a forerunner of Pickwick.

concerned with a female. He then concluded her to be a witch, and said, he fancied those breasts gave suck to a legion of devils. Slipslop seeing Lady Booby enter the room, cried, *Help! or I am ravished*, with a most audible voice; and Adams, perceiving the light, turned hastily, and saw the lady . . . just as she came to the feet of the bed; nor did her modesty, when she found the naked condition of Adams, suffer her to approach farther.—She then began to revile the parson as the wickedest of all men, and particularly railed at his impudence in chusing her house for the scene of his debaucheries, and her own woman for the object of his bestiality. Poor Adams had before discovered the countenance of his bedfellow, and now first recollecting he was naked, he was no less confounded than Lady Booby herself, and immediately whipt under the bed-clothes, whence the chaste Slipslop endeavoured in vain to shut him out. Then putting forth his head, on which, by way of ornament, he wore a flannel nightcap, he protested his innocence, and asked ten thousand pardons of Mrs. Slipslop for the blows he had struck her, vowing he had mistaken her for a witch. . . .[1]

Writing 'in imitation of the manner of Cervantes', Fielding would certainly seem to have conceived Parson Adams in the image of Don Quixote. Adams, rushing gallantly to the aid of the distressed, mistaking (though pardonably, given the beau's soft skin and Slipslop's rough beard) the roles of ravisher and (would-be) ravished, is clearly a quixotic figure; and nowhere more so than in his recourse to devils and witches (as Don Quixote to enchanters) to explain the discrepancy between reality and his own apprehension of it. But, as is indicated by the rest of the scene, Fielding ends by creating his own distinctive comic type; and it is this type that Dickens takes over from him (even down to the nightcap). Fielding, like Dickens, delightedly exploits the comic victim's initial mistake to make him ridiculous in his own eyes—and to malign him in the eyes of others: desperately trying to hide 'under the bed-clothes', the virtuous parson—made humiliatingly subject to the misunderstanding of Lady Booby—is reviled as 'the wickedest of all men'. That this is the essence of Fielding's comedy is suggested by the way in which he immediately proceeds to duplicate the situation, just as Dickens makes his bedroom scene burgeon into further misunderstandings. Adams leaves Slipslop's room only to go by mistake into

[1] Shakespeare Head edition (Oxford, 1926), II, 183–5.

Fanny's room, where he curls up in a corner of her bed and falls asleep. In the morning Joseph comes into the room:

> Fanny waking at the same instant, and stretching out her hand on Adams's beard, she cry'd out.—'O heavens! where am I?' 'Bless me! where am I?' said the parson. Then Fanny screamed, Adams leapt out of bed, and Joseph stood, as the tragedians call it, like the *statue of surprize*. '*How came she into my room?*' cry'd Adams. '*How came you into hers?*' cry'd Joseph, in an astonishment. 'I know nothing of the matter,' answered Adams, 'but that she is a vestal to me. As I am a Christian, I know not whether she is a man or a woman. He is an infidel who doth not believe in witchcraft. They as surely exist now as in the days of Saul. My clothes are bewitched away too, and Fanny's brought into their place.' ... (p. 187)

And Adams's reactions to the predicaments he finds himself in precisely prefigure those of Pickwick in analogous circumstances: he too tries to justify himself, '[protesting] his innocence' both to Lady Booby and to Joseph; he too is greatly embarrassed, being 'no less confounded than Lady Booby herself' and leaping out of Fanny's bed.

At the beginning of Chapter 3, Book I, of *Joseph Andrews* there is the following description of Parson Adams:

> Mr. Abraham Adams was an excellent scholar. He was a perfect master of the Greek and Latin languages; to which he added a great share of knowledge in the Oriental tongues; and could read and translate French, Italian, and Spanish. He had applied many years to the most severe study, and had treasured up a fund of learning rarely to be met with in a university. He was, besides, a man of good sense, good parts, and good nature; but was at the same time as entirely ignorant of the ways of this world as an infant just entered into it could possibly be. As he had never any intention to deceive, so he never suspected such a design in others. He was generous, friendly, and brave to an excess; but simplicity was his characteristick ...

It seems clear enough that Pickwick is initially presented, *mutatis mutandis*, as the same character-type as Adams. The author of the paper on Hampstead Ponds and Tittlebats, he is the same type of good,

24

generous man, with the same kind of simplicity and ignorance of the world. We might say, therefore, that the measure of Dickens's originality is what he makes of the Adams-type that he takes over from Fielding; and the immediate measure of this is the fact that, while Adams remains the same kind of man at the end of *Joseph Andrews*, Pickwick is transformed by the end of *Pickwick Papers*. Dickens himself was aware of the change in Pickwick, though it seems to have made him uneasy; and in his preface to the novel he ingeniously contrived to defend it:

> It has been observed of Mr. Pickwick, that there is a decided change in his character, as these pages proceed, and that he becomes more good and more sensible. I do not think this change will appear forced or unnatural to my readers, if they will reflect that in real life the peculiarities and oddities of a man who has anything whimsical about him, generally impress us first, and that it is not until we are better acquainted with him that we usually begin to look below these superficial traits, and to know the better part of him. (p. xii)

Ingenuity apart, what Dickens's defence of his procedure suggests is the fact of real development in Pickwick, and what it points to is the growth of Dickens's initial conception as he worked. What it points to, indeed, is Pickwick's outgrowing of his original model. It is this development that I wish to pursue in some detail, but before I do so I should like to remark briefly on another measure of Dickens's originality in relation to both Cervantes and Fielding—his conception of Sam.

Sam's function is most clearly defined on the night of Pickwick's misadventure in Miss Witherfield's room. Leaving her room, Pickwick despairs of finding his way to his own room in the dark and settles down in the passage for the night. Suddenly, to his great joy, Sam appears:

> 'Sam,' said Mr. Pickwick, suddenly appearing before him, 'where's my bed-room?'
> Mr. Weller stared at his master with the most emphatic surprise; and it was not until the question had been repeated three several times, that he turned round, and led the way to the long-sought apartment.
> 'Sam,' said Mr. Pickwick as he got into bed, 'I have made one

of the most extraordinary mistakes to-night, that ever were heard of.'

'Wery likely, sir,' replied Mr. Weller drily.

'But of this I am determined, Sam,' said Mr. Pickwick; 'that if I were to stop in this house for six months, I would never trust myself about it, alone, again.'

'That's the wery prudentest resolution as you could come to, sir,' replied Mr. Weller. 'You rayther want somebody to look arter you, sir, wen your judgment goes out a wisitin'.' (p. 312)

Sam's obvious function, as he himself sees, is 'to look arter' Pickwick; Dostoevski's Prince Myshkin being a good example of what happens when innocence and goodness are let loose on the world untended. But at the same time Sam, with his knowing canniness, is not only an effective foil to Pickwick's simplicity; the goodwill with which he is always prepared to bring Pickwick back to the fold, as it were, when his judgment goes a visiting, his loyalty to Pickwick and his admiration of him, serve to counterbalance his master's ridiculousness. Moreover, if Pickwick turns to Sam like a child to a father in the quoted passage, transforming the servant into the guardian of his master; at other times, especially towards the end of the novel, he is in turn like a father to Sam. In his presentation of this unique relationship Dickens's departure from his models is obvious. There is nothing like it in Fielding; and though Sam may appear to bear a resemblance to Sancho (especially in so far as his characteristic verbal tag—'as——said, when . . .'—can be thought of as parallel to Sancho's proverbs), Sancho's relationship to Don Quixote, if equally complex, is different in kind.

II

Dickens parts company from Fielding in the way in which he uses the character-type of the good, simple man for purposes of social criticism. We are better able to register the difference between the two writers, to follow Dickens in his movement beyond Fielding, when we see that once again he starts by imitating the earlier novelist.

In Book II, Chapter 11 of *Joseph Andrews* Adams, together with Fanny, is brought before a justice and accused of robbery. In actual fact he has just saved Fanny from being raped, but her quick-witted assailant has contrived to turn the tables on him. As the justice proceeds

26

to commit Adams to gaol, pending the assizes which are not due to be held for several months, the parson is again a victim of the misunderstanding of others—but his predicament is no longer a comic one. At the last moment, however, he is saved when he is recognized by a squire and consequently accepted as a gentleman by the justice. Clearly, Fielding's object in bringing Adams before the justice is to satirize this representative of the law, who is shown to be thoroughly unfitted for his position. If Adams, a virtuous man exposed to the ways of the world, is thus an 'effective instrument of social criticism', as Maynard Mack asserts;[1] it seems to me we should add that Fielding's social criticism is not profound. It is too much a matter of surfaces, being restricted, as in this instance, to the individual, and not pursuing the larger implications to which the near miscarriage of justice gives rise. It is symptomatic of the incidental quality of the social criticism that Adams, having been saved, is at once propelled into his next adventure, and by the beginning of the following chapter has contentedly (and 'utterly') forgotten 'everything that [has] happened'—and that Fanny's assailant, having 'privily withdrawn' when the squire intervenes, is heard of no more.

In Chapter 25 of *Pickwick Papers* the encounter of Pickwick and Nupkins, the magistrate, corresponds in all essentials to that of Adams and the justice. Arraigned before Nupkins (at the behest of the apprehensive Miss Witherfield) and charged with intending to fight a duel, than which nothing could be further from his mind, Pickwick is in danger of being sent to gaol since he cannot produce the sureties which Nupkins demands for his bail. Like Adams, he is saved in the nick of time, Dickens improving on Fielding, however, in making use to this end not of a convenient *deus ex machina* but of the resourceful Sam. As in *Joseph Andrews*, the incident provides an opportunity for a satirical exposure of the magistrate; and Dickens, like Fielding, is content to leave the matter at that. If Dickens can thus be seen to follow in Fielding's footsteps in this type of incidental social criticism, he breaks away from him—and sets out on his own individual path as a novelist—in his pursuance of the more devious functioning of the judicial process in the case of Pickwick and Mrs. Bardell.

As Pickwick's trial proceeds, our attention is drawn by a subtle complication of the main pattern of comic misadventure in the novel. As comic victim, Pickwick's typical desire is to establish his innocence;

---

[1] '*Joseph Andrews* and *Pamela*', *Fielding: A Collection of Critical Essays*, ed. Ronald Paulson (Eaglewood Cliffs, N.J., 1962), p. 55.

here, in a court of law, he is positively required to do so on pain of conviction. Whereas, moreover, he has previously been exposed to what might be called the bona fide misunderstanding of others, it soon becomes clear in court that he is now subject to the deliberate, wilful misunderstanding of counsel. 'Chops and Tomata sauce!' exclaims Serjeant Buzfuz, quoting a crucial phrase in Pickwick's correspondence with Mrs. Bardell, and adding: 'Gentlemen, is the happiness of a sensitive and confiding female to be trifled away, by such shallow artifices as these?' (p. 473). The superb Buzfuz is not to be taken too seriously, but by the time he has done with Pickwick, Dickens has moved from a comedy of circumstance—'We are all the victims of circumstances, and I the greatest,' says Pickwick, when he receives the letter from Dodson and Fogg that initiates the action for breach of promise (p. 245) —to a work of social engagement.

Dickens begins the move in his presentation of the men behind Buzfuz, the attorneys who brief him. The kind of practice in which Dodson and Fogg excel is intimated in their treatment of Ramsey. Coming to their office to settle a debt of 'two pound ten, and . . . costs [of] three pound five', Ramsey is informed by Fogg (as his clerk reports) that a declaration has already been filed against him, and that this considerably increases the costs:

> 'Well, Ramsey tried to speak, but Fogg wouldn't let him, so he put the money in his pocket, and sneaked out. The door was scarcely shut, when old Fogg turned round to me, with a sweet smile on his face, and drew the declaration out of his coat pocket. "Here, Wicks," says Fogg, "take a cab and go down to the Temple as quick as you can, and file that. The costs are quite safe, for he's a steady man with a large family, at a salary of five-and-twenty shillings a week, and if he gives us a warrant of attorney, as he must in the end, I know his employers will see it paid; so we may as well get all we can out of him, Mr. Wicks; it's a Christian act to do it, Mr. Wicks, for with his large family and small income, he'll be all the better for a good lesson against getting into debt,—won't he, Mr. Wicks, won't he?"—and he smiled so good-naturedly as he went away, that it was delightful to see him. He is a capital man of business,' said Wicks, in a tone of the deepest admiration, 'capital, isn't he?' (p. 264)

Dickens's specification of the size of Ramsey's debt and of the amount of costs he has incurred should not be thought of as yet another example of his passion for unnecessary detail—the quality that George Orwell has singled out as the distinguishing feature of his style.[1] The detail, in this case, points to a fundamental disjunction between the abstract concept of justice, according to which debts must be paid, and the quotidian practice of the law, whereby costs may legally be larger than the debt. It is in the free space, so to speak, of this disjunction that we are to see Dodson and Fogg as operating; for the mark of 'a capital man of business', such as Fogg, is his ability to manipulate the disjunction to his advantage. The room left him for manoeuvre, moreover, is so large that manipulation readily slides over into extortion, as here, and legal practice becomes 'sharp practice' (p. 276). At the same time, a concomitant of the system that enables Dodson and Fogg to operate at least nominally within the law is that 'a steady man' such as Ramsey, a good citizen, becomes their ideal victim. And Dodson and Fogg, we see, make a business of victimization, as their champertous procedure in the case of Pickwick indicates: acting for Mrs. Bardell 'on speculation', as Sam elicits (p. 362), they deliberately exploit her misunderstanding of Pickwick's declaration for their own gain.

The point to be registered here is that Dodson and Fogg should not be regarded merely as unscrupulous lawyers; they are representative in a way that Fielding's justice and Dickens's own Nupkins are not. Their victimization of Pickwick is representative of what is referred to (in 'The Tale about the Queer Client') as 'the open oppression of the law, aided by all the craft of its most ingenious practitioners' (p. 293); and (in an authorial comment on the general tendency of the 'ingenious machines' which are 'put in motion' in the Temple) as 'the torture and torment of His Majesty's liege subjects [for] the comfort and emolument of the practitioners of the law' (p. 418). Pickwick, that is to say, is to be seen as a victim of 'the law'; and the law, as Mr. Grummer points out, is 'law, civil power, and exekative' (p. 333). It is the state that Pickwick finally confronts as he stands his trial; and it is in making this kind of confrontation the centre of his novel that Dickens moves beyond or away from Fielding. An obvious sign of this move, as I have remarked, is the growth of the conception of Pickwick—for Pickwick, the amiable butt, is ready for the confrontation when it comes.

---

[1] 'Charles Dickens', *Critical Essays* (London, 1946), pp. 45–8. The detail in Dickens, I should say, is never strictly 'unnecessary' since, at the least, it contributes to the vividness and solidity of his descriptions.

We can most easily chart the extent of the change in Pickwick when we bear in mind that he is first presented as the epitome of the 'Pickwickian', in the sense in which Dickens uses the term. The phrase 'in a Pickwickian sense' is defined in the first chapter of the novel, and has a somewhat different meaning from that in general currency.[1] At the opening meeting of the Pickwick Club, Blotton calls Pickwick 'a humbug'; and then there follows this exchange:

> 'The CHAIRMAN felt it his imperative duty to demand of the honourable gentleman, whether he had used the expression which had just escaped him in a common sense.
>
> 'Mr. BLOTTON had no hesitation in saying that he had not—he had used the word in its Pickwickian sense. (Hear, hear.) He was bound to acknowledge that, personally, he entertained the highest regard and esteem for the honourable gentleman; he had merely considered him a humbug in a Pickwickian point of view. (Hear, hear.)
>
> 'Mr. PICKWICK felt much gratified by the fair, candid, and full explanation of his honourable friend. He begged it to be at once understood, that his own observations had been merely intended to bear a Pickwickian construction. (Cheers.)' (p. 5)

Whatever connotation the term may now bear, this passage makes it clear that, as far as Dickens is concerned, to take something in 'a Pickwickian sense' (or 'point of view' or 'construction') is to transform insult into compliment; to be 'Pickwickian', in a word, is to be both prudent and evasive. This meaning is reinforced soon after with reference to Tupman:

---

[1] It also has a different meaning from that advanced by J. Hillis Miller. He says that when he speaks (in his chapter on *Pickwick Papers*) 'of "Pickwick", [he] must be understood to be using the term in a Pickwickian sense, and to be including within that term all Pickwick's avatars in the novel, all those characters who have analogous experiences'. *Charles Dickens: The World of His Novels* (Cambridge, Massachusetts, 1959), p. 4. However he interprets 'in a Pickwickian sense', Miller is scarcely justified in reducing Pickwick, an individual character, to a 'term'. It may be remarked, moreover, that Miller's procedure here is representative of what is open to question in his general critical method. The running together of separate characters is analogous to his method of 'putting together moments from many different parts of the novel' (p. 4). Such a method is surely untenable when it leads, as in the following instance, to a statement about Pickwick which is made by 'putting together' in a single sentence quotations from four different chapters of the novel: 'Pickwick, like everyone else in *Pickwick Papers*, is, in spite of his philosophical calm, "a gentleman of excitable temperament" (53). "Roused" (15) by the "exciting spectacle" (52), which "light[s] up a glow of enthusiasm within him" (11), he "start[s] into full life and animation" (1)' (p. 17).

Now general benevolence was one of the leading features of the Pickwickian theory, and no one was more remarkable for the zealous manner in which he observed so noble a principle than Mr. Tracy Tupman. The number of instances, recorded on the Transactions of the Society, in which that excellent man referred objects of charity to the houses of other members for left-off garments or pecuniary relief is almost incredible. (p. 16)

When Tupman, moreover, is 'ignominiously compared to a dismounted Bacchus' by Jingle, he is notably 'Pickwickian' in his response:

He passed the wine, coughed twice, and looked at the stranger for several seconds with a stern intensity; as that individual, however, appeared perfectly collected, and quite calm under his searching glance, he gradually relaxed, and reverted to the subject of the ball. (pp. 16–17)

There are a number of milestones along the road that leads a non-Pickwickian Pickwick to the Fleet. The first one is passed when Pickwick expresses his amazement at Tupman's intention to go in 'a green velvet jacket, with a two-inch tail' to Mrs. Leo Hunter's breakfast:

'Such *is* my intention, sir,' replied Mr. Tupman warmly. 'And why not, sir?'
'Because, sir,' said Mr. Pickwick, considerably excited, 'because you are too old, sir.'
'Too old!' exclaimed Mr. Tupman.
'And if any further ground of objection be wanting,' continued Mr. Pickwick, 'you are too fat, sir.'
'Sir,' said Mr. Tupman, his face suffused with a crimson glow. 'This is an insult.'
'Sir,' replied Mr. Pickwick in the same tone, 'it is not half the insult to you, that your appearance in my presence in a green velvet jacket, with a two-inch tail, would be to me.' (pp. 196–7)

This is pure comedy, of course, and the dispute is amicably settled in the end, but it is worth noting that Pickwick, in circumstances analogous to those at the meeting of the Club, refuses here either to palliate or evade—even though a Pickwickian way out is clearly offered him

31

when Tupman uses the dreaded word 'insult'. This incident, indeed, is a prelude to a significant development in the action. At Mrs. Leo Hunter's Pickwick spots Jingle, and at once determines to follow him. 'He deceived a worthy man once,' he says, 'and we were the innocent cause. He shall not do it again, if I can help it; I'll expose him!' (p. 206). Far from evading issues, we see, Pickwick is already at this stage actively confronting them; and the seriousness of his purpose begins to move the action away from the plane of comedy. It is thus a different Pickwick who denounces Dodson and Fogg when he calls on them for an explanation of their letter to him. The lawyers prudently summon their clerks as witnesses:

> 'I merely want you to hear what this gentleman says,' replied Dodson. 'Pray, go on, sir—disgraceful and rascally proceedings, I think you said?'
> 'I did,' said Mr. Pickwick, thoroughly roused. 'I said, sir, that of all the disgraceful and rascally proceedings that ever were attempted, this is the most so. I repeat it, sir.'
> 'You hear that, Mr. Wicks?' said Dodson.
> 'You won't forget these expressions, Mr. Jackson?' said Fogg.
> 'Perhaps you would like to call us swindlers, sir,' said Dodson. 'Pray do, sir, if you feel disposed; now pray do, sir.'
> 'I do,' said Mr. Pickwick. 'You *are* swindlers.' (p. 268)

The offices of Dodson and Fogg are far removed from the charmed world of the Pickwick Club, and the distance that Pickwick has travelled is suggested by the way in which he positively courts trouble here, reckless of consequences. When the verdict goes against him in his trial for breach of promise, it is not a suddenly changed Pickwick who refuses to pay 'one farthing of costs or damages' even if this means that he must 'spend the rest of [his] existence in a debtor's prison' (p. 487). But in terms of the original conception of his character, what Pickwick does at this critical moment is untypically to refuse to avail himself of the chance of a settlement. In electing to go to prison in order to express his protest against injustice, Pickwick is so far transformed as to have ceased altogether to be a 'Pickwickian'.

The change in *Pickwick Papers* by the time Pickwick goes to gaol is manifested in a number of ways. As he enters the prison, Perker's description of him as 'a most extraordinary man' (p. 570) underlines the change not only in our response to him but in that of those with whom he comes in contact: still very much a victim, Pickwick is decidedly no longer a comic butt. This change in his status (and in the general direction of the novel) is given a structural pointing, as it were. Whereas, at the start of his adventures, it is Pickwick who needs rescuing and is saved from the cabman by Jingle; in prison (and thereafter) it is Jingle who is first supported and then redeemed by Pickwick. Even the mode of characterization changes once Pickwick is in prison. When he admits to Sam that 'old men may come here [i.e., to the Fleet], through their own heedlessness and unsuspicion: and young men may be brought here by the selfishness of those they serve' (p. 599), his self-criticism indicates that, as a character, he has been developed to the point of having an inner life. This change is in turn suggestive of a more fundamental change of mode. Maynard Mack has well said that 'comedy presents us with life apprehended in the form of spectacle rather than in the form of experience';[1] in the prison scenes we can watch *Pickwick Papers* changing form under our eyes. Finally, this change involves the tacit abandonment by Dickens of what might be called the Jane Austen fictional ethos, the Jane Austen of the well-known opening of Chapter 48 of *Mansfield Park*: 'Let other pens dwell on guilt and misery. I quit such odious subjects as soon as I can, impatient to restore everybody, not greatly in fault themselves, to tolerable comfort, and to have done with all the rest.' As Dickens precisely proceeds in the prison scenes to dwell on guilt and misery, it is of some interest to recall an earlier passage from the novel: 'It is painful to reflect upon the perfidy of our species; and we will not, therefore, pursue the thread of Mr. Jingle's meditations . . .' (p. 123).

In the prison scenes Dickens exploits previously established comic patterns for serious purposes. This, for instance, is how he uses Pickwick to indict prison conditions:

'This,' said the gentleman . . . 'this here is the hall flight.'

'Oh,' replied Mr. Pickwick, looking down a dark and filthy staircase, which appeared to lead to a range of damp and gloomy stone vaults, beneath the ground, 'and those, I suppose, are the ittle cellars where the prisoners keep their small quantities of coals. Unpleasant places to have to go down to; but very convenient, I dare say.'

'Yes, I shouldn't wonder if they was convenient,' replied the

[1] '*Joseph Andrews* and *Pamela*', *loc. cit.*, p. 57.

gentleman, 'seeing that a few people live there, pretty snug. That's the Fair, that is.'

'My friend,' said Mr. Pickwick, 'you don't really mean to say that human beings live down in those wretched dungeons?'

'Don't I?' replied Mr. Roker, with indignant astonishment; 'why shouldn't I?'

'Live! Live down there!' exclaimed Mr. Pickwick.

'Live down there! Yes, and die down there, too, wery often!' replied Mr. Roker; 'and what of that? Who's got to say anything agin it? Live down there! Yes, and a wery good place it is to live in, ain't it?' (p. 573)

This, we realize, is the Pickwick of the 'Bill Stumps, His Mark' fiasco, Pickwick as Don Quixote. But if Pickwick misunderstands what he sees because he views reality in the light of his own (humane) assumptions, it is now prison conditions—and the society that tolerates them—that are exposed, not he.

In a similar manner, Dickens exploits Sam's position as the guide and mentor of his innocent and unworldly master:

'It strikes me, Sam,' said Mr. Pickwick . . . 'that imprisonment for debt is scarcely any punishment at all.'

'Think not, sir?' inquired Mr. Weller.

'You see how these fellows drink, and smoke, and roar,' replied Mr. Pickwick. 'It's quite impossible that they can mind it much.'

'Ah, that's just the wery thing, sir,' rejoined Sam, '*they* don't mind it; it's a regular holiday to them—all porter and skittles. It's the t'other vuns as gets done over, vith this sort o' thing: them down-hearted fellers as can't svig away at the beer, nor play at skittles neither; them as vould pay if they could, and gets low by being boxed up. I'll tell you wot it is, sir; them as is always a idlin' in public-houses it don't damage at all, and them as is always a workin' wen they can, it damages too much. "It's unekal", as my father used to say wen his grog warn't made half-and-half: "It's unekal, and that's the fault on it."'

'I think you're right, Sam,' said Mr. Pickwick, after a few moments' reflection, 'quite right.' (pp. 576–7)

Sam's homely eloquence does not disguise the fact that Dickens is leading Pickwick into deep and unaccustomed waters here. When Pickwick finally concedes that Sam is 'right', he has been led far beyond a recognition of the injustice of his own treatment by the law and of the villainy of Dodson and Fogg; what he subscribes to, in effect, is a condemnation of the whole system of imprisonment for debt. (In passing, it may be remarked that Sam's eloquence is preferable to Dickens's own hortatory voice, which we see him in the process of discovering in these pages—and trying to disown by making it echo in Pickwick's thoughts: '. . . we still leave unblotted in the leaves of our statute book, for the reverence and admiration of succeeding ages, the just and wholesome law which declares that the sturdy felon shall be fed and clothed, and that the penniless debtor shall be left to die of starvation and nakedness. . . . Turning these things in his mind . . . Mr. Pickwick gradually worked himself to the boiling-over point . . .' (p. 595).) It is not only to an indictment of debtors' prisons that Pickwick is led, however. When Roker tells him that his landlord, 'the Chancery prisoner', is dying, and that the doctor has said, six months previously, that only a change of air could save him, Pickwick is taken as far as he can go: 'Great Heaven!' he exclaims; 'has this man been slowly murdered by the law for six months?' (p. 626). This moment marks the end of Pickwick's innocence. It is also at the thematic heart of the novel, for the question that Pickwick asks is, in its paradoxical bluntness, subversive of the very concept of the rule of law.

The immediate consequence for Pickwick of the loss of his innocence is that he is overwhelmed by his knowledge and by the sense of his own impotence. Having really seen, he wishes to see no more:

> 'I have seen enough,' said Mr. Pickwick, as he threw himself into a chair in his little apartment. 'My head aches with these scenes, and my heart too. Henceforth I will be a prisoner in my own room.'
>
> And Mr. Pickwick steadfastly adhered to this determination. For three long months he remained shut up, all day; only stealing out at night to breathe the air when the greater part of his fellow prisoners were in bed or carousing in their rooms. . . . (p. 645)

Commenting on Pickwick's decision, Alexander Welsh says that 'the revolutionary character of [Pickwick's having gone to prison] is underlined when he subsequently shuts himself in his own room at the Fleet for three months to protest the injustice to others that he has witnessed since his incarceration. These are the disturbing tactics of "passive resistance" and "nonviolent action" with which we have renewed acquaintance in the twentieth century.'[1] This interpretation is hardly in accord with the facts as we have them. Pickwick shuts himself up because he finds the 'scenes' in the prison too painful to bear, not because he wishes to protest against injustice. We must rather agree, I think, with J. Hillis Miller, who calls Pickwick's retirement to his room a 'definitive act of withdrawal', and relates it to Pickwick's subsequent withdrawal from the world at the end of the novel.[2] I should even say that Pickwick's retirement signifies a return to a 'Pickwickian' evasiveness, an opting out of the new kind of experience that has been forced on him. What lies behind this, it seems to me, is Dickens's own inability, his unpreparedness, at this stage of his career, to develop further the subversive implications of his tale. The rest of the novel is accordingly conceived in terms of devising a means to bring about Pickwick's release from prison—and of restoring everyone to happiness.

When Mrs. Bardell, having given a cognovit for the amount of her costs to Dodson and Fogg, is herself thrown into the Fleet by them, Sam is quick to see that the situation can be exploited for his master's good. Perker is summoned, and he informs Pickwick that he can obtain a release from the damages if he agrees to pay the costs of both plaintiff and defendant; and that he can furthermore obtain a statement from Mrs. Bardell that 'this business was, from the very first, fomented, and encouraged, and brought about', by Dodson and Fogg. Perker then goes on to say:

> 'I . . . say, however, that the whole facts, taken together, will be sufficient to justify you, in the minds of all reasonable men. And now, my dear sir, I put it to you. This one hundred and fifty pounds, or whatever it may be—take it in round numbers—is nothing to you. A jury has decided against you; well, their verdict is wrong, but still they decided as they thought right, and it *is* against you. . . . Can you hesitate to avail yourself of [the chance of release], when it restores you to your friends, your old pursuits, your health and amusements; when it liberates your faithful and attached servant, whom you otherwise doom to imprisonment for the whole of your life; and above all, when it enables you to take

---

[1] 'Waverley, Pickwick, and Don Quixote', *loc. cit.*, p. 26.
[2] *Charles Dickens*, p. 31.

the very magnanimous revenge . . . of releasing this woman from a scene of misery and debauchery, to which no man should ever be consigned, if I had my will, but the infliction of which on any woman, is even more frightful and barbarous. Now I ask you, my dear sir, not only as your legal adviser, but as your very true friend, will you let slip the occasion of attaining all these objects, and doing all this good, for the paltry consideration of a few pounds finding their way into the pockets of a couple of rascals, to whom it makes no manner of difference, except that the more they gain, the more they'll seek, and so the sooner be led into some piece of knavery that must end in a crash? . . .' (pp. 661–2)

Perker's arguments are so persuasive that, in the end, Pickwick agrees to do what he is asked; but we should be aware of the elements of special pleading in Perker's presentation of the case. If Pickwick is 'justified' in 'the minds of all reasonable men'; if he is justified, more-over, in availing himself of the opportunity of 'doing all this good' by releasing both Sam and Mrs. Bardell as well as himself, and also of helping Arabella and Winkle; the central fact remains that justice has not been done. Ultimately, indeed, it is money which proves to be the only effective counter to injustice, the injustice which was the cause of Pickwick's bold protest. Being a man to whom the amount involved is (fortunately) 'nothing', Pickwick is in a position, even if he does not obtain justice, to buy his freedom. The corollary of this is that Pickwick, on his release, is no longer concerned with questions of principle; and he uses his money to do what justice he can in numerous acts of individual benevolence, of which Jingle and Job, Arabella and Winkle, and Sam and Mary are the beneficiaries. Finally, as Perker presents the matter, it is merely a 'paltry consideration' that the costs are to be paid to Dodson and Fogg, and it is a comforting reflection that they can safely be left to undo themselves; but these arguments simply obscure the fact that they get away with their knavery: they have been 'too clever' to enable 'an indictment for conspiracy' to be brought against them (p. 661). When Pickwick later has the satisfaction of roundly denouncing Dodson and Fogg to their faces, he declares that he has 'now removed a great weight from his mind', and he is left feeling 'perfectly comfortable and happy' (p. 751)—but his denunciation leaves them where they were, with the law of the country behind them. Indeed, the last we hear of Dodson and Fogg is that they continue to prosper: they are 'universally considered among the sharpest of the sharp', but they remain 'in business, from which they realise a large income' (p. 800).

G. K. Chesterton has said that 'it is doubtful' whether Dickens 'ever afterwards rose' to 'the level of *The Pickwick Papers*'.[1] Chesterton's 'level', in other words, is more like a peak, but it would seem more reasonable to regard *Pickwick Papers* as what it so obviously is—a beginning. It is an important beginning, however, not merely because it is radiant with Dickens's genius but because it is so directly related to the work that follows. What Dickens does in *Pickwick Papers* is to discover his theme, the broad theme of social injustice, which it becomes his life's work to develop in manifold ways. The social criticism in *Pickwick Papers* may be limited in force, but, with the later work in mind, we cannot help being struck by the comprehensiveness of its implications. By the end of the novel Dickens is already on the way to understanding, as he does with complete assurance in *Bleak House*, that if the Dodsons and Foggs of this world are simply left to themselves, it is a whole society which is corrupted by its acceptance of them. He is also on the way to understanding, as he does in *Little Dorrit*, that a debtors' prison may be a microcosm of the respectable world (outside its walls) that tolerates it. And with Pickwick's unanswerable question about the murdered Chancery prisoner he sets out on the road that is to lead to the final, great, subversive vision of *Our Mutual Friend*.

But it is not only large issues that are raised by the impetus of the tale Dickens has to tell in *Pickwick Papers*. It is also instructive to watch his creative imagination almost incidentally alighting on material that he is to exploit later. Early on, for instance, what is to become the grim fact of *Oliver Twist* is encapsulated in a comic metaphor: 'It is an established axiom, that "every bullet has its billet." If it apply in an equal degree to shot, those of Mr. Winkle were unfortunate foundlings, deprived of their natural rights, cast loose upon the world, and billeted nowhere' (p. 254). If there is nothing else so vividly and incidentally suggestive as this, there are a number of lines that stretch out to the later work, particularly *Bleak House*. There is the Chancery prisoner; there are the 'green parasols' distributed to the 'five-and-forty women' of Eatanswill (p. 161) that open out, as it were, under

---

[1] '*The Pickwick Papers*', *The Dickens Critics*, ed. George H. Ford and Lauriat Lane (Ithaca, N.Y., 1961), p. 109. Chesterton's essay is reprinted from his chapter on *Pickwick Papers* in his less readily available book, *Charles Dickens*, first published in 1906.

the 'auriferous showers' that fall on electors in the later novel; there is the objection, concisely formulated by Mr. Weller, senior, to the philanthropic activities of Stiggins's 'noble society' that comes in the fullness of time to embrace Mrs. Jellyby: '. . . wot aggrawates me, Samivel, is to see 'em a wastin' all their time and labour in making clothes for copper-coloured people as don't want 'em, and taking no notice of flesh-coloured Christians as do' (p. 371). Nor is it only *Bleak House* of which there are anticipations. There is also Jingle, the mercenary adventurer in Miss Rachael's affections, who fathers Edith Dombey, Lady Dedlock, Gowan, and the unreformed Bella Wilfer—and whose designing amorousness is the obverse of that 'disinterested attachment' which gratifies Pickwick (p. 780), and which—made more passionately a matter of love—is to become the *summum bonum* in the Dickens world.

Dickens not only discovers his themes in his first novel; he also discovers a central character-type which differs from that which he starts with. Pickwick begins as a victim of comic misadventure, but he ends as a victim of social injustice. The far-reaching significance of this change may be gauged by comparing Pickwick with another representative victim of the times—the central character of Surtees's *Jorrocks's Jaunts and Jollities*. The last of Surtees's papers in the *New Sporting Magazine* was published in September 1834, that is, less than eighteen months before Dickens began his novel; and the success of these papers is some indication of the nature of contemporary taste. I quote a passage which exemplifies the way in which Surtees handles Jorrocks's misadventures:

> A stopper appears—a gate locked and spiked, with a downward hinge to prevent its being lifted. To the right is a rail, and a ha-ha beyond it—to the left a quick fence. Tom glances at both, but turns short, and, backing his horse, rides at the rail. The Yorkshireman follows, but Jorrocks, who espies a weak place in the fence a few yards from the gate, turns short, and, jumping off, prepares to lead over. It is an old gap, and the farmer has placed a sheep-hurdle on the far side. Just as Jorrocks has pulled that out, his horse, who is a bit of a rusher, and has now got his 'monkey' completely up, pushes forward while his master is yet stooping—and hitting him in the rear, knocks him clean through the fence, head-foremost into a squire-trap beyond it!—'Non *redolet* sed *olet*!' exclaims the Yorkshireman, who dismounts in

a twinkling, lending his friend a hand out of the unsavoury cess-pool. 'That's what comes of hunting in a new saddle, you see,' added he, holding his nose. Jorrocks scrambles upon terra firma, and exhibits such a spectacle as provokes the shout of the field. He has lost his wig, his hat hangs to his back, and one side of his person and face is completely japanned with black, odoriferous mixture. 'My vig!' exclaims he, spitting and spluttering, 'but that's the nastiest hole I ever was in; Fleet ditch is lavendar-water compared to it! Hooi yonder!' hailing a lad; 'catch my 'oss, boouy!...'[1]

The immediate cause of Jorrocks's misadventure is, no doubt, his horse, which is temperamentally 'a bit of a rusher', but it is clear enough that it is his own limitations as a horseman which bring about his downfall: he does not leap the rail, as Tom (the professional hunts-man) and the Yorkshireman do—and as a sportsman should—but 'prepares to lead over'. Indulging in the sport of gentlemen, aping his betters while dropping his aitches, Jorrocks (the grocer of St. Botolph-Lane and Great Coram-Street) at all points fails ludicrously to be genteel; characteristically, he gives up the hunt shortly after his fall, solacing himself with thoughts of 'the quarter of house-lamb' to be served 'at half-past five to a *minute*' (p. 29). Surtees's comedy, in other words, is rooted in the discrepancy between Jorrocks's aspirations and his performance—the discrepancy between the real thing and an imitation. But Surtees's humour for the most part is a matter—as indeed in the quoted passage it literally is—of horseplay, a slapstick humour which depends on physical discomfiture. The 'spectacle' that Jorrocks finally 'exhibits' is of a man who is the ridiculous victim of his own ineptitude and grossness, a sportsman who, instead of covering himself with glory, is covered with the contents of a cesspool. The satire, moreover, has strong class overtones, and the ridiculing of the antics of the grocer and his friends is conducted in the spirit of traditional low comedy.[2]

George H. Ford maintains that *Jorrocks's Jaunts and Jollities* is 'one of the important sources' of *Pickwick Papers*;[3] and Steven Marcus asserts that it provides 'something of the substratum of the novel, the

---

[1] Robert Smith Surtees, *Jorrocks's Jaunts and Jollities* (London, 1924), pp. 28–9.
[2] See Erich Auerbach's *Mimesis*, tr. Willard Trask (New York, 1957), for an illuminating discussion of the permutations of this tradition.
[3] *Dickens and His Readers* (Princeton, 1955), p. 17.

material with which Dickens began.'[1] It should be clear, I think, that Surtees is neither as significant nor as fundamental an influence as these statements suggest. *Jorrocks* should rather be considered as a convenient yardstick for measuring the difference between Pickwick and what the age had to offer in the way of comic victims. Of an entirely different order as a comic creation, Pickwick, as he is transformed into the defiant victim of social injustice, himself spans the gap between the neoclassical separation of the styles.

Dickens's future course as a novelist would seem to have been determined by his creation of Pickwick. Certainly in all the novels that follow *Pickwick Papers* the central character is a victim of one kind or another, *Oliver Twist* (which he began while he was still writing the earlier novel) being an immediate case in point. Dickens's development in this connection can be regarded as his continually deepening understanding of the concept of victimization—and of the nature of the alternatives open to the victim. That the figure of the victim should have obtruded into his most sunny work is no doubt attributable to his strong and continuing sense of his own victimization as a child. We have only to recall a much-quoted passage from the autobiographical fragment which he gave to Forster to see where his preoccupation with the victim has its roots:

> It is wonderful to me how I could have been so easily cast away at such an age. It is wonderful to me, that, even after my descent into the poor little drudge I had been since we came to London, no one had compassion enough on me—a child of singular abilities, quick, eager, delicate, and soon hurt, bodily or mentally— to suggest that something might have been spared, as certainly it might have been, to place me at any common school. Our friends, I take it, were tired out. No one made any sign. My father and mother were quite satisfied. They could hardly have been more so, if I had been twenty years of age, distinguished at a grammar-school, and going to Cambridge.[2]

To root Dickens's art in his childhood experiences, and particularly in his spell at the blacking warehouse and in his father's imprisonment (which followed his 'descent into the poor little drudge'), is to see— with Edmund Wilson—that the large impulse behind his art is to

---

[1] *Dickens: from Pickwick to Dombey* (London, 1965), p. 24
[2] John Forster, *Charles Dickens*, I, 31.

understand 'a world in which such things could occur'.[1] But it is also to recognize that Dickens's development of the victim as a central type is a matter not only of his personal history but of the history of his times. It is almost as if the victim is a product of the *Zeitgeist*: following the security of Jane Austen's central characters, there proceeds a line of nineteenth-century victims—in Thackeray, in the Brontës, in George Eliot, in Henry James, in Hardy—and it is a line which culminates in the archetypal victim of Kafka.

III

It is also worth considering some of the technical features of *Pickwick Papers* because Dickens's first novel reveals in striking combination both the artlessness of his narrative procedure and the natural tendencies of his art. The artlessness is most apparent in his narrative stance. Though the full title of the novel is *The Posthumous Papers of the Pickwick Club*, and though Dickens accordingly adopts the point of view of an 'editor' of 'multifarious documents confided to him' by members of the Club (p. 1), his pursuit of his chosen method is, to say the least, cavalier. He sticks to the method for Chapters 1–9, artlessly drops it at the beginning of Chapter 10 with the exchange between Jingle and Sam, and as artlessly returns to Pickwick's 'note-book' as a source in the same chapter; thereafter, he maintains the method, giving scattered references to sources, until Chapter 19 (in which is to be found the last such reference); with the description of Mr. Weller, senior, in Chapter 23, he quietly and finally abandons the method. 'The machinery of the Club,' Dickens tells us in the Preface, 'proving cumbrous in the management, was gradually abandoned as the work progressed' (p. x); thereby marking the ground, as it were, both as regards attitude and performance, for an estimate of the distance he was to travel to the sustained and revolutionary experiment in point of view in *Bleak House*.

At the beginning of the novel, Pickwick and his friends undertake to send 'authenticated accounts' of 'their adventures, together with all tales and papers to which local scenery or associations may give rise' to the Club in London (p. 2). The last clause of the quotation suggests the mood in which the youthful Dickens plunged into the project that

---

[1] 'Dickens: The Two Scrooges', *The Wound and the Bow* (London, 1952, revised edition first published 1941), p. 7.

had been proposed to him, trusting to time, circumstance, and inspiration to shape his novel for him within a loose picaresque frame.
As it was to turn out, the picaresque form had a virtue other than its
amenability to a writer without a plan; as Fielding had realized, it
provided a ready means of bringing about a confrontation between an
unworldly hero and the world, of bringing the two poles around which
the narrative circles into easy conjunction. But, however suited to
Pickwick's adventures, the picaresque remains episodic in effect and
fails to yield an overall unity. Looking back on his work some ten
years later, Dickens himself (in the revised Preface to the novel) re-
gretted its lack of unity: '. . . I could perhaps wish now that these
chapters were strung together on a stronger thread of general interest'
(p. x). We might add that the novel shows more signs of 'stringing
together' than Dickens apparently discerned; and that it contains in
embryo the two structurally unifying devices which were to become
characteristic of his full-fledged work.

The first device has been generally recognized. Within the looseness
of the picaresque form, Dickens does in fact make some effort to tie
certain incidents together by constructing a number of plotlets, as it
were. Amid random elections and cricket matches, there are unified
clusters of incidents—such as those concerned with the Pickwickians
and Jingle, with Pickwick and Mrs. Bardell, with Winkle and Arabella, and so on. Clearly it was more congenial for Dickens to work
within the frame of a unifying plot, and his art reveals a steady development of this natural tendency till it culminates in the complex, and
symbolically meaningful, plots of some of the later novels.

Commenting on the fragmentary structure of *Pickwick Papers*, J.
Hillis Miller says that 'the total rhythm of the novel is apparently not
really a rhythm at all, but rather a discontinuous succession of experiences whose only unity is that they happen to the same person.'[1]
The novel has a greater unity than this, however, and it is provided by
its structure of analogies, the second device of which Dickens instinctively makes use. I am indebted for this insight to Steven Marcus,
who says that Dickens has an 'analogical imagination', the working of
which he defines as follows:

> By multiplying a particular character or situation, and embodying
> within a single work manifold and significantly diversified images
> of the same kind of person or relationship, he was able to render

[1] *Charles Dickens*, p. 22.

43

the conceptions in his novels more dramatic, subtle and complex than he could have done through any other resource compatible with his kind of genius.[1]

This seems to me to be a seminal observation in Dickens criticism, and we can only regret that Marcus does not develop it more fruitfully, either in his discussion of *Pickwick Papers* or in the rest of his book. He does provide us with a valuable tool for analysis of the late novels, which are not included within the scope of his book, when he says that 'in all his later writing the discovery of the connections between social and personal disorders becomes Dickens's chief preoccupation', and that Dickens uses the 'analogical method' to explore such connections (pp. 47–8); but in his description of Dickens's 'initial experiment with [the] technique' in *Pickwick Papers*, he restricts himself to examples of the 'multiplication' of a 'particular character': he refers to the 'tribe of shrewish, predatory women' (Mrs. Weller, Miss Witherfield, Mrs. Bardell, Mrs. Pott, Mrs. Leo Hunter, Mrs. Nupkins, Mrs. Raddle and Mrs. Wardle) and to the 'witty, resourceful, imperturbable and socially marginal young men' (Sam, Jingle and Bob Sawyer) (p. 40). It seems to me that the analogical method (to adopt Marcus's term) has more extensive dimensions. Pickwick, briefing Peter Magnus on how to press his suit with Miss Witherfield, advises that he 'should argue, by analogy' that he is 'a very desirable object' (p. 323); I suggest that, underlying the random, picaresque features of *Pickwick Papers*, there is a sustained argument by analogy.

There are three main groups of analogues in the novel. First, and most obviously, there are the comic predicaments, which are the basis of the narrative. These typically involve misunderstanding of one kind or another; and, as I have remarked in a different connection, the opening incident with the cabman can be regarded in this respect as a comic paradigm. On this level, the novel can be viewed as a series of analogous comic situations. In addition to all the instances of misunderstanding previously referred to, we may note the following analogues: Pickwick's benevolently observing some drunken soldiers and reflecting how 'truly delightful' it is 'to a philanthropic mind, to see these gallant men staggering along under the influence of an overflow, both of animal and ardent spirits' (p. 14); Winkle's acceptance of a challenge to a duel with Dr. Slammer (pp. 23–5); the belief of the public-house woman and the red-headed man that the 'depressed Pickwickians' have

---

[1] *Dickens*, p. 40.

stolen the horse they want to 'put up' at their establishment (p. 64); Pickwick's being taken to be in fancy dress when he appears in his usual clothes at Mrs. Leo Hunter's party (p. 200); Winkle's imputed liaison with Mrs. Pott (p. 238); Wardle's donation of a 'reputation' to Tupman when that sportsman '[shuts] his eyes firmly', fires 'into the air'—and kills a partridge (p. 253); Captain Boldwig's taking of Pickwick for 'a drunken plebeian', and his despatching of him to the pound (p. 259); Mrs. Dowler's 'running away' with Winkle (p. 515); Winkle's meeting with Dowler (pp. 538–40); and 'the scientific gentleman's' view of Pickwick's lantern (pp. 556–9).

Second, there is a group of analogues that is used for satirical purposes. On this level, the narrative swings between two poles which are first adumbrated in the report of Pickwick's address to the Club: '... but this he would say, that if ever the fire of self-importance broke out in his bosom, the desire to benefit the human race in preference effectually quenched it' (p. 4). The inner contest between self-importance and benevolence adverted to here is externalized in the narrative as Pickwick, the exemplar of benevolence, is brought into contact with self-important people. This confrontation, itself analogous to that between unworldliness and worldliness, which is the *raison d'être* of the picaresque form of the novel, provides the occasion for a good deal of satire. The satire is directed, in a series of analogues, against the self-important, especially those engaged in some kind of public activity. At the military review at Rochester, there is Colonel Bulder, who is seen 'galloping first to one place and then to another, and backing his horse among the people, and prancing, and curvetting, and shouting in a most alarming manner, and making himself very hoarse in the voice, and very red in the face, without any assignable cause or reason whatever' (p. 46); there is Perker, who, emphatically resisting Pickwick's attempts to take the initiative in tracing Jingle, insists that 'the very first principle to be observed in these cases, is this: if you place a matter in the hands of a professional man, you must in no way interfere in the progress of the business' (p. 124); there is Pott, the editor of the Eatanswill Gazette:

> 'The contest,' said Pott, 'shall be prolonged so long as I have
> health and strength, and that portion of talent with which I am
> gifted. From that contest, sir, although it may unsettle men's
> minds and excite their feelings, and render them incapable for
> the discharge of the every-day duties of ordinary life; from that

contest, sir, I will never shrink, till I have set my heel upon the Eatanswill Independent. I wish the people of London, and the people of this country to know, sir, that they may rely upon me; —that I will not desert them, that I am resolved to stand by them, sir, to the last.' (p. 162);

there is Mrs. Leo Hunter, whose 'ambition' is 'to have no other acquaintance' than those 'who have rendered themselves celebrated by their works and talents' (p. 194); there is Captain Boldwig, who gives orders 'with all due grandeur and ferocity: for Captain Boldwig's wife's sister had married a Marquis, and the Captain's house was a villa, and his land "grounds", and it was all very high, and mighty, and great' (p. 257); and there is Nupkins, who, when Pickwick (charged with intent to disturb the peace) requests a private interview, turns pale: 'Could the man Weller, in a moment of remorse, have divulged some secret conspiracy for his assassination? It was a dreadful thought. He was a public man: and he turned paler, as he thought of Julius Caesar and Mr. Perceval' (p. 344).

Nupkins and Pott are related by a further analogy, their self-importance in their public function being neatly juxtaposed to their hen-pecked condition as husbands (pp. 347–8, 163). Another form of satirical analogy is parody. The 'swarry' held by a 'select company of Bath footmen' (Chapter 37) is a comic parody of the rituals of polite society at Bath; and it functions, by analogy, to ridicule not only the footmen but also what is parodied—a technique that Dickens subtly extends in *Little Dorrit*.[1]

Third, there is the most important of the various groups of analogues —that of the victim. The central theme of the novel is the victimization of Pickwick, and the idea of victimization is kept before the reader in a number of episodes in which characters figure as victims. On the level of comedy, there are, first, all the various victims of misunderstanding. There is also Mr. Weller, senior, whom Sam describes as a 'wictim o' connubiality' (p. 273), and who is consequently the victim of Stiggins. There are also the young ladies, the chapel-followers of 'the shepherd', whose heads (according to Mr. Weller) are 'reg'larly [turned]' by him, and who are 'the wictims o' gammon' (p. 371). Miss Rachael mediates between the comic victims and those who really suffer: ridiculous in the way in which she is trapped by Jingle, she is nevertheless a pathetic victim of his schemes. Perker's client, 'a

---

[1] See Ch. 6, pp. 208–9 below.

rustily-clad, miserable-looking man, in boots without toes and gloves without fingers', on whom there are 'traces of privation and suffering —almost of despair' (p. 424), is a victim of Chancery (and a forerunner of the man from Shropshire in *Bleak House*). Mrs. Bardell, in the end, is herself the victim of Dodson and Fogg, as is Ramsey. But it is the interpolated tales which, in this respect, most repay examination. Once dismissed as excrescences, their general significance has been established by Edmund Wilson:

> There are in *Pickwick Papers*, especially in the early part, a whole set of interpolated short stories which make a contrast with the narrative proper. These stories are mostly pretty bad and deserve from the literary point of view no more attention than they usually get; but, even allowing here also for an element of the conventional and popular, of the still-thriving school of Gothic horror, we are surprised to find rising to the surface already the themes which were to dominate his later work.[1]

It is worth adding, I think, that victims figure prominently in six out of the nine tales (of the remaining three, two—those concerned with Bath and Christmas—are 'occasion' pieces); and that a specific significance of the tales is their reinforcement of the victim-image. In all four of the 'dark' tales there are victims: in 'The Stroller's Tale' there is the wife, who is the victim of the drunken clown; in 'The Story of the Convict's Return' it is the convict who is the victim of his dissipated father and returns to seek him out 'in fierce and deadly passion' (p. 80); in 'A Madman's Manuscript' the woman is the victim of the madman, who buys her; and in 'The Old Man's Tale about the Queer Client' Heyling is the victim of his father-in-law. Even in 'The Parish Clerk' the clerk is the comic victim of the daughter of the saddler; and in 'The Story of the Bagman's Uncle' the young lady is the victim of her melodramatic and 'supernatural' abductors.

The analogues, then, make for a comparative density of texture, for a closer weave than we might expect to find in a picaresque design. But the drawback of Dickens's method in this novel is that there is ultimately no real analogy between the proceedings of the individual and the procedures of society. In his peregrinations Pickwick is regularly the victim of misunderstanding, but he encounters (as I have previously pointed out) misunderstanding in good faith; in his brush

---

[1] 'Dickens', *loc. cit.*, p. 9.

with the law he is the victim of the deliberate exploitation of mis-understanding. Dickens's development, in this respect, may be seen as an attempt to understand and probe more deeply the analogies between private and public conduct, to use analogy, as Steven Marcus suggests, to link together the individual and social spheres—a technique which he perfects in *Bleak House, Little Dorrit* and *Our Mutual Friend*. It may also be viewed as an attempt to find a satisfactory form to contain the analogues; and since analogy is implicit metaphor, we might expect a development in which images and symbols are used analogically as additional unifying devices within a plot.

2

OLIVER TWIST

I

Oliver Twist is two novels. It is an imaginative evocation of a social problem that is consistently presented in terms of two central images; it is also an affirmation of a moral belief in Virtue Triumphant that is articulated by means of a plot which is inconsistent with the imaginative apprehension of the subject. This bifurcation is responsible for the thematic confusions of a novel of undoubted imaginative power.

It is perhaps an indication of the devious workings of the imagination that the structure of the novel is also bifurcated, though not in a way that is directly related to the thematic division of interest. The action is rooted in the workhouse, with which the book begins; but thereafter it branches out into two areas which have generally been characterized as distinct 'worlds', the underworld of Fagin and his gang, and the middle-class milieu of Mr. Brownlow and of the Maylies. These worlds are only fleetingly brought together by the action in Nancy's surreptitious contacts with Rose and in Brownlow's visit to Fagin in the condemned cell. They are firmly held together, however, by a vision which sees in them alternative possibilities of the human condition, and which projects them throughout in terms of two related images. The images occur together in a passage which may be thought of as at the imaginative centre of the novel:

> The night was bitter cold. The snow lay on the ground, frozen into a hard thick crust; so that only the heaps that had drifted into by-ways and corners were affected by the sharp wind that howled abroad: which, as if expending increased fury on such prey as it found, caught it savagely up in clouds, and, whirling

it into a thousand misty eddies, scattered it in air. Bleak, dark, and piercing cold, it was a night for the well-housed and fed to draw round the bright fire and thank God they were at home; and for the homeless starving wretch to lay him down and die. Many hunger-worn outcasts close their eyes in our bare streets, at such times, who, let their crimes have been what they may, can hardly open them in a more bitter world. (pp. 145–6)

In this passage the manifold differences of condition that distinguish the lot of one man from another are starkly narrowed to one fundamental distinction: that between 'the homeless' and 'the well-housed', between poor naked wretches and accommodated man. The distinction is thus between a man's having a 'home', which provides him with shelter, food, warmth and light; and being condemned to be out in the 'bare streets', which means being exposed not only to the cold and the dark but also to starvation. To be out in the streets, moreover, is to move through the darkness of a hell on earth, for those who die in the streets, 'let their crimes have been what they may, can hardly open [their eyes] in a more bitter world'. To have a home, by contrast, is a sign of grace, and the well-housed may duly 'thank God' they are at home.

The opposed images of home and the streets function as analogues of the two opposed worlds of the novel, the worlds of civilized order and of crime. We are adverted to this dimension of the imagery by the curious use of the word 'crimes' in the quoted passage. The use of this word (rather than 'sins', which, in the context, suggests itself as a more natural choice) associates the 'outcasts' not only with the destitute but with the criminal. And indeed the impression of the criminals that we carry away, when we look back on the novel as a whole, is of men who are essentially homeless, who are continually moving from one 'den' to another, who are constantly on the run. Nor need we rely only on such impressions.

In the Preface which he wrote for the third edition of *Oliver Twist* in 1841, Dickens was at some pains to clarify his own moral attitude to the criminals he had depicted. Though he specifically excluded his friend Bulwer Lytton's *Paul Clifford* from having 'any bearing on . . . the subject' (p. lxiii), it seems clear enough that he was out to dissociate his novel from the genre of the Newgate novel, which *Paul Clifford* might be said to have inaugurated:

What manner of life is that which is described in these pages,

as the every-day existence of a Thief? What charms has it for the
young and ill-disposed, what allurements for the most jolter-
headed of juveniles? Here are no canterings upon moonlit heaths,
no merry-makings in the snuggest of all possible caverns, none
of the attractions of dress, no embroidery, no lace, no jack-boots,
no crimson coats and ruffles, none of the dash and freedom with
which 'the road' has been, time out of mind, invested. The cold,
wet, shelterless midnight streets of London; the foul and frowsy
dens, where vice is closely packed and lacks the room to turn;
the haunts of hunger and disease, the shabby rags that scarcely
hold together: where are the attractions of these things? Have
they no lesson, and do they not whisper something beyond the
little-regarded warning of a moral precept? (p. lxiii)

It is striking that Dickens, in seeking to describe the habitat of his
thieves, should seize first on 'the cold, wet, shelterless midnight streets
of London'. And time and again, in the novel, the thieves are typically
shown pursuing their way through these streets. Even when 'the sharp
wind' seems to have 'cleared' the streets 'of passengers, as of dust and
mud', and it is 'within an hour of midnight', Fagin hurries through
them 'trembling, and shivering', for 'the weather [is] dark and piercing
cold' (p. 168). Out in the streets on another occasion, he is described
in terms which point to the significance of the collocation of street and
criminal:

> The mud lay thick upon the stones: and a black mist hung
> over the streets; the rain fell sluggishly down: and everything
> felt cold and clammy to the touch. It seemed just the night when
> it befitted such a being as the Jew, to be abroad. As he glided
> stealthily along, creeping beneath the shelter of the walls and
> doorways, the hideous old man seemed like some loathsome rep-
> tile, engendered in the slime and darkness through which he
> moved: crawling forth, by night, in search of some rich offal for
> a meal. (pp. 120–1)

Clearly it befits Fagin 'to be abroad' on such a night not because he is
a Jew and a 'hideous old man' but because he is a criminal; and he has
his 'being' in the streets because he is produced by them, 'engendered',
it seems, in their 'slime and darkness'. The streets are as much the
natural home of Fagin and his like as the moors round Wuthering

Heights are that of Cathy and Heathcliff. Nancy, indeed, bitterly accuses Fagin of being responsible for the fact that 'the cold, wet, dirty streets are [her] home' (p. 104). The streets, moreover, are seen to lead the criminals, twist and turn as they may, inexorably in one direction: when Fagin is finally brought to trial, the court is said to be 'paved, from floor to roof, with human faces' (p. 358); and Fagin makes his last appearance in the streets when he is hanged (p. 364).

But it is, of course, not only the criminals and prostitutes who walk the streets; the 'hunger-worn outcasts' of the previously quoted passage, who, as often as not, 'close their eyes in [the] bare streets', are also the law-abiding poor. Oliver, when he runs away from the undertaker, is one of them; and he reflects that London is 'the very place for a homeless boy, who must die in the streets, unless someone [helps] him' (p. 44). That a life in 'the cold, wet, shelterless midnight streets' is made to project a life in the underworld is thus not merely a means of countering the 'allurements' of romantic 'canterings upon moonlit heaths'; it is primarily a means of insisting on the connection between poverty and crime. Receiving the efflux of the poor, the streets engender criminals. Implied throughout by the repeated use of the street image, this process—or, at least, the first stage in the process—is dramatized in the case of Oliver. It is precisely when Oliver finds himself in the streets, homeless and starving, that he is approached by the Dodger; and, having been provided by him with a 'hearty meal', Oliver is induced to follow that solicitous youth by his promise to introduce him to 'a 'spectable old genelman . . . wot'll give [him] lodgings for nothink' (pp. 47–8).

A further feature of life in the underworld is that the thieves' houses have more in common with the street than with a home. Monks, on being received in one of Fagin's dens, complains that 'it's as dark as the grave', and is informed by his host that he and his friends 'never shew lights to [their] neighbours'; Fagin then takes him into a room which is 'destitute of all moveables save a broken armchair, and an old couch or sofa without covering . . .' (pp. 169–70). After the Chertsey expedition, Bill Sikes takes up his quarters in 'a mean and badly-furnished apartment, of very limited size: lighted only by one small window in the shelving roof, and abutting on a close and dirty lane'; in this apartment there is not only 'a great scarcity of furniture' but a 'total absence of comfort' (p. 257). Fagin, in the end, like 'all the men he [has] known who [have] died upon the scaffold', comes to '[inhabit]' a condemned cell (p. 360).

By contrast the world of civilized order is characterized by the amenities of its homes. Mr. Brownlow takes Oliver home to 'a neat house, in a quiet shady street', where he is 'carefully and comfortably deposited' and 'tended with a kindness and solicitude that [know] no bounds'; a 'motherly old lady' constantly looks 'kindly and lovingly' at him and feeds him broth which is 'strong enough to furnish an ample dinner, when reduced to the regulation strength: for three hundred and fifty paupers, at the very lowest computation' (pp. 67–70). Mrs. Maylie and Rose are first shown together sitting at 'a well-spread breakfast-table' in 'a handsome room: though its furniture [has] rather the air of old-fashioned comfort, than of modern elegance' (p. 187). When Oliver goes with them to a cottage in the country, the room in which he works at his lessons is 'quite a cottage-room, with a lattice-window', around which there are 'clusters of jessamine and honeysuckle' that creep 'over the casement' and fill 'the place with their delicious perfume'; the room looks into a garden, and 'all beyond' is 'fine meadow-land and wood' (p. 227).

These descriptions are not in themselves especially noteworthy, but they are given force by the very vividness of that to which they are quietly opposed. Heaven, even in Milton, is a more prosaic place than Hell. And in *Oliver Twist* Dickens seems to think of home as a heaven as well as a haven. It is not merely, as I have pointed out, that the streets are presented as hell. Harry Maylie tells Rose that 'when the young, the beautiful, and good, are visited with sickness, their pure spirits insensibly turn towards their bright home of lasting rest' (p. 231). Now that the Clarendon edition of the novel enables us to watch Dickens at work, moreover, we can see how another such identification was originally made explicit—though Dickens finally thought better of it. Oliver is described as sometimes thinking of his dead mother and sobbing unseen, but being comforted when he raises his eyes 'to the deep sky overhead' and ceases 'to think of her as lying in the ground'; in his manuscript Dickens first had Oliver raise his eyes to the sky 'and [remember] that there [is] a home beyond' (p. 211). The 'long home' of Ecclesiastes is no doubt behind what may well be merely a traditional use of the word 'home' in these two passages, but that does not mean to say that we should brush aside the associations which it gathers in the novel. Certainly Dickens repeatedly suggests that home, like heaven, is a concentration of all good. In early editions of the novel, Rose is described as follows:

The very intelligence that shone in her deep blue eye, and was stamped upon her noble head, seemed scarcely of her age or of the world; and yet the changing expression of sweetness and good humour; the thousand lights that played about the face, and left no shadow there; above all, the smile; the cheerful happy smile— were intwined with the best sympathies and affections of our nature. (pp. 187–8)

In the 1846 edition (on which Kathleen Tillotson has based the Clarendon text) the last part of this passage was amended to: '. . . the cheerful, happy smile; were made for Home; for fireside peace and happiness' (p. 188). And at the end of the novel, Harry Maylie— having renounced all worldly ambition—proposes to Rose in the following terms:

> 'I offer you, now, no distinction among a bustling crowd; no mingling with a world of malice and detraction, where the blood is called into honest cheeks by aught but real disgrace and shame; but a home—a heart and a home—yes, dearest Rose, and those, and those alone, are all I have to offer.' (p. 357)

When we have registered the significance of the home and street analogues, which are at the heart of the novel, we are better able to appreciate the importance of the workhouse in the narrative.[1] The workhouse is the home which is provided for the poor by the secure; and it is the last refuge of the unhoused poor from a life in the streets. The workhouse, in a word, mediates between the images of home and street, and it thus may also be said to mediate between the two worlds which the images in turn project. Starting life in the workhouse, Oliver—once he has left his birthplace—moves backwards and forwards between the two worlds; and the question posed by the narrative is which world, the respectable or the criminal, he will finally come to inhabit. The main action of the novel, that is to say, is concerned, quite simply, with Oliver's search for a home. This, at any rate, is the way in which he sees his plight. When Mr. Brownlow tells

---

[1] Humphry House, for instance, does not believe that the opening section on the workhouse is properly integrated in the novel: 'We now read for other reasons the novels in which [Dickens's treatment of the Poor Law] is chiefly discussed. Some adjustment of attention is needed to see the frighteningly evil world of the later part of *Oliver Twist*, which has the private emotional quality of a bad dream, as a proper development of the opening chapters. We tend rather to think of the first part as a detached tract, preliminary to the novel that matters.' *The Dickens World* (London, 1960; first published 1941), p. 92.

Oliver that he wants to have a serious talk with him, the boy at once takes alarm:

> 'Oh, don't tell me you are going to send me away, sir, pray!' exclaimed Oliver, alarmed at the serious tone of the old gentle-man's commencement; 'don't turn me out of doors to wander in the streets again. Let me stay here, and be a servant. Don't send me back to the wretched place I came from. Have mercy upon a poor boy, sir!' (p. 85)

After three months in the country with Mrs. Maylie and Rose, Oliver is said to have 'become completely domesticated with the old lady and her niece' (p. 212). And at the end of the novel, when he returns to his birthplace, the essential change in his condition is made clear:

> But if Oliver, under these influences, had remained silent while they journeyed towards his birthplace by a road he had never seen, how the whole current of his recollections ran back to old times, and what a crowd of emotions were wakened up in his breast, when they turned into that which he had traversed on foot: a poor houseless wandering boy, without a friend to help him, or a roof to shelter his head. (p. 348)

A recognition of the structural and imaginative importance of the analogues inclines us to trust the tale, rather than the artist, in postulating the central theme of the work. The tale suggests that the central theme is the fate of the homeless in early nineteenth-century England; and in turning to it, Dickens was proceeding further along the road on which he had set out in *Pickwick Papers*. Social injustice was the theme he had discovered in the writing of *Pickwick*; and it should come as no surprise that he fixed in his second novel on so obvious a manifestation of it as the treatment of the poor. Pickwick becomes a victim of social injustice—Oliver is born one.

This view of the theme is similar to that advanced by Arnold Kettle in what seems to me to be the best critical account of *Oliver Twist*; but I would urge that we bear in mind the close connection between theme and structure, and so read the novel with an altogether different emphasis from that given it by Kettle. He says that the 'pattern' of the novel 'is the contrasted relation of two worlds—the underworld of the workhouse, the funeral, the thieves' kitchen, and the comfortable world of the Brownlows and Maylies'; and he maintains that 'the power of the book . . . proceeds from the wonderful evocation of the underworld and the engagement of our sympathy on behalf of the inhabitants of that world.'[1] I think it essential to see that the workhouse is not part of the underworld, is not on a par with the thieves' kitchen. The poor in this novel are poised between its two worlds—whether we call them 'the comfortable world' and 'the underworld' or the worlds of civilized order and crime—not relegated from the start to the latter. And because their fate is made to hang in the balance, as it were, it is by them, in the person of Oliver, that our sympathy is engaged, not by the inhabitants of the underworld at large, and certainly not by its typical representatives, Fagin and Bill Sikes. Dickens, at any rate, would have been surprised by Kettle's sympathies. In his Preface, he says that he drew some of his characters 'from the most criminal and degraded of London's population' (p. lxi); and he adds:

> It appeared to me that to draw a knot of such associates in crime as really do exist; to paint them in all their deformity, in all their wretchedness, in all the squalid poverty of their lives; to shew them as they really are, for ever skulking uneasily through the dirtiest paths of life, with the great, black, ghastly gallows closing up their prospect, turn them where they may; it appeared to me that to do this, would be to attempt a something which was greatly needed, and which would be a service to society. And therefore I did it as I best could. (p. lxii)

It seems to me, furthermore, that Kettle's failure to locate the poor in relation to the two worlds of the novel leads him to mistake its general drift. I fully agree with his contention that 'the core of the novel, and what gives it value, is its consideration of the plight of the poor' (p. 130); but must dissent when he goes on to say that the 'living . . . conflict of the book . . .—symbolized . . . by the gruel scene—is the struggle of the poor against the bourgeois state . . .' (p. 132), and that 'the central theme' is 'what are the poor to do against the oppressive state?' (p. 134). The poor in this novel do not struggle against the state. Oliver, after all, is the representative figure here; and if he rebels against the workhouse in asking for more, that is the

---

[1] 'Dickens: *Oliver Twist*', *An Introduction to the English Novel* (London, 1951), Vol. I, pp. 130, 131. The essay is reprinted in *The Dickens Critics*, ed. George H. Ford and Lauriat Lane.

full extent of his civil disobedience. What the plot suggests is that the poor, as in the case of Oliver, are finally forced on to the streets; and what happens to them thereafter, which world they come in the end to inhabit, is largely a matter of chance. The novel is not concerned with what the poor should do against the oppressive state, but, I shall argue, with what the well-housed and the well-fed should do to ensure that the poor do not opt for the criminal. To view the Artful Dodger's defiance of the court that tries him as representative of the struggle of the poor against the state, as Kettle does, is to blur the fundamental distinction between the poor and the criminal. And to imply, as I think Kettle does, that criminal existence is itself part of that struggle, a protest against the bourgeois state, is to impose a reading on the novel that is too revolutionary by far for the work of the young Dickens, who, viewing his presentation of the criminals as a deterrent, intended their depiction to be 'a service' to the bourgeois society for which he was writing.

Dickens's social criticism is effective, if limited, because it is conveyed in terms of the two main images of the novel, the striking but simple images of home and street. This, for instance, is how we are made to view the workhouse:

> The members of this board were very sage, deep, philosophical men; and when they came to turn their attention to the workhouse, they found out at once, what ordinary folks would never have discovered—the poor people liked it! It was a regular place of public entertainment for the poorer classes; a tavern where there was nothing to pay; a public breakfast, dinner, tea, and supper all the year round; a brick-and-mortar elysium, where it was all play and no work. 'Oho!' said the board, looking very knowing; 'we are the fellows to set this to rights; we'll stop it all, in no time.' So, they established the rule, that all poor people should have the alternative (for they would compel nobody, not they,) of being starved by a gradual process in the house, or by a quick one out of it. With this view, they contracted with the water-works to lay on an unlimited supply of water; and with a corn-factor to supply periodically small quantities of oatmeal; and issued three meals of thin gruel a day, with an onion twice a week, and half a roll on Sundays. They made a great many other wise and humane regulations, having reference to the ladies, which it is not necessary to repeat; kindly undertook to

divorce poor married people, in consequence of the great expense of a suit in Doctors' Commons; and, instead of compelling a man to support his family, as they had theretofore done, took his family away from him, and made him a bachelor! There is no saying how many applicants for relief under these last two heads, might have started up in all classes of society, if it had not been coupled with the workhouse; but the board were long-headed men, and had provided for this difficulty. The relief was inseparable from the workhouse and the gruel; and that frightened people. (pp. 9–10)

The first point to note is the way in which Dickens simplifies issues. If under the new Poor Law of 1834 life in the workhouse was indeed made 'miserable as a matter of policy',[1] he makes no attempt to do justice to the Benthamites (here ingloriously represented by the 'philosophical men' of the board), who were endeavouring to counter the widespread pauperization of labourers under the system which the new law replaced. What Dickens characteristically does is to appeal, as Trevelyan says, 'from the Benthamite abstractions in which the Commissioners dealt, to the flesh and blood realities which interested the more sensitive public of the Victorian era';[2] and so succeed with equally characteristic satirical humour in reducing proffered aid to the poor to a system of unwanted matrimonial relief. It must be said, however, that the flesh and blood realities he presents are not grossly exaggerated. As late as 1850 the diet of paupers in St. Pancras Workhouse was shown to be markedly inferior to that of convicts in Pentonville Prison;[3] and in the same year Dickens himself forcefully drew attention to the fact that convicts were better off than paupers:

> If this girl [i.e., a domestic servant in her early twenties, who was subject to epilepsy and had consequently been sent to the workhouse by her employer] had stolen her mistress's watch, I do not hesitate to say she would, in all probability, have been infinitely better off. Bearing in mind, in the present brief description of this walk, not only the facts already stated in this Journal, in reference to the Model Prison at Pentonville, but the general treatment of convicted prisoners under the associated silent system

[1] George Macaulay Trevelyan, *British History in the Nineteenth Century and After (1782–1919)* (London, 1944; revised edition first published 1937), p. 250.
[2] *Ibid.*
[3] See 'Pet Prisoners', *Household Words*, I (27 April 1850).

too, it must be once more distinctly set before the reader that we have come to this absurd, this dangerous, this monstrous pass, that the dishonest felon is, in respect of cleanliness, order, diet, and accommodation, better provided for, and taken care of, than the honest pauper.[1]

The indictment of the workhouse in *Oliver Twist* is effective because it is focussed on its specific failure to be a home for the indigent: it is a place in which the married man is separated from his family 'and made . . . a bachelor', and the alternative to a life in the streets that it offers is to be 'starved by a gradual process' rather than 'by a quick one'. Far from being made at home, the inmates of the workhouse are depersonalized by it: born in the workhouse, Oliver—an 'item of mortality' (p. 1)—is 'badged and ticketed' a parish child (p. 3); and is finally put out 'To Let', five pounds being offered 'to anybody who [will] take possession of him' (p. 19). It is for the midnight streets that he is schooled by the 'want and cold' (p. 4) he suffers at the baby-farm to which he is sent and by 'the gloom of his infant years' (p. 8).

It is in this light that the most famous incident in the book should, I think, be viewed. J. Hillis Miller maintains that 'the fame of the scene in which Oliver asks for "more" derives . . . from the way it expresses dynamically Oliver's revolt against the hostile social and material world';[2] but it seems to me that the scene above all dramatizes, in the most direct and simple manner, the extent to which what is taken for granted at home is denied in the workhouse. Hence the enormity of the response to Oliver's request; and hence the power of the scene, which appeals to our own deepest sense of the right to ask for more as a natural perquisite of home and childhood. In this incident Oliver no doubt does revolt against the workhouse system, but it is not as a rebel that he is cast in the novel; indeed, his single act of rebellion against the sort of authority represented by the workhouse even falls to him by lot (p. 11). He is throughout, rather, the exemplar of a boy without a home; and it is on its failure to provide him with one, to save him from the streets, that Dickens's indictment of the workhouse rests.

Dickens's treatment of the workhouse as the central institution depicted in the novel foreshadows the way in which institutions are pre-

---

[1] 'A Walk in a Workhouse', *Household Words*, I (25 May 1850), 205. The article is attributed to Dickens by Frederic G. Kitton, *The Minor Writings of Charles Dickens: A Bibliography and Sketch* (London, 1900), p. 124.
[2] *Charles Dickens*, p. 38.

sented in later novels such as *Bleak House* and *Little Dorrit*, yet reveals the limitations of his method at this stage of his career. The workhouse is not treated as an isolated social abuse, as Dotheboys Hall is in *Nicholas Nickleby* (which followed *Oliver Twist*); but, at the same time, it is not established as representative of the society that has produced it in the way that the Court of Chancery and the Circumlocution Office are. The structure of the novel, with its polarized worlds, cannot accommodate such an effect, for the workhouse is not part of either. Thus, though the failure of the workhouse is symbolic of the wider failure of society to make adequate provision for the poor, and this failure is fraught with the dangers that are dramatized in Oliver's story; the attitudes that lie behind the failure have no correlative in the world that, we must assume, has brought the workhouse into being. The representative inhabitants of this world are the Brownlows and the Maylies, but there is no indication that they share in a social responsibility for the workhouse. Responsibility is simply attributed, in a kind of limbo, to disembodied 'philosophers' and to fat but insubstantial gentlemen of the board. Dickens's social criticism in *Oliver Twist*, in other words, is limited in force because, though it probes, it does not probe home. The workhouse may mediate between the two worlds of the novel, but it does not link them; whereas in the later novels, as I shall try to show, the institutions that are attacked function as the foci of multifarious worlds that radiate from them, and the analogical method is used to relate public failure and private complaisance.

In *Oliver Twist* Dickens's social criticism is accordingly less subversive in its implications than in the later novels. It seems to presuppose a fundamental good will on the part of those with power, and therefore to be directed towards two simple prescriptions. The first of these is symbolized in the scene in which Oliver, having been put out To Let and claimed by Mr. Gamfield, is brought before the magistrate in order to be formally apprenticed to the sweep:

> 'And this man that's to be his master—you, sir—you'll treat him well, and feed him, and do all that sort of thing,—will you?' said the old gentleman.
>
> 'When I says I will, I means I will,' replied Mr. Gamfield doggedly.
>
> 'You're a rough speaker, my friend, but you look an honest, open-hearted man,' said the old gentleman: turning his spectacles

in the direction of the candidate for Oliver's premium, whose
villainous countenance was a regular stamped receipt for cruelty.
But, the magistrate was half blind and half childish, so he
couldn't reasonably be expected to discern what other people did.

'I hope I am, sir,' said Mr. Gamfield with an ugly leer.

'I have no doubt you are, my friend,' replied the old gentleman: fixing his spectacles more firmly on his nose, and looking
about him for the inkstand.

It was the critical moment of Oliver's fate. If the inkstand
had been where the old gentleman thought it was, he would
have dipped his pen into it, and signed the indentures; and Oliver
would have been straightway hurried off. But, as it chanced to
be immediately under his nose, it followed, as a matter of course,
that he looked all over his desk for it, without finding it; and
happening in the course of his search to look straight before him,
his gaze encountered the pale and terrified face of Oliver Twist:
who, despite all the admonitory looks and pinches of Bumble,
was regarding the repulsive countenance of his future master:
with a mingled expression of horror and fear, too palpable to be
mistaken, even by a half-blind magistrate. (pp. 17–18)

If this is to be regarded as 'the critical moment of Oliver's fate', then
it is clear what saves him. It is when the magistrate really sees Oliver
for the first time that his plight becomes 'too palpable to be mistaken',
and he responds to it by refusing to sanction the indentures (p. 19).
The novel as a whole seems to imply that what is required on the part
of authority in regard to the workhouse, and so in regard to the treatment of the poor, is, for a start, simply a recognition of the true state
of affairs. Dickens appears to assume that such a recognition, like that
of the 'half-blind magistrate', who does not see things 'immediately
under his nose', will be sufficient for natural decency to assert itself.
Hence his advocacy of realism in the novel—his own kind of realism—
suggests more than a predilection for a particular literary mode; it is
the assumption of a weapon, and the aim (announced in the Preface)
of showing things 'as they really are' has a wider frame of reference
than the defence of his procedure in his depiction of the criminals
in *Oliver Twist*. The extent to which Dickens thought of his work
in terms of the exposure of abuse, a 'showing up' of what needed to
be attacked, and therefore in terms of a fidelity to things as they are,
is directly revealed in a letter which discloses how Mr. Laing, a

magistrate notorious for his severity, sat for Mr. Fang, the magistrate who tries Oliver on a charge of pickpocketing. The letter is to Thomas Haines, a reporter at the Mansion House police office:

> In my next number of *Oliver Twist*, I must have a magistrate; and casting about for a magistrate whose harshness and insolence would render him a fit subject to be 'shewn up' I have, as a necessary consequence, stumbled upon Mr. Laing of Hatton Garden celebrity. I know the man's character perfectly well, but as it would be necessary to describe his appearance also, I ought to have seen him, which (fortunately or unfortunately as the case may be) I have never done.
>
> In this dilemma it occurred to me that perhaps I might under your auspices be smuggled into the Hatton Garden office for a few moments some morning. If you can further my object, I shall be really very greatly obliged to you.[1]

Showing things as they are, then, is designed to ensure the kind of recognition that leads to action. Just what action should be taken by those who look at the scenes of *Oliver Twist*, scenes under *their* noses, is implicit in the structure and imagery of the novel. It is vividly suggested in the following passage:

> In such a neighbourhood, beyond Dockhead in the Borough of Southwark, stands Jacob's Island, surrounded by a muddy ditch, six or eight feet deep and fifteen or twenty wide when the tide is in, once called Mill Pond, but known in these days as Folly Ditch. It is a creek or inlet from the Thames, and can always be filled at high water by opening the sluices at the Lead Mills from which it took its old name. At such times, a stranger, looking from one of the wooden bridges thrown across it at Mill-lane, will see the inhabitants of the houses on either side lowering from their back-doors and windows, buckets, pails, domestic utensils of all kinds, in which to haul the water up; and when his eye is turned from these operations to the houses themselves, his utmost astonishment will be excited by the scene before him. Crazy wooden galleries common to the backs of half a dozen houses, with holes from which to look upon the

---

[1] The Pilgrim edition of *The Letters*, ed. Madeline House and Graham Storey (London, 1965), Vol. I, p. 267.

slime beneath; windows, broken and patched: with poles thrust out, on which to dry the linen that is never there; rooms so small, so filthy, so confined, that the air would seem too tainted even for the dirt and squalor which they shelter; wooden chambers thrusting themselves out above the mud, and threatening to fall into it—as some have done; dirt-besmeared walls and decaying foundations; every repulsive lineament of poverty, every loathsome indication of filth, rot, and garbage; all these ornament the banks of Folly Ditch.

In Jacob's Island, the warehouses are roofless and empty; the walls are crumbling down; the windows are windows no more; the doors are falling into the streets; the chimneys are blackened, but they yield no smoke. Thirty or forty years ago, before losses and chancery suits came upon it, it was a thriving place; but now it is a desolate island indeed. The houses have no owners; they are broken open, and entered upon by those who have the courage; and there they live, and there they die. They must have powerful motives for a secret residence, or be reduced to a destitute condition indeed, who seek a refuge in Jacob's Island. (p. 339)

The central motive of this passage, the decay of the houses in Jacob's Island, is at once apparent. It is insisted on again and again with fierce intensity: the 'crazy wooden galleries' with holes in them; the 'broken and patched' windows; the wooden chambers 'threatening to fall' into the mud; the 'decaying foundations'; the 'roofless and empty' warehouses; the walls that are 'crumbling down'; the windows that are 'windows no more'; the doors that are 'falling into the streets'. Whole houses, as well as doors, are falling into the streets—or seem about to do so. Jacob's Island, that is to say, is the place where the two worlds of the novel meet, where a home is only barely distinguishable from the street; and it is no accident that the action should converge on it in the climatic pages of the narrative. But Jacob's Island is not only the meeting-place of home and street; it is the nexus of crime and poverty, for those who 'seek a refuge' in it either have 'powerful motives for a secret residence' or are 'reduced to a destitute condition indeed'. What the narrative asserts, in other words, is that the workhouse leads to Jacob's Island, that for the likes of Oliver there is no other home (though he himself is providentially provided with one); and that, once they take up residence there, closely lodged with the criminal, the 'repulsive lineament[s] of poverty' are likely to be a 'loathsome indication' of more than an outer 'rot'. It is not the air alone that is 'tainted' in the 'dirt and squalor'.

Kathleen Tillotson maintains that since the 1841 Preface 'says nothing about the more specific social and political purposes of the novel', this 'perhaps suggests that Dickens felt them relatively incidental and temporary'.[1] It seems to me, rather, that the passion invested in the description of Jacob's Island, not to mention the general tenor of the narrative, suggests that Dickens's 'social purpose' in the novel is not only fundamental but its animating principle. And though it is not part of the novelist's job to specify the kind of political action that should be taken to counter social ills, I should say, moreover, that the Jacob's Island passage, given the context of the novel as a whole, shouts the need to provide homes for the poor. This is the second prescription of *Oliver Twist*. And this is how Dickens himself viewed the matter, as the Preface to the 1850 edition of the novel makes clear:

> At page 267 of this present edition of OLIVER TWIST, there is a description of 'the filthiest, the strangest, the most extraordinary, of the many localities that are hidden in London.' And the name of this place is JACOB'S ISLAND.
>
> Eleven or twelve years have elapsed, since the description was first published. I was as well convinced then, as I am now, that nothing effectual can be done for the elevation of the poor in England, until their dwelling-places are made decent and wholesome. I have always been convinced that this Reform must precede all other Social Reforms; that it must prepare the way for Education, even for Religion; and that, without it, those classes of people which increase the fastest, must become so desperate and be made so miserable, as to bear within themselves the certain seeds of ruin to the whole community. (Appendix B, p. 382)

Written by the mature Dickens, the concluding lines of this passage go further than anything in *Oliver Twist*: they not only assert a connection between poverty and crime but postulate the retributive effects of such a connection on a society that neglects its poor. The vision, indeed, is the vision of *Bleak House*, which Dickens began to write in 1851; and the 1850 Preface points to a link between the description of Jacob's Island and the later novel which may be discerned

[1] *'Oliver Twist'*, *Essays and Studies* (New Series), XII (1959), 101.

in the description itself. Jacob's Island, which has been ruined by 'chancery suits', is a first version of Tom-all-Alone's; and though it would seem to be safely cut off from the comfortable homes of London by the 'muddy ditch' which surrounds it, its 'tainted' air is the air which will work the corruption of Tom's blood, against which none of those homes will be proof. Its decaying houses, moreover, fore-shadow the falling houses in the *Bleak House* slum—and the social collapse they portend.[1] Dickens's imagination, in other words, seized in *Oliver Twist* on material which his art could not yet fully encompass and discipline.

II

If we consider the novel I have been discussing as the first (because primary) of the two novels *Oliver Twist* comprises, Dickens 'intended' the second and very different novel that he describes in his Preface:

> ... when I wished to shew, in little Oliver, the principle of Good surviving through every adverse circumstance, and triumphing at last; and when I considered among what companions I could try him best, having regard to that kind of men into whose hands he would most naturally fall; I bethought myself of those who figure in these volumes. (p. lxii)

This view of the novel is also given Forster's imprimatur:

> It is ... the primary purpose of the tale to show its little hero, jostled as he is in the miserable crowd, preserved everywhere from the vice of its pollution, by an exquisite delicacy of natural sentiment which clings to him under every disadvantage.[2]

Granting that we should attend to what is actually done in the novel rather than to what the novelist intended to do, we must nevertheless recognize that Dickens's overt intention has left its mark and is re-sponsible for the thematic bifurcation of the work. The quoted state-ments emphasize how great the division is. If it is conceded that Oliver's search for a home is at the centre of the narrative, then

[1] See Ch. 5, p. 176 below.
[2] John Forster, *Charles Dickens*, I, 136.

whether he finds one or not is made dependent on two factors which are in no way necessarily connected. It is made dependent, if we follow Dickens and Forster, on the quality of Oilver's virtue; but the tale suggests, rather, that it depends on the operation of social circumstance Similarly, the fact of crime, which is central to the novel, is subject to two different, and exclusive views. If we go by the Preface, crime i merely incidental to the trial of goodness—'I considered among what companions I could try him best'—and it is virtue which is put on trial in the novel. If we respond to the structure, however, we see that crime is a fundamental feature of life in the society depicted; and since Oliver, the illegitimate foundling and responsibility of the state very nearly falls a victim to it, it is society which is put on trial. Faced by these contradictions, the critic, I think, must distinguish art from artifice

Dickens's attempt, for the first time, to establish a form by con structing a plot is the most obvious sign of artifice in the novel. The plot, as has been often remarked, is thoroughly inept. It is melodramatic the stage-villain Monks (a king-pin of the machinery) being a repre sentative instance here: he is unconvincingly motivated, and his pre sentation throughout is sensational and theatrical. The plot has not even a decent minimum of verisimilitude: Monks starts his machina tions when he 'accidentally [encounters]' Oliver, whom he has never seen before, and has his 'suspicions . . . awakened' by Oliver's 're semblance to his father' (p. 336); for good measure, Mr. Brownlow is struck by Oliver's 'strong resemblance' to a picture of his mother on the strength of which he determines to track down Monks and set off on a journey to the West Indies (p. 335). Finally, the plot is made to depend on an immoderate use of coincidence: Brownlow, the oldest friend of Oliver's father, is the man of all the men in the streets of London with whom Oliver becomes involved as a suspected pick pocket; the Maylie home, the residence of the sister of Oliver's mother is the house of all the houses available for the purpose that Sikes choose to burgle.

Kathleen Tillotson declares that these coincidences are 'designed by Dickens precisely to illustrate the power of the principle of Good Mr. Brownlow says it was a "stronger hand than chance" that brought Oliver to his door, and the sophisticated reader is not meant to add that the stronger hand was the author's.'[1] But since the principle of Good as I shall argue, is not satisfactorily embodied 'in little Oliver', the putatively virtuous object of the stronger hand's ministrations, I, for

---

[1] '*Oliver Twist*', loc. cit., p. 93.

one, find that I cannot help making the prohibited addition. For the same reason, and also because *Oliver Twist* seems to me to be grounded in the social if ever novel was, I find it difficult to allow for the co-incidences, as Steven Marcus does, by accepting that 'in effect there is . . . no reality, no existence in *Oliver Twist* other than the parabolic one the characters inhabit and serve'; by reading the novel, that is to say, as a moral fable 'in the tradition of Bunyan', with Oliver 'essentially the incarnation of a moral quality'.[1]

The mundane coincidences should not be moralized away, the more especially since melodrama and coincidence are features of most of Dickens's plots—they are the marks of the Dickens world, of the under-world, as it were, of his fiction—though in his later work, at least, they are never as crude as here; and the late plots are themselves impressively integrated in wider designs. The plot of *Oliver Twist*, however, is so manifestly weak as to undermine belief in that part of the action which is concerned with the salvation of Oliver; and his salvation consequently appears to be arbitrary rather than the reward of virtue. His salvation, indeed, is forcibly superimposed on the action by the plot; and as Arnold Kettle, among others, has pointed out,[2] it runs counter to the main movement of the narrative. This, as we have seen, would seem to propel Oliver along a path that leads irrevocably from the workhouse to Jacob's Island or its like.

Our belief in Oliver as an embodiment of the principle of Good has first of all to overcome what elsewhere in Dickens we do well to respond to—the force of analogy. On the occasion of the fight with Noah Claypole, which leads Oliver to take to the streets, Noah is described as provoking him, 'like [the] malicious and ill-conditioned charity-boy' that he is (p. 36). 'Ill-conditioned' is doubtless meant merely to refer to Noah's wicked disposition, but its association with 'charity-boy' makes it suggest that Noah has been subject to something like the modern notion of conditioning. And this is precisely what Oliver, a charity-boy by birth if not education, and against all the odds, is shown to be immune to. It is true we are told, when Oliver leaves the workhouse for the undertaker's, that he is 'in a fair way of [having been] reduced, for life, to a state of brutal stupidity and sullenness by the ill-usage he [has] received' (pp. 22–3); but these qualities are not otherwise in evidence, and the ill-usage proves to be less lasting in its effects. If Oliver has indeed 'been brought up bad', as the Dodger

[1] *Dickens*, pp. 79, 67, 80.
[2] *The English Novel*, I, 131–2

asserts in response to his innocence of the meaning of the word 'scragged', he lives to confound the latter's prognostication: 'Fagin will make something of you, though, or you'll be the first he ever had that turned out unprofitable' (p. 118). Oliver's unassailable virtue, in other words, simply has to be taken, in spite of all that is implied about the corrupting power of his environment, as Dickens's donnée; but we need a large measure of credulity to find it acceptable.

Doubt is furthermore cast on the unassailability of Oliver's virtue by the symbolism of two powerful scenes, which are not adequately accounted for in terms of the plot but suggest, however, a more convincing view of his experience. On the first morning of his stay with Fagin, Oliver wakes from 'a sound, long sleep' and finds himself alone with the old man:

> Although Oliver had roused himself from sleep, he was not thoroughly awake. There is a drowsy state, between sleeping and waking, when you dream more in five minutes with your eyes half open, and yourself half conscious of everything that is passing around you, than you would in five nights with your eyes fast closed, and your senses wrapt in perfect unconsciousness. At such times, a mortal knows just enough of what his mind is doing, to form some glimmering conception of its mighty powers: its bounding from earth and spurning time and space: when freed from the restraint of its corporeal associate.
>
> Oliver was precisely in this condition. He saw the Jew with his half-closed eyes; heard his low whistling; and recognised the sound of the spoon, grating against the saucepan's sides; and yet the self-same senses were mentally engaged, at the same time, in busy action with almost everybody he had ever known.

Believing Oliver to be asleep, Fagin takes a small box from a trap in the floor, and '[surveys] with . . . pleasure' a number of magnificent watches and articles of costly jewellery that he draws from it:

> Having replaced these trinkets, the Jew took out another: so small that it lay in the palm of his hand. There seemed to be some very minute inscription on it; for the Jew laid it flat upon the table: and shading it with his hand: pored over it, long and earnestly. At length he put it down, as if despairing of success; and, leaning back in his chair, muttered,

'What a fine thing capital punishment is! Dead men never repent; dead men never bring awkward stories to light. Ah, it's a fine thing for the trade! Five of 'em strung up in a row; and none left to play booty, or turn white-livered!' (pp. 51–2)

The description of Fagin examining his stolen treasure is so deliberately heightened by the account given of Oliver, who is watching him, that we are led to believe that the trinket with 'some very minute inscription on it' must have a special significance. This, indeed, is how J. Hillis Miller explains the scene: 'For what Oliver sees is Fagin gloating over his stolen jewels, and "poring long and earnestly" over a tiny trinket which may be a clue to his origin, and to his lost identity. This trinket functions as a magic talisman in whose presence the half-dreaming Oliver is put in touch with his past.'[1] But the fact of the matter is that the trinket has no such significance; Fagin does not yet know who Oliver is, since Monks has not yet encountered and identified him, and nothing more is made of the trinket. We can only conclude that the scene has no special function in the plot, and that significance is to be sought in Oliver's condition rather than in the trinket.

Though he is half-asleep, Oliver's state is clearly one of heightened consciousness: in such a state one is said to dream more in five minutes than in five nights. Freed from 'the restraint of its corporeal associate', and so 'spurning time and space', his mind, moreover, is a mind receptive to visionary experience. The vision is one that Oliver does not understand, that Dickens himself, perhaps, understands only imaginatively, not intellectually, for it negates a great deal of what he consciously asserts in regard to Oliver. It is a vision in which Fagin the thief is inextricably entwined with 'almost everybody' Oliver has 'ever known', is inextricably entwined, that is, with Oliver's past life. What is conveyed is that Oliver's whole past has led inevitably to Fagin; and what is implied is that, if in the future he is to be separated from the thief, it will not be by way of a Brownlow but of the gallows, with which Fagin's mind is busy.

This scene, as has been pointed out, bears a close resemblance to one that follows much later in the novel. Secure with the Maylies in their country retreat, Oliver is working at his books one evening when he falls into a half-sleep that is described in much the same terms as in the previously quoted passage, it even being explicitly stated that his

[1] *Charles Dickens*, p. 75.

is a condition in which 'visionary scenes . . . pass before' one. Suddenly he becomes aware of Fagin and Monks peering at him through the open window. They disappear at once, but 'their look' is 'as firmly impressed upon his memory, as if it had been deeply carved in stone, and set before him from his birth' (pp. 227–8). Once again we are ready to assume that the incident will have some significance in the plot, Colin Williamson even maintaining that it 'was to lead to Oliver's second and nearly catastrophic period of captivity', but that Dickens changed his plans.[1] All that is actually made of the incident in the plot, however, is Mr. Brownlow's later revelation that 'the Jew . . . had [received] a large reward [from Monks] for keeping Oliver ensnared: of which some part was to be given up, in the event of his being rescued: and that a dispute on this head had led to their visit to the country house for the purpose of identifying him' (p. 352). This ties threads together, but hardly accounts for the weight given the incident and for the powerful impression it makes. What the scene would appear to convey, therefore, is that Oliver, even in his snug retreat, is unable to shut out Fagin, that his bond with him is as ineffaceable as if it too had been 'deeply carved in stone, and set before him from his birth'. When 'the inmates of the house, attracted by Oliver's cries', attempt to pursue the men, they can find no trace of them: 'The grass was long; but it was trodden down nowhere, save where their own feet had crushed it. The sides and brinks of the ditches, were of damp clay; but in no one place could they discern the print of men's shoes, or the slightest mark which would indicate that any feet had pressed the ground for hours before' (pp. 229–30). We are provoked into commenting that the only marks Fagin leaves are those he has left on Oliver—but of these too there are, miraculously, no trace.

If Oliver's innocence must nevertheless be taken as impermeable, we cannot help noticing, however, that it is sometimes made to appear less like a manifestation of his virtue than of the stupidity he is said to have been reduced to by the workhouse. Not only does he fail to understand the meaning of the 'game' that Fagin plays with his boys and then with him (pp. 55–6); when he is finally allowed to accompany the Dodger and Master Bates on one of their excursions, he wonders 'where they [are] going, and what branch of manufacture he [will] be instructed in, first' (p. 57). Similarly, on another and later occasion

---

[1] 'Two Missing Links in *Oliver Twist*', *Nineteenth-Century Fiction*, XXII (December 1967), 229.

'when he has learnt what industry Fagin and his gang are engaged in), he watches Bill Sikes and Toby Crackit stow away the tools of their trade in preparation for their assault on the Maylie household; but it is only when they have actually climbed the wall of the house and are '[stealing] cautiously' towards it that he registers 'for the first time' what 'the objects of the expedition' are (pp. 142–3).

This expedition is the occasion of a climactic scene in which Dickens shows 'in little Oliver, the principle of Good . . . triumphing at last', but the scene does not have quite the effect that was apparently intended:

> And now, for the first time, Oliver, well nigh mad with grief and terror, saw that housebreaking and robbery, if not murder, were the objects of the expedition. He clasped his hands together, and involuntarily uttered a subdued exclamation of horror. A mist came before his eyes; the cold sweat stood upon his ashy face; his limbs failed him; and he sunk upon his knees.
>
> 'Get up!' murmured Sikes, trembling with rage, and drawing the pistol from his pocket; 'get up, or I'll strew your brains upon the grass.'
>
> 'Oh! for God's sake let me go!' cried Oliver; 'let me run away and die in the fields. I will never come near London; never, never! Oh! pray have mercy on me, and do not make me steal. For the love of all the bright Angels that rest in Heaven, have mercy upon me!' (p. 143)

The first thing we notice about the presentation of Oliver at this crisis in his fortunes is its utter banality. The scene of his appeal to Sikes is conceived in clichés of language and action: he is 'well nigh mad with grief and terror', he clasps his hands together and utters (involuntarily) an 'exclamation of horror', a mist comes before his eyes, the 'cold sweat' stands on his 'ashy face', his limbs fail him, he sinks upon his knees and, begging not to be made to steal, invokes 'the bright Angels that rest in Heaven'. The best that we can say of this sort of thing, of the sense of the second-hand and of a striving for effect that the passage communicates, is that, though Dickens has taken embattled virtue for a subject, it has certainly not caught his imagination. Nor is virtue in fact shown to be efficacious. Forcibly put into the house through a small window by Sikes, and instructed at pistol-point to open the street door, Oliver 'firmly [resolves] that, whether he [die] in the attempt or not, he [will] make one effort to dart up stairs from the hall, and alarm the family' (p. 145)—but it is not by this resolution that he is saved after all. Fired at and wounded, not by Sikes but by the aroused Giles, he is once again a passive victim of forces beyond his control.

Oliver is saved from committing a criminal act, then, by external circumstance—in a word, by the plot. He is thereafter established in his own right in the world of the respectable through the endeavours of Nancy; but, in devising this part of the plot, Dickens is led to subvert his ostensible moral theme. Several critics have commented on the weakness of Nancy's characterization, declaring, for instance, that she is 'finally null',[1] or quite '[unreal] as a literary creation';[2] but, though until late in his career Dickens's young women (like Rose in this novel) are generally idealized and romanticized with abandon, it seems to me that Nancy is convincing enough. Despite some sentimental touches in her presentation, I find it easier to assent to Dickens's claim in the Preface that 'IT IS TRUE', though 'a contradiction, an anomaly, an apparent impossibility' (p. lxv), than to accept his view of Oliver. What requires consideration, however, is not the anomaly of her character but of her position in relation to Oliver.

Nancy's ultimate befriending of Oliver at considerable risk to herself—at what proves to be the cost of her own life—is prepared for in the plot. She is first shown to be different from Fagin and Sikes when, having herself been instrumental in Oliver's recapture, she seeks to protect him as he makes a vain bid to escape. Both Sikes and Fagin are presented as unremittingly brutal, the former being ready to turn his dog on Oliver, though Nancy fears 'he'll tear the boy to pieces'; and the latter beating him, when he has been caught, with 'a jagged and knotted club'. Nancy, however, struggles with Sikes in order to prevent him from releasing the dog, though he threatens to 'split [her] head against the wall'; and, wresting the club from Fagin's hand, she throws it into the fire, declaring that she 'won't stand by' and see Oliver beaten now that he has 'got the boy' again (pp. 102–3). Nancy thus not only shows a warm human compassion for Oliver, in contrast to the brutality of the men, but is also completely disinterested and regardless of self. The qualities of character she displays, that is to say, and they are the same as those she manifests in her later, and fatal,

---

[1] Angus Wilson, Introduction to Penguin English Library edition of *Oliver Twist*, ed. Peter Fairclough (Harmondsworth, 1966), p. 22.
[2] Philip Collins, *Dickens and Crime* (London, 1962), p. 261.

attempt to establish Oliver's rights, are not adequately described as being 'the last fair drop of water at the bottom of the dried-up weed-choked well' (Preface, p. lxv). They seem to me to amount, for all practical purposes, to a 'principle of Good surviving through every adverse circumstance'. What the tale suggests, therefore, is that, though Nancy, the prostitute, is said to belong to a 'particular species of humanity' (p. 102), she does not belong to it because of a natural depravity; and, equally, that her genuine goodness has not sufficed to save her from so belonging.

The description of Nancy, as she prepares herself to meet Rose for the first time, clearly indicates what has made her what she is:

> The girl's life had been squandered in the streets, and among the most noisome of the stews and dens of London, but there was something of the woman's original nature left in her still; and when she heard a light step approaching the door opposite to that by which she had entered, and thought of the wide contrast which the small room would in another moment contain, she felt burdened with the sense of her own deep shame: and shrunk as though she could scarcely bear the presence of her with whom she had sought this interview.
>
> But struggling with these better feelings was pride,—the vice of the lowest and most debased creatures no less than of the high and self-assured. The miserable companion of thieves and ruffians, the fallen outcast of low haunts, the associate of the scourings of the jails and hulks, living within the shadow of the gallows itself, —even this degraded being felt too proud to betray a feeble gleam of the womanly feeling which she thought a weakness, but which alone connected her with that humanity, of which her wasting life had obliterated so many, many traces when a very child.

Nancy tells Rose that she is an 'infamous creature', and that 'the poorest women fall back, as [she makes her] way along the crowded pavement'. When Rose herself 'involuntarily [falls] from her strange companion', Nancy cries out:

> 'Thank heaven upon your knees, dear lady . . . that you had friends to care for and keep you in your childhood, and that you were never in the midst of cold and hunger, and riot and drunken-ness, and—and something worse than all—as I have been from

my cradle; I may use the word, for the alley and gutter were
mine, as they will be my death-bed.' (pp. 270–1)

There is an interesting connection between the first of these passages
and the scene in which Nancy defends Oliver from Sikes and Fagin.
If there is said to be 'something of the woman's original nature' still
left in Nancy, this quality is clearly 'the womanly feeling' which she
thinks a weakness but which 'alone [connects] her with . . . humanity';
it is thus that which distinguishes man from brute—that is, it is the
kind of natural human goodness she displays in her earlier defence of
Oliver. The 'wide contrast' between herself and Rose that Nancy
anticipates is developed in terms of this implicit definition. Nancy's
'original nature' or natural goodness has been 'squandered', and she
has been left with a 'wasting life'; Rose's has been husbanded and preserved. Nancy's goodness has been squandered because she has been
exposed since childhood to the streets—it has, indeed, been 'squandered
in the streets'; Rose's has been preserved because she has had 'friends
to care for and keep' her in her childhood, in a word, because she has
had a home in which it has been sheltered and nurtured. Nancy consistently projects the difference between herself and Rose in terms which
in turn project the two contrasted worlds of the novel. A street-
walker, she herself is a product of the streets: she says that her 'eyes
and senses [opened] on London streets' (p. 271), that 'the alley and
the gutter' were her 'cradle', and that she has 'no certain roof but
the coffin-lid' (p. 275). Her homelessness is repeatedly stressed, and
it is our sense of it that makes her determination to return home to
Sikes, even though Mr. Brownlow offers her 'a quiet asylum, either
in England, or . . . in some foreign country', so poignant: 'I must go
home,' she says, and when Rose incredulously repeats the word 'home',
she insists on it—'Home, lady . . . To such a home as I have raised
for myself with the work of my whole life' (pp. 315–16). It is a fine
psychological touch, one of many in the presentation of Nancy. Rose,
on the other hand, has known only the amenities of a home, and has
been provided by it with more than physical shelter: she has never
been 'in the midst of cold and hunger, and riot and drunkenness, and
something worse than all'.

John Bayley maintains that 'the imaginative principle of *Oliver
Twist*' is a 'waking nightmare' which 'dispels any true distinction
between the world of darkness which Oliver is in, and the world of
light which he longs for'; in line with this argument, he says that the

meeting between Nancy and Rose is 'dream-like': 'another novelist would make such a confrontation of worlds the most reality-enhancing note in his tale, but in *Oliver Twist* they only confirm the dream atmosphere.'[1] I should say, however, that 'the world of darkness', which is the darkness of the midnight streets, and 'the world of light', which is the light of home, *are* effectively distinguished in the meeting of Nancy and Rose. There is nothing 'dreamlike' about the meeting because it solidly counterposes figures who are representative products of the two worlds of the novel, which both here and elsewhere are rooted in the realities—strongly enough evoked if not enhanced—of street and home. The meeting, indeed, is so firmly grounded in the true stuff of the novel that, though it is necessitated by the plot, it undermines that view of reality which the plot is designed to convey.

At the end of the novel we discover that Rose, like Nancy, may be said to have opened her eyes on the streets, in the sense that she was left helpless and abandoned in childhood; and we may infer that she would have been likely to go the way of Nancy if she had not been provided with a home, first by the 'poor cottagers' who took her in, and then by Mrs. Maylie. Rose and Nancy, in other words, are counterparts—'Two Sister-Women' is the descriptive headline (added in the 1867 edition) to the chapter which describes their first meeting (Appendix C, p. 387)—and the fact that Rose is respectable and Nancy a fallen woman is in no way to be attributed to the operation of a principle of Good. Nancy is a victim not of her nature but of social circumstance—she, indeed, rather than Oliver, carries the victim theme of the novel; Rose, on the other hand is saved if not by luck, then by the grace of God—and home. Both of the girls, moreover, are dramatic counterparts of Oliver. Rose is an Oliver who is saved from the workhouse; Nancy is an Oliver whose goodness does not save her from the streets.

The creation of a convincingly good Nancy, who finally secures Oliver a home, is dictated by the needs of the plot, which is superimposed on the action in the interests of the moral theme; but Nancy herself is a disruptive force, for her story offers an ironic comment on the triumph of the principle of Good in the kind of adverse circumstances in which it is set in the novel. Dickens's first attempt at a plot must be considered a failure on more than one count, but it is in part attributable to his failure to make provision within a plot for

[1] '*Oliver Twist*: "Things as They Really Are"', *Dickens and the Twentieth Century*, ed. John Gross and Gabriel Pearson (London, 1962), pp. 57, 51.

the play of analogy. The elaborate plots of the late novels, with their unifying clusters of analogues, are one measure of the growth of his art.

III

The bifurcation of the novel also means that we are presented with two views of the criminals. On the one hand, in accordance with the spiritual drama that the novel ostensibly enacts, the criminals (and especially Fagin) are presented as an incarnation of the principle of Evil. Fagin, from the moment of his first appearance when he is shown complete with red hair, fire and fork (p. 50), is meant, as Lauriat Lane points out,[1] to be seen as the devil. At one point Sikes says quite explicitly that when Fagin lays his 'withered old claw' on his shoulder, it reminds him of 'being nabbed by the devil' (p. 302); and there are a host of similar references throughout. Though Fagin, however, is convincingly presented as a villainous character, he is not an impressive devil, the embodiment in him of a principle of Evil—like that of a principle of Good in Oliver—being asserted rather than demonstrated. The enduring impression we have of Fagin, who, it will be remembered, seems to have been 'engendered in the slime and darkness' of the streets, 'like some loathsome reptile', is of a man who has ceased to be a man not because he is the devil but because he has become a beast; and this, indeed, is the final impression we carry away of him: in the condemned cell he is shown 'rocking himself from side to side, with a countenance more like that of a snared beast than the face of a man' (p. 363). Bill Sikes is an even more strikingly brutal figure than Fagin. From the moment he '[drops] on his knees' in order to 'assail' his dog (p. 93) to his savage murder of Nancy, he is consistently beast-like in all his actions; and Dickens emphasized the point by the descriptive headlines he added to the chapters which describe the murder and Sikes's own death: 'Goading the Wild Beast', 'The Wild Beast Springs'; 'The Wild Beast hemmed in', 'The Wild Beast laid low' (Appendix C, p. 387). It is, of course, within the social perspective of the novel that we are given this more vivid view of the criminals as beasts. Living in 'dens' and 'lairs', they are less than men because they lack the minimum requirement for a life of civilized order.

[1] 'The Devil in *Oliver Twist*', *The Dickensian*, LII (June 1956), 133.

Dickens's own fascination with the criminal—and no reader of *Oliver Twist* can fail to respond to the intensity of the sections which deal with the murder of Nancy and with the flight and death of Sikes —has been revealingly commented on, from a psychological point of view, by Edmund Wilson:

> For the man of spirit whose childhood has been crushed by the cruelty of organized society, one of two attitudes is natural: that of the criminal or that of the rebel. Charles Dickens, in imagination, was to play the rôles of both, and to continue up to his death to put into them all that was most passionate in his feeling.[1]

I should merely like to add that Dickens's imaginative immersion in the world of the criminal is also of interest in regard to the development of his social criticism. The criminal ethos that is evoked in the novel is characterized by attitudes that are made manifest on the two occasions when Oliver has some direct experience of crime—the stealing of Mr. Brownlow's handkerchief, and the attempted burglary of the Maylie household. On the first occasion, 'confused and frightened' by what he has seen, Oliver '[takes] to his heels' to shouts of 'Stop thief!' and is thoroughly 'alarmed' to find that the Dodger and Master Bates have joined in pursuit of him (pp. 58–9). On the second occasion, after he has been wounded by Giles, Oliver is picked up by Sikes and is at first carried by him in his flight from the house, but is finally left 'lying in a ditch' (p. 161). The twice-enacted abandonment of Oliver reveals clearly enough that the animating principle of the criminal world is not evil for its own sake but a belief, as Toby Crackit puts it, in 'every man for himself' (p. 161); and a consequent readiness on the part of the criminal to betray his fellow. Fagin is equally trenchant: 'Some conjurers,' he tells Mr. Bolter, 'say that number three is the magic number, and some say number seven. It's neither, my friend, neither. It's number one' (p. 293). And the fear of betrayal, of someone's 'playing booty', is the fear that haunts the underworld.

Dickens's presentation of criminal values is at one point made more complex by his use of what at first appears to be a perfectly straightforward simile: when the Dodger and Master Bates join in the pursuit of Oliver on the occasion referred to, they are said to do so 'like good citizens' (p. 58). Though the simile is obviously intended to indicate

[1] 'Dickens: The Two Scrooges', *The Wound and the Bow*, p. 13.

that they pursue Oliver as if they were good citizens, it also obliquely suggests that good citizens might conceivably be actuated by motives such as theirs. It is no more than an oblique suggestion; and, indeed, the representative 'good citizens' in the novel, such as Mr. Brownlow and Rose, are characterized, especially in relation to Oliver, by their selflessness and by their fidelity to him. That good citizens too, however, may be prone to the allurements of Fagin's magic number—if not to playing booty—is indicated in an unguarded moment by Mrs. Maylie. When Rose is apparently dying, Mrs. Maylie says to Oliver: 'It may be time that I should meet with some misfortune; but I hope it is not this'; and when he asks what she means, she replies: 'The heavy blow . . . of losing the dear girl who has so long been my comfort and happiness' (p. 214). Mrs. Maylie, respectably established in her comfortable home, is not exposed to criticism here, it being doubtful whether Dickens himself is aware of the implications of her attitude. The sharpening of his awareness, however, leads in the novels that follow to the realization that what in *Oliver Twist* is taken to be the ethos of the criminal, may, more deviously, also be that of the solid citizen. In *Martin Chuzzlewit* Pecksniff, with his concern for number one and suave readiness to betray all around him in the interests of that number, could serve as a model for Fagin's unsophisticated gang. And Pecksniff is bourgeois man.

3

MARTIN CHUZZLEWIT

I

The outcome of the intentional fallacy, says W. K. Wimsatt, is that the work itself, 'as an object of specifically critical judgment, tends to disappear'.[1] In recent Dickens criticism *Martin Chuzzlewit* is the prime instance of such a disappearance. Critics appear to have relied on one or other of two authoritative statements of 'intention'. In the Preface which he wrote for the first cheap edition of the novel, Dickens defined his aim as follows:

> My main object in this story was, to exhibit in a variety of aspects the commonest of all the vices; to show how Selfishness propagates itself; and to what a grim giant it may grow, from small beginnings.[2]

This declaration was later enlarged on by John Forster:

> . . . the notion of taking Pecksniff for a type of character was really the origin of the book; the design being to show, more or less by every person introduced, the number and variety of humours and vices that have their root in selfishness.[3]

The difficulty of reading *Martin Chuzzlewit* as a 'vast series of multiple perspectives on selfishness'[4] is that Pecksniff, as 'a type of

---

[1] *The Verbal Icon* (New York, 1964), p. 22. Wimsatt's essays on The Intentional Fallacy and The Affective Fallacy (from which the quotation is taken) were written in collaboration with Monroe C. Beardsley.
[2] *Martin Chuzzlewit* (London, 1850), p. vii.
[3] *Charles Dickens*, II, 24.
[4] Edgar Johnson, *Charles Dickens*, I, 470.

character' (and 'the origin of the book') is clearly an exemplar of hypocrisy rather than selfishness, it being in this sense that his name has passed into the language. Some critics, accordingly, have attempted to have their intentional cake and eat it: 'The theme of *Martin Chuzzlewit* is a sort of selfish hypocrisy, and the unity of the book lies in the panoramic picture of this vice';[1] the novel is 'a study in selfishness and hypocrisy'.[2] There is no intrinsic connection, however, between selfishness and hypocrisy; and readings of the novel which are productive of even such cautious modifications of 'the design' point to the existence of a discrepancy between the supposed intention and the impression actually made by the work itself.

J. Hillis Miller approvingly quotes Dickens's statement of intention, but then goes on to say that 'selfishness exists in the novel not only as the ethical bent of the characters, but also as the state of isolation in which they live. The novel is full of people who are wholly enclosed in themselves . . .'[3] This, it seems to me, is critical legerdemain. To equate 'selfishness' (through the mediating idea of 'self-enclosure') with a metaphysical 'state of isolation' is to do violence to common usage. The equation, indeed, is a means of providing authorial sanction for a view of the novel which is manifestly different from that which the author says was intended: 'The problem which faces the characters of *Martin Chuzzlewit* is . . . how to achieve an authentic self, a self which, while resting solidly on something outside of itself, does not simply submit to a definition imposed from without' (p. 103). Though the critic may view the characters as being faced by such a problem, there is scant evidence in the text that they themselves are concerned with it. It is not till much later in his career that Dickens faces the problem; and in *Martin Chuzzlewit* it is not the direct concern even of young Martin, the only character who may be said to assay (however perfunctorily) such an achievement. The characters are concerned, I shall argue, with more mundane matters. That Miller himself is perhaps submitting the novel to a definition imposed from without is suggested by the following representative instance of his procedure. Mr. Mould, it is stated, exemplifies a 'total enclosure' within his own life:

[1] Edwin B. Benjamin, 'The Structure of *Martin Chuzzlewit*', *Philological Quarterly*, 34 (1955), 40.
[2] R. C. Churchill, 'Charles Dickens', *The Pelican Guide to English Literature*, Vol. VI (Harmondsworth, 1958), p. 120.
[3] *Charles Dickens*, p. 104.

The lack of a division into subjective and objective worlds is suggested by the recurrence of an unusual grammatical form. Instead of saying 'Mr. Mould's legs,' Dickens says 'the legs of Mr. Mould.' Mr. Mould's legs are not appendages possessed by him, and therefore in a way separate; they are *of* him, within the intimate circle of his existence. Dickens goes on to speak of 'the hand of Mr. Mould,' and finally uses the locution in a way which strikingly suggests that everything surrounding Mr. Mould has equal status as an extension of himself: he speaks of 'the premises of Mr. Mould.' (p. 100)

It is difficult to envisage in what way (other than by amputation) Mr. Mould's legs and hands may be thought of as 'separate' from himself. And, though the precise force of the distinction between the two forms of the possessive is a moot point, it may well be argued that Mr. Mould's premises may more readily be considered 'an extension of himself' when attached to him by an apostrophe.

Like Miller, Steven Marcus invokes the theme of selfishness, but then proceeds to analyse the novel in terms remote from it. He says that *Martin Chuzzlewit* 'may be seen as a supreme dramatization of selfishness in all its varieties';[1] but he maintains that 'for Dickens selfishness implies . . . all the deformations consequent upon the assumption that the source of all right judgment and truth is in the self'. Consequently 'the problem of self in *Martin Chuzzlewit*', is said to be 'synonymous with the problem of authority', and the novel to be 'concerned with the question of authority and obedience' (pp. 224–5). The 'dramatization of selfishness', it turns out, is viewed as a drama of self-assertion; but misgivings about the general drift of the analysis are strengthened by what seems to be the inappropriateness of specific comments on the action. 'In Jonas,' we are told, 'all the limiting inner contradictions of the desire for unconditional self-hood and power are represented; and finally they lead him to commit the most desperate act of self-assertion known to civilized society' (p. 234). Jonas's murder of Tigg, in common with any other murder, may no doubt be viewed as an act of self-assertion, but it is not presented as such. Jonas is no Raskolnikov, and he commits murder not out of a desire for unconditional selfhood but (more prosaically) in order to protect himself from a blackmailer and safeguard his guilty secret. Similarly, it is difficult to think of Pecksniff and Mrs. Gamp as 'the

---

[1] *Dickens*, p. 213.

finest examples' of 'the self attempting to establish unconditional an
absolute authority' (p. 235). Both Pecksniff and Mrs. Gamp no doub
try to get their own way, but they are presented as doing so in orde
(quite simply) to feather their nests—and by means of a consisten
obsequiousness that hardly accords with an attempt to establish un
conditional and absolute authority.

Faced with the gap between the fact of criticism and the fact of fic
tion, we can, with Barbara Hardy, only deplore the 'strange images o
Dickens . . . so freely bred by post-Jamesian criticism'.[1] But if, lik
her, we wish to take a close and straight look at the work itself, it i
essential that we first rid ourselves of intentional blinders. This sh
fails to do. 'I would of course agree,' she says, 'that the characters hav
this extensive moral commitment to the general theme of selfishnes
and often to the more specialized variant of hypocrisy'; and she pro
ceeds to expose the weakness of the novel by pointing to 'the ga
between moral theme and action' (p. 110). A more rewarding ap
proach, surely, is to proceed not from external evidence of the them
to the action but from the action to a formulation of theme.

II

Justice has not been seen to be done to Dickens's plots. Though it i
now usually argued that his mature work has a thematic unity, hi
violent and melodramatic plots are still commonly regarded as the las
infirmity of a rehabilitated but irritating genius. Violent and melo
dramatic they well may be, but they are not simply a crude mechanisn
for linking together a large number of characters. They are integra
to Dickens's purpose, the means by which the word is made flesh
From *Martin Chuzzlewit* on—and, flawed though it is, I regard thi
as Dickens's first mature work—we do well to consider the plot as
necessary vehicle of the novelist's thought; and, consequently, as th
most readily available guide to the nature of the imaginative visio
embodied in the novel.

What, we may therefore ask, are the mainsprings of the plot o
Martin Chuzzlewit? What do such diverse major characters as Peck
sniff, Jonas, Tigg and the two Martins have in common in terms no
of selfishness but of the action? All these characters, with the exceptio

---

[1] '*Martin Chuzzlewit*', *Dickens and the Twentieth Century*, ed. John Gross and Gabri
Pearson, p. 107.

of old Martin, may be said to be fortune-hunters, to set out in one way
or another to make their fortunes; while old Martin devotes himself
to foiling those who would lay hands on his particular fortune. And
fortune-hunting, it appears, is at the centre of all the main ramifications of the plot. It is a desire for money that leads Pecksniff first to
take on young Martin and then to dismiss him; to marry off Merry
to Jonas and then himself to make his repulsive advances to Mary;
to take old Martin into his home and to be so readily deceived by him;
and to invest all he has in the Anglo-Bengalee. It is a desire for money
that leads Jonas to attempt to murder his father, and then to become
involved with the Anglo-Bengalee and Tigg, who himself proposes to
make a fortune through the fraudulent company he has established. It
is a desire to make his fortune that leads young Martin to America
and to Eden. Pecksniff, in other words, scheming for legacies and
deviously speculating, is at the centre of the novel not as a type of
selfishness but as a quintessential fortune-hunter, a man avid of making
a fortune in both the ways that are dramatized in the novel.

The widespread fortune-hunting posits a mercenary society, a
society in which supreme value is accorded to money. What a ravenous
desire for money brings with it is explicitly indicated on two occasions
by old Martin in conversations with Pecksniff:

'. . . I tell you, man,' he added, with increasing bitterness, 'that
I have gone, a rich man, among people of all grades and kinds;
relatives, friends, and strangers; among people in whom, when I
was poor, I had confidence, and justly, for they never once deceived
me then, or, to me, wronged each other. But I have never found
one nature, no, not one, in which, being wealthy and alone, I
was not forced to detect the latent corruption that lay hid within
it, waiting for such as I to bring it forth. . . . I have . . . corrupted
and changed the nature of all those who have ever attended on
me, by breeding avaricious plots and hopes within them . . .'
(pp. 39–40)
'. . . My brother had in his wealth the usual doom of wealth, and
root of misery. He carried his corrupting influence with him, go
where he would; and shed it round him, even on his hearth. . . .'
(p. 386)

Money, old Martin sees—and this is the vision of the novelist—
activates 'the latent corruption' in those who believe it is the highest

good to acquire it. Money, repeatedly associated in Martin's words with corruption, is in such a society a corrupting principle. This is what *Martin Chuzzlewit* is about.[1] It accordingly marks an important stage in Dickens's development. The 'corrupting influence' of wealth becomes from this point on his major theme, and he continues to explore it with an ever-increasing complexity of treatment until its final triumphant statement in *Our Mutual Friend*.

Mr. Pecksniff, we are informed time and again, is 'a moral man'. In dismissing young Martin, he typically presents himself as 'an honest man, seeking to do [his] duty in this carnal universe'; and, striking himself 'upon his breast or moral garden', he deplores the withdrawal of Martin 'from the flowery paths of purity and peace' (p. 210). The way in which Pecksniff cultivates his moral garden in the universe of *Martin Chuzzlewit* is indicated early on in the novel:

> It has been remarked that Mr. Pecksniff was a moral man. So he was. Perhaps there never was a more moral man than Mr. Pecksniff: especially in his conversation and correspondence. It was once said of him by a homely admirer, that he had a Fortunatus's purse of good sentiments in his inside. In this particular he was like the girl in the fairy tale, except that if they were not actual diamonds which fell from his lips, they were the very brightest paste, and shone prodigiously. (p. 12)

Though the coin in which Pecksniff freely trades is counterfeit, he—like Fortunatus—has an inexhaustible store of it, his ability to produce 'good sentiments' at will testifying to the fertility of his garden. The image vividly epitomizes Pecksniff; but it is also worth noting that thus early in the novel it associates Pecksniff's morality, and 'through [him], morality in general' (p. 33), with money. Of money, of course,

---

[1] Ross H. Dabney in *Love and Property in the Novels of Dickens* (London, 1967) comes close to subscribing to this view. He maintains that 'the book is about selfishness' (p. 48); but he also says that 'selfishness and unselfishness are primarily represented through the characters' attitudes towards love and money' (p. 36), and that 'the main plot, if Dickens had followed through with it, would have shown the effects of the power of money in corrupting the relationship between the generations' (p. 42). J. Hillis Miller also says that 'the novel could be defined as Dickens's first elaborate attack on the money worship of commercialized man', but he insists on making this subsidiary to the theme of selfhood: 'It is because [the characters] have submitted to money as the sole yardstick of value that they have only superficial and inauthentic identities. In *Martin Chuzzlewit* people are at once wholly turned in upon themselves and wholly dependent upon the value they have in other people's eyes.' *Charles Dickens*, p. 132.

Pecksniff does not deign to be publicly aware. 'Money,' he tells John Westlock, 'is the root of all evil. I grieve to see that it is already bearing evil fruit in you. But I will not remember its existence' (pp. 19–20); thus annihilating money to a green shade. That Pecksniff's own morality, however, is rooted in an earthy preoccupation with money is constantly suggested, the stuff of his benevolence being nowhere more strikingly revealed than in his negotiations with his prospective son-in-law. Jonas bluntly asks him what he means to give his daughters when they marry:

> 'Indeed, my dear friend,' said Mr. Pecksniff, 'you may well inquire. The heart is not always a royal mint, with patent machinery to work its metal into current coin. Sometimes it throws it out in strange forms, not easily recognised as coin at all. But it is sterling gold. It has at least that merit. It is sterling gold.' (p. 326)

And, when Jonas finally elicits from him that 'in the event of such a man as he proposing for his daughter's hand, he would endow her with a fortune of four thousand pounds', Pecksniff cannot forbear from adding a 'fatherly remark':

> 'I should sadly pinch and cramp myself to do so . . . but that would be my duty, and my conscience would reward me. For myself, my conscience is my bank. I have a trifle invested there, a mere trifle, Mr. Jonas; but I prize it as a store of value, I assure you.' (p. 328)

The language Pecksniff employs in these two passages evokes the distinctive ethos of the world of *Martin Chuzzlewit*, a world in which what might (in view of the moral Pecksniff) be called the moral life of its inhabitants is consistently expressed in terms of money or business. In *Howards End* E. M. Forster opposes an 'outer life' of business, of telegrams and anger, to an 'inner life' of personal relations, of moral sensibility and discrimination; in *Martin Chuzzlewit* the two are fused through the recurring metaphors of money and business, the novel offering a special instance of what Dorothy Van Ghent calls 'the law of conversion of spirit into matter that operates in the Dickens world'.[1]

[1] 'The Dickens World: A View from Todgers's', *The Dickens Critics*, ed. George H. Ford and Lauriat Lane, p. 217.

But, for the moment, it is not with the metaphysical implications of this 'law' that I am concerned; the money and business metaphors are an index of a wholly commercialized society. The commercial imagery, moreover, is pervasive, and applies not only to Pecksniff but to a number of other characters in such a way that it is part of the texture of the novel.

In ironically elaborating his assertion that Pecksniff 'gets no credit' from Tom Pinch, 'not he', John Westlock says to Tom: 'Who but a madman would suppose you advertised him hereabouts, much cheaper and much better than a chalker on the walls could, eh, Tom?' —and he insists that 'Pecksniff [has] traded in [Tom's] nature' (p. 23). When Mrs. Lupin tells Pecksniff that old Martin 'is far from easy in his thoughts, and wants some proper advice from those whose goodness makes it worth his having', this is Pecksniff's response: ' "Then," said Mr. Pecksniff, "he is the sort of customer for me." But though he said this in the plainest language, he didn't speak a word. He only shook his head: disparagingly of himself too' (p. 33). Assembled at Pecksniff's house, the Chuzzlewit relations heap 'bullyings and denunciations' on their host when news of old Martin's disappearance is brought them: 'Mr. Pecksniff had, in short, but one comfort, and that was the knowledge that all these his relations and friends had hated him to the very utmost extent before; and that he, for his part, had not distributed among them any more love than, with his ample capital in that respect, he could comfortably afford to part with' (p. 62). This is how Pecksniff introduces himself to Tom's sister:

> 'Don't be alarmed, Miss Pinch,' said Mr. Pecksniff, taking her hand condescendingly in one of his, and patting it with the other. 'I have called to see you, in pursuance of a promise given to your brother, Thomas Pinch. My name—compose yourself, Miss Pinch—is Pecksniff.'
>
> The good man emphasised these words as though he would have said, 'You see in me, young person, the benefactor of your race; the patron of your house; the preserver of your brother, who is fed with manna daily from my table; and in right of whom there is a considerable balance in my favour at present standing in the books beyond the sky. But I have no pride, for I can afford to do without it!' (p. 135)

At Todgers's, Pecksniff begs Martin to excuse his daughters' agitation as they fly to wait on the old man: 'They are made up of feeling,' he says. 'A bad commodity to go through the world with, Mr. Chuzzlewit!' (p. 164). Courting Mary, Pecksniff asks 'in playful accents' and 'as a parting fancy' whether he should bite her little finger, which he holds up: 'Receiving no reply, he kissed it instead; and then stooping down, inclined his flabby face to hers (he had a flabby face, although he *was* a good man), and with a blessing, which from such a source was quite enough to set her up in life, and prosper her from that time forth, permitted her to leave him' (p. 484). With young Martin's scorn 'fresh and hot upon him', Pecksniff is especially 'tender in his humanity' and 'dignified and exalted in his virtue': 'Having this large stock of superfluous sentiment and morality on hand which must positively be cleared off at any sacrifice, Mr. Pecksniff no sooner heard his son-in-law announced, than he regarded him as a kind of wholesale or general order, to be immediately executed' (p. 677). It is a case of the seller sold, however, for Jonas has brought Tigg with him, and Pecksniff is duly drawn into the Anglo-Bengalee: 'The sum which would complete the proprietorship in this snug concern, was nearly equal to Mr. Pecksniff's whole hoard: not counting Mr. Chuzzlewit, that is to say, whom he looked upon as money in the Bank, the possession of which inclined him the more to make a dash with his own private sprats for the capture of such a whale as Mr. Montague described' (pp. 683–4). And when old Martin finally denounces Pecksniff in the closing pages of the novel, he says, *inter alia:* 'Counting on the restoration of the love you knew I bore [young Martin], you designed him for one of your two daughters, did ye? Or failing that, you traded in him as a speculation which at any rate should blind me with the lustre of your charity, and found a claim upon me!' (pp. 804–5).[1]

Part of the distinctive humorous flavour of Pecksniff as a character is attributable to the use of these metaphors either by, or in relation to, him; just as the revelation through the metaphors of the worldliness of this unworldly man is an unfailing sign of his hypocrisy. The metaphors are thus a suggestive indication of the springs of the novelist's imaginative conception of Pecksniff as a character; and their recurrence throughout the novel in relation to other characters as well justifies us in regarding Pecksniff as 'the origin of the book' in a sense somewhat different from that recorded by Forster.

It is perhaps only to be expected that Charity and Mercy, the flowers of the moral garden, should be presented in their father's image:

---

[1] Some further instances of the use of this kind of imagery in connection with Pecksniff are to be found on pp. 41, 145, 200, 305, 470, 497, 678.

What a pleasant sight was that, the contrast they presented: to see each loved and loving one sympathising with, and devoted to, and leaning on, and yet correcting and counter-checking, and, as it were, antidoting, the other! To behold each damsel, in her very admiration of her sister, setting up in business for herself on an entirely different principle, and announcing no connexion with over-the-way, and if the quality of goods at that establishment don't please you, you are respectfully invited to favour ME with a call! (p. 12)

Young Martin, of course, is a prospective customer; and when it is revealed that he has secretly 'made his matrimonial choice', their anger is delightfully (and characteristically) evoked: 'What! Had they taken to their hearth and home a secretly contracted serpent; a crocodile, who had made a furtive offer of his hand; an imposition on society; a bankrupt bachelor with no effects, trading with the spinster world on false pretences!' (p. 160). The Pecksniff girls, however, have inner resources, and, despite their shock, are at once able to respond to old Martin's appeal for a kind reception of Mary: 'Where was the orphan whom the two Miss Pecksniffs would not have cherished in their sisterly bosom! But when that orphan was commended to their care by one on whom the damned-up love of years was gushing forth, what exhaustless stores of pure affection yearned to expend themselves upon her!' (pp. 161–2).

Jonas is a man who does not waste his breath on a show of morality. He has early got into the habit 'of considering everything as a question of property', and consequently has 'gradually come to look, with impatience, on his parent as a certain amount of personal estate, which [has] no right whatever to be going at large, but ought to be secured in that particular description of iron safe which is commonly called a coffin, and banked in the grave' (p. 119). He sets out to realize this asset by attempting to poison his father; and Anthony Chuzzlewit, having discovered his plan, makes explicit that connection between 'crime' and 'business' which the novel as a whole elaborates (going, in this respect, a stage further than *Oliver Twist*, in which the more palpable connection between crime and poverty is established): 'Oh, Chuff,' Chuffey reports him as having said, 'oh, dear old Chuff! a voice came into my room to-night, and told me that this crime began with me. It began when I taught [Jonas] to be too covetous of what I have to leave, and made the expectation of it his great business!'

(p. 784). Unexposed in his crime, if not undetected, Jonas gives himself to business as usual. Dining with the Pecksniffs at a wayside hotel, he takes the opportunity of whispering in Cherry's ear that 'the supper' is 'a contract business, and therefore the more she [eats], the better the bargain [is]' (p. 121); and, indeed, it is as a tasty morsel that he contracts for Merry: pressed by Jonas, Merry declares that if she could ever bring herself to say that she would marry him, it should only be that she 'might hate and tease' him all her life; to which he replies: 'That's as good as saying it right out. It's a bargain, cousin. We're a pair, if ever there was one' (p. 336). And since the union of this mutual pair was not the one that Pecksniff had in mind in proposing to bestow his daughter and four thousand pounds on Jonas, the voracious suitor is quick to draw on the fund of his prospective father-in-law's benevolence: 'As it ain't the one you're so fond of, you must come down with another thousand, Pecksniff. You must make it up to five. It's worth that, to keep your treasure to yourself, you know. You get off very cheap that way, and haven't a sacrifice to make' (p. 337).

Even old Martin is infected to cynicism by the corruption he despises. Mrs. Lupin's disinterested and good-hearted attempt to cheer him up is met with: "Ah! you begin too soon," he said, in so low a voice that he seemed to be thinking it, rather than addressing her. "But you lose no time. You do your errand, and you earn your fee. Now, who may be *your* client?" (p. 31). And the change in old Martin, when he appears at the end of the novel as the scourge of Pecksniff, is appropriately marked by a climactic use of the central image:

> The old man received Mary no less tenderly than he had received Tom Pinch's sister. A look of friendly recognition passed between himself and Mrs. Lupin, which implied the existence of a perfect understanding between them. It engendered no astonishment in Mr. Tapley; for, as he afterwards observed, he had retired from the business, and sold off the stock. (p. 801)

This, then, is the way in which the moral climate of the main fortune-hunters and of their antagonist is evoked. Of the other main characters, Tigg (I shall argue) figures in a different but related verbal pattern; and young Martin, though it is true that he refers to his relations with his grandfather as having been 'a fair exchange, a barter, and no more' (p. 242), is not otherwise indicted by the commercial imagery, a discrimination which emphasises that his attempt to make his fortune is different in kind from that of Pecksniff, Jonas and Tigg. Even a minor character such as Mrs. Gamp is shown to breathe the same air as the fortune-hunters, though the oppressiveness of the atmosphere is relieved by Dickens's continued exuberance of language and freshness of invention.

The rich linguistic fertility of the presentation of Mrs. Gamp, her astonishing flow of talk, has been justly celebrated, her 'rich folks may ride on camels, but it ain't so easy for 'em to see out of a needle's eye' (p. 407) being only one of her unageing monuments. But she is shown to cultivate personal relations with as nice a calculation as Pecksniff his garden:

> 'Why, goodness me!' she said, 'Mrs. Chuzzlewit! To think as I should see beneath this blessed ouse, which well I know it, Miss Pecksniff, my sweet young lady, to be a ouse as there is not a many like, worse luck, and wishin' it ware not so, which then this tearful walley would be changed into a flowerin' guardian, Mr. Chuffey; to think as I should see beneath this indiwidgle roof, identically comin', Mr. Pinch (I take the liberty, though almost unbeknown), and do assure you of it, sir, the smilinest and sweetest face as ever, Mrs. Chuzzlewit, I see, exceptin' yourn, my dear good lady, and *your* good lady's too, sir, Mr. Moddle, if I may make so bold as speak so plain of what is plain enough to them as needn't look through mill-stones, Mrs. Todgers, to find out wot is wrote upon the wall behind. Which no offence is meant, ladies and gentlemen; none bein' took, I hope. To think as I should see that smilinest and sweetest face which me and another friend of mine, took notige of among the packages down London Bridge, in this promiscuous place, is a surprige in-deed!'

> Having contrived, in this happy manner, to invest every member of her audience with an individual share and immediate personal interest in her address, Mrs. Gamp dropped several curtseys to Ruth, and smilingly shaking her head a great many times, pursued the thread of her discourse . . . (pp. 703–4)

Her parting from her fellow-nurse, Betsey Prig, 'as from a cherished member of the sisterhood', is worthy of a Jonas: 'Wishin' you lots of sickness, my darlin' creetur,' she observes, 'and good places. It won't be long, I hope, afore we works together, off and on, Betsey;

and may our next meetin' be at a large family's, where they all takes it reg'lar, one from another, turn and turn about, and has it business-like' (p. 468). Businesslike, indeed, is her approach to Jonas himself:

> 'Me and a friend of mine, one off, one on, could do it, Mr. Chuzzlewit,' replied the nurse; 'our charges not bein' high, but wishin' they was lower, and allowance made considerin' not strangers. Me and Betsey Prig, sir, would undertake Mr. Chuffey reasonable,' said Mrs. Gamp, looking at him with her head on one side, as if he had been a piece of goods, for which she was driving a bargain; 'and give every satigefaction. Betsey Prig has nussed a many lunacies, and well she knows their ways, which puttin' 'em right close afore the fire, when fractious, is the certainest and most compoging.' (p. 716)

If we look, therefore, for a motif in the imaginative world of *Martin Chuzzlewit*, it is the commercialization of life (rather than selfishness) that suggests itself. The recurrent commercial imagery exemplifies a more complex use of the analogical method than any we have yet seen. The commercial analogues, by presenting us with an insistent view of a society, are—at least in the English sections of the novel—a unifying factor; and indeed they enable us to think of the overall structure in terms of an implicit commercial metaphor. The novel, says Edwin B. Benjamin, 'falls naturally into three parts, showing the rise, triumph, and fall of hypocrisy . . .'[1] I would agree that it has a three-part structure, but suggest that it may be described differently. The first part, in which old Martin is taken ill at the Blue Dragon and the Chuzzlewit clan descends on Pecksniff's village, may be thought of as the convergence of the fortune-hunters: 'In a word, things came to that pass that nearly the whole family sat down before the Blue Dragon, and formally invested it; and Martin Chuzzlewit was in a state of siege' (p. 53). But the word 'invested' is, in this novel, a loaded word; and we may think of the fortune-hunters' besieging of old Martin as an investment in a sense that suggests the commercial meta-phor for the structure. The second part begins with old Martin's disappearance and extends to his reappearance, a changed man, as Tom's unknown employer. This part deals, then, with the dispersal of the fortune-hunters and with their various schemes—with their

---

[1] 'The Structure of *Martin Chuzzlewit*', *loc. cit.*, p. 45.

speculations, as it were. The third part is a reassembly: with the arrest of Jonas, the denunciation of Pecksniff, and the 'marriage' of Cherry, it brings the dispersed fortune-hunters together again. Their coming together, however, marks the frustration of their schemes, Cherry's last-minute desertion by Moddle in the presence of the Chuzzlewits, assembled at Todgers's, being yet another dramatization of their general frustration. The third part, that is, is the pay-off, the return on the original investment.

Dorothy Van Ghent's excellent essay, 'The Dickens World: A View from Todgers's', draws our attention, among other things, to the significance of Todgers's Commercial Boarding-House. If the view from Todgers's is, in her terms, at the centre of the Dickens world, I would suggest that the view we are given of the firm of Anthony Chuzzlewit and Son is at the centre of the world of *Martin Chuzzlewit*:

> The old-established firm of Anthony Chuzzlewit and Son, Manchester Warehousemen, and so forth, had its place of business in a very narrow street somewhere behind the Post Office; where every house was in the brightest summer morning very gloomy . .
> A dim, dirty, smoky, tumble-down, rotten old house it was, as anybody would desire to see; but there the firm of Anthony Chuzzlewit and Son transacted all their business and their pleasure too, such as it was; for neither the young man nor the old had any other residence, or any care or thought beyond its narrow limits.
> Business, as may be readily supposed, was the main thing in this establishment; insomuch indeed that it shouldered comfort out of doors, and jostled the domestic arrangements at every turn. Thus in the miserable bedrooms there were files of moth-eaten letters hanging up against the walls; and linen rollers, and fragments of old patterns, and odds and ends of spoiled goods, strewed upon the ground; while the meagre bedsteads, washing-stands, and scraps of carpet, were huddled away into corners as objects of secondary consideration, not to be thought of but as disagreeable necessities, furnishing no profit, and intruding on the one affair of life. The single sitting-room was on the same principle, a chaos of boxes and old papers, and had more counting-house stools in it than chairs: not to mention a great monster of a desk straddling over the middle of the floor, and an iron safe

sunk into the wall above the fire-place. The solitary little table for purposes of refection and social enjoyment, bore as fair a proportion to the desk and other business furniture, as the graces and harmless relaxations of life had ever done, in the persons of the old man and his son, to their pursuit of wealth.... (pp. 175–6)

What is evoked here, in the description of 'the miserable bedrooms' in which pieces of bedroom furniture are 'huddled away into corners as objects of secondary consideration', and of the sitting-room which, 'on the same principle', has (with its counting-house stools rather than chairs, and with its great desk and iron safe) a preponderance of 'business furniture', is the transformation of a home into a counting-house—a transformation which is anticipatory of the novelist's later view of London itself.[1] The 'narrow limits' of the Chuzzlewit residence, in accordance with the characteristic definition, in Dickens, of a man by his environment, are expressive of the narrowness of the lives of father and son. The principle which directs their lives, as well as the furnishing of their home, is the principle of profit; and the 'pursuit of wealth' has become for them 'the one affair of life'. The business of making money, in other words, has for the directors of Chuzzlewit and Son become a monomania. It is this monomania which is at the centre of the novel, and which, radiating out from there, informs the activities of the various fortune-hunters. As Tigg inimitably puts it, thrusting his words down the throat of Jonas after he has prevented him from escaping abroad, 'that confounded bee-hive of ours in the city must be paramount to every other consideration, when there is honey to be made...' (p. 630). And the word which comes out of the house of Chuzzlewit and Son, 'the true business precept' enunciated by Jonas, is that which, though unavowed, directs the moral Pecksniff as well as Tigg:

> 'There's another thing that's not easily overdone, father,' remarked Jonas, after a short silence.
> 'What's that?' asked the father; grinning already in anticipation.
> 'A bargain,' said the son. 'Here's the rule for bargains. "Do other men, for they would do you." That's the true business precept. All others are counterfeits.' (p. 181)

[1] See Ch. 8, p. 282 below.

A concern with this monomania, indeed, may be regarded as being at the centre of most of Dickens's mature work. Certainly the firm of Anthony Chuzzlewit and Son leads straight to the firm of Dombey and Son, it being with Mould's question at the funeral of Anthony that *Dombey and Son* may be said to begin:

> . . . the whole of Mr. Mould's establishment were on duty within the house or without; feathers waved, horses snorted, silks and velvets fluttered; in a word, as Mr. Mould emphatically said, 'everything that money could do was done.'
>
> 'And what can do more, Mrs. Gamp?' exclaimed the undertaker, as he emptied his glass and smacked his lips. (p. 320)

The description of the Chuzzlewit house, furthermore, vividly suggests what the effect of such a monomania is, and in a way that relates the view of Chuzzlewit and Son to the view from Todgers's. The description of 'the relatively innocent prospect from the roof of Todgers's boarding-house,' says Dorothy Van Ghent, 'bears a curious resemblance to passages in M. Sartre's *La Nausée* and other writings, where non-human existences rage with an indiscriminate life of their own.'[1] The indiscriminate life of chimney-pots, which (among other things) are seen from the roof of Todgers's, exemplifies, in part, 'the principle of relationship between things and people in the novels of Dickens'. This principle is 'a transposition of attributes', whereby things that are 'demonically possessed . . . imitate the human', while 'it is as if the life absorbed by things had been drained out of people who have become incapable of their humanity', and who 'develop thing-attributes' (pp. 213, 214). In the description of the Chuzzlewit household, the 'great monster of a desk straddling over the middle of the floor' may be taken as an instance of the kind of 'demonic possession' that is apparent from the roof of Todgers's. But we are also told that 'business', which is 'the main thing in this establishment', 'shouldered comfort out of doors, and jostled the domestic arrangements at every turn'. In the world of *Martin Chuzzlewit*, in other words, it is not only inanimate things that are endowed with life but also the concept of business. It is as if business has itself become a demonic force.

A hint of the consequences of the monomania that has vitalized business is given us in the assertion that every house in the vicinity of

[1] 'The Dickens World', *loc. cit.*, p. 219.

Chuzzlewit and Son is 'in the brightest summer morning very gloomy'. This intimation that the life of the Chuzzlewits, in the house of business beyond which they have no other 'care or thought', is deprived of light and warmth is further elaborated towards the end of the novel. Old Martin, under the impression that Jonas has in fact murdered his father, apostrophises his dead brother in terms that recall the gloomy house in which Jonas has grown up:

> 'Oh, brother!' cried old Martin, clasping his hands and lifting up his eyes. 'Oh, brother, brother! Were we strangers half our lives that you might breed a wretch like this, and I make life a desert by withering every flower that grew about me! Is it the natural end of your precepts and mine, that this should be the creature of your rearing, training, teaching, hoarding, striving for: and I the means of bringing him to punishment, when nothing can repair the wasted past!' (p. 781)

Anthony, who saw that Jonas's crime began with himself, may be said to have generated his own death, and certainly to have 'bred a wretch' who (as his progress from the attempted poisoning to the actual murder of Tigg and his own suicide demonstrates) is compounded of death; while old Martin, who has himself 'withered in the shell of his suspicion and distrust for . . . many years' (p. 479), has also dealt out death, as it were, making 'life a desert by withering every flower that grew' about him. Death, it appears, is 'the natural end' of their 'precepts', which are none other than Jonas's 'true business precept'. What we have in *Martin Chuzzlewit*, in other words, is a 'transposition of attributes' of a different kind from that remarked by Dorothy Van Ghent: business is endowed with life; and life, as a result, is destroyed or goes insolvent. This view of the businessman's life emerges clearly in what Tom tells Ruth's employer, the brass-and-copper founder: 'If you imagine that the payment of an annual sum of money gives [you the right to employ her], you immensely exaggerate its power and value. Your money is the least part of your bargain in such a case. You may be punctual in that to half a second on the clock, and yet be Bankrupt' (p. 574). The vision indeed, with its components of spiritual and moral bankruptcy and of a loss of life figured in images of the desert and withering and wasting, is essentially the vision of *Our Mutual Friend*, which Dickens may be said to have begun to write with *Martin Chuzzlewit*.

The violence of that part of the action which relates to Jonas is not evidence, as Ross H. Dabney claims it is, of a 'Bill Sikes syndrome',[1] but a fitting dramatization of the loss of life with which the novel is fundamentally concerned. This loss of life is also manifested, of course, in the transformation of men into things—things of a commercial turn, as the gentlemen at Todgers's might say. To regard a man as 'a kind of wholesale or general order' or as 'money in the Bank' or as 'a certain amount of personal estate' or as 'a piece of goods' is to devitalize him and so to prepare the way for his conversion into an instrument. 'By little and little', we are told, Pecksniff 'began to try whether Mr. Chuzzlewit gave any promise of becoming an instrument in his hands, and finding that he did, and indeed that he was very supple in his plastic fingers, he made it the business of his life, kind soul! to establish an ascendancy over him . . .' (p. 475). Old Martin, though he has 'escaped so many snares from needy fortune-hunters', nevertheless seems in fact to have 'become the good man's tool and plaything' (p. 479); and he later tells Tom that, while he was staying at Pecksniff's house, he suffered his host to treat him 'like his tool and instrument' (p. 772). Tigg, explaining the working of the Anglo-Bengalee to Jonas, says: ' ". . . in short, my good fellow, we stick it into B, up hill and down dale, and make a devilish comfortable little property out of him. Ha, ha, ha! I drive B, in point of fact," said Tigg, pointing to the cabriolet, "and a thoroughbred horse he is" ' (pp. 445–6); but Jonas does not really need such instruction, as Tigg comes to realize: 'Instead of Jonas being his tool and instrument, their places seemed to be reversed' (p. 648). There is, indeed, 'nothing personal in morality', as Pecksniff says (p. 14), once it is informed by the true business ethic; but the propensity to depersonalize in the interests of 'business' is not as easily controlled as Tigg's horse, being liable, rather, to a galloping inflation. Despatched for Jonas's portmanteau, a messenger 'duly [brings] his luggage back, with a short note from that other piece of luggage, his wife' (p. 639); Jonas earlier tells the wife of his bosom that he hates himself 'for having been fool enough to strap a pack upon [his] back for the pleasure of treading on it' whenever he chooses (p. 458); and, driving down to Pecksniff's with Tigg, he furiously asks his partner, when told that Bailey is 'drenched to the skin', whether he intends stopping in order 'to spread him out to dry' (p. 647).

It is significant that, when Pecksniff determines to make it the

---

[1] *Love and Property*, p. 45.

business of his life to twist old Martin round his plastic finger, he does so because he cannot 'but foresee the probability of his respected relative being made the victim of designing persons, and of his riches falling into worthless hands' (p. 475). Accordingly, the worthy man decides to make a victim of Martin himself. There is, in other words, a clear connection, in this novel, between the victim theme which we have seen emerging in Dickens's earlier work and the notion of instrumentality. To use a man as an instrument is, in effect, to victimize him. In *Martin Chuzzlewit*, therefore, the number of victims is large, each of the main fortune-hunters progressively adding his tools and instruments to the total. Thus Pecksniff successively victimizes young Martin, Merry, old Martin and Tom, and attempts to make a victim of Mary; Jonas victimizes his father, his wife, Pecksniff, Tigg—and tries to do the same to Chuffey; Tigg victimizes Jonas and Pecksniff, not to mention other investors in the Anglo-Bengalee. The fact that all the main victimizers are themselves victimized, and that the other victims (with the exception of the dead Anthony and the unnamed investors in the Anglo-Bengalee) are in the end restored to happiness makes for a neat pattern; but the incidence of victimization is so pronounced, as we read, that it leaves an impression of a society at large that is the victim of its own business precepts.

The vitalization of business at the expense of life is related to a further transposition that is prominent in the novel, to what might be called a transposition of terminology. The personal, 'moral' life that consistently expresses itself in the language of commerce has as a counterpart a world of business that advertises itself in moral terms. In a sphere more exalted than that of Anthony Chuzzlewit and Son, the Anglo-Bengalee exemplifies this phenomenon in the business world:

> The secretary smiled again; laughed, indeed, this time; and said, rubbing his nose slily with one end of the portfolio:
> 'It was a capital thought, wasn't it?'
> 'What was a capital thought, David?' Mr. Montague inquired.
> 'The Anglo-Bengalee,' tittered the secretary.
> 'The Anglo-Bengalee Disinterested Loan and Life Assurance Company is rather a capital concern, I hope, David,' said Montague.
> 'Capital indeed!' cried the secretary, with another laugh—'in one sense.'

'In the only important one,' observed the chairman; 'which is number one, David.'

'What,' asked the secretary, bursting into another laugh, 'what will be the paid-up capital, according to the next prospectus?'

'A figure of two, and as many oughts after it as the printer can get into the same line,' replied his friend. 'Ha, ha!' (p. 429)

The transformation of Montague Tigg into Tigg Montague, complete with false hair and black dye and every inch the gentleman—like the metamorphosis of Bailey Junior from Todgers's boy into 'a young gentleman in [the Company's] livery' (p. 420), a 'highly-condensed embodiment of all the sporting grooms in London, an abstract of all the stable-knowledge of the time' (p. 422)—is expressive of the world in which the Anglo-Bengalee successfully imposes its image, a world in which appearance is everything. It is a world, indeed, in which Mrs. Gamp confidently celebrates her friendship with Mrs. Harris, winning everyone, apart from the dastardly Betsey Prig, to a belief in her existence; and in which young Bailey, likewise through the sheer force of the image he projects, can compel Poll Sweedlepipe to go through the motions of shaving him:

> The barber stood aghast; but Mr. Bailey divested himself of his neck-cloth, and sat down in the easy shaving chair with all the dignity and confidence in life. There was no resisting his manner. The evidence of sight and touch became as nothing. His chin was as smooth as a new-laid egg or a scraped Dutch cheese; but Poll Sweedlepipe wouldn't have ventured to deny, on affidavit, that he had the beard of a Jewish rabbi. (p. 460)

It is in this world of false appearances that Pecksniff's hypocrisy is grounded. His hypocrisy, however vividly conceived and presented, has its place in the economy of the novel not as an isolated vice, nor as a mysteriously 'specialized variant' of selfishness, but as a personal correlative of the image-projection that is the breath of big business.

In *Martin Chuzzlewit*, therefore, Dickens may be regarded as standing by the determination, announced in the Preface to *Oliver Twist*, to show things 'as they really are'; though he penetrates here not into 'the foul and frowsy dens' of outcast criminals but into the opulent establishments of such as Tigg, a 'man of business', as Jonas calls him (and the successor of Fogg, the 'capital man of business' in

98

Pickwick Papers). The change of milieu is great, but Dickens has come to see that behind the façade of middle-class wealth and power and respectability there prowl the ghosts of Fagin and his like. Tigg's capital concern with 'number one' is not only a variant of Jonas's 'do other men, for they would do you', the guiding precept of Anthony Chuzzlewit and Son, Manchester Warehousemen, of the Martin Chuzzlewit who withered every flower that grew about him, and of the moral Pecksniff; it is also Fagin's 'magic number'. And Tigg, of course, is a precursor of Mr. Merdle, the still more eminent business-man of *Little Dorrit*. The respectable is seen to shade so perceptibly into the criminal that, by the time of *Little Dorrit*, it needs for its encompassment the image of a ubiquitous prison.

The way in which Tigg and the secretary of the Anglo-Bengalee play on the word 'capital' in the quoted discussion between them is illustrative of their more devious game with the public. Their whole enterprise is an elaborate play on words—from the nominal capital of the Company (with its numerous 'oughts' that are naught) to its very name. It is in his choice of a name for the Company—The Anglo-Bengalee Disinterested Loan and Life Assurance Company—that Tigg, a 'man of business' but 'not a moral man', as he tells Jonas (p. 636), shows his understanding of a world of appearances. In the name of assuring life, the Company's ethic of the magic number is disguised as a moral disinterestedness. The Anglo-Bengalee is, as it were, an in-stitutionalized Mrs. Todgers, who looks at the Pecksniff girls 'with affection beaming in one eye, and calculation shining out of the other' (p. 126).

Tigg, in his sphere, is as adept at executing a wholesale or general order as Pecksniff (with his 'large stock of superfluous sentiment and morality') is in his:

> 'My dear fellow!' cried Tigg, clapping [Jonas] on the shoulder, 'I applaud your frankness. If men like you and I speak openly at first, all possible misunderstanding is avoided. Why should I disguise what you know so well, but what the crowd never dream of? We companies are all birds of prey: mere birds of prey. The only question is, whether, in serving our own turn, we can serve yours too: whether in double-lining our own nest, we can put a single lining into yours. Oh, you're in our secret. You're behind the scenes. We'll make a merit of dealing plainly with you, when we know we can't help it.' (p. 441)

It is mere concidence that Jonas is the order which, in their several ways, is executed by both Pecksniff and Tigg; but, linking them as he does, we become aware of a connection between Pecksniff's grandiloquence and Tigg's plainness. The counterfeit coin in which the moral Pecksniff trades is simply the obverse of the counterfeit disinterestedness with which the man of business lays bare his soul. The moral man and the man of business meet, furthermore, in the image of the bird of prey, for John Westlock regards Pecksniff as having 'scraped and clawed into his pouch' all the 'hard savings' of Tom's grandmother (p. 22). It is an image, indeed, that recurs in relation to fortune-hunters as a species. Old Martin tells Pecksniff that rich men are 'fit objects to be robbed and preyed upon and plotted against and adulated by . . . knaves' (p. 39); and Mr. George Chuzzlewit pointedly asks some members of the Chuzzlewit family (assembled at Pecksniff's) to 'refrain from acting the part of vultures in regard to other members of this family who are living' (p. 60). The bird of prey image is yet another means of suggesting the death that is the natural end of 'business' precepts—and, as used in *Our Mutual Friend*, it leads, finally, to the dust and ashes of the dust-mounds.[1]

Pecksniff, in contradistinction to the commercial colouring of his moral discourse, exhibits the disinterestedness of a very Tigg when he is business-like. The terms, he informs his daughters, on which 'a new inmate' is to be admitted as a pupil-architect to the Pecksniff establishment, are unusual:

'Is he handsome, Pa?' inquired the younger daughter.
'Silly Merry!' said the eldest: Merry being fond for Mercy. 'What is the premium, Pa? tell us that.' . . .
'He is well looking,' said Mr. Pecksniff, slowly and distinctly: 'well looking enough. I do not positively expect any immediate premium with him.'
Notwithstanding their different natures, both Charity and Mercy concurred in opening their eyes uncommonly wide at this announcement, and in looking for the moment as blank as if their thoughts had actually had a direct bearing on the main chance.
'But what of that!' said Mr. Pecksniff, still smiling at the fire. 'There is disinterestedness in the world, I hope? We are not all arrayed in two opposite ranks: the *off*ensive and the *def*ensive.

[1] See Ch. 8, p. 283–4 below.

Some few there are who walk between; who help the needy as they go; and take no part with either side. Umph!'

There was something in these morsels of philanthropy which reassured the sisters. They exchanged glances, and brightened very much.

'Oh! let us not be for ever calculating, devising, and plotting for the future,' said Mr. Pecksniff, smiling more and more, and looking at the fire as a man might, who was cracking a joke with it: 'I am weary of such arts. If our inclinations are but good and open-hearted, let us gratify them boldly, though they bring upon us Loss instead of Profit. Eh, Charity?' (pp. 15–16)

The Pecksniff girls, of course, are momentarily disconcerted by their father's foregoing of the 'premium' that he usually exacts from his pupils only because they are as yet unaware that the pupil in question is young Martin—and that Pecksniff has therefore already embarked on a long-term speculation in him as heir-apparent to his grandfather. It is notable, however, that they are at once 'reassured' by the 'morsels of philanthropy' he provides for them. The philanthropy is an infallible indication that Pecksniff, like Tigg, is engaging in his own kind of life assurance. For this purpose, and again like Tigg, he appropriates terms from the moral lexicon, the chief of which, significantly, is 'disinterestedness'. As he says to his daughters, even 'worldly goods' such as cream, sugar, tea, toast, ham and eggs 'have their moral' (p. 14).

Disinterestedness is a quality that Pecksniff, a 'disinterested gentleman' (p. 670), continues to demonstrate and to proclaim. Mrs. Lupin is 'fairly melted by his disinterested anxiety' for the well-being of old Martin (p. 43). Before he is rudely cut short by Mrs. Ned at the war-council of the investing Chuzzlewits, he tries to win them to his ways: 'Now we must not lose sight of the fact that our esteemed friend has a grandson, to whom he was, until lately, very much attached . . . I would submit to you, whether we might not remove Mr. Chuzzlewit's distrust of us, and vindicate our own disinterestedness by—'(pp. 59–60). In London, humbly pressing 'his hot hands together', he assures old Martin that he has spoken 'quite disinterestedly' to him on behalf of his grandson (p. 159). And then, finally, moments only before his downfall, he swoops on old Martin, feathers spread, asserting his own disinterestedness in a superb flight:

'Oh, vermin!' said Mr. Pecksniff. 'Oh, bloodsuckers! Is it not enough that you have embittered the existence of an individual, wholly unparalleled in the biographical records of amiable persons; but must you now, even now, when he has made his election, and reposed his trust in a Numble, but at least sincere and disinterested relative; must you now, vermin and swarmers (I regret to make use of these strong expressions, my dear sir, but these are times when honest indignation will not be controlled), must you now, vermin and swarmers (for I WILL repeat it), taking advantage of his unprotected state, assemble round him from all quarters, as wolves and vultures, and other animals of the feathered tribe assemble round—I will not say round carrion or a carcass, for Mr. Chuzzlewit is quite the contrary—but round their prey—their prey—to rifle and despoil; gorging their voracious maws, and staining their offensive beaks, with every description of carnivorous enjoyment!' (p. 802)

The transposition of terminology that I have documented is evidence of a widespread transvaluation of value in the society in which it occurs. Accordingly, it seems to me, the statements of intention of Dickens and Forster notwithstanding, that it is the loss of a viable sense of value by a whole society that is the true theme of *Martin Chuzzlewit*.

That it is a whole society Dickens has in mind is indicated on a number of occasions. Pecksniff, righteously angry with Mrs. Todgers for having propitiated a troublesome boarder, provides an opportunity for one such extension of the view:

'And do you mean to say, ma'am, is it possible, Mrs. Todgers, that for such a miserable consideration as eighteen shillings a week, a female of your understanding can so far demean herself as to wear a double face, even for an instant?'

'I am forced to keep things on the square if I can, sir,' faltered Mrs. Todgers. 'I must preserve peace among them, and keep my connexion together, if possible, Mr. Pecksniff. The profit is very small.' . . .

'The profit!' repeated Mr. Pecksniff. 'The profit of dissimulation! To worship the golden calf of Baal, for eighteen shillings a week!' . . .

Eighteen shillings a week! Just, most just, thy censure, upright Pecksniff! Had it been for the sake of a ribbon, star, or garter; sleeves of lawn, a great man's smile, a seat in parliament, a tap upon the shoulder from a courtly sword; a place, a party, or a thriving lie, or eighteen thousand pounds, or even eighteen hundred;—but to worship the golden calf for eighteen shillings a week! Oh pitiful, pitiful! (pp. 168–9)

The fact that it is not only Pecksniff (and poor Mrs. Todgers) who are exposed to censure here but also, by implication, the numerous followers of Baal in high places points to the re-enactment off-stage, as it were, of the drama that is played out in the novel. The Pecksniffian 'process of reasoning', it is further intimated, is by no means *sui generis*: 'That many undertakings, national as well as individual—but especially the former—are held to be specially brought to a glorious and successful issue, which never could be so regarded on any other process of reasoning, must be clear to all men' (p. 329). And Tigg says to Jonas, 'Everybody profits by the indiscretion of his neighbour; and the people in the best repute, the most' (p. 636). Within its limits, *Martin Chuzzlewit* cannot accommodate such larger effects—hence the need, in two of the instances cited, for so direct and heavy an irony on the novelist's part—but the indication that the false and golden god is an object of general worship posits the absence of a true sense of value in all walks of society. Dickens, it would appear, was already being faced by the need to devise a structure which could contain a more comprehensive working-out of his theme. This he was to do, with conspicuous success, in *Bleak House, Little Dorrit* and *Our Mutual Friend*.

An alternative scale of value is adumbrated in the closing pages of the novel in the description of the coming together of John Westlock and Ruth Pinch. John, who says he hopes he knows 'the value' of Ruth's heart and 'the worth' of her nature (p. 818), emerges as a merchant of love: 'See,' old Martin says to Ruth, 'what Tom and I purchased this morning while you were dealing in exchange with that young merchant there' (p. 821); and, giving Ruth the jewels he has bought her, Martin adds that he does not know 'which becomes the other most', but that it is no use asking John, 'for he is bribed' (p. 822). This twist to the prevailing commercial imagery is followed by an explicit juxtaposition of love and money:

'. . . It would be unjust to you,' [Tom says to John], 'to speak of your having chosen a portionless girl, for I feel that you know her worth; I am sure you know her worth. Nor will it diminish in your estimation, John, which money might.'

'Which money would, Tom,' he returned. 'Her worth! Oh, who could see her here, and not love her! Who could know her, Tom, and not honour her! Who could ever stand possessed of such a heart as hers, and grow indifferent to the treasure! . . .' (p. 824)

The love passages in this novel, as in most of Dickens's work until late in his career, are not strongly realized; but what is said here is given force by all that has gone before. The only hope in the world of Pecksniff and Jonas and Tigg, it is implied, lies in the establishment of a currency that is beyond debasement. In setting love against money as true wealth at the end of the novel, Dickens had cleared the way for a direct testing of the proposition in *Dombey and Son*.

III

Martin Chuzzlewit is like *Oliver Twist* in that the novelist's consistent imaginative presentation of a subject is overlaid by a consciously planned but more superficial apprehension of that subject. The imaginative vision reveals itself in the recurring images and the crucial transpositions to which I have drawn attention; the simpler definition of the subject is grafted on to this material in a number of set pieces throughout the novel. The result is a kind of double exposure, which may be clearly observed early on in the action when (in the first of the set pieces) old Martin's suspicions are aroused by Pecksniff's championship of his grandson:

Martin lay for some time, with an expression on his face of silent wonder, not unmixed with rage: at length he muttered in a whisper:

'What does this mean? Can the false-hearted boy have chosen such a tool as yonder fellow who has just gone out? Why not! He has conspired against me, like the rest, and they are but birds of one feather. A new plot; a new plot! Oh self, self, self! At every turn nothing but self!' (p. 42)

The images old Martin employs here align his grandson with the men of business as well as with the fortune-hunters: he is a bird of prey, 'like the rest'; he, too, is ready to use others as his tools and instruments. Young Martin seems, that is, to have the makings of a capital fellow— the first instances of a transposition of terminology occur in the previous chapter, which describes the Pecksniffs at home—but his propensities are at the same time viewed, more narrowly, as marks of his selfishness. He turns out, in fact, to be neither a man of business nor a fortune-hunter, but the passage is illustrative of the way in which the restricted, 'intended' theme of selfishness is imposed on the larger imaginative vision. From the outset the imposed theme is inextricably bound up with motives it does not subsume.

The theme of selfishness, moreover, is itself developed without coherence, the term 'self' unavailingly being used in the set pieces to wed incompatible actions that constantly strain apart. On the one hand, the term is used in a sense that relates the theme to the novelist's imaginative preoccupation. Old Martin, on the occasion already referred to, continues to brood on the 'foul uses' to which his money is likely to 'be put at last':

> '. . . after filling me with cares and miseries all my life, it will perpetuate discord and bad passions when I am dead. So it always is. What lawsuits grow out of the graves of rich men, every day: sowing perjury, hatred, and lies among near kindred, where there should be nothing but love! Heaven help us, we have much to answer for! Oh self, self, self! Every man for himself, and no creature for me!' (p. 42)

The phrase 'every man for himself', as used here, is equivalent to Jonas's 'do other men, for they would do you' and to Tigg's 'number one'. The word 'self', that is, evokes the kind of mercenary self-seeking in which the fortune-hunters are shown to engage, 'the principle of self', as Shelley puts it, 'of which money is the visible incarnation'; and it is used in this sense in two further passages towards the end of the novel:

> 'Aye,' [Slyme] said, with a sulky nod. 'You may deny your nephews till you die, but Chevy Slyme is Chevy Slyme still, all the world over. Perhaps even you may feel it some disgrace to your own blood to be employed in this way. I'm to be bought off.'

'At every turn!' cried Martin. 'Self, self, self. Every one among them for himself!' (p. 788)

In every single circumstance, whether it were cruel, cowardly, or false, [old Martin] saw the flowering of the same pregnant seed. Self; grasping, eager, narrow-ranging, over-reaching self; with its long train of suspicions, lusts, deceits, and all their growing consequences; was the root of the vile tree. Mr. Pecksniff had so presented his character before the old man's eyes, that he—the good, the tolerant, enduring Pecksniff—had become the incarnation of all selfishness and treachery . . . (p. 796)

On the other hand, in three equally emphatic passages the word 'self' is used in a markedly different sense. Prior to the first passage, young Martin (about to set sail for America) is shown taking an exuberant farewell of Mary, being full of thoughts of the 'change of scene and change of place, change of people, change of manners, change of cares and hopes' awaiting him:

> Was he thinking solely of her care for him, when he took so little heed of her share in the separation; of her quiet monotonous endurance, and her slow anxiety from day to day? Was there nothing jarring and discordant even in his tone of courage, with this one note 'self' for ever audible, however high the strain? Not in her ears. It had been better otherwise, perhaps, but so it was. She heard the same bold spirit which had flung away as dross all gain and profit for her sake, making light of peril and privation that she might be calm and happy; and she heard no more. That heart where self has found no place and raised no throne, is slow to recognise its ugly presence when it looks upon it. . . . (p. 241)

The use of the word 'self' here clearly sounds an altogether different note from that sounded in the previously quoted passages. That Martin is precisely not an exemplar of mercenary self-seeking, like Pecksniff or Jonas or Tigg, is dramatized in his having placed his love for Mary above the fortune he has hoped to inherit, in his having 'flung away as dross all gain and profit for her sake'. Preoccupied only with himself, Martin here exemplifies a radically different kind of 'selfishness', an egotistic self-centredness. It is this, as Mark Tapley soon sees, that is 'the one absorbing principle of Martin's character' (p. 244); and it is to a realization of his selfishness in this sense and of Mark's selflessness by contrast that Martin eventually comes after being 'very near his death' in Eden:

> It was natural for him to reflect—he had months to do it in—upon his own escape, and Mark's extremity. This led him to consider which of them could be the better spared, and why? Then the curtain slowly rose a very little way; and Self, Self, Self, was shown below.
>
> He asked himself, besides, when dreading Mark's decease (as all men do and must, at such a time), whether he had done his duty by him, and had deserved and made a good response to his fidelity and zeal. No. Short as their companionship had been, he felt in many, many instances, that there was blame against himself; and still inquiring why, the curtain slowly rose a little more, and Self, Self, Self, dilated on the scene. (pp. 524–5)

Of the shallow, unconvincing insubstantiality of this as a rendering of spiritual experience I shall have more to say later; suffice it now to note that the 'self' which is disclosed by the rising curtain is a replica of that which has dilated in old Martin, as the old man is eventually led to see. Reconciled with his grandson, admitting that 'the fault' has been his own 'no less' than the young man's, he says: 'The curse of our house . . . has been the love of self; has ever been the love of self. How often have I said so, when I never knew that I had wrought it upon others!' (p. 804)

The use of the word 'self' as a unifying thematic counter in these passages in fact sets up a false analogy in the novel between self-seeking and self-centredness. The motive of self-seeking is subsumed by the large social theme, the loss of a viable sense of value in a society in which such mercenary self-seeking is prevalent; but the motive of self-centredness, of an individual moral imperfection of which the two Martins are the chief exemplars, has no organic connection with the main theme. That the analogy is forced is indirectly reflected in the structure of the book: Dickens's need to resolve the drama of spiritual conversion (which is what the story of the two Martins develops into) results in the two major contrivances of the plot, which are its two major weaknesses.

The first such contrivance is old Martin's deception of Pecksniff, an unsubtle attempt, by indirections to find directions out. He conceives his plan of pretending senility and apparently submitting to Pecksniff, he later reveals, in order 'to probe . . . Pecksniff, and to prove the constancy and truth of Mary (to himself no less than Martin)' (p. 808). The plan, however, cannot but appear to be a singularly masochistic means of establishing what is sufficiently known already: that Martin has long seen through Pecksniff is clearly shown at their first meeting in the Blue Dragon; and that he has faith in Mary is evidenced by his choice of her as a wife for his grandson. Martin is from the start an implausible Boffin; if (in *Our Mutual Friend*) it is possible to accept that Boffin is sustained in his pretence by the object he has in view, it is difficult to believe that Martin is kept going by the prospect of his eventual scourging of Pecksniff: 'I never could have undergone such torture,' he tells Tom, 'but for looking forward to this time' (p. 772). The game simply does not seem to be worth the candle. Nor is it, indeed, as far as the novelist is concerned. Dickens, of course, gains his great scene of denunciation; but since he has taken care that we should realize Martin is only playing a part at Pecksniff's, the scenes in which the good man is inveigled into his trap are deprived of all real drama. As Ross H. Dabney says, 'There is no real threat or tension; we know that Old Martin is not really senile and will protect Mary. Whatever Pecksniff and Mary say or do to each other is deprived of importance—even of reality—by Old Martin's deception and manifest intentions.'[1]

How is it, we wonder, that Dickens should have been so blind to this weakness? The answer, I think, is that Martin's involvement with Pecksniff is meant to serve a further, and more important, purpose. If Martin's close association with Pecksniff brings together two exponents of 'self', though of the imperfectly related self-centred and self-seeking variety, his deception of him, which results in Pecksniff's final exposure, is also made the occasion of his own moral transformation. It is suggested, since he undertakes the deception shortly after having broken with his grandson, that he is then still unregenerately 'selfish':

> 'There is a kind of selfishness,' said Martin: 'I have learned it in my own experience of my own breast: which is constantly upon the watch for selfishness in others; and holding others at a distance by suspicions and distrusts, wonders why they don't

[1] *Love and Property*, p. 40.

approach, and don't confide, and calls that selfishness in them. Thus I once doubted those about me—not without reason in the beginning—and thus I once doubted you, Martin.' (p. 804)

It is during his stay at Pecksniff's house, we are given to understand, that a decisive change occurs:

> 'The penance I have done in his house,' said Mr. Chuzzlewit, 'has carried this reflection with it constantly, above all others. That if it had pleased Heaven to visit such infirmity on my old age as really had reduced me to the state in which I feigned to be, I should have brought its misery upon myself. Oh you whose wealth, like mine, has been a source of continual unhappiness, leading you to distrust the nearest and dearest, and to dig yourself a living grave of suspicion and reserve; take heed that, having cast off all whom you might have bound to you, and tenderly, you do not become in your decay the instrument of such a man as this, and waken in another world to the knowledge of such wrong as would embitter Heaven itself, if wrong or you could ever reach it!' (pp. 807–8)

The period of the deception, in other words, is also meant to be seen as a time of 'penance', during which Martin awakes to the error of his ways. Indeed, it appears that the deception is necessitated not so much by the need to expose Pecksniff as to provide an experience which can account for the change in Martin. That the experience itself did not deeply engage Dickens may be inferred from the way in which it is left, as it were, to speak for itself in Martin's retrospective summary. But in fact it does not. Since the aims of the deception are commendably selfless, and since the practice of it forces on Martin a continual self-abnegation, it would appear that the change in him is effectually wrought of its own accord.

The change in young Martin is recorded almost as perfunctorily. In the swamps of Eden the curtain rises on Self and reveals to him 'the failing of his life':

> It was long before he fixed the knowledge of himself so firmly in his mind that he could thoroughly discern the truth; but in the hideous solitude of that most hideous place, with Hope so far removed, Ambition quenched, and Death beside him rattling

at the very door, reflection came, as in a plague-beleagured town; and so he felt and knew the failing of his life, and saw distinctly what an ugly spot it was.

Eden was a hard school to learn so hard a lesson in; but there were teachers in the swamp and thicket, and the pestilential air, who had a searching method of their own.

He made a solemn resolution that when his strength returned he would not dispute the point or resist the conviction, but would look upon it as an established fact, that selfishness was in his breast, and must be rooted out. He was so doubtful (and with justice) of his own character, that he determined not to say one word of vain regret or good resolve to Mark, but steadily to keep his purpose before his own eyes solely: and there was not a jot of pride in this; nothing but humility and steadfastness: the best armour he could wear. So low had Eden brought him. So high had Eden raised him up. (p. 525)

It is an unfortunate implication that we are perhaps to view Martin's spiritual progress as following the pattern of a fortunate fall, for this only emphasizes the utter triviality of his experience. The deep tonal chords of the prose are the more inappropriate in that Martin's selfishness, his 'ugly spot', has for the most part been represented as a matter of hogging the fire (p. 73) or sitting in the most comfortable chair (p. 92) or, at worst, forgetting all about the loyal servant whom he has left in charge of his luggage (p. 278). This kind of action is an imperfect substitute for a more profound characterization which could alone justify the fanfare of a moral conversion. But then the description of the conversion is itself a substitute for the real thing. The strenuousness of the assertion here is reminiscent of that by which Oliver Twist's virtue is vindicated, and it similarly suggests that Dickens was not deeply concerned with what he was doing. The repetitions, the capitalized abstractions, the cliché of phrase and image alike indicate a lack of imaginative vitality; the thinness of the treatment being matched by the insubstantiality of the subsequent presentation of the change in Martin:

'. . . But, my life, how wet you are, Mark!' [said Martin].
'*I* am! What do you consider yourself, sir?'
'Oh, not half as bad,' said his fellow-traveller, with an air of great vexation. 'I told you not to keep on the windy side, Mark,

but to let us change and change about. The rain has been beating
on you ever since it began.'

'You don't know how it pleases me, sir,' said Mark, after a
short silence: 'if I may make so bold as say so, to hear you a-going
on in that there uncommon considerate way of yours; which I
don't mean to attend to, never, but which, ever since that time
when I was floored in Eden, you have showed.' (pp. 658–9)

The portrayal of the chastening of Martin is thus both perfunctory
and superficial; and yet, in order to bring it about, Dickens has recourse
to the second major contrivance in the plot—the sending of Martin to
America. John Forster has pointed out that there were extra-literary
considerations behind this development:

> [Sales] rose somewhat on Martin's ominous announcement, at
> the end of the fourth number, *that he'd go to America*; but though
> it was believed that this resolve, which Dickens adopted as sud-
> denly as his hero, might increase the number of his readers, that
> reason influenced him less than the challenge to make good his
> *Notes* which every mail had been bringing him from unsparing
> assailants beyond the Atlantic. . . .[1]

Whatever the extra-literary considerations, the fact remains that, in
the novel as it stands, the *raison d'être* of the American section is, as
Forster puts it, Martin's 'casting off his slough of selfishness in the
poisonous swamp of Eden'.[2] The American episodes, comprising
nearly one-sixth of the novel, thus illustrate the tendency of the subsidiary action that is concerned with self-centredness to strain apart
from the main action. An immediate sign of this is that Martin's
American adventure is implausibly motivated, for his contention that
his grandfather 'will not suffer [him] to live . . . if he can help it, in
[his] own land' (p. 238) is wildly exaggerated. More significantly, the
adventure is concerned, as it turns out, less with his moral and spiritual
development than with Dickens's satirizing of America, with a 'making good' of *American Notes*—and that is a thoroughly disintegrative
element in the novel.

Forster quotes an interesting confession that Dickens made to him
while he was working on one of the American sections: 'I write in
haste, for I have been at work all day; and, it being against the grain

---

[1] *Charles Dickens*, Vol. II (London, 1873), p. 42.   [2] *Ibid.*, p. 53.

with me to go back to America when my interest is strong in the other parts of the tale, have got on but slowly.'[1] Dickens's imagination, apparently, was not really gripped by the American material. Playing fitfully, it may be inferred, on the American scene, it here and there seizes on America as a kind of commercialized England writ large in a way that might have been successfully incorporated within the over-all design; but the vision is never steady and the opportunity is lost.

One of Martin's first impressions of America is of a land of dollars:

> [The conversation of the busy gentlemen] was rather barren of interest, to say the truth; and the greater part of it may be summed up in one word. Dollars. All their cares, hopes, joys, affections, virtues, and associations, seemed to be melted down into dollars. Whatever the chance contributions that fell into the slow cauldron of their talk, they made the gruel thick and slab with dollars. Men were weighed by their dollars; life was auctioneered, appraised, put up, and knocked down for its dollars. The next respectable thing to dollars was any venture having their attainment for its end. The more of that worthless ballast, honour and fair-dealing, which any man cast overboard from the ship of his Good Name and Good Intent, the more ample stowage-room he had for dollars. Make commerce one huge lie and mighty theft. Deface the banner of the nation for an idle rag; pollute it star by star; and cut out stripe by stripe as from the arm of a degraded soldier. Do anything for dollars! What is a flag to *them*! (p. 273)

The land in which everything is 'melted down into dollars' and where life itself is 'auctioneered' is not as far removed from the land of Pecksniff and Jonas and Tigg as the novelist appears to believe. It is Dickens's lack of awareness of the resemblance, betrayed in the tone of hectoring superiority, that is disconcerting here; the lack of aware-ness pointing to the separation, in his imagination, of the two 'worlds' of the novel. That the imaginative worlds are potentially homogeneous is suggested by the sporadic recurrence in the American sections of the kind of image that is characteristically used to evoke the English ethos.[2] Major Pawkins, we are told, is a man who, 'trading on his

---

[1] *Ibid.*

[2] I am indebted to a student of mine, Mr. Alan Marbé, for drawing my attention to these images.

stock of wisdom', invariably proceeds 'on the principle of putting all the goods he [has] (and more) into his window'; he is also (having 'a most distinguished genius for swindling') an 'admirable man of business' (pp. 267–8). The 'sterling coin' of General Choke's 'benevolence' (p. 349) manifests itself in his introducing Martin to Mr. Scadder, agent of the Eden Land Corporation; Scadder is himself like 'a bird of prey' (p. 353), and he runs the Land Corporation in as businesslike a manner as Tigg the Anglo-Bengalee. Finally, American slave-owners actualize the tendency noted in England to convert men into personal estate, Mark Tapley remarking that 'they're so fond of Liberty in this part of the globe, that they buy her and sell her and carry her to market with 'em' (p. 283).

If the American pages in *Martin Chuzzlewit*, in other words, were not informed by Dickens's aggressive response to the hostile reception accorded *American Notes*, they might have been used to extend the scope of his evocation of the return of Baal. As it is, however, the passages quoted do not bulk large enough in the American sections to constitute a weighty parallel to the business transacted in England. Their effect, in fact, is diffused in the general anatomy of folly that Dickens seems impelled to undertake in defiance of an American abomination of satire that Mr. Bevan is made to describe to Martin:

> '. . . I believe no satirist could breathe this air. If another Juvenal or Swift could rise up among us to-morrow, he would be hunted down. If you have any knowledge of our literature, and can give me the name of any man, American born and bred, who has anatomised our follies as a people, and not as this or that party; and who has escaped the foulest and most brutal slander, the most inveterate hatred and intolerant pursuit; it will be a strange name in my ears, believe me. In some cases I could name to you, where a native writer has ventured on the most harmless and good-humoured illustrations of our vices or defects, it has been found necessary to announce, that in a second edition the passage has been expunged, or altered, or explained away, or patched into praise.' (p. 276)

Barbara Hardy maintains that 'there is no visible relation between Martin's selfishness and the dramatization on a national scale of the hypocritical and aggressive selfishness of America', but she also says that 'there is, indeed, as we all know, this thematic connection between the social satire and the individual types of selfishness . . .'[1] It seems to me that, if the idea of 'self' is to be invoked in the American episodes (and it is significant that the novelist himself does not invoke it other than in relation to its dilation in Martin), it is best referred to in terms (unconnected though they may be with 'selfishness') of national self-conceit. This is the 'note' that is constantly sounded in Martin's encounters with Americans, whether in Colonel Diver's reference to American newspapers as 'the Palladium of rational Liberty at home . . . and the dread of Foreign oppression abroad . . . the Envy of the world . . . and the leaders of Human Civilization' (p. 257) or in Mr. Jefferson Brick's belief that Broadway '[whips] the universe' (p. 265); whether in Mr. Chollop's view that Americans are 'the intellect and virtue of the airth, the cream Of human natur', and the flower Of moral force' (p. 522) or in the Pogram Defiance which, as Mr. Pogram says, 'defied the world . . . Defied the world in general to com-pete with our country upon any hook; and devellop'd our internal resources for making war upon the universal airth' (p. 532). Martin soon discovers that Americans 'as a body' are 'ready to make oath upon the Evangelists at any hour of the day or night, that [America] is the most thriving and prosperous of all countries on the habitable globe' (p. 268); and Mark describes Eden as 'a reg'lar little United States in itself' because the 'two or three American settlers left . . . coolly comes over one, even here . . . as if it was the wholesomest and loveliest spot in the world' (p. 517).

Nor is the thematic irrelevance of the American scenes compensated for by the quality of the satire. It is widely held that the satire is brilliant;[2] but I must confess that with every re-reading of the novel I find the American episodes of less and less interest. There are admittedly fine moments but, on the whole, it seems to me that the satire tends to be either too patent, as when General Fladdock expatiates on the enormity of English class distinctions only to be outraged when he finds that he is 'expected to know' Martin, 'a fellow who [has] come over in the steerage of a line-of-packet ship, at the cost of four pound ten' (pp. 289–90); or too crude, as in the following not unrepresentative example:

They were walking back very leisurely; Martin arm-in-arm

---

[1] '*Martin Chuzzlewit*', loc. cit., p. 115.
[2] See, for instance, Edgar Johnson, *Charles Dickens*, I, 469, 471, 475; Barbara Hardy, '*Martin Chuzzlewit*', loc. cit., p. 120; and Steven Marcus, *Dickens*, p. 219.

with Mr. Jefferson Brick, and the major and the colonel side-by-side before them; when, as they came within a house or two of the major's residence, they heard a bell ringing violently. The instant this sound struck upon their ears, the colonel and the major darted off, dashed up the steps and in at the street-door (which stood ajar) like lunatics; while Mr. Jefferson Brick, detaching his arm from Martin's, made a precipitate dive in the same direction, and vanished also.

'Good Heaven!' thought Martin. 'The premises are on fire! It was an alarm bell!'

But there was no smoke to be seen, nor any flame, nor was there any smell of fire. As Martin faltered on the pavement, three more gentlemen, with horror and agitation depicted in their faces, came plunging wildly round the street corner; jostled each other on the steps; struggled for an instant; and rushed into the house, a confused heap of arms and legs. Unable to bear it any longer, Martin followed. Even in his rapid progress he was run down, thrust aside, and passed, by two more gentlemen, stark mad, as it appeared, with fierce excitement.

'Where is it?' cried Martin, breathlessly, to a negro whom he encountered in the passage.

'In a eatin room, sa. 'Kernell, sa, him kep a seat 'side himself, sa.'

'A seat!' cried Martin.

'For a dinnar, sa.' (pp. 269–70)

The burlesque that falls a little flat, the grossness of the exaggeration and the triteness of the writing accord ill with the subtleties of the Pecksniffian scene.

4

DOMBEY AND SON

I

Lord Jeffrey referred to Mr. Dombey as 'a mitigated Jonas';[1] and, indeed, as he is first presented, Dombey might have come straight out of the pages of *Martin Chuzzlewit*. Married for ten years and with a daughter aged six, Dombey thinks of himself as having had no issue—'to speak of': '. . . what was a girl to Dombey and Son! In the capital of the House's name and dignity, such a child was merely a piece of base coin that couldn't be invested—a bad Boy—nothing more' (p. 3). And contemplating the possibility of his wife's death, he feels 'sincere regret' at the prospect of finding 'a something gone from among his plate and furniture, and other household possessions', a something 'well worth the having' (p. 5). This, we recognize, is the language of the earlier novel, and Dombey's business-like sentiments evoke the distinctive ethos of the society portrayed in it, manifesting a similar confusion of values. But whereas in *Martin Chuzzlewit* Dickens shows how business precepts corrupt moral values, in *Dombey and Son* he considers the effect of such precepts on the emotional being of his characters, particularly and centrally on that of Mr. Dombey himself. The title of Chapter III—'In which Mr. Dombey, as a Man and a Father, is seen at the Head of the Home-Department'— points to the perspective in which 'business' is viewed in this novel.

That Dombey is kept so firmly at the centre of the novel is an immediate indication of the discipline of its organization. It has been generally remarked that *Dombey and Son* is Dickens's first carefully planned novel, and it is also commonly regarded as his first mature work, 'the first in which a pervasive uneasiness about contemporary

---

[1] Letter to Dickens, 14. 12. 1846, quoted by John Forster, *Charles Dickens*, II, 330.

society takes the place of an intermittent concern with specific social wrongs'.[1] I believe that *Martin Chuzzlewit*, rather than *Dombey and Son*, both in respect of its considerable achievement (its weaknesses notwithstanding) and its concern with themes that are central to Dickens's work as a novelist, marks the end of his apprenticeship; but it is certainly true that the later novel is the first in which an elaborate plot is successfully used as a unifying principle. In *Dombey and Son* the plot is not compounded of confusions of theme, as in Dickens's earlier work, but is integral to it. In his handling of crucial turns in the plot, however, such as Paul's death or Edith's abandonment of Dombey and subsequent confrontation with Carker or Florence's return in the nick of time to her suicidal father, Dickens still succumbs to the sentimental and theatrical seductions of his art. Nor is the plot negotiated without an immoderate allowance of coincidence, most notably in episodes such as the return of Walter Gay on the very day of Florence's flight from home or the reappearance of Solomon Gills on the night before the wedding of the young couple. But these weaknesses of temperament and craft are more than compensated for by the coherence which the plot provides.

The plot may be thought of as having the shape of a circle, making *Dombey and Son* the kind of 'round world' which the novelist himself invokes some half-way through the novel:

> Were this miserable mother, and this miserable daughter [i.e., Mrs. Brown and her daughter Alice], only the reduction to their lowest grade, of certain social vices sometimes prevailing higher up? In this round world of many circles within circles, do we make a weary journey from the high grade to the low, to find at last that they lie close together, that the two extremes touch, and that our journey's end is but our starting-place? Allowing for great difference of stuff and texture, was the pattern of this woof repeated among gentle blood at all?
> Say, Edith Dombey! And Cleopatra, best of mothers, let us have your testimony! (pp. 495–6)

Dickens is over-explicit here, but the passage illuminates his method not only in this novel but also in subsequent, more ambitious work. The method is grounded in his belief in the interconnection of distinct

---

[1] Kathleen Tillotson, *Novels of the Eighteen-Forties* (London, 1961; first published 1954), p. 157.

social classes, of 'high grades' and low; and it consists, in the first
instance, of so constructing a plot as to make this connection palpable
on the narrative level. The characteristic structure of Dickens's large
'social' novels—of *Bleak House*, *Little Dorrit* and *Our Mutual Friend*,
I shall argue, as well as of *Dombey and Son*—is that of a 'round world
of many circles within circles'. But such a structure, where plot effectively bodies forth theme, implies a firm thematic, as well as narrative,
centre. It is Dickens's particular genius to establish not only a narrative
but also a thematic movement from circle to circle by means of the
analogical method, by repeating 'the pattern' of the 'woof' amid all
'the difference of stuff and texture'. It is a recognition of the thematic
analogues at the centre of these novels that takes us to their heart—
and that also makes them appear altogether tighter and suppler
organisms than the 'large loose baggy monsters' of Henry James's
disdain.[1]

The short title of the novel, *Dombey and Son*, with its implied
reference to the Dombey family as well as to the family firm, is more
evocative of the central concerns of the narrative than the full title,
Dealings with the Firm of Dombey and Son, *Wholesale, Retail, and for
Exportation*. Dombey and Son, with its Home-Department prominent
among its other branches, is solidly at the centre of the plot. The narrative moves out from that centre to various social circles, encompassing
Mrs. Skewton (an aged and withered Cleopatra), her daughter Edith,
Cousin Feenix and Sir Barnet and Lady Skettles at the highest 'grade'
and Mrs. Brown and Alice at the lowest, all the characters being connected in one way or another either with the Dombey family or the
firm. But Edith and Cleopatra, we remember, are authorially enjoined
to recognize a further connection between themselves and Mrs. Brown
and Alice. The analogy between their situations is so clear that it
hardly needs to have attention drawn to it; but if the readiness of both
mothers to sell their daughters epitomizes the kind of preoccupation
with money that is common in the world of Dombey and Son, the
value of money itself is questioned early on in the novel. When Paul
is about five years old, he places his father 'in a difficulty' by asking
him what money is. Deciding against a technical explanation, Mr.
Dombey answers: 'Gold, and silver, and copper. Guineas, shillings,
half-pence. You know what they are?':

---

[1] The phrase refers specifically to *The Newcomes*, *Les Trois Mousquetaires*, and 'Tolstoi's
"Peace and War"', but James would have been ready, I imagine, to incorporate Dickens's
work in his condemnation. See 'Preface to *The Tragic Muse*', *The Art of the Novel* (New
York, 1934), p. 84.

'Oh yes, I know what they are,' said Paul. 'I don't mean that, Papa. I mean what's money after all?' . . .

'What is money after all!' said Mr. Dombey, backing his chair a little, that he might the better gaze in sheer amazement at the presumptuous atom that propounded such an inquiry.

'I mean, Papa, what can it do?' returned Paul . . .

Mr. Dombey drew his chair back to its former place, and patted him on the head. 'You'll know better by-and-by, my man,' he said. 'Money, Paul, can do anything.' He took hold of the little hand, and beat it softly against one of his own, as he said so.

But Paul got his hand free as soon as he could; and rubbing it gently to and fro on the elbow of his chair, as if his wit were in the palm, and he were sharpening it—and looking at the fire again, as though the fire had been his adviser and prompter—repeated, after a short pause:

'Anything, Papa?'

'Yes. Anything—almost,' said Mr. Dombey.

'Anything means everything, don't it, Papa?' asked his son: not observing, or possibly not understanding, the qualification.

'It includes it: yes,' said Mr. Dombey.

'Why didn't money save me my Mama?' returned the child. 'It isn't cruel, is it?'

'Cruel!' said Mr. Dombey, settling his neckcloth, and seeming to resent the idea. 'No. A good thing can't be cruel.'

'If it's a good thing, and can do anything,' said the little fellow, thoughtfully, as he looked back at the fire, 'I wonder why it didn't save me my Mama.' (pp. 92–3)

The question that Paul has the presumption to propound not only links up with that of Mr. Mould in *Martin Chuzzlewit*—'And what can do more [than money], Mrs. Gamp?'; it is also one that continues to preoccupy Dickens hereafter, receiving its final answer only in *Our Mutual Friend*. It is a question that demands an answer in *Dombey and Son*, for it is rhythmically recalled throughout the novel. When Dombey decides to lend money to Walter's uncle, he says to his son: 'And you see, Paul, how powerful money is, and how anxious people are to get it,' Paul's face showing 'a sharp understanding of the reference conveyed in these words' (pp. 132–3). The 'feebleness of wealth' is 'direfully impressed' on Dombey after Paul's death: 'What could it do, his boy had asked him. Sometimes, thinking of the baby question, he could hardly forbear inquiring, himself, what *could* it do indeed: what had it done?' (p. 272). 'Do you know nothing more powerful than money?' Alice asks Dombey when he asserts that 'money will bring about unlikely things' (p. 725). Finally, when Dombey is near death, his 'distracted' mind fastens on the question: 'He would repeat that childish question, "What is money?" and ponder on it, and think about it, and reason with himself, more or less connectedly, for a good answer; as if it had never been proposed to him until that moment' (p. 860).

The 'good answer', of course, is provided by the novel as a whole. The book is, in effect, an extended answer to Paul's questions about money, dramatizing what money can do not only *for* the man who has it but also *to* him, and suggesting what money amounts to after all. What money has done for Dombey is strikingly evoked in Miss Tox's early reference to him as 'a pecuniary Duke of York' (p. 9); some idea of what it has done to him is conveyed in the quoted discussion between him and Paul. Dombey's belief in the power of money, in what it can do, has made him blind to the obvious limitations of that power. A general blindness to what is going on around him, both at home and in his business, is, indeed, one of his constantly disabling characteristics; and it further manifests itself here in his inability to see the drift of Paul's questions. Paul, however, persists in dwelling on what money cannot do, intimating, with a sick child's intuition, that it is likely to be no more efficacious in preserving his own life than it has been in the case of his mother:

> 'It can't make me strong and quite well, either, Papa; can it?' asked Paul, after a short silence; rubbing his tiny hands.
>
> 'Why, you *are* strong and quite well,' returned Mr. Dombey. 'Are you not?'
>
> Oh! the age of the face that was turned up again, with an expression, half of melancholy, half of slyness, on it! (pp. 93–4)

If Paul's own death makes it abundantly clear that money cannot buy life, Dombey's second marriage demonstrates that it equally cannot buy love. Complimented by Mrs. Skewton on having made 'a perfect palace' of his refurbished house, Dombey's response is characteristic:

> 'It is handsome,' said Mr. Dombey, looking round. 'I directed that no expense should be spared; and all that money could do, has been done, I believe.'

'And what can it not do, dear Dombey?' observed Cleopatra.

'It is powerful, madam,' said Mr. Dombey.

He looked in his solemn way towards his wife, but not a word said she. (p. 500)

In thus delineating areas where money is of no value, Dickens sets up an opposition in the novel between money on the one hand and life and love on the other. This opposition is made apparent in different but related terms when Polly Toodle thanks Mr. Carker, with a 'mother's prayers and blessings', for having been so good as to take an interest in her son—'thanks so rich when paid out of the Heart's mint, especially for any service Mr. Carker had rendered, that he might have given back a large amount of change, and yet been overpaid' (p. 311). This placing of the wealth of the heart against that of a more material mintage makes explicit the opposed criteria of value that are examined in the novel. The heart, evoking not only feeling but also life and love, is set against money in the central opposition on which the book is based. Characters are ranged round this centre in two opposing camps, those whom (in view of a vivid statement of the opposition) we may regard as dealing in hearts and those who deal, as it were, in hides: 'Dombey and Son,' we are told in the opening pages, 'had often dealt in hides, but never in hearts' (p. 2). These are the dealings with Dombey and Son that the book treats. They are treated, as I have suggested, analogically, the hide-merchants being shown, by way of connecting images and ideas, to conform to an outlook that (with Edgar Johnson) we may call 'Dombeyism'; and the merchants in love to adhere to 'Heart'.

John Westlock, it will be recalled, is presented as a merchant of love at the end of *Martin Chuzzlewit*. It is not surprising that the phrase should arise in a discussion of *Dombey and Son* because the themes of the two novels are closely related. If the central theme of *Martin Chuzzlewit* is the loss of a viable sense of value in a commercialized society, that of *Dombey and Son* is the recognition of true value—the need to know value right, as Susan Nipper indignantly tells Dombey:

'Miss Floy,' said Susan Nipper, 'is the most devoted and most patient and most dutiful and beautiful of daughters, there an't no gentleman, no Sir, though as great and rich as all the greatest and richest of England put together, but might be proud of her and would and ought. If he knew her value right, he'd rather lose his greatness and his fortune piece by piece and beg his way in rags from door to door, I say to some and all, he would!' cried Susan Nipper, bursting into tears, 'than bring the sorrow on her tender heart that I have seen it suffer in this house!' (p. 615)

Florence's 'tender heart', as Dombey has to learn, is worth more than all 'his greatness and his fortune'. The action of the novel is concerned with the opening of Dombey's own heart—Florence's enduring study is of 'how to win her father's heart' (p. 509)—and with his liberation from his restricted code of values when he recognizes what she means to him. Prior to that time he remains 'shut up within himself', a man who rarely '[oversteps] the enchanted circle within which the operations of Dombey and Son [are] conducted' (p. 285). At the centre of many circles, Dombey is a prisoner in his round world.

II

The first words that Dombey speaks to his wife on the birth of his son are: 'The house will once again, Mrs. Dombey, be not only in name but in fact Dombey and Son; Dom-bey and Son!' (p. 1); and he goes on:

'He will be christened Paul, my—Mrs. Dombey—of course. . . . His father's name, Mrs. Dombey, and his grandfather's! I wish his grandfather were alive this day!' And again he said 'Dom-bey and Son', in exactly the same tone as before.

Those three words conveyed the one idea of Mr. Dombey's life. The earth was made for Dombey and Son to trade in, and the sun and moon were made to give them light. Rivers and seas were formed to float their ships; rainbows gave them promise of fair weather; winds blew for or against their enterprises; stars and planets circled in their orbits, to preserve inviolate a system of which they were the centre. Common abbreviations took new meanings in his eyes, and had sole reference to them: A.D. had no concern with anno Domini, but stood for anno Dombei—and Son. (pp. 1–2)

The essential grotesquerie of the 'handsome well-made man' that Dombey is said to be (p. 1) is at once vividly suggested as he views the birth of his son—the beating of a new heart—exclusively in relation to the continued life of his firm. Nor is his preoccupation with Dombey and Son merely evidence of a crass materialism; it is obsessive, the three words conveying 'the one idea' of his life. Anthony Chuzzlewit and Son, whose transactions constitute 'the one affair of life' for its directors, has suffered a sea change, we see, into Dombey and Son. Dombey's monomania, however, is even more reductive than that of the Chuzzlewits, reducing everything—the very world itself (as the novelist wittily intimates)—to its terms. This, it seems to me, is what 'Dombeyism' is; not, as Edgar Johnson maintains, 'a cynical economic system' (created by 'competitive greed and indifference to the welfare of others') that 'spawns all the vices and cruelties of society. And of that system—it might even be called Dombeyism—Mr. Dombey is the symbolic embodiment.'[1] Dombeyism, though no doubt the product of an economic system, is evocative of a set of attitudes rather than a system. It is only in the novels from *Bleak House* on that Dickens begins to come to grips with systems.

Dombeyism is more comprehensively defined in the magnificent scene in which Dombey hires Polly Toodle as a wet nurse for Paul. The scene, providing much matter for analysis, needs to be quoted at length:

'My good woman,' said Mr. Dombey, turning round in his easy chair, as one piece, and not as a man with limbs and joints, 'I understand you are poor, and wish to earn money by nursing the little boy, my son, who has been so prematurely deprived of what can never be replaced. I have no objection to your adding to the comforts of your family by that means. So far as I can tell, you seem to be a deserving object. But I must impose one or two conditions on you, before you enter my house in that capacity. While you are here, I must stipulate that you are always known as—say as Richards—an ordinary name, and convenient. Have you any objection to be known as Richards? You had better consult your husband.'

As the husband did nothing but chuckle and grin, and continually draw his right hand across his mouth, moistening the palm, Mrs. Toodle, after nudging him twice or thrice in vain, dropped a curtsey and replied 'that perhaps if she was to be called out of her name, it would be considered in the wages.'

'Oh, of course,' said Mr. Dombey. 'I desire to make it a

---

[1] *Charles Dickens*, II, 635.

question of wages, altogether. Now, Richards, if you nurse my bereaved child, I wish you to remember this always. You will receive a liberal stipend in return for the discharge of certain duties, in the performance of which, I wish you to see as little of your family as possible. When those duties cease to be required and rendered, and the stipend ceases to be paid, there is an end of all relations between us. Do you understand me?'

Mrs. Toodle seemed doubtful about it; and as to Toodle himself, he had evidently no doubt whatever, that he was all abroad.

'You have children of your own,' said Mr. Dombey. 'It is not at all in this bargain that you need become attached to my child, or that my child need become attached to you. I don't expect or desire anything of the kind. Quite the reverse. When you go away from here, you will have concluded what is a mere matter of bargain and sale, hiring and letting: and will stay away. The child will cease to remember you; and you will cease, if you please, to remember the child.'

Mrs. Toodle, with a little more colour in her cheeks than she had had before, said 'she hoped she knew her place.'

'I hope you do, Richards,' said Mr. Dombey. 'I have no doubt you know it very well. Indeed it is so plain and obvious that it could hardly be otherwise. Louisa, my dear, arrange with Richards about money, and let her have it when and how she pleases. Mr. what's-your-name, a word with you, if you please!'

Thus arrested on the threshold as he was following his wife out of the room, Toodle returned and confronted Mr. Dombey alone. He was a strong, loose, round-shouldered, shuffling, shaggy fellow, on whom his clothes sat negligently: with a good deal of hair and whisker, deepened in its natural tint, perhaps by smoke and coal-dust; hard knotty hands: and a square forehead, as coarse in grain as the bark of an oak. A thorough contrast in all respects to Mr. Dombey, who was one of those close-shaved close-cut moneyed gentlemen who are glossy and crisp like new banknotes, and who seem to be artificially braced and tightened as by the stimulating action of golden shower-baths. . . . (pp. 15–17)

Dickens's control of tone here is superb. It is allied, moreover, with a precision of detail that gives the scene as a whole a solid particularity, and that richly establishes Dombey as a character. The images used to describe Dombey admirably combine with what he says to reveal the man. When he turns round in his chair to Polly, 'as one piece, and not as a man with limbs and joints', his physical presence is strikingly evoked. Dombey's stiffness is characteristic, and it is repeatedly insisted on. He has a 'starched, impenetrable dignity and composure' (p. 18); he is an 'austere, stiff gentleman . . . a hard-looking gentleman' (p. 28); the 'stiff and stark fire-irons' in his library appear 'to claim a nearer relationship than anything else there' to him (p. 52); he turns his head in his cravat 'as if it were a socket' (p. 53); he lays himself on a sofa 'like a man of wood, without a hinge or joint in him' (p. 378); in his 'unbending form', he is 'no bad representation of [a] body' (p. 429); the Chicken tells Mr. Toots that Dombey is 'as stiff a cove as ever he see, but that it is within the resources of Science to double him up, with one blow in the waistcoat' (p. 442); and Toots himself refers to Dombey in an excited moment as 'a marble monument' (p. 705). Stiffness is one of the two main images that constitute the imaginative frame, as it were, of the Dombey analogue; and it is suggestive of much that is represented by Dombeyism.

It is suggestive, first, in relation to the man of wood who is not like a man with limbs and joints, of his inhumanity. The inhumanity of his attitudes is immediately apparent in the quoted scene in his insistence that Polly see as little as possible of her family, Dombey simply remaining impervious to the fact that Polly herself has a baby, not to mention four other children. Polly, to him, is not a mother but a feeding-machine; and when she incurs his displeasure by not only going to visit her family but taking his son with her, she is summarily thrown out—and Paul as summarily weaned, being 'prematurely deprived', as Mrs. Chick says, of his 'natural nourishment' (p. 82). Dombey's attitude to Polly is, of course, representative of his larger inhumanity to his daughter Florence. His outer stiffness, indeed, is analogous to the paralysis of Clifford Chatterley in *Lady Chatterley's Lover*, suggesting, like it, the paralysis of his emotional self. It comes as somewhat of a surprise to think of Dombey as a forerunner of Clifford Chatterley, but, quite apart from the runaway wife, there are a number of striking analogies between the two. Not only Clifford but Mellors is brought to mind in the 'confrontation' of Dombey and Toodle. Dombey's stiffness, in relation to Toodle's obvious vitality, his 'loose, round-shouldered, shuffling' shagginess, is furthermore suggestive of the blocking of the free flow of life in him, of an inner deadness that is the counterpart of his inhumanity to others. But, at the same time, since Dombey seems to be 'artificially braced and tightened as by the stimulating action of golden shower-baths', his stiffness is also arrogantly assumed, a posture deliberately adopted as alone becoming the glossy crispness ('like new bank-notes') of a 'moneyed gentleman'. 'Stiff with starch and arrogance', as he is later said to be (p. 91), his arrogance to Polly in this scene is appalling. Not only does he assure her of the plainness and obviousness of 'her place' (a relegation subtly emphasized by Dickens in throughout presenting Polly's responses to Dombey in indirect speech); by alluding to her poverty and declaring that he has no objection to her adding to the comforts of her family by nursing his boy, Dombey contrives to do Polly a service in permitting her to serve him and his. Since Dombey, moreover, is described as living 'encased' in a 'cold hard armour of pride' (p. 560), his stiff arrogance is not only offensive; it is also assumed defensively, as a protective casing against the life of feeling that he denies in himself. Steven Marcus, commenting on the armour image and some of the other images of Dombey's stiffness quoted above, interestingly suggests that Dombey is 'alienated from his body', and that his 'rigidity . . . is the armor and disguise of his impotence';[1] a reading which, in view of the facts, is no doubt exaggerated, but may profitably be applied in modified form to the hints we are given about the nature of Dombey's sexual relations with Edith—and to the part played by Carker in the breakup of their marriage.

Dombey's arrogance, in the quoted scene, is further exemplified in his stipulation that Mrs. Polly Toodle be known as Richards. This stipulation should be related to his addressing of Polly's husband as 'Mr. what's-your-name'. Since Toodle is not to be employed by him, he has no need of a name; and the phrase used to address him effectively denies his existence in relation to Dombey, as it denies his existence as the husband of the woman from whom he is about to be parted by Dombey's money. Similarly, calling Polly 'Richards' effaces the woman and the mother, and converts her into a functionary. Asserting the impersonality of his relationship with her, it is intended to ensure her constant awareness of the impersonality he desires in her relationship with his child, a relationship which is to exclude a 'need' for Polly to 'become attached' to Paul, or him to her. As F. R. Leavis says, Dombey's substitution of Richards for Polly's real name is indicative of his 'will to preclude as far as possible any but the barest functional

---

[1] *Dickens*, p. 339.

relation between the stoker's wife and the infant of class . . .'[1] It is also representative of one of the main tendencies of Dombeyism, the readiness to reduce human beings to an economic function; Dombey's attitudes, in this regard, being once again analogous to those of Clifford Chatterley in respect of his colliers. Encased in the armour of his wealth as well as his pride, Dombey can deal safely with Richards: though she is, in effect, to give his son life, her service is made 'a question of wages, altogether'. Dombey, indeed, contrives to make all life 'a mere matter of bargain and sale, hiring and letting'.

Dombey's adherence to an economic functionalism in the case of Polly has a parallel in his relationship with his daughter. 'Some weeks' after Polly has commenced her duties, Florence returns home from her aunt's and, seeking out the nurse, demands to know 'what they have done' with her mother. The ensuing conversation makes it clear that Florence has not even been informed of her mother's death, and Susan Nipper tells Polly that Dombey has not seen Florence since that event, 'not once since' (pp. 23–6). His ignoring of Florence, his leaving her to learn of her mother's death from 'a strange nurse', reveals that, to all intents and purposes, she does not exist for him: having had the misfortune to be born a bad boy, she is simply beyond the purview of 'the one idea'. After Paul's death, Dombey's Freudian slip in writing out the inscription for his son's tablet graphically emphasizes the point:

'Will you be so good as read it over again?' [said the statuary]. 'I think there's a mistake.'
'Where?'
The statuary gives him back the paper, and points out, with his pocket rule, the words 'beloved and only child.'
'It should be, "son," I think, Sir?'
'You are right. Of course. Make the correction.' (p. 241)

Polly's conversation with Florence on the occasion referred to is productive of collocations that are natural and simple but important in the novel. Gently trying to lead Florence to a realization of her mother's death, Polly tells her a story of 'a lady' who 'was taken ill and died' and 'was buried in the ground where the trees grow':

'The cold ground?' said the child, shuddering again.

[1] *'Dombey and Son'*, *The Sewanee Review*, 70 (1962), 188.

'No! The warm ground,' returned Polly, seizing her advantage, 'where the ugly little seeds turn into beautiful flowers, and into grass, and corn, and I don't know what all besides. Where good people turn into bright angels, and fly away to Heaven!' (p. 24)

The collocation of warmth and life has an obvious bearing on Polly's role here. Her instinctive compassion for the child is seen to function as a life-sustaining warmth—characteristically, she draws Florence 'to her breast' when she finally grasps the purport of the story—a warmth which Dickens, like D. H. Lawrence, suggests has been preserved by the working class and lost by their betters. Alternatively, the collocation of cold and death, when related to Dombey's inhuman coldness to Florence (which makes Polly's story necessary), implies that in the end it is life itself that Dombeyism denies and negates, a judgement that is dramatically enforced, I shall argue, in the presentation of Paul's death.

Coldness is the second main image by which Dombeyism is imaginatively evoked. Dombey's coldness and stiffness, indeed, are interdependent:

> In all his life, [Mr. Dombey] had never made a friend. His cold and distant nature had neither sought one, nor found one. And now when that nature concentrated its whole force so strongly on a partial scheme of parental interest and ambition, it seemed as if its icy current, instead of being released by this influence, and running clear and free, had thawed for but an instant to admit its burden, and then frozen with it into one unyielding block. (p. 47)

The image of the freezing of the 'current' of Dombey's nature, the blocking in him of the free flow of feeling, implies his lack of 'heart', a heart to move the warm blood. Dombey's coldness, in other words, like his stiffness, is a manifestation of his inner deadness; and the two images are combined in that of the 'frozen unyielding block'. Numerous references are made to Dombey's coldness. He has a 'cool heart' (p. 15); at Paul's christening he assists in 'making it so cold, that the young curate [smokes] at the mouth' as he reads (p. 56); unmoved by the 'cold collation' ('set forth in a cold pomp of glass and silver, and looking more like a dead dinner lying in state than a social refreshment'), that chills his guests after the christening, he 'might have been hung up for sale at a Russian fair as a specimen of a frozen gentleman' (p. 57); he has a 'frosty heart' (p. 91); he is the 'icy patron' of Mr. Carker (p. 379); on his return home from his honeymoon, his characteristic reply to Mrs. Skewton, who enquires how he found 'that delightfullest of cities, Paris', is: 'It was cold' (p. 500); ice is said to be an 'unnecessary article in Mr. Dombey's banquets' (pp. 514–15). Not unexpectedly, his house is cold too:

> They were black, cold rooms; and seemed to be in mourning, like the inmates of the house. The books precisely matched as to size, and drawn up in a line, like soldiers, looked in their cold, hard, slippery uniforms, as if they had but one idea among them, and that was a freezer. The bookcase, glazed and locked, repudiated all familiarities. . . . (p. 52)

The reference to the locked bookcase, to that which should be open being kept shut, adverts us to a subsidiary line of imagery that evokes Dombey's closed quality. Typically, he himself is often shown behind closed or locked doors. After Paul's death Florence repeatedly approaches 'her father's door', but the door is 'ever closed, and he shut up within' (p. 249); and Florence envies children who have 'won their household places' and do not 'stand without', as she does, 'with a bar across the door' (p. 347). Dombey mourns his 'lost child . . . allied with whom he was to have shut out all the world as with a double door of gold . . .' (p. 280); and is left to live 'shut up in his towering supremacy' (p. 716). Dombey's eventual liberation from the enchanted circle in which he is confined is manifested as an opening of self—just as it is also an unbending and unfreezing.

These, then, are the main components of Dombeyism. Dombey's connections with a representative group of characters who, like him, view life as a matter of bargain and sale are riveted by analogy. Major Bagstock, for instance, though retired from the army, is still active as a soldier of fortune. Establishing himself as 'Dombey's right-hand man', he helps to arrange his friend's marriage to Edith, buying a share, as it were, in 'the elegance and wealth of Edith Dombey's establishment' (p. 371). A product of Sandhurst—'We were iron, Sir, and it forged us', he tells Dombey (p. 127)—he is, as he admits, 'not in general a man of sentiment' (p. 271). He is also 'a wooden-featured' man, with 'a very rigid pair of jaw-bones', which he exercises, however, to good effect: ' "Old Joe, Sir, needn't look far for a wife even now, if he was on the look-out; but he's hard-hearted, Sir, is Joe—he's tough, Sir, tough, and de-vilish sly!" ' . . . It may be doubted whether there ever was a more entirely selfish person at heart; or at stomach is perhaps a better expression, seeing that he was more decidedly endowed with that latter organ than with the former' (pp. 83–5). The Major is aided and abetted in his plans for Dombey by Edith's mother, Mrs. Skewton, who shares even more actively in her daughter's establishment by going to live in it. Mrs. Skewton has 'a mortal aversion' for 'the low word business' (p. 527), and declares that she 'would have [her] world all heart' (p. 294). She asserts that what she wants is heart (this being 'frightfully true in one sense, if not in that in which she used the phrase') (p. 289), and frankly confesses her weakness to Dombey and the Major:

'. . . I acknowledge—let me be open—that it is my failing to be the creature of impulse, and to wear my heart, as it were, outside. I know my failing full well. My enemy cannot know it better. But I am not penitent; I would rather not be frozen by the heart-less world, and am content to bear this imputation justly.' (p. 368)

Appropriately, Mrs. Skewton appears for the first time in the novel in 'a wheeled chair' that is propelled by a page named Withers, though there is 'nothing whatever, except the attitude, to prevent her from walking' (pp. 286, 288). At night, however, under the ministrations of her maid, she seems to '[take] off her manner with her charms, and to . . . put on paralysis with her flannel gown', the maid collecting 'the ashes of Cleopatra' and carrying them away, ready for the following day's 'revivification' (p. 396). And in the end Mrs. Skewton suffers a 'paralytic stroke': '. . . Paralysis was not to be deceived, had known her for the object of its errand, and had struck her at her glass, where she lay like a horrible doll that had tumbled down' (p. 528). 'Making mouths' and '[mowing]' before her death (pp. 584–5), Mrs. Skewton is not unlike Mrs. Brown, who has 'a mouth that [mumbles] and [chatters] of itself' when she is not speaking, and works 'her shrivelled yellow face and throat into all sorts of contortions' (p. 69). Mrs. Brown, as her daughter Alice says, 'would sell . . . anything, or anybody, for money', and has 'thought to make a sort of property' of Alice herself (pp. 725, 752). Not surprisingly, Alice comes back to

England 'harder than she went', and 'coldly' suffering her mother's embrace, looks 'coldly on her with her stern, regardless, hardy, beautiful face' (pp. 486–7). Encountering Edith, and asked by her what it is she has to sell, Alice replies: ' "Only this," '... holding out her wares, without looking at them. "I sold myself long ago" ' (p. 574). Alice's relation to Edith is sufficiently clear for there to have been no need for Dickens to assert it artificially in the plot by eventually revealing them to be cousins.

Mr. Dombey entrusts the care of Paul to those who may be expected to ensure that he grow up in his father's image. Mrs. Pipchin, who, as Miss Tox puts it, keeps 'an infantine Boarding-House of a very select description' (p. 98), is 'generally spoken of as "a great manager" of children' (p. 99). Her 'scale of charges' is 'high' (p. 100), for though the 'frosty glistening of her hard grey eye' sometimes gives way to the 'shrewd [twinkling]' of a 'frosty eye' (p. 139), the 'hard grey eye [is] sharp enough' always to see the main chance (p. 140). Her husband having 'broken his heart' in 'pumping water out of the Peruvian Mines', she still wears black for him some forty years later, her presence being 'a quencher to any number of candles'; it also appears that there has been 'some mistake in the application of the Peruvian machinery, and that all her waters of gladness and milk of human kindness' have been 'pumped out dry, instead of the mines' (pp. 97, 99). Her own 'constitution' being 'made of . . . hard metal' (p. 136), it is part of her system 'not to encourage a child's mind to develop and expand itself like a young flower, but to open it by force like an oyster' (p. 102). The plant imagery here leads back, I shall show, to the way in which Dombey rears his son, and on to Doctor Blimber, to whom Paul moves from Mrs. Pipchin's. Doctor Blimber's establishment is a 'very expensive' one:

> In fact, Doctor Blimber's establishment was a great hot-house, in which there was a forcing apparatus incessantly at work. All the boys blew before their time. Mental green-peas were produced at Christmas, and intellectual asparagus all the year round. . . . Every description of Greek and Latin vegetable was got off the driest twigs of boys, under the frostiest circumstances. . . . (p. 141)

Doctor Blimber, who has 'a determined, unimpassioned, inflexible, cold-blooded' way of reading (p. 148), is (like Mr. Gradgrind in *Hard*

Times) a very Dombey of education, reducing poetry and the wisdom of the ages to a business of facts and forms: his pupils know no rest from 'stony-hearted verbs' and 'inflexible syntactic passages', and irrevocably conclude that 'all the fancies of the poets, and lessons of the sages' are 'a mere collection of words and grammar,' and have 'no other meaning in the world' (p. 143).

Viewed in relation to Dickens's development as a novelist, the Dombey analogue figures most interestingly in a sudden extension of the world of Dombey and Son. Our attention is drawn from a consideration of whether Dombey's 'master-vice' (his being bound a 'prisoner to one idea') is 'an unnatural characteristic' to other unnatural phenomena:

> Alas! are there so few things in the world, about us, most unnatural, and yet most natural in being so? Hear the magistrate or judge admonish the unnatural outcasts of society . . . But follow the good clergyman or doctor, who, with his life imperilled at every breath he draws, goes down into their dens, lying within the echoes of our carriage wheels and daily tread upon the pavement stones. Look round upon the world of odious sights—millions of immortal creatures have no other world on earth—at the lightest mention of which humanity revolts, and dainty delicacy living in the next street, stops her ears, and lisps 'I don't believe it!' Breathe the polluted air, foul with every impurity that is poisonous to health and life; and have every sense, conferred upon our race for its delight and happiness, offended, sickened and disgusted, and made a channel by which misery and death alone can enter. Vainly attempt to think of any simple plant, or flower, or wholesome weed, that, set in this foetid bed, could have its natural growth, or put its little leaves off to the sun as GOD designed it. And then, calling up some ghastly child, with stunted form and wicked face, hold forth on its unnatural sinfulness, and lament its being, so early, far away from Heaven—but think a little of its having been conceived, and born and bred, in Hell!
>
> . . .
>
> [If men would only try 'to make the world a better place'], not the less bright and blest would that day be for rousing some who never have looked out upon the world of human life around them, to a knowledge of their own relation to it, and for making

them acquainted with a perversion of nature in their own contracted sympathies and estimates; as great, and yet as natural in
its development when once begun, as the lowest degradation
known. (pp. 647, 648)

If the novelist's eloquence is directed (rather too strenuously, perhaps) to insisting that it is natural, not unnatural, for 'outcasts of
society' brought up in the slums to be depraved; what is considered
unnatural, indeed 'a perversion of nature', is the 'contracted sympathies
and estimates' of those who have never been roused to a knowledge
of their relation to 'the world of human life around them'. But 'contracted sympathies and estimates', we realize, might serve as a concise
description of Dombeyism, contracted sympathies standing for Dombey's characteristic shrinking of feeling, his cold imperviousness to
others, and contracted estimates for the tight spirit of calculation by
which he is animated in a world of bargain and sale. The plant imagery
in the passage reinforces such a connection: the products of the 'foetid
bed' of the slums, cheated of their 'natural growth', recall the boys
who come under the ministrations of Mrs. Pipchin and Doctor Blimber, not to mention Paul's experience in his father's house (which
remains to be discussed). The refusal, moreover, of 'dainty delicacy
living in the next street' to believe in the existence of the slums and
the general lack of awareness of such 'dens' posit a blindness that is not
unlike that of Dombey in his dealings with the world round him.[1] It
seems to me imperceptive, therefore, to refer to this passage, as Humphry House does, as 'a curiously sudden, inept, and passionate piece
of propaganda for Public Health', and to maintain that it is, 'of course,
ludicrously detached from the theme and mood of the novel'.[2] The
novel suggests, rather, that such slums are brought into existence and
left as they are through what we may call the operation of Dombeyism
in public life.

With this passage, therefore, Dickens once again, as in *Pickwick
Papers* and *Oliver Twist*, is drawn to the theme of social injustice.
It is significant that, though some ten years had intervened since the
writing of *Oliver Twist*, his conception of the immediate action re-

[1] In a letter written some years before the novel, Dickens refers to a 'delicacy' that 'shuts
its eyes': 'There is a kind of delicacy which is not at all shocked by the existence of such
things [as Ragged Schools], but is excessively shocked to know of them; and I am afraid it
will shut its eyes on Ragged Schools until the Ragged Scholars are perfect in their learning
out of doors, when woe to whole garments.' The letter is dated 16. 9. 1843, *Letters from
Charles Dickens to Angela Burdett-Coutts*, ed. Edgar Johnson (London, 1953), p. 54.
[2] *The Dickens World*, pp. 192, 193.

quired to counter social abuse is still exposure of it. Injustice and abuse have only to be shown as they are, he still seems to believe, for them to be at once remedied:

> Oh for a good spirit who would take the house-tops off . . . and show a Christian people what dark shapes issue from amidst their homes, to swell the retinue of the Destroying Angel as he moves forth among them! For only one night's view of the pale phantoms rising from the scenes of our too-long neglect; and from the thick and sullen air where Vice and Fever propagate together, raining the tremendous social retributions which are ever pouring down, and ever coming thicker! Bright and blest the morning that should rise on such a night: for men, delayed no more by stumbling-blocks of their own making . . . would then apply themselves . . . to make the world a better place! (p. 648)

By the time Dickens next pursues the theme of social injustice in *Bleak House*, as we shall see, he is no longer so optimistic. His treatment of the theme in *Dombey and Son*, however, sustained by no more than an implied connection between the slums referred to above and the haunts of such as Mrs. Brown, is seminal. His vision of 'Vice and Fever propagating together' in the 'sullen air' of the slums, of a 'moral pestilence' and contagious disease sweeping together over the whole city, may be regarded as the imaginative genesis of *Bleak House*:[1]

> Those who study the physical sciences . . . tell us that if the noxious particles that rise from vitiated air were palpable to the sight, we should see them lowering in a dense black cloud above such haunts, and rolling slowly on to corrupt the better portions of a town. But if the moral pestilence that rises with them, and in the eternal laws of outraged Nature, is inseparable from them, could be made discernible too, how terrible the revelation! Then should we see depravity, impiety, drunkenness, theft, murder, and a long train of nameless sins against the natural affections and repulsions of mankind, overhanging the devoted spots, and creeping on, to blight the innocent and spread contagion among the pure. . . . (pp. 647–8)

[1] Humphry House also points to a connection with *Bleak House*, though in terms of plot. *Ibid.*

The likely consequence of a continued blindness to the existence of the slums, it is intimated, is that a whole society will blight its own stock—as Dombey does.

III

The domestic blight of Dombeyism is most strikingly evidenced in the life and death of Paul. After the banishment of Polly the nursery is 'put into commission', the 'Commissioners' being Mrs. Chick and Miss Tox, but to no avail:

> . . . in spite of his early promise, all this vigilance and care could not make little Paul a thriving boy. Naturally delicate, perhaps, he pined and wasted after the dismissal of his nurse, and, for a long time, seemed but to wait his opportunity of gliding through their hands, and seeking his lost mother. . . .
>
> The chill of Paul's christening had struck home, perhaps to some sensitive part of his nature, which could not recover itself in the cold shade of his father; but he was an unfortunate child, from that day. Mrs. Wickham often said she never see a dear so put upon. (pp. 89–90)

Paul, exposed to 'chill' from the time of his christening, is like a delicate plant which can only blossom if it gets sufficient sun and warmth, but does not 'thrive' in 'the cold shade'. His physical frailty and sickliness, his 'want of vital power' (p. 190), is clearly attributable to emotional deprivation. Deprived of the warmth of parental love that is essential to his well-being and, though provided for a while by Polly, is incompatible with the coldness of Dombey (who, in his own way, genuinely cares for his son), Paul 'pines and wastes'. The flourishing condition of Polly's own children is an ironic comment on that of the rich man's son: on the fateful occasion on which Polly visits her family, her 'own honest apple face [becomes] immediately the centre of a bunch of smaller pippins, all laying their rosy cheeks close to it, and all evidently the growth of the same tree' (p. 65). Dombey's presence, by contrast, it is indicated, is positively inimical to growth:

> Mr. Dombey represented in himself the wind, the shade, and the autumn of the christening. He stood in his library to receive

the company, as hard and cold as the weather; and when he looked out through the glass room, at the trees in the little garden, their brown and yellow leaves came fluttering down, as if he blighted them.

. . .

It was a bleak autumnal afternoon indeed; and as [Polly] walked, and hushed, and, glancing through the dreary windows, pressed the little fellow closer to her breast, the withered leaves came showering down. (pp. 52, 61)

If Dombey, with a characteristic stroke of the novelist, is viewed as blighting the leaves that come fluttering down; the association of Paul with 'the withered leaves' is ominously anticipatory of his fate when, without a Polly to press him close, he is exposed to the wind and the shade that Dombey 'represents in himself'. The plant imagery culminates, indeed, with the emphatic implication that it is the 'frozen gentleman' who is ultimately responsible for the death of his son: summoning Polly to Paul's deathbed, Susan Nipper asks her to come 'and do a kindness to the sweet dear that is withering away. Oh, Mrs. Richards, withering away!' (p. 220); and, taken to Paul, Polly lifts 'his wasted hand' and calls him 'her dear boy, her pretty boy, her own poor blighted child' (p. 224). Paul dies, we realize, a victim of Dombeyism. The fact that a number of victims in *Dombey and Son* are the victims of inadequate parents—not only Paul but also Florence, Edith and Alice—is a further indication of the domestic and emotional perspectives of the business theme in this novel.

The actual description of Paul's death was much admired by contemporaries of Dickens. Thackeray, for instance, is reported to have said to Mark Lemon: 'There's no writing against such power as this— One has no chance! Read that chapter describing young Paul's death: it is unsurpassed—it is stupendous!'[1] Forster maintains that 'there is nothing in all [Dickens's] writings more perfect, for what it shows of his best qualities, than the life and death of Paul Dombey.'[2] And Jeffrey, Byron's 'immortal' Jeffrey, 'skill'd to condemn', and the critic of Wordsworth, wrote to Dickens: 'Oh, my dear, dear Dickens! what a No. 5 you have now given us! I have so cried and sobbed over it last night, and again this morning; and felt my heart purified by those tears, and blessed and loved you for making me shed them; and I

---

[1] Edgar Johnson, *Charles Dickens*, II, 611.
[2] *Charles Dickens*, II, 323.

never can bless and love you enough. Since the divine Nelly was found dead on her humble couch, beneath the snow and the ivy, there has been nothing like the actual dying of that sweet Paul, in the summer sunshine of that lofty room. . . .'[1] More recent responses to the dying of Paul have not generally been so favourable. If we tend to believe that the description of Paul's death is sentimental, it seems to me to be a matter of some critical importance to demonstrate that this is not merely a question of changing taste.

After Polly has 'stooped down' by Paul's bed, Walter Gay is also 'brought into the room':

> His open face and manner, and his cheerful eyes, had always made him a favourite with Paul; and when Paul saw him, he stretched out his hand, and said, 'Good-bye!'
>
> 'Good-bye, my child!' said Mrs. Pipchin, hurrying to his bed's head. 'Not good-bye?'
>
> For an instant, Paul looked at her with the wistful face with which he had so often gazed upon her in his corner by the fire. 'Ah yes,' he said placidly, 'good-bye! Walter dear, good-bye!'— turning his head to where he stood, and putting out his hand again. 'Where's Papa?'
>
> He felt his father's breath upon his cheek, before the words had parted from his lips.
>
> 'Remember Walter, dear Papa,' he whispered, looking in his face. 'Remember Walter. I was fond of Walter!' The feeble hand waved in the air, as if it cried 'good-bye!' to Walter once again.
>
> 'Now lay me down,' he said, 'and, Floy, come close to me, and let me see you!'
>
> Sister and brother wound their arms around each other, and the golden light came streaming in, and fell upon them, locked together.
>
> 'How fast the river runs, between its green banks and the rushes, Floy! But it's very near the sea. I hear the waves! They always said so!'
>
> Presently he told her that the motion of the boat upon the stream was lulling him to rest. How green the banks were now, how bright the flowers growing on them, and how tall the rushes! Now the boat was out at sea, but gliding smoothly on. And now there was a shore before him. Who stood on the bank!—

[1] Quoted by John Forster, *ibid.*, p. 333.

He put his hands together, as he had been used to do at his prayers. He did not remove his arms to do it; but they saw him fold them so, behind her neck.

'Mama is like you, Floy. I know her by the face! But tell them that the print upon the stairs at school is not divine enough. The light about the head is shining on me as I go!' (pp. 225–6)

I. A. Richards's criteria of sentimentality[1] help us to pinpoint the weaknesses in this passage. That there is a 'quantitative' sentimentality here, a preoccupation on the part of the novelist with emotion for its own sake that betrays itself in an imprecision of detail in the description, is at once suggested by the reference to Walter's face and manner and eyes having 'always' made him 'a favourite with Paul'. This is simply not true to the facts as we have them: so far as we know, Paul has met Walter only once—when he travels to Brighton to borrow money from Dombey. Clearly, both Walter and Polly are introduced to exploit the sympathy which they readily command, and to give Paul the opportunity of a fond farewell. The manner in which he is made to bid Walter farewell, moreover—'Ah yes, good-bye!'; 'Remember Walter, dear Papa. I was fond of Walter!'—lacks all verisimilitude: that a child of Paul's age should be shown to possess the degree of knowledge, resignation, and worldliness that this implies, not to mention a capacity for speaking of his affection for Walter as if he were already dead, suggests that the novelist's attention has strayed from its object. And, indeed, with the ten-line authorial announcement of Death that follows the quoted passage (and that concludes with the sentence 'And look upon us, angels of young children, with regards not quite estranged, when the swift river bears us to the ocean!'), we are left looking, as it were, solely at the novelist and his emotion. Premature death, it would appear, always awoke in Dickens the memory of the death of his beloved sister-in-law, Mary Hogarth; and 'the memory of her death', as Edgar Johnson says, 'deepened the pathos with which [he] was always to contemplate youth or innocence condemned to die'.[2]

There is evidence, too, of a 'qualitative' sentimentality, of an inappropriateness of emotion that stems from the substitution of a factitious situation for the purported situation. The references to Paul and

---

[1] See *Practical Criticism: A Study of Literary Judgment* (London, 1929), Part III, Ch. VI.

[2] *Charles Dickens*, I, 203.

Florence being 'locked together' and to his sense of being 'lulled to rest'
effectively evoke the coming of Paul's death in terms of a wrenching
apart and a gradual ebbing of consciousness. But his dying vision of
the mother he has not known and his report from 'a shore' beyond
'the sea' suggest a state of heightened consciousness and soothingly
convert separation into reunion. That the novelist may wish us to
accept that this is what death means is not to the point; Paul is still
alive. What Dickens actually does is factitiously to bring into play
emotions relating to an age-old image of mother and child and to the
dead mother. Finally, for good measure, as Paul passes from the cold
shade of his father to a divine light, 'the print upon the stairs at school'
is also invoked, the print in which, 'in the centre of a wondering group',
a figure 'with a light about its head—benignant, mild, and merciful—
stood pointing upward' (p. 194).

If the death of Paul deprives Dombey of a son for his firm, it
appears that Dombey and Son is efficiently managed by Mr. Carker.
Carker, who is 'Grand Vizier' to Dombey's 'Sultan', affects 'a stiff
white cravat, after the example of his principal', and is 'always closely
buttoned up and tightly dressed' (pp. 170, 171). The kind of relationship that subsists between the two men is economically indicated:

> 'How do you do this morning?' said Mr. Carker the Manager,
> entering Mr. Dombey's room soon after his arrival one day:
> with a bundle of papers in his hand.
> 'How do you do, Carker?' said Mr. Dombey, rising from his
> chair, and standing with his back to the fire. 'Have you anything
> there for me?'
> 'I don't know that I need trouble you,' returned Carker,
> turning over the papers in his hand. 'You have a committee to-
> day at three, you know.'
> 'And one at three, three-quarters,' added Mr. Dombey.
> 'Catch you forgetting anything!' exclaimed Carker, still turn-
> ing over his papers. 'If Mr. Paul inherits your memory, he'll be
> a troublesome customer in the house. One of you is enough.'
> 'You have an accurate memory of your own,' said Mr. Dombey.
> 'Oh! I!' returned the manager. 'It's the only capital of a man
> like *me*.'
> Mr. Dombey did not look less pompous or at all displeased,
> as he stood leaning against the chimneypiece, surveying his (of

course unconscious) clerk, from head to foot. The stiffness and nicety of Mr. Carker's dress, and a certain arrogance of manner, either natural to him or imitated from a pattern not far off, gave great additional effect to his humility. He seemed a man who would contend against the power that vanquished him, if he could, but who was utterly borne down by the greatness and superiority of Mr. Dombey. (p. 172)

At the end of the conversation, Dombey, we are told, 'surveys' Carker from head to foot. What he sees, in the 'stiffness' of Carker's dress and in the 'arrogance' of his manner, is a flattering imitation of himself, as if he has produced—to the greater good of Dombey and Son—not only a son but a manager in his own image. Dombey, however, is characteristically blind to the 'unconscious' clerk; nor does he register the import of what Carker says before he begins his survey of him. If Carker's assumed humility is designed to perform a function equivalent to that of the fire which is warming Dombey's back (and from which he is excluded), the ironic emphasis with which he refers to himself betrays a real arrogance, a conviction of the superiority of the 'capital' he commands over that of his patron, and hints, therefore, at a resentment of his position. Two kinds of wealth having been set in opposition in the sphere of personal relations, it is now suggested that, in the sphere of business, the possession of what we might call natural resources is posed against that of cash. And Carker, with a dedicated Dombeyism, is out to make the most of what he possesses, reducing, if not the whole world, then what primarily concerns him to a sophisticated variety of bargain and sale: 'We have partnerships of interest and convenience,' he tells Edith, 'friendships of interest and convenience, dealings of interest and convenience, marriages of interest and convenience, every day' (p. 627). What Dombeyism produces in the world of business, it emerges, is ruthless competition, for Carker 'the Manager' is bent on managing Dombey as well as his firm. Carker, as Kathleen Tillotson points out, is a type of the 'new man', a 'forerunner of the managerial revolution'.[1]

Seen alone at his desk, Carker presents a somewhat different appearance from that which Dombey surveys. His stiffness, it seems, is something which, like his clothes, he puts on, for he is 'smooth and soft'. Looking over some papers, he might 'easily suggest some whimsi-

---

[1] *Novels of the Eighteen-Forties*, p. 177. The phrases used are quotations, which the writer says she has been unable to trace.

cal resemblance to a player at cards'. His face is that 'of a man who [studies] his play, warily'; though, 'something too deep for a partner, and much too deep for an adversary', he sits 'playing his game alone' (p. 298). Dombey and Son is what he gambles with, for not only (as Mr. Morfin tells Harriet Carker) does he '[abuse] his trust', dealing and speculating 'to advantage for himself' more often than 'for the House' he represents; he also leads the firm on to 'prodigious ventures', which ultimately result in the 'ruinous consequences' that Morfin anticipates. Before he abandons Dombey and Son, however, Carker so arranges things that it is perfectly plain what sort of manager he has been: 'as if he had resolved to show his employer at one broad view what has been brought upon him by ministration to his ruling passion' (pp. 748–9). Dombey, that is to say, is, in the end, himself the victim of Dombeyism.

Carker may not do anything that is technically criminal, but, 'playing his game alone', he is a further embodiment of Fagin's ideology of 'number one'. Acting on the belief that it is the 'interest and convenience' of number one alone that matters, and consequently regarding everyone round him as potentially his prey, he is also in the line of the 'men of business' in *Martin Chuzzlewit*. Apart from repeated references to his 'wide show of . . . teeth' (p. 300), a number of images present him as a predator: 'feline from soul to crown', with 'long nails, nicely pared and sharpened', he sits at his work 'as if he were waiting at a mouse's hole' (pp. 298–9); his 'favourite attitude' presents 'a singularly crouching appearance' (p. 303); he grins 'like a shark', and keeps his 'shining eye' on Florence 'like a scaly monster of the deep' (pp. 303, 399); 'coiled up snugly at certain feet', he is 'ready for a spring, or for a tear, or for a scratch, or for a velvet touch', as the humour takes him and occasion serves (p. 313); he has a 'wolf's face' (p. 365); and he rides a horse 'as if he hunted men and women' (p. 600). The woman he hunts, of course, is Edith Dombey, for it is not only in business that he competes with his master. Just as he would swallow both Dombey and Dombey and Son, he wishes to devour Edith; and perhaps the most striking of all these images is that which describes him as he approaches his 'wife' in the rooms he has taken in the French hotel: he comes, 'with his gleaming teeth, through the dark rooms, like a mouth' (p. 757).

Talking to her mother on the night before she agrees to marry Dombey, Edith is quite explicit about her attitude to him:

'... Who takes me, refuse that I am, and as I well deserve to be,' she answered, raising her head, and trembling in her energy of shame and stormy pride, 'shall take me, as this man does, with no art of mine put forth to lure him. He sees me at the auction, and he thinks it well to buy me. Let him! When he came to view me—perhaps to bid—he required to see the roll of my accomplishments. I gave it to him. When he would have me show one of them, to justify his purchase to his men, I require of him to say which he demands, and I exhibit it. I will do no more. He makes the purchase of his own will, and with his own sense of its worth, and the power of his money; and I hope it may never disappoint him. *I* have not vaunted and pressed the bargain; neither have you, so far as I have been able to prevent you.' (p. 395)

Edith, it is clear, is a first working of the more lively and complex portrait of Bella Wilfer in *Our Mutual Friend*. If her extraction of the last ounce of value out of the metaphor of Dombey's purchase of her is representative of the broad and heavy strokes with which for the most part she is drawn, the imagery of bargain and sale here nevertheless has its thematic significance. Reduced by her mother's promotion and Dombey's courtship to so much merchandise, Edith, in agreeing to marry on such terms, attempts (like Carker) to meet Dombeyism with Dombeyism, so to speak. And she is correspondingly strict in her part of the bargain, not only disdaining to 'vaunt and press' it but excluding 'heart' from its scope: 'Did you think I loved you?' she later asks Dombey during one of their altercations. '... Did you ever care, Man! for my heart, or propose to yourself to win the worthless thing? Was there any poor pretence of any in our bargain? Upon your side, or on mine?' (p. 566). Wanting heart in her marriage, like her paralytic mother in everything, Edith is repeatedly imaged as a statue, sitting, for instance (a fit mate for the wooden Dombey), 'like a handsome statue; as cold, as silent, and as still' (p. 428). Despite this impassivity, however, she does respond to Florence's plight: though looking like 'a marble image' as she promises Florence that she will 'cherish' her, she assures the girl that there in no one 'whose heart could beat with greater truth' to her than her own does (pp. 506–7). Edith's 'natural heart', we are given to understand, has been 'undermined, corrupted, and perverted' by her mother (p. 433), but it still beats. What is more difficult to understand is why, if she is not altogether deadened, if, on the contrary, the sense of her own worthlessness and shame ('refuse that I am') is so strong within her, she should have contracted such a marriage in the first place. The way in which she is presented scarcely accords with her purported indifference: 'Grown too indifferent,' she tells Carker, 'for any opposition but indifference, to the daily working of the hands that had moulded me to this; and knowing that my marriage would at least prevent their hawking of me up and down; I suffered myself to be sold as infamously as any woman with a halter round her neck is sold in any market-place' (p. 761).

Edith's marriage to Dombey, as she speedily discovers, does not turn out to be quite the bargain she anticipates. Following the wedding journey, she returns with her husband to the refurbished house that arouses her mother's admiration. Dombey tries to elicit some enthusiasm on her part for the handsome and expensive alterations that have been made, but with no success:

> He might have read in [her glance] that, ever baring her own head for the lightning of her own contempt and pride to strike, the most innocent allusion to the power of his riches degraded her anew, sunk her deeper in her own respect, and made the blight and waste within her more complete.
>
> But dinner was announced, and Mr. Dombey led down Cleopatra; Edith and his daughter following. Sweeping past the gold and silver demonstration on the sideboard as if it were heaped-up dirt, and deigning to bestow no look upon the elegancies around her, she took her place at his board for the first time, and sat, like a statue, at the feast. (p. 501)

Edith is soon constrained, we see, into wondering (with Paul) what money is after all, her disregarding of 'the gold and silver demonstration on the sideboard' suggesting a rather different sense of value from that which she has been brought up to hold. Like Bella in *Our Mutual Friend*, she has begun to understand that wealth may be as dirt (the phrase 'heaped-up dirt' itself being evocative of the dust mounds in the later novel). It appears, moreover, that her attempt to meet Dombey on his chosen ground is more dangerous than she has considered. Already contaminated by her contact with Dombeyism in the person of her mother, once she is exposed to Dombey himself, 'the blight' is 'made more complete', and, like Paul, she wastes within.

If the marriage of Edith and Dombey, then, scarcely survives the

honeymoon, and if it is clear enough, as Steven Marcus says, that
'there is no erotic feeling between them',[1] it is not unexpected that
the marriage hearse should be blighted with plagues. Perhaps the most
interesting and most unsatisfactory aspect of Dickens's treatment of
the marriage is the development of Edith's relationship with Carker.
Though Carker at once shows a decided interest in her, Dombey
himself, in deciding to make use of him as an intermediary in order to
express his dissatisfaction with his wife (and so to humble her), pre-
cipitates matters. After a confidential breakfast with Carker, during
the course of which Dombey asks him to undertake the 'charge', the
two men ride off for the City together:

> . . . Mr. Dombey, in his dignity, rode with very long stirrups,
> and a very loose rein, and very rarely deigned to look down to
> see where his horse went. In consequence of which it happened
> that Mr. Dombey's horse, while going at a round trot, stumbled
> on some loose stones, threw him, rolled over him, and lashing
> out with his iron-shod feet, in his struggles to get up, kicked
> him. (p. 600)

Dombey, it is evident, is riding for a fall in his marriage too, and due
to a similar arrogant heedlessness and blindness and looseness of rein.
Edith's eventual abandonment of Dombey for Carker, after her husband has completely alienated her and his man has subtly persisted in
his advances, has a dramatic appropriateness when it comes—but
thereafter Dickens suddenly and unfortunately changed his plans:

> Note from Jeffrey this morning, who won't believe (positively
> refuses) that Edith is Carker's mistress. What do you think of a
> kind of inverted Maid's Tragedy, and a tremendous scene of her
> undeceiving Carker, and giving him to know that she never
> meant that?[2]

In the event Edith is allowed to humiliate both Dombey and Carker,
and Dickens has his tremendous scene, but the inverted *Maid's*

---

[1] *Dickens*, p. 343. Marcus quotes a telling piece of 'allegory' here: 'The quality of their
marital relation is suggested in Dickens's description of Dombey's dining-table: Dombey sits
at one end, "and the long plateau of precious metal frosted, separating him from Mrs.
Dombey, whereon frosted Cupids offered scentless flowers to each of them, was allegorical
to see" (Ch. 36).'
[2] Letter to John Forster, 21. 12. 1847, quoted by Forster, *Charles Dickens*, II, 336.

Tragedy turns out to be a disappointingly melodramatic affair. It is perhaps a measure of Dickens's having burked issues inherent in a Dombey marriage that the themes of chastity and of marital fidelity figure prominently in his next novel, *David Copperfield*.

Dickens's original conception of Edith was evidently of some complexity and more in line with *The Changeling* than an inverted *Maid's Tragedy*. Writing to Forster about a month before the letter quoted in part above, he said:

> Of course she hates Carker in the most deadly degree. I have not elaborated that, now, because (as I was explaining to Browne the other day) I have relied on it very much for the effect of her death. . . .[1]

Forster's remark that Jeffrey's intervention raised 'the question whether the end might not come by other means than her death, and [bring] with it a more bitter humiliation for her destroyer'[2] suggests that Edith was originally intended to die at Carker's hands, a development which no doubt had its own potential for melodrama; but what is also intimated is Dickens's apprehension of Edith's hatred of Carker coexisting with sexual desire for him. This possibility is interestingly explored, and in a way that makes F. R. Leavis's criticism of the second half of the novel appear too severe: he says that the theme of the Bought Bride 'takes Dickens into a realm where he *knows* nothing. What he takes for knowledge is wholly external and conventional; determined, therefore, unresistingly by all the theatrical clichés and sentimental banalities of the high-life novelette and the equivalent drama'; and he maintains that the relationships of Dombey and Edith and Carker belong to a general 'ethos of unreality'.[3] I have earlier remarked that dramatic turns in this part of the plot tempted Dickens to theatricality, and I would agree that even in the passages I now want to consider there is a banality of expression; but I think that the presentation of Edith's response to Carker (before its 'inversion') is at times both subtle and complex.

At the wedding of Edith and Dombey all the men in the family party kiss the bride. Carker approaches her too:

---

[1] *Ibid.*, p. 335. These letters incidentally reveal the degree to which serial publication both allowed for and encouraged consultation between the novelist and his intimates in regard to the direction of his work.

[2] *Ibid.*

[3] '*Dombey and Son*', *loc. cit.*, pp. 193, 194.

There is a glow upon her proud cheek, and a flashing in her eyes, that may be meant to stay him; but it does not, for he salutes her as the rest have done, and wishes her all happiness.

'If wishes,' says he in a low voice, 'are not superfluous, applied to such a union.'

'I thank you, Sir,' she answers, with a curled lip, and a heaving bosom.

But, does Edith feel still, as on the night when she knew that Mr. Dombey would return to offer his alliance, that Carker knows her thoroughly, and reads her right, and that she is more degraded by his knowledge of her, than by aught else? Is it for this reason that her haughtiness shrinks beneath his smile, like snow within the hand that grasps it firmly, and that her imperious glance droops in meeting his, and seeks the ground? (p. 444)

Florence's eyes, we are told on another occasion, are drawn to Carker 'by an attraction of dislike and distrust that she [cannot] resist' (p. 515); what we are invited to witness in the glow on Edith's cheek and in her flashing eyes and heaving bosom is a similar phenomenon though in a decidedly sexual context. And if the language here strikes us as banal, that is not the case with the suddenly arresting snow simile. Edith's 'haughtiness', it will repeatedly be shown, is impervious to anything that Dombey can muster against it; but Carker, we are made to realize, has the power not only to quell it, for 'her imperious glance droops in meeting his', but also to thaw it, for the simile implies that the hand which is prepared to maintain its firm grasp on snow will eventually melt as well as 'shrink' it. Carker, moreover, knows how to hold her in his power. Threatening to disclose to Dombey the 'circumstances' of Florence's 'folly about . . . Walter' and 'very undesirable association' with Captain Cuttle and Mr. Gills, a disclosure, he assures Edith, which will be attended by the 'separation and alienation' of Florence from the Dombey home, he declares that his knowledge of her special 'interest' in Florence gives him pause: 'It so far shakes me, if I may make the confession, in my allegiance, that on the intimation of the least desire to that effect from you, I would suppress [the circumstances]' (pp. 525–6). Skilfully undermined, Edith succumbs to this blackmail; and Carker succeeds in demonstrating that not only his 'allegiance' to Dombey but hers too may be called into question. Thereafter he insidiously and persistently prepares the

ground for her betrayal of Dombey, and she becomes more and more
hatefully attracted to him:

> 'I have learnt from your mother, Mrs. Dombey,' said Mr.
> Dombey, with magisterial importance, 'what no doubt you know,
> namely, that Brighton is recommended for her health. Mr.
> Carker has been so good—'
> She changed suddenly. Her face and bosom glowed as if the
> red light of an angry sunset had been flung upon them. Not un-
> observant of the change, and putting his own interpretation upon
> it, Mr. Dombey resumed . . . (p. 565)

If we read this as implying that the mere mention of Carker's name
arouses in Edith only an angry hatred of him, we shall be doing as
little justice to the scene as Dombey, who is sure the name humiliates
her. What her angry glowing also indicates is that even the thought
of Carker suddenly animates her. There is, indeed, a suggestion that,
in finally deserting Dombey, Edith, who is habitually so cold and
statue-like in her relationship with him, has (like Hermione in *The
Winter's Tale*) bequeathed her numbness to death and is roused to life.
It is only a faint suggestion, of course, for it accords neither with
Carker's devouring sexuality nor with the inverted *Maid's Tragedy*;
but it is a measure of the new depths, muddy though they may be, of
Dickens's art.

IV

Julian Moynahan remarks that the values opposed to those of Dombey
are 'simple good nature and simple-mindedness', and that these leave
'out of account intelligence, forceful maculine energy . . . as well as
sensuality'.[1] In the world of Dombey, however, intelligence, masculine
energy and sensuality are easily perverted, as the case of Carker
demonstrates; and good nature and simple-mindedness are not to be
sneered at, as a short scene which concludes the hiring of Polly
suggests:

> 'You'll take a glass yourself, Sir, won't you?' said Miss Tox,
> as Toodle appeared.

[1] *'Dealings with the Firm of Dombey and Son: Firmness versus Wetness', Dickens and the
Twentieth Century*, ed. John Gross and Gabriel Pearson, p. 129.

'Thankee, Mum,' said Toodle, 'since you *are* suppressing.'

'And you're very glad to leave your dear good wife in such a comfortable home, ain't you, Sir?' said Miss Tox, nodding and winking at him stealthily.

'No, Mum,' said Toodle. 'Here's wishing of her back agin.'

Polly cried more than ever at this. So Mrs. Chick, who had her matronly apprehensions that this indulgence in grief might be prejudicial to the little Dombey ('acid, indeed,' she whispered Miss Tox), hastened to the rescue.

'Your little child will thrive charmingly with your sister Jemima, Richards,' said Mrs. Chick; 'and you have only to make an effort—this is a world of effort, you know, Richards—to be very happy indeed. You have been already measured for your mourning, haven't you, Richards?'

'Ye-es, Ma'am,' sobbed Polly.

'And it'll fit beautifully. I know,' said Mrs. Chick, 'for the same young person has made me many dresses. The very best materials, too!'

'Lor, you'll be so smart,' said Miss Tox, 'that your husband won't know you; will you, Sir?'

'I should know her,' said Toodle, gruffly, 'anyhows and any-wheres.'

Toodle was evidently not to be bought over. (p. 19)

Though Toodle's intelligence is apparently somewhat devious, it registers firmly enough what both Miss Tox and Mrs. Chick are 'suppressing'; and though his simple-mindedness makes him impervious to the benefits that are being heaped on his wife, it ensures that he is 'not to be bought over', a quality, given an Edith Dombey, that is not to be despised. And though Polly, crying and sobbing, cuts a poor figure in 'a world of effort', and though her 'indulgence in grief' regrettably manifests the kind of 'wetness' that Moynahan objects to; her simple good nature, it emerges, is of no little consolation to the cold and desolate Dombey whom she nurses. Toodle, speaking straight from the heart in simple, stolid indifference to the blandishments offered it, and Polly, not to be persuaded into parting from her family 'with a light heart and a smile', as Mrs. Chick recommends (p. 20), are representative of what is opposed to Dombeyism in the novel. All the characters ranged round Florence (and Paul), as distinguished from those grouped round Dombey, are characterized by the possession of 'heart', which, as I have remarked, naturally opposes life, love and feeling to more worldly possessions.

The value of that which is 'paid out of the Heart's mint' is asserted when Florence, having been struck by her father and told to follow the woman who has deserted him, makes her way to the shop of Walter's uncle. There she finds Captain Cuttle, and faints at his feet:

> The Captain, pale as Florence, pale in the very knobs upon his face, raised her like a baby, and laid her on the same old sofa upon which she had slumbered long ago.
>
> 'It's Heart's Delight!' said the Captain, looking intently in her face. 'It's the sweet creetur grow'd a woman!'
>
> Captain Cuttle was so respectful of her, and had such a reverence for her, in this new character, that he would not have held her in his arms, while she was unconscious, for a thousand pounds. . . .
>
> . . . Captain Cuttle snatched from his breakfast-table a basin of cold water, and sprinkled some upon her face. Yielding to the urgency of the case, the Captain then, using his immense hand with extraordinary gentleness, relieved her of her bonnet, moistened her lips and forehead, put back her hair, covered her feet with his own coat which he pulled off for the purpose, patted her hand—so small in his, that he was struck with wonder when he touched it—and seeing that her eyelids quivered, and that her lips began to move, continued these restorative applications with a better heart.
>
> . . .
>
> 'Oh, Captain Cuttle!' cried Florence, putting her hands together, and speaking wildly. 'Save me! keep me here! Let no one know where I am! I'll tell you what has happened by-and-by, when I can. I have no one in the world to go to. Do not send me away!'
>
> 'Send *you* away, my lady lass!' exclaimed the Captain. '*You*, my Heart's Delight! Stay a bit! We'll put up this here dead-light, and take a double turn on the key!'
>
> With these words, the Captain, using his one hand and his hook with the greatest dexterity, got out the shutter of the door, put it up, made it all fast, and locked the door itself.
>
> When he came back to the side of Florence, she took his hand, and kissed it. The helplessness of the action, the appeal it made to

him, the confidence it expressed, the unspeakable sorrow in her
face, the pain of mind she had too plainly suffered, and was
suffering then, his knowledge of her past history, her present
lonely, worn, and unprotected appearance, all so rushed upon the
good Captain together, that he fairly overflowed with compassion
and gentleness. (pp. 668–70)

When we are told that Captain Cuttle raises Florence 'like a baby',
it is clear how we are intended to view the part he plays in this scene,
Dombey's inadequacy in relation to his children being exposed by those,
like Polly and Cuttle, who step into the parental breach, as it were.
Certainly Cuttle here gives Florence what she has never had from her
father. The 'knobs upon his face', his 'immense hand', and his iron
hook are alien to Dombey's smooth crispness ('like new bank-notes'),
but the gentleness with which he lifts 'the sweet creetur grow'd a
woman' posits a kind of strength on which she can rely in her need.
And when he covers her feet 'with his own coat which he [pulls] off
for the purpose', it is significantly warmth that he provides her with.
The Captain wears his heart in his face, if not on his sleeve, the face
(we are told on another occasion) which is 'like an amiable warming-
pan' (p. 714); and it is, of course, from a warm heart that his compassion and gentleness 'fairly overflow', this flow being strongly contrasted with the 'contracted sympathies' of the 'frozen gentleman'.
The kind of strength Dombey has is recalled by the reference to the
'thousand pounds' which would offer no temptation to the reverent
Captain to hold the unconscious Florence in his arms; just as the
generous, disinterested wholeheartedness of his response to the girl's
appeal is set against the spirit of calculation that goes with Dombey's
strength. What the scene dramatizes, in other words, is the meaning
of 'heart'; and what it symbolizes, as the Captain takes heart from the
success of his 'restorative applications', is its vitalizing power.

This power is further affirmed in the outcome of Florence's painful
relationship with her father. Despite his habitual cold indifference to
her, Dombey, it is early on suggested, is actually ambivalent to
Florence:

The last time he had seen his slighted child, there had been that
in the sad embrace between her and her dying mother, which was
at once a revelation and a reproach to him. Let him be absorbed
as he would in the Son on whom he built such high hopes, he

could not forget that closing scene. He could not forget that he
had had no part in it. That, at the bottom of its clear depths of
tenderness and truth, lay those two figures clasped in each other's
arms, while he stood on the bank above them, looking down a
mere spectator—not a sharer with them—quite shut out.

Unable to exclude these things from his remembrance, or to
keep his mind free from such imperfect shapes of the meaning
with which they were fraught, as were able to make themselves
visible to him through the mist of his pride, his previous feelings
of indifference towards little Florence changed into an uneasiness
of an extraordinary kind. He almost felt as if she watched and
distrusted him. As if she held the clue to something secret in his
breast, of the nature of which he was hardly informed himself.
As if she had an innate knowledge of one jarring and discordant
string within him, and her very breath could sound it. (p. 29)

Julian Moynahan has drawn attention to this passage and commented
revealingly on part of it, but he unaccountably maintains that Dombey's
fear of feeling is 'never explained'.[1] An explanation is suggested, it
seems to me, in Dombey's sense of the embrace between Florence and
her dying mother constituting not only a 'revelation' but 'a reproach
to him'. The embrace has strikingly revealed to him the existence of a
kind of feeling that his whole way of life denies; and he thinks of it as
a reproach because it figures a tacit criticism of his own lack of feeling
on the same occasion, and of a general deficiency in him. But it is
even more than a reproach. The living Florence, remembered always
as giving herself to that embrace, represents a threat to the values by
which he lives: as Moynahan himself says, Dombey 'sees the two
figures as if they lay drowned at the bottom of a body of water', and
he is 'afraid that if he once lets go he will be dissolved or drowned in
a sea of feeling' (p. 124). At the same time it is not only fear that
Dombey feels, and the water image implies an ambivalence to Florence
that is thereafter projected in two opposed responses to her. On the
one hand, the fact that he remains standing 'on the bank' above the
'two figures clasped in each other's arms' suggests that, at this crucial
moment, he clings above all to his own safety; and as he comes to
register more sharply the threat that Florence constitutes to that safety
—in a re-enactment of the scene with the dying mother, she is 'locked
together' in an embrace with the dying Paul while he stands looking

[1] *Ibid.*, p. 123.

on—his 'negative' feeling towards her slowly changes to hatred: recalling the embrace between mother and daughter, he is 'afraid that he [may] come to hate her' (p. 29). On the other hand, he cannot forget that he 'had no part' in 'that closing scene', that he was 'a mere spectator—not a sharer with them—quite shut out'; and this regret expresses a secret hankering for such an embrace, a desire to share in such feeling. This is the 'secret' to which Florence holds 'the clue', the 'one jarring and discordant string within him' that her 'very breath' can sound. The water image thus also suggests that Dombey may one day wish strongly enough for the embrace to risk jumping from the bank, and so convincingly prepares for a change in his attitude to Florence. Such a change is further prefigured when, on the night of his return home with his second wife, Dombey sits observing Florence while pretending to be asleep and with his face covered by a handkerchief. It is implied then that Dombey, in his blindness, really sees Florence for the first time, and seeing, 'he [softens] to her, more and more' (p. 503). He feels 'inclined to speak to her, and call her to him' when his wife enters the room (p. 504), Edith thus unwittingly coming between father and daughter on this occasion as on the night when she leaves her husband.

When Dombey (in the scene referred to) pretends to be asleep and Florence sits opposite him, she finds herself 'for the first time in her life—for the very first time within her memory from her infancy to that hour—alone with her father, as his companion'; in her 'lonely life and grief', all she has known has been 'the suffering of a breaking heart' (p. 502). Her response to the coldness and hatred of 'his alienated heart' is to make it the perpetual 'study of a loving heart' (the title of Chapter XXIV) to 'learn the road to a hard parent's heart' (p. 322); and she sets out doggedly on the pilgrimage that will 'lead her bleeding feet along that stony road which ended in her father's heart' (p. 399). The account of her relationship with her father, it will be observed, cannot be said, like Mrs. Skewton, to want heart. Florence, indeed, Captain Cuttle's 'Heart's Delight', is cloyingly presented as being all heart; and her loving and undeterred persistence in the face of her father's continued rejection of her is neither convincing nor consistent with the imagery that is used to describe her suffering: her tears, as a child, are said to be 'frozen by the expression' of her father (p. 30); when she tries to approach him after the death of Paul, he 'freezes' the 'glowing love within the breast of his young daughter', and she stands and looks at him 'as if stricken into stone' (p. 256); and the hope that 'flutters' within her when Dombey re-marries is said, some two years later, to be 'quite gone' from her heart, for even her 'patient trust' cannot 'survive the daily blight of such experience' (p. 649). She still has enough love for her father, however, to yield to 'the impulse of her affection' when Edith deserts him (p. 665); and it is only when he meets her proffered love with a savage blow that she finally accepts that he has 'murdered' the 'fond idea' to which she has held 'in spite of him', and runs out, 'orphaned, from his house':

> Ran out of his house. A moment, and her hand was on the lock, the cry was on her lips, his face was there, made paler by the yellow candles hastily put down and guttering away, and by the daylight coming in above the door. Another moment, and the close darkness of the shut-up house (forgotten to be opened, though it was long since day) yielded to the unexpected glare and freedom of the morning; and Florence, with her head bent down to hide her agony of tears, was in the streets. (p. 666)

Florence's flight is described as a movement from the 'darkness' and confinement of the 'shut-up' house to the light and freedom of the morning; it is a movement, in a word, from Dombeyism to Walter and love.

The relationship of Florence and Walter, like that of Ruth Pinch and John Westlock in *Martin Chuzzlewit*, does not have much substance, but it similarly asserts the value of love in a world of business. Walter knows that, though Florence is 'a homeless wandering fugitive', she is 'richer to him so, than in all the wealth and pride of her right station' (p. 696); when she tells him that she has been thinking 'what a charge' she is to him and 'how much poorer' she will make him, he replies: 'And how much richer, Florence' (p. 789); and this note is again sounded on their wedding day:

> Riches are uncovering in shops; jewels, gold, and silver flash in the goldsmith's sunny windows; and great houses cast a stately shade upon them as they pass. But through the light, and through the shade, they go on lovingly together, lost to everything around; thinking of no other riches, and no prouder home, than they have now in one another. (p. 806)

The answer to Paul's question is implied as Florence and Walter make their way through the allegorical light and shade: money is as nothing to the 'whole heart' which they reciprocally give each other (pp. 712, 787). But heart is not only true wealth; it has also earlier been shown to have a revivifying power, and Walter's love completes the restoration that Captain Cuttle begins: 'When she, cast out of home, come here to me,' Cuttle tells Toots, 'and dropped upon them planks, her wownded heart was broke. I know it. I, Ed'ard Cuttle, see it. There's nowt but true, kind, steady love, as can ever piece it up again' (p. 784).

This power is once more apparent when Florence returns to her father and so saves him from suicide. Bankrupt and abandoned by his daughter as well as his wife, Dombey, a 'poor broken man', with 'stooping shoulders' and 'his chin dropped on his breast', is at last brought to his knees; and, 'thrown upon the bare boards', he at last lets 'his tears flow' as they will, weeping alone 'in the dead of night' (p. 841). But his unbending and unfreezing is a release that brings him insight, for he now sees the blight he has made: 'He knew, now, what it was to be rejected and deserted; now, when every loving blossom he had withered in his innocent daughter's heart was snowing down in ashes on him'; and when 'the mist' through which he has seen her clears, 'her true self' is revealed (p. 839). Florence's appearance just as Dombey rises 'with a terrible face' and a 'guilty hand grasping what [is] in [his] breast' (p. 843) is excruciatingly theatrical, but he is ready for it:

> As she clung closer to him, in another burst of tears, he kissed her on her lips, and, lifting up his eyes, said, 'Oh my God, forgive me, for I need it very much!'
> With that he dropped his head again, lamenting over and caressing her, and there was not a sound in all the house for a long, long time; they remained clasped in one another's arms, in the glorious sunshine that had crept in with Florence. (pp. 844–5)

It is as easy to sneer at this as it is at simple good nature and simplemindedness; and, indeed, Julian Moynahan remarks (though not with direct reference to this passage) that 'at the end of *Dombey and Son* Dickens is saying that things would be all right if men of Dombey's class and function made their daughters their mothers and lay down'.[1] That there should be so strong an echo of *King Lear* in the quoted passage, however, suggests that Dickens is saying something rather more profound. 'Clasped' in his daughter's arms, Dombey is at last

[1] *Ibid.*, p. 131.

able to give himself to the embrace of love; and if this recalls the earlier water image and intimates that he has now had the courage to jump from the bank, it is to risk a 'drowning' that is the necessary prelude to renewed life—a life in which, with a sounder sense of value, it is Florence's daughter, rather than Dombey and Son, that 'he hoards . . . in his heart' (p. 878). Incapsulated in the water image and its implicit extension in this passage is the kernel of the complex imaginative vision of *Our Mutual Friend* with its near-drownings that precede spiritual rebirth and its presentation of love as a regenerative force.

5

BLEAK HOUSE

I

What connexion can there be, between the place in Lincoln-shire, the house in town, the Mercury in powder, and the where-about of Jo the outlaw with the broom, who had that distant ray of light upon him when he swept the churchyard-step? What connexion can there have been between many people in the in-numerable histories of this world, who, from opposite sides of great gulfs, have, nevertheless, been very curiously brought to-gether! (p. 219)

Curious connections are so prominent in *Bleak House* that we scarcely deserve so rude an authorial nudging. Indeed, as we read the novel for the first time, the sense of connections being mysteriously made in a way that we cannot quite comprehend is what is principally offered to our bewilderment. (When we reread the novel, our awareness of the mastery with which the connections are prepared for and established is a constant source of pleasure.) Dickens's narrative technique, moreover, is designed to maintain our initial sense of ex-pectant bewilderment, our alertness for connection. It is not merely that we are slowly led to see that 'the whole bileing of people', in Mr. Bucket's phrase, is 'mixed up in the same business' (p. 806), such an effect being common to any novel with an elaborate plot; the double narrative throughout quietly posits a large connection, a connection between the apparently exclusive worlds of Esther Summerson and Lady Dedlock, and testifies (with pre-Jamesian innocence) to the virtues in this instance of a mixed point of view. The nature of these virtues, however, has been so variously described[1] that it is worth considering in some detail how the double narrative functions.

It has been asserted that the Chancery case of Jarndyce and Jarndyce is at the centre of the plot, 'almost every character' in one way or another being 'caught up in [its] convolutions'.[2] It seems to me, however, that the immediate effect of the double narrative is precisely to deny the existence of a single fixed centre. Though the narrative of the omniscient author opens with the evocation of Chancery in fog, it has little to say thereafter of Jarndyce and Jarndyce. The omniscient narrative is primarily concerned with 'the world of fashion' (p. 8) and the world of squalor; and with Lady Dedlock, who mediates between the two and may be thought of as at the centre of this narrative. The first-person narrative, with Esther Summerson (the narrator) at its centre, is on the whole concerned with the Bleak House world of middle-class respectability, and it is in this narrative that the working of Chancery is most closely scrutinized.[3] The juxtaposition of the two narratives has a curious effect. Taking our bearings, as it were, by two different and alternating centres, following two different time sequences (the historic present of the omniscient narrative and the retrospective past of the first-person narrative), moving in strongly differentiated social circles, we are impressed with a sense of the distinctiveness and separateness of the worlds that cohere round the narrative centres; and our attention, moreover, is equally held by what we apprehend as two main actions, that concerned with Lady Dedlock's secret, and that related to the case of Jarndyce and Jarndyce. The narrative method thus ensures that our sense of unrelated parts, of dissociation, is far stronger than it is in a work such as *Middlemarch*, for instance, where Dorothea Brooke and Lydgate may be thought of as constituting analogous centres of interest but where the homogeneity of the narrative is never in doubt. At the same time the omniscient and first-person narratives, like two adjacent, intersecting circles,

---

[1] See, most notably, the analyses of the narrative technique in J. Hillis Miller, *Charles Dickens*, pp. 164, 176–9; W. J. Harvey, 'Chance and Design in *Bleak House*', *Dickens and the Twentieth Century*, ed. John Gross and Gabriel Pearson, pp. 147–53; and Morton Dauwen Zabel, '*Bleak House*', *Craft and Character in Modern Fiction* (New York, 1957), pp. 38–40.

[2] Edgar Johnson, *Charles Dickens*, II, 764.

[3] Dickens is not altogether consistent in his handling of the two narratives. Though Richard's history is throughout traced by Esther in her narrative, the account of one meeting between Richard and Vholes (pp. 547–55) is arbitrarily assigned to the omniscient narrative, it being difficult to justify the departure from a well-defined narrative 'area' on the grounds of the narrator's omniscience. This kind of carelessness is also manifest in the way in which Dickens sometimes fails to maintain Esther's distinctive style, lapsing into sudden vividness —as W. J. Harvey has pointed out. See 'Chance and Design in *Bleak House*', *loc. cit.*, p. 147.

overlap, characters such as Miss Flite or Mr. Guppy appearing in both; and our initial impression of the structure is of two 'round worlds' rather than one, as in *Dombey and Son*.

Once the novel gets under way, however, we become aware of a further characteristic of the narrative movement. On the one hand, the movement, centring alternately in Esther and Lady Dedlock, is in both cases strongly centrifugal; that is to say, we move out in an apparently random manner from Esther and Bleak House and Jarndyce and Jarndyce to the lives of characters such as the Skimpoles, the Turveydrops and the Jellybies; and, similarly, we move out from Lady Dedlock and her mansions in town and country to the world of such as Krook and the Smallweeds and the Snagsbies. On the other hand, the first-person narrative moves with ever-increasing urgency to repeated meetings between Esther and Lady Dedlock—to their first meeting, with its undertones of obscure significance, at the keeper's lodge (pp. 254–7); to their second meeting and the revelation of their relationship (pp. 508–13); and, finally, to Esther's discovery of her mother's body towards the end of the novel (pp. 811–12). This movement on the part of Esther and Lady Dedlock is, as it were, reciprocally centripetal, each moving towards the centre of the other's world, though to speak in such terms at once suggests the inadequacy of our initial conception of the structure. The narratives, we realize, not only overlap but converge; and the point at which they converge, the point at which the connection between Esther and Lady Dedlock is established, is seen to constitute the centre of a unified structure, of a circle that after all encompasses the 'many circles within circles' of the two narratives in a single 'round world'.

The point at which the two narratives become inextricably linked is also the thematic centre of the novel. Since it is a point at which apparently exclusive worlds are symbolically shown to be kith and kin, the theme suggested is the inescapable oneness of various social classes or groups, Dickens revealing how an obsession with money may infest a whole society. *Bleak House*, therefore, is thematically continuous with *Martin Chuzzlewit* and *Dombey and Son*, but in it the theme is treated with a new and admirable comprehensiveness. For the first time in Dickens individual attitudes are related to those of organized society; and, furthermore, the likely fate of such a society is related to that of individuals in it. These connections are effected, as we might expect, by means of the analogical method, the method being used with great skill to link not only the manifold preoccupations of a large number of characters but also, and most strikingly, the representative public activity of Jarndyce and Jarndyce and the private drama of Lady Dedlock. The two main actions, which the double narrative leads us to apprehend as separate, are also shown, in the end, to converge.

The form of the novel is thus neither meretricious nor productive of merely minor felicities[1] but the necessary and indivisible expression of its substance. Indeed, though Esther is made to tell the story of the Jarndyces and Chancery, *her* story is an integral part of the narrative that is concerned with Lady Dedlock; the omniscient narrative, in other words, is also *Esther's* story, and once again what appears to be separate is not.[2] It is all one, and the plot, with its central revelation of the relationship between Esther and Lady Dedlock, is an organic part of the whole conception. Dickens's use of the plot, moreover, to evoke an atmosphere of mystery, which—like the fog—hangs over the novel to the end, should not be dismissed as evidence of an inferior art or tolerated as the price to be paid for other rewards by the adult reader, but should rather be regarded as contributive to the novel's imperative drive towards exposure—towards the exposure not only of Lady Dedlock and of Tulkinghorn's murderer and of Chancery practice but of the rottenness of a whole society, of which the large number of individual deaths is ominously symbolic.[3] The plot itself, that is to say, is a symbolic structure, and it tells us a great deal more what the book is about than the much-praised symbol of the fog. This should not be taken to suggest that it is fully meaningful and convincing. Woven into the brilliant imaginative design, there is the palpably melodramatic and distractingly irrelevant figure of an Hortense.

II

Discerning in Dickens a tendency, like that of Jacobean dramatists, to

[1] One of the intermittent and paradoxical products of the employment of a mixed point of view is an increased verisimilitude in the area where the narratives overlap. Having become accustomed, for instance, to the way in which the delightful Snagsby is presented by the omniscient author, it is with a recognition of the kind we experience in real life when we suddenly see someone we know well in a new light that we respond to Esther's view of him towards the end of the novel: 'In the passage behind the door, stood a scared, sorrowful-looking little man in a grey coat, who seemed to have a naturally polite manner, and spoke meekly' (p. 805).

[2] I am indebted for this suggestion to a student of mine, Mrs. Lillian Reichstein.

[3] If we include the deaths (off-stage, so to speak) of Tom Jarndyce and Miss Barbary, there are altogether eleven deaths in the novel: in addition to these two, there are those of Hawdon, the brickmaker's baby, 'Coavinses' (Charley's father), Gridley, Krook, Jo, Tulkinghorn, Lady Dedlock, and Richard.

'episodic intensification', a tendency, that is, 'to exploit to the full possibilities of any particular scene, situation or action without too much regard for the relevance of such local intensities to the total work of art', W. J. Harvey denies that *Bleak House* has the 'organic unity' of a work such as *Great Expectations*. In *Bleak House*, he maintains, an 'extreme tension' is set up between 'the centrifugal vigour' of the parts and 'the centripetal demands of the whole'; and the impression finally made by the book is one of 'immense and potential anarchic energy being brought—but only just—under control'.[1] This estimate, I feel, fails to do justice either to the imaginative coherence of the novel or to its smoothness. If part of the action does have a strongly centrifugal movement in the sense I have suggested, it is not by way of episodic intensification. The action that takes place at the periphery of the two main narrative areas is closely and directly related to that which proceeds more obviously at the centre of things. So careful is the organization, that an analysis of the function of circumferential figures leads us straight to the complex of ideas that is at the thematic centre of the novel, and that constitutes the nuclear analogue of its structure of analogies.

Harold Skimpole, to consider Esther's narrative first, would appear to be sufficiently remote from the central activities of this section of the book to make him a representative figure in this respect. A typical Dickens 'character', of scant importance in the plot, Skimpole might be thought to have no particular business in *Bleak House* and to exist barefacedly as testimony to his creator's exuberance (if not to his ambivalence towards Leigh Hunt). Yet Skimpole's first words prove—as we discover—to be of decided relevance to the large concerns of the novel:

> . . . he must confess to two of the oldest infirmities in the world: one was, that he had no idea of time; the other, that he had no idea of money. In consequence of which he never kept an appointment, never could transact any business, and never knew the value of anything! Well! So he had got on in life, and here he was! He was very fond of reading the papers, very fond of making fancy sketches with a pencil, very fond of nature, very fond of art. All he asked of society was, to let him live. *That* wasn't much. His wants were few. Give him the papers, conversation, music, mutton, coffee, landscape, fruit in the season, a few

[1] 'Chance and Design in *Bleak House*', *loc. cit.*, pp. 145–6.

sheets of Bristol-board, and a little claret, and he asked no more. He was a mere child in the world, but he didn't cry for the moon. He said to the world, 'Go your several ways in peace! Wear red coats, blue coats, lawn sleeves, put pens behind your ears, wear aprons; go after glory, holiness, commerce, trade, any object you prefer; only let Harold Skimpole live!' (pp. 69–70)

Skimpole, we see, opposes to the pursuit of money in the world of commerce and trade the satisfaction of his cultivated tastes (which range, with fine impartiality, over realms of both flesh and spirit). Since the world that he bids go its way in peace is the world, among other things, of Chancery and Jarndyce and Jarndyce, his opting out of its commitments has a certain charm; and his dilettantism seems relatively harmless. But, as Esther and Richard very soon discover, his demand that the world at large 'let Harold Skimpole live' turns out to be more sharply directed to that portion of it with cash to spare—and to mean: 'Let Harold Skimpole live by letting him live on you.' By presenting himself as 'a mere child in the world', Skimpole further-more absolves himself from all responsibility for his actions, leaving himself the freedom not only to practise but (in a subsequent 'discourse about Bees') to preach 'the Drone philosophy' (p. 93). His pained withdrawal from the world, it is apparent, is simply a strategy for accosting it by other means, and his twin 'infirmities' are no more otherworldly than the Court of Chancery, which proceeds with a comparable indifference to time and the conservation of other people's money.

Skimpole's oblivious self-centredness is perhaps most strikingly in-dicated when he secretly hands the sick Jo over to Bucket. His response, when his part in Jo's strange disappearance is revealed and Esther taxes him with it, is a marvel of perverted logic:

'Observe the case, my dear Miss Summerson. Here is a boy received into the house and put to bed, in a state that I strongly object to. The boy being in bed, a man arrives—like the house that Jack built. . . . Here is the Skimpole who accepts the bank-note produced by the man who demands the boy who is received into the house and put to bed in a state that I strongly object to. Those are the facts. Very well. Should the Skimpole have refused the note? *Why* should the Skimpole have refused the note? Skimpole protests to Bucket; "what's this for? I don't

understand it, it is of no use to me, take it away." Bucket still
entreats Skimpole to accept it. Are there reasons why Skimpole
not being warped by prejudices, should accept it? Yes. Skimpole
perceives them. What are they? Skimpole reasons with himself,
this is a tamed lynx, an active police-officer, an intelligent man
. . . [who] has acquired, in the exercise of his art, a strong faith
in money; he finds it very useful to him, and he makes it very
useful to society. Shall I shake that faith in Bucket, because I
want it myself; shall I deliberately blunt one of Bucket's weapons;
shall I positively paralyse Bucket in his next detective operation?
And again. If it is blameable in Skimpole to take the note, it is
blameable in Bucket to offer the note—much more blameable
in Bucket, because he is the knowing man. Now, Skimpole
wishes to think well of Bucket; Skimpole deems it essential, in
its little place, to the general cohesion of things, that he *should*
think well of Bucket. The State expressly asks him to trust to
Bucket. And he does. And that's all he does!' (p. 830)

If, in his juggling of 'the facts', Skimpole here clearly enjoys playing
Falstaff after Gadshill, his self-exposure is complete. The logical extension of his parasitism, of his readiness to snap up all unconsidered
trifles, is an insidious moral corruption, of which his acceptance of
Bucket's bribe is only one instance, for he also evidences a like fond-
ness for five-pound notes in relieving Vholes of one in return for
introducing him to Richard (p. 533). Unwarped by prejudice, Skimpole contrives both to have his cake and eat it, to admit the facts and
yet to evade all moral responsibility for his behaviour by denying it to
be questionable, and then by anyway fixing responsibility, with im-
peccable logic, on Bucket. His attitude, in this respect, is of a piece
with his initial refusal to take responsibility for Jo, with his placid
indifference to his fate. By confining the matter at issue to his acceptance of the money, moreover, he also manages to ignore other implications of his handing over of Jo, to ignore the fact that his action is a
betrayal of his host's confidence, as Esther tells him (p. 829); and, still
more important, that it represents, as we see, a betrayal of the sick
boy himself. Skimpole's betrayal of Jo is a specific dramatization, an
enactment in miniature, as it were, of the large breach of faith in
respect of Jo that is perpetrated by the society he lives in; and that
breach of faith, I shall argue, is likewise attributable to a moral corruption that is associated with parasitism and an evasion of responsibility.

An apparently peripheral figure such as Skimpole, in other words, is of central importance, and the way in which Dickens handles him is some evidence of the 'organic unity' of the novel.

A figure in the omniscient narrative who might be thought of as occupying an analogous position to that of Skimpole in Esther's narrative is Grandfather Smallweed, though it is true that, serving as Tulkinghorn's instrument, he has a more clearly defined function in the plot. If Skimpole is a typical Dickens 'character', Smallweed is one of Dickens's typical grotesques, 'a mere clothes-bag with a black skull-cap on the top of it', constantly requiring to undergo at the hands of his granddaughter 'the two operations . . . of being shaken up like a great bottle, and poked and punched like a great bolster' in order to be restored to some animation, and constantly discharging missiles at 'the venerable partner of his respected age whenever she makes an allusion to money' (p. 289). But Smallweed, we soon perceive, has not simply strayed out of *The Old Curiosity Shop*. His occupation, for one thing, has the authentic *Bleak House* stamp. A moneylender, living on other people with the persistence if not the suavity of Skimpole— George complains that he has paid him 'half as much again as [the] principal, in interest and one thing and another' (p. 473)—Smallweed engages in a business which we may regard as the archetype of parasitic activity in the novel. Appropriately, making use of the kind of image that we will find recurring in other contexts, Phil Squod (when George makes his complaint) proclaims Smallweed to be 'a leech in his dispositions'. And the moneylender's eagerness (like that of a large number of characters in the book) to lay his hands on someone else's property is not confined to the call of professional duty, as he reveals in a memorable gesture when he asserts his right to inherit the worldly remains of the late Mr. Krook: ' "I have come down," repeats Grandfather Smallweed, hooking the air towards him with all his ten fingers at once, "to look after the property" ' (p. 465).

Smallweed, furthermore, is as prone to passing the buck as Skimpole, habitually seeking to evade responsibility for the squeezing of his clients by maintaining that he is merely the agent of a 'friend in the city'—a prefiguration, this, of the more involved game that Fledgeby plays with Riah in *Our Mutual Friend*. Nor is integrity one of Smallweed's virtues. He is not at all averse (under Tulkinghorn's direction) to breaking faith with George, for instance, leaving the trooper with a sense of having been unaccountably betrayed: 'There has always been an understanding that this bill was to be what they call Renewed,'

George tells Phil. 'And it has been renewed, no end of times' (p. 473) The way in which Smallweed brings pressure to bear on George, moreover, is a prelude to his open blackmailing of Sir Leicester when he obtains possession of Lady Dedlock's letters to Hawdon (pp. 730–2).

The narrative excursions, then, are designed to evoke a varied but recurring image of a corrupt and parasitic society, of a society in which people do not so much live with one another as on one another. On the periphery of things, Skimpole and Smallweed are simply the most striking instances of a widespread tendency. There is also, for instance, Mr. Turveydrop, who having suffered his wife to work herself to death 'to maintain him in those expenses which were indispensable to his position', not only allows his small, shabby, hard-working son to keep him but seems, in his fat resplendence, to be absorbing his son's substance; a distinguished man, he does 'nothing whatever' but serve as 'a model of Deportment' (pp. 191–2). There are, too, the Dedlock relations, foremost among them being that *memento mori*, Miss Volumnia, who lives 'slenderly' in Bath 'on an annual present from Sir Leicester', making 'occasional resurrections in the country houses of her cousins' (p. 390); and the Honourable Bob Stables, who in his desire 'to serve his country in a post of good emoluments, unaccompanied by any trouble or responsibility' (pp. 390–1) looks ahead to the Barnacles of *Little Dorrit*.[1] There are, in addition, the philanthropists, those acquaintances of Mr. Jarndyce, who are ready 'to do anything with anybody else's money' (p. 99). Of these the most notable for 'rapacious benevolence' is Mrs. Pardiggle, 'a formidable style of lady', who has the effect 'of wanting a great deal of room', swelling, it would seem, on the enforced contributions to good causes of her 'weazened and shrivelled' children; in the world of commerce and trade that Skimpole rejects she makes a show 'of doing charity by wholesale, and of dealing in it to a large extent' (pp. 100–1, 108). There are Mr. Quale and Mr. Gusher, who originate testimonials to each other, soliciting donations from 'charity schools of small boys and girls, who [are] specially reminded of the widow's mite, and requested to come forward with halfpence and be acceptable sacrifices' (p. 204). The extent to which parasitism is corrupting is not demonstrated, in respect of the instances of it that have just been noted, with the finality that characterizes the presentation of Skimpole and Smallweed, but it is firmly enough implied; it is further indicated in the depiction of the

---

[1] As does Sir Thomas Doodle, who 'comes in' after Lord Coodle has gone out, 'bringing in with him all his nephews, all his male cousins, and all his brothers-in-law' (p. 562).

institutions of the society of which Mr. Turveydrop, the Dedlock relations and Mrs. Pardgiggle are respected members.

III

The most prominent institution of this society is, of course, Chancery, and the representative example of its procedure its handling of the cause of Jarndyce and Jarndyce. Jarndyce and Jarndyce, it is at once brought to our notice, is a rich picking for the lawyers engaged in the suit, 'some two or three of whom have inherited it from their fathers, who made a fortune by it' (p. 2). Jarndyce and Jarndyce, indeed, exemplifies that 'the one great principle of the English law is, to make business for itself' at the expense of 'the laity' (p. 548). The practice of law, in other words, has little to do with justice and is simply a socially condoned form of parasitism—as is graphically confirmed by the eventual lot of the Jarndyce estate, which is eaten up in costs (another instance, this, of the symbolic dimensions of the plot). This view of the legal process is reinforced by that taken of lawyers in a series of images. The house Tulkinghorn lives in is divided into sets of chambers in which 'lawyers lie like maggots in nuts' (p. 130). The quintessential lawyer is Vholes, and his name, as Louis Crompton has pointed out,[1] evokes that of the parasitic field mouse that destroys crops. There is 'something of the Vampire' in Vholes (p. 820); he looks at Richard 'as if he were making a lingering meal of him with his eyes as well as with his professional appetite' (p. 550), and, when Jarndyce and Jarndyce has run its course, he gasps 'as if he [has] swallowed the last morsel of his client' (p. 867). The toleration by 'the laity' of this legal voraciousness, albeit with some grumbling, is seen as an insane condonation of social cannibalism: 'As though, Mr. Vholes and his relations being minor cannibal chiefs, and it being proposed to abolish cannibalism, indignant champions were to put the case thus: Make man-eating unlawful, and you starve the Vholeses!' (p. 549)

An essential condition of this legal parasitism being the protraction of proceedings, it is not unexpected that Jarndyce and Jarndyce should appear to be 'an endless cause' (p. 2). But the dilatoriness of Chancery also points to its evasiveness, to its failure to take decisions, its failure, that is, to fulfil its social function of taking responsibility in issues brought before it. And this evasiveness ramifies, for 'shirking and shark-

[1] 'Satire and Symbolism in *Bleak House*', *Nineteenth-Century Fiction*, 12 (March 1958), 300.

ing, in all their many varieties' are 'sown broadcast by the ill-fated cause' (p. 5); and the Lord Chancellor and the lawyers, as Gridley complains, assert that they are not responsible for injustices—'It's the system' (p. 215). If the system of justice that 'gives to monied might, the means abundantly of wearying out the right' (p. 3) is clearly rotten at the core, we are also shown (moving yet once again, as it were, from centre to fringe) how the corruption spreads. We see this notably in the equivocal position of Bucket, that amiable representative of the forces of law and order, the 'tamed lynx' of Skimpole's disquisition. Bucket is as efficient and decisive as Chancery is confusedly procrastinatory, and he is capable of adhering with some delicacy to a code of honour (as when he delays George's arrest at the Bagnet birthday); but he is also not above lying to Snagsby (with 'an engaging appearance of frankness') about the nature of Tulkinghorn's interest in Jo's encounter with the lady (p. 309); nor above bribing Skimpole and abducting the sick Jo; nor bargaining with Smallweed about the sum he aims to extort from Sir Leicester (pp. 732, 735); nor recommending to that baronet that he capitulate to the blackmail (p. 735).

If this, then, is the way in which the Court of Chancery is presented to us, it is important to note two further points relative to that presentation. First, though Dickens's case against Chancery may appear to be poetically heightened, it was not untrue to the facts. Jarndyce and Jarndyce was suggested, says Edgar Johnson, by 'the notorious Jennings case, involving the disputed property of an old miser of Acton who had died intestate in 1798, leaving almost £1,500,000. When one of the claimants died in 1915 the case was still unsettled and the costs amounted to £250,000.'[1] Second, it should be clear that the attack on Chancery is intended to be more than an attack on a single antiquated institution.[2] Chancery is throughout presented as a representative national establishment: as such, as 'a slow, expensive, British, con-

---

[1] *Charles Dickens*, II, 771. Dickens himself, in his Preface to the novel, insists on the truth of his account: '. . . I mention here that everything set forth in these pages concerning the Court of Chancery is substantially true, and within the truth' (p. xiii); and John Butt and Kathleen Tillotson quote a passage from *The Times* of 28th March 1851 that lends support to his insistence. See *Dickens at Work*, p. 185.

[2] A typically defensive reaction of some of Dickens's contemporaries was both to attempt to localize the attack in this way and to discredit it by asserting its redundance. George H. Ford refers to a review of *Little Dorrit* by Fitzjames Stephen (the elder brother of Leslie Stephen) in 1857, in which Stephen 'makes one hit against the social criticism which was to persist among later critics: that Dickens was simply whipping dead horses. "He seems . . . to get his first notions of an abuse from the discussions which accompany its removal. . . . This was his course with respect both to imprisonment for debt and to Chancery reform."' *Dickens and His Readers*, p. 105. Edgar Johnson quotes Lord Chief Justice Denman's description of the attack on Chancery as 'belated and now unnecessary'. *Charles Dickens*, II, 760.

stitutional kind of thing', it commands Sir Leicester's tacit support
(p. 13); and as such it evokes Mr. Kenge's defensive pride: 'We are
a great country, Mr. Jarndyce, we are a very great country. This is a
great system, Mr. Jarndyce, and would you wish a great country to
have a little system?' (p. 844). To regard Chancery as being at the
heart not only of the fog that covers London at the beginning of the
novel but of a whole social system, to regard it, that is, as symbolic
of the functioning of a parasitic society, is to register the difference
between Dickens's social criticism in *Bleak House* and that in *Nicholas
Nickleby*, for instance, with its restricted attack on Dotheboys Hall;
and also that, as we have seen, in *Oliver Twist*, with its more limited
denunciation of the workhouse. To see that Chancery, and not the
fog, is the central symbol of *Bleak House* is both to recognize the
opening move in the analogical strategy of the late novels and to do
justice to the nature and scope of Dickens's first major assault on the
England of his day.

That Chancery is intended to have this kind of representative significance is borne out not alone (as I shall indicate) by the development of the action that connects it with Jo and Tom-all-Alone's but
by the glancing reflection of its image in another central institution
of state—parliament. The politicians, it emerges, are also not concerned with exercising the responsibilities of their office but only,
again like the lawyers, with graciously living on the 'people', the
'supernumeraries' of the drama that is enacted between Boodle and
Buffy and their retinues, of the drama that makes politics the art of
providing for Noodle (p. 161). To ensure that he and his are provided
for, moreover, Sir Thomas Doodle finds, during an election, that he
'must throw himself upon the country—chiefly in the form of
sovereigns and beer', the 'auriferous and malty shower' being later
'unpleasantly connected with the word bribery' in some two hundred
election petitions (pp. 562–8). In addition, it is perhaps not irrelevant
to mention that in the industrial society in which Chancery and
Parliament so effectively maintain themselves smoke is described (in
a passing reference) as 'the London ivy', an 'affectionate parasite' that
wreathes itself so clingingly round the sign PEFFER (later PEFFER and
SNAGSBY) as to 'overpower' it (p. 127).

Smoke, together with mud and fog, is also linked to Chancery in
the much-discussed description with which the novel begins, the description in which Chancery (by means of a richness of association that
has not perhaps had its due) is given a memorable habitation:

Bleak House

London. Michaelmas Term lately over, and the Lord Chancellor sitting in Lincoln's Inn Hall. Implacable November weather. As much mud in the streets, as if the waters had but newly retired from the face of the earth, and it would not be wonderful to meet a Megalosaurus, forty feet long or so, waddling like an elephantine lizard up Holborn Hill. Smoke lowering down from chimney-pots, making a soft black drizzle, with flakes of soot in it as big as full-grown snowflakes—gone into mourning, one might imagine, for the death of the sun. Dogs, undistinguishable in mire. Horses, scarcely better; splashed to their very blinkers. Foot passengers, jostling one another's umbrellas, in a general infection of ill-temper, and losing their foot-hold at street-corners, where tens of thousands of other foot passengers have been slipping and sliding since the day broke (if this day ever broke), adding new deposits to the crust upon crust of mud, sticking at those points tenaciously to the pavement, and accumulating at compound interest.

Fog everywhere. Fog up the river, where it flows among green aits and meadows; fog down the river, where it rolls defiled among the tiers of shipping, and the waterside pollutions of a great (and dirty) city. . . .

The raw afternoon is rawest, and the dense fog is densest, and the muddy streets are muddiest, near that leaden-headed old obstruction, appropriate ornament for the threshold of a leaden-headed old corporation: Temple Bar. And hard by Temple Bar, in Lincoln's Inn Hall, at the very heart of the fog, sits the Lord High Chancellor in his High Court of Chancery.

Never can there come fog too thick, never can there come mud and mire too deep, to assort with the groping and floundering condition which this High Court of Chancery, most pestilent of hoary sinners, holds, this day, in the sight of heaven and earth. (pp. 1–2)

Bearing in mind the complacency of mid-century optimism about progress, we cannot help being struck by the dark harshness of this evocation of the Victorian scene. What is suggested, indeed, is the difficulty of making any progress at all in the fog and smoke and mud, the predicament of a 'groping and floundering condition' being general. The ramifications of this condition are far-reaching. In the first place the mud, which is in part responsible for it, is associated with an accumula-

168

tion 'at compound interest', and with a state in which 'it would not be wonderful to meet a Megalosaurus'; the accumulation of money, that is, is tacitly associated with a reversion to a lower form of life, and (by a further extension of the image) with a retrogressive Chancery, which is situated where 'the muddy streets are muddiest'. Second, the mud is linked, in terms of the imagery, with a 'black drizzle' of smoke and soot, those emblems of industrial civilization; and what this posits is not just a retrogression but a blotting out of life, for one might imagine the flakes of soot mourning 'the death of the sun', and it is doubtful 'if this day ever broke'. Chancery itself, it hardly needs saying, is 'at the very heart of the fog'; and the court is 'dim', with 'wasting candles here and there' and fog hanging 'heavy' in it and stained-glass windows that 'admit no light of day into the place' (p. 2). Third, the dual movement of the narrative as a whole is reflected in the development of one of the images in this passage. The fog that is 'defiled' by the 'waterside pollutions' of the great city is responsible, together with the mud and the smoke, for a general 'infection' of ill-temper among foot passengers; at the centre of the fog, where 'the dense fog is densest', there is the Court of Chancery, that most 'pestilent' of sinners. Moving out from that centre to the country at large, we are told that Chancery 'has its decaying houses and its blighted lands in every shire' (pp. 2–3), and that Jarndyce and Jarndyce 'has stretched forth its unwholesome hand to soil and corrupt' untold numbers of people (p. 5). Chancery, that is, is from the outset associated with the spread of a noxious infection and corruption in the body politic. If Dombeyism, as we have seen, is the blight of domestic life, then Chancery and all its works is presented as the blight of public life, the parasite that consumes the social organism.[1]

The image that radiates from the pestilent sinner should be related to a passage in which Mr. Jarndyce tells Esther of the decay of some Jarndyce property in London:

'There is, in that city of London there, some property of ours, which is much at this day what Bleak House was then [i.e., in the time of Tom Jarndyce]—I say property of ours, meaning of the Suit's, but I ought to call it the property of Costs; for Costs is the only power on earth that will ever get anything out of it

---

[1] This effect is strengthened by the repetition of the same image in the first-person narrative: Esther thinks of Jarndyce and Jarndyce as 'that blight' (p. 523), this being the typical term used by Mr. Jarndyce as well as Esther to refer to the suit.

now, or will ever know it for anything but an eyesore and a heartsore. It is a street of perishing blind houses, with their eyes stoned out; without a pane of glass, without so much as a windowframe, with the bare blank shutters tumbling from their hinges and falling asunder; the iron rails peeling away in flakes of rust; the chimneys sinking in; the stone steps to every door (and every door might be Death's Door) turning stagnant green; the very crutches on which the ruins are propped, decaying. Although Bleak House was not in Chancery, its master was, and it was stamped with the same seal. These are the Great Seal's impressions, my dear, all over England—the children know them! '(pp. 96–7)

Here, figured persistently in detail after detail of the imagery, is plainly a manifestation of social blight, of Chancery's 'decaying houses and blighted lands'. And the property referred to, though Mr. Jarndyce does not mention its name, is equally clearly Tom-all-Alone's, the London slum in dispute in Jarndyce and Jarndyce and the home of Jo. Mr. Jarndyce's sudden reference to children implies one of the most disturbing aspects of the Great Seal's imprint—the blighting of the lives of children (like Jo) who are born and bred in such slums. It is, indeed, in his exposure of the way in which the lives of the innocent are blighted that Dickens's attack on Chancery (and the society of his day) is centred. Certainly Tom-all-Alone's is at the centre of the world of *Bleak House*, it being no coincidence that a surviving list of projected titles of the novel should so insistently point to it. John Forster notes the following titles which were 'successively proposed for *Bleak House*. 1. "Tom-all-Alone's. The Ruined House"; 2. "Tom-All-Alone's. The Solitary House that was always shut up"; 3. "Bleak House Academy"; 4. "The East Wind"; 5. "Tom-all-Alone's. The Ruined [House, Building, Factory, Mill] that got into Chancery and never got out"; 6. "Tom-all-Alone's. The Solitary House where the Grass grew"; 7. "Tom-all-Alone's. The Solitary House that was always shut up and never Lighted"; 8. "Tom-all-Alone's. The Ruined Mill, that got into Chancery and never got out"; 9. "Tom-all-Alone's. The Solitary House where the Wind howled"; 10. "Tom-all-Alone's. The Ruined House that got into Chancery and never got out"; 11. "Bleak House and the East Wind. How they both got into Chancery and never got out"; 12. "Bleak House".'[1]

[1] *Charles Dickens*, Vol. III (London, 1874), pp. 31–2.

If Mr. Jarndyce's description of Tom-all-Alone's points pre-
dominantly to its deterioration as property, the omniscient narrative
gives us some indication of the condition of its human inhabitants:

> Jo lives—that is to say, Jo has not yet died—in a ruinous
> place, known to the like of him by the name of Tom-all-Alone's.
> It is a black, dilapidated street, avoided by all decent people; where
> the crazy houses were seized upon, when their decay was far
> advanced, by some bold vagrants, who, after establishing their
> own possession, took to letting them out in lodgings. Now, these
> tumbling tenements contain, by night, a swarm of misery. As, on
> the ruined human wretch, vermin parasites appear, so these
> ruined shelters have bred a crowd of foul existence that crawls
> in and out of gaps in walls and boards; and coils itself to sleep,
> in maggot numbers, where the rain drips in; and comes and goes,
> fetching and carrying fever, and sowing more evil in its every
> footprint than Lord Coodle, and Sir Thomas Doodle, and the
> Duke of Foodle, and all the fine gentlemen in office, down to
> Zoodle, shall set right in five hundred years—though born ex-
> pressly to do it. . . .
> This desirable property is in Chancery, of course. It would
> be an insult to the discernment of any man with half an eye, to
> tell him so. Whether 'Tom' is the popular representative of the
> original plaintiff or defendant in Jarndyce and Jarndyce; or
> whether Tom lived here when the suit had laid the street waste,
> all alone, until other settlers came to join him; or whether the
> traditional title is a comprehensive name for a retreat cut off from
> honest company and put out of the pale of hope; perhaps nobody
> knows. Certainly, Jo don't know.
> 'For *I* don't,' says Jo, '*I* don't know nothink.' (pp. 219–20)

It is a further measure of the organic unity of the novel that in this
centrally significant passage there should appear the simile of the
vermin parasites. In terms of the simile, the 'crowd of foul existence'
that the slum has bred 'in maggot numbers' is clearly a crowd of human
parasites, of miserable mendicants whose begging exemplifies the most
primitive and precarious form of social parasitism. Of such a tribe is
Jo, dumbly sweeping his crossing and depending on the charity of men
like Hawdon and Snagsby. Of such is Jo, who, like 'the other lower
animals', gets on as well as he can in 'the unintelligible mess' of city

life; who, listening to 'a band of music' together with a drover's dog, is said to derive 'probably . . . the same amount of animal satisfaction' as the dog and to be 'probably upon a par' with it 'as to awakened association, aspiration or regret, melancholy or joyful reference to things beyond the senses', but to be 'otherwise' far beneath 'the brute': 'Turn that dog's descendants wild, like Jo, and in a very few years they will so degenerate that they will lose even their bark—but not their bite' (pp. 221–2). In his low, degenerate state, in other words, Jo (tiny parasite) points to the existence of a muddy Megalosaurus at the heart of civilization.[1]

Orphaned, defenceless, knowing nothink, Jo is an inevitable victim of exploitation. He, and others like him, it is implied, are in their turn parasitically battened on by the 'bold vagrants' who have 'seized' the houses in Tom-all-Alone's and let them out in lodgings. And the vagrants remain undisturbed in their illegal possession of the houses, of course, because the property is 'in Chancery', because, consequently, it as good as belongs to no one and no one is to be found both willing and able to take responsibility for it. Certainly not the lawyers, for those maggots in nuts are not only far removed from the maggot numbers of Tom-all-Alone's but otherwise engaged in the consuming suit of Jarndyce and Jarndyce. Certainly not the politicians, for though Lord Coodle and Sir Thomas Doodle and their fellows participate in 'much mighty speech-making . . . both in and out of Parliament, concerning Tom', they are really preoccupied with providing for Noodle; and 'Tom' is accordingly left to go 'to perdition head foremost in his old determined spirit' (p. 627). The street is 'laid waste' under the joint auspices, as it were, of legislature and judiciary. The image of being of this society, it becomes clear, is a chain of parasites.

Since it is Chancery that is responsible, in the first instance, for the desolation of Tom-all-Alone's, and since Jo is viewed as having been 'bred' by the 'ruined shelters', it seems reasonable to regard him as the direct responsibility of Chancery. Jo, we might say, the poor naked wretch who has to bide the pelting of the storm, is as much a ward of Chancery as Ada and Richard. Yet the long arm of the law, when it

[1] Another (related) aspect of the retrogressive tendency of this society is pointed to in the description of the churchyard in which Hawdon is buried: 'With houses looking on, on every side, save where a reeking little tunnel of a court gives access to the iron gate—with every villainy of life in action close on death, and every poisonous element of death in action close on life—here, they lower our dear brother down a foot or two: here, sow him in corruption, to be raised in corruption: an avenging ghost at many a sick bedside: a shameful testimony to future ages, how civilisation and barbarism walked this boastful island together' (p. 151).

concerns itself with Jo at all, is intent only to push him out of sight: the police constable's instructions, as the wistful Snagsby is informed, are that Jo is 'to move on' (p. 265). The injunction is a concise indication of the way in which the authorities evade their obligation towards Jo; and this passing of the buck typifies the official response he meets with elsewhere when he moves on. Worn-out and ill, he is befriended by the brickmakers' women at St. Albans, but they can find no 'proper refuge' for him (as Esther reports):

> The friend had been here and there, and had been played about from hand to hand, and had come back as she went. At first it was too early for the boy to be received into the proper refuge, and at last it was too late. One official sent her to another, and the other sent her back again to the first, and so backward and forward; until it appeared to me as if both must have been appointed for their skill in evading their duties, instead of performing them. (pp. 431–2)

And when Allan Woodcourt later finds Jo in London, so 'deplorably low and reduced' as probably to be 'too far gone to recover' (p. 640), he reflects (considering where to 'bestow' him) on the 'strange fact' that 'in the heart of a civilised world this creature in human form should be more difficult to dispose of than an unowned dog' (p. 636). The failure on the part of organized society to provide for Jo (as distinct from providing for Noodle) amounts to a betrayal of him, to a betrayal of the trust reposed in it to care for a ward; and this failure, as Woodcourt's thought implies, is symptomatic of that of the 'civilised world' which will not own him.

The immediate consequence for Jo of this failure is his untimely death. Taken in, eventually, by George, he is not prepossessing: 'Homely filth begrimes him, homely parasites devour him, homely sores are in him, homely rags are on him: native ignorance, the growth of English soil and climate, sinks his immortal nature lower than the beasts that perish' (p. 641). Jo, we realize, has been devoured by a parasitic society as well as by the homely parasites. And his death, Dickens insists, is representative, exemplfying the fate of the unprotected in such a society:

> Dead, your Majesty. Dead, my lords and gentlemen. Dead, Right Reverends and Wrong Reverends of every order. Dead,

men and women, born with Heavenly compassion in your hearts.
And dying thus around us every day. (p. 649)

The tone of this is uncertain (though even its mixture of effects is
preferable to the sentimentality of that recital of the Lord's Prayer
which it follows), but its emphasis is unmistakable: it is a whole society
that shares in the guilt of Jo's death.

The general social consequences of the existence of a slum such as
Tom-all-Alone's are first adverted to in the passage (quoted on p. 171
above) in which the 'crowd of foul existence' is said to come and go,
'fetching and carrying fever, and sowing more evil in its every foot-
print' than the Lord Coodles can ever set right. These consequences
are elaborated on in the description of the revenge 'Tom' takes on
being left to go to perdition:

> But he has his revenge. Even the winds are his messengers,
> and they serve him in these hours of darkness. There is not a
> drop of Tom's corrupted blood but propagates infection and con-
> tagion somewhere. It shall pollute, this very night, the choice
> stream (in which chemists on analysis would find the genuine
> nobility) of a Norman house, and his Grace shall not be able to
> say Nay to the infamous alliance. There is not an atom of Tom's
> slime, not a cubic inch of any pestilential gas in which he lives,
> not one obscenity or degradation about him, not an ignorance,
> not a wickedness, not a brutality of his committing, but shall
> work its retribution, through every order of society, up to the
> proudest of the proud, and to the highest of the high. Verily,
> what with tainting, plundering, and spoiling, Tom has his re-
> venge. (pp. 627–8)

The central image of the insidious contagion which is Tom's revenge
is the actual disease that is disseminated by the slum, 'Tom's corrupted
blood . . . [propagating] infection and contagion' in the society that has
propagated it. The image admirably conveys a number of related
significances. The infection and contagion are, first, a direct physical
manifestation of the 'alliance' (no matter how 'infamous') of 'every
order of society', of their interdependence; the image, in other words,
points directly to what is indirectly insisted on by the narrative method.
The spread of the disease also demonstrates what the alliance entails:
it is a dramatic assertion that a gangrened limb cannot safely be left

unattended, that a society which leaves its slums to go to perdition head foremost will ineluctably be dragged down after them. But the fact that the society which disregards the signs of its own disorder in this way is a 'pestilent sinner' at heart, and the fact that the disease which corrupts its blood originates in Tom-all-Alone's suggest, furthermore, that the infection and contagion are symbolic of the specific disease that is Chancery. The spread of the disease, that is, symbolizes the way in which Chancery functions to blight the lives of those it touches, irrespective of how remote their connection with it may appear to be. In the plot this process is directly exemplified by the career of Richard (which I shall discuss later); it is symbolized by Jo's contraction of the (unnamed) disease and by the way he infects Esther and Charley. Esther and Jo (the latest in a line of victims that starts with Pickwick) are both equally innocent victims of Chancery. Finally, the spread of the infectious disease is intended to represent in tangible physical terms the analogous spread in such a society of a moral corruption, of what Dickens in *Dombey and Son* calls a 'moral pestilence'. The dissemination of this pestilence is shown to have a characteristic dual movement. It is Chancery that produces the specific parasitic blight of Tom-all-Alone's; stewing in its corruption, it is the slum that pours back into society the more general (but equally contaminating) mess of 'obscenity' and 'degradation', of 'ignorance', 'wickedness' and 'brutality'.

In *Barnaby Rudge* there is an interesting parallel to this vein of imagery. The Gordon rioters are described as follows:

> One other circumstance is worthy of remark; and that is, that from the moment of their first outbreak at Westminster, every symptom of order or preconcerted arrangement among them vanished. When they divided into parties and ran to different quarters of the town, it was on the spontaneous suggestion of the moment. Each party swelled as it went along, like rivers as they roll towards the sea; new leaders sprang up as they were wanted, disappeared when the necessity was over, and reappeared at the next crisis. Each tumult took shape and form from the circumstances of the moment; sober workmen, going home from their day's labour, were seen to cast down their baskets of tools and become rioters in an instant; mere boys on errands did the like. In a word, a moral plague ran through the city. The noise, and hurry, and excitement, had for hundreds and hundreds an attrac-

tion they had no firmness to resist. The contagion spread like a dread fever: an infectious madness, as yet not near its height, seized on new victims every hour, and society began to tremble at their ravings. (p. 403)

Since Dickens's preoccupation with the eighteenth-century Gordon riots reflects, at least in part, a concern with the Chartist agitation of his own day, as Edmund Wilson has pointed out;[1] the quoted passage suggests the possibility of another dimension to the disease imagery that is central in *Bleak House*. Are we to understand, that is to say, that the continued disregard of Tom may lead to the violent eruption of his corrupted blood, to insurrection? There is certainly at least one passage that hints at this:

> Twice, lately, there has been a crash and a cloud of dust, like the springing of a mine, in Tom-all-Alone's; and, each time, a house has fallen. These accidents have made a paragraph in the newspapers, and have filled a bed or two in the nearest hospital. The gaps remain, and there are not unpopular lodgings among the rubbish. As several more houses are nearly ready to go, the next crash in Tom-all-Alone's may be expected to be a good one. (p. 220)

The collapse of slum houses, it may be argued, is not an uncommon occurrence, but the opening simile is so forcefully evocative of violent and unnatural explosion as to charge the reference to 'the next crash in Tom-all-Alone's' with ominous threat. The explosive potentiality of the slum, however, is not further developed; the representative inhabitant of Tom-all-Alone's is poor, defenceless Jo, and adult residents are only dimly seen as skulking figures in the dark.

Though Dickens, therefore, does not ignore the possibility of revolution, he posits a rather different fate for this unregenerate society. Characteristically, he communicates his sense of this fate through a daring and grotesque image, an image, however, that subtly combines elements of two other major images—those of the corrupted blood and the parasite—the image of Krook's death by Spontaneous Combustion. Krook's representative significance is baldly asserted: Miss Flite tells Esther's party that 'among the neighbours' Krook is called 'the Lord Chancellor', and that his junk-shop is called 'the

---

[1] See 'Dickens: The Two Scrooges', *The Wound and the Bow*, p. 16.

Court of Chancery' (p. 51). His physical appearance is clearly intended
to evoke the aura of his illustrious namesake at the heart of the mud
and the fog: he is 'short, cadaverous, and withered' (p. 50); he spreads
his lean hands 'like a vampire's wings' (p. 138). His breath, moreover,
issues 'in visible smoke from his mouth, as if he were on fire within'
(p. 50)—a phenomenon that leads straight to his later grisly disintegra-
tion:

> The Lord Chancellor of that Court, true to his title in his last
> act, has died the death of all Lord Chancellors in all Courts,
> and of all authorities in all places under all names soever, where
> false pretences are made, and where injustice is done. Call the
> death by any name Your Highness will, attribute it to whom
> you will, or say it might have been prevented how you will, it
> is the same death eternally—inborn, inbred, engendered in the
> corrupted humours of the vicious body itself, and that only—
> Spontaneous Combustion, and none other of all the deaths that
> can be died. (pp. 455–6)

Though George Henry Lewes at once roundly declared that no
authoritative organic chemist would countenance the possibility of
spontaneous combustion (in which Dickens sincerely believed),[1]
Krook's death retains the imaginative, if not the scientific, validity it
was originally intended to have. 'Inborn, inbred, engendered in the
corrupted humours of the body itself', Krook's death leaves him, as it
were, self-consumed, 'represented' only by what looks like 'the cinder
of a small charred and broken log of wood sprinkled with white
ashes' (p. 455). This, then, rather than revolution, is the postulated
end of a world that condones Chancery and Tom-all-Alone's—as
though the parasitic society were at last to turn universal wolf and eat
up itself.

[1] See Gordon S. Haight, 'Dickens and Lewes on Spontaneous Combustion', *Nineteenth-Century Fiction*, 10 (June 1955), 53–63. Cf. Dickens: 'I am very truly obliged to you for the loan of your remarkable and learned Lecture on Spontaneous Combustion; and I am not a little pleased to find myself fortified by such high authority. Before writing that chapter of *Bleak House*, I had looked up all the more famous cases you quote . . .; but three or four of those you incidentally mention . . . are new to me—and your explanation is so beautifully clear, that I could particularly desire to repeat it several times before I come to the last No. and the Preface. . . .
'It is inconceivable to me how people can reject such evidence, supported by so much familiar knowledge, and such reasonable analogy. But I suppose the long and short of it is, that they don't know, and don't want to know, anything about the matter.' Letter to Dr. John Elliotson, 7. 2. 1853, *The Letters of Charles Dickens*, ed. Walter Dexter (Bloomsbury, 1938), II, 446–7. See, too) Preface to *Bleak House*, p. xiv.

IV

The way in which Chancery blights all it touches is directly exemplified, as I have remarked, by the case of Richard. Richard, indeed, is rather too much of a 'case', too predictable in his behaviour, to be really interesting; but as an *exemplum* to what is said more imaginatively elsewhere in the novel, he has his place. His place, from birth, is in Chancery:

> 'My dear Esther, I am a very unfortunate dog not to be more settled, but how *can* I be more settled? If you lived in an unfinished house, you couldn't settle down in it; if you were condemned to leave everything you undertook, unfinished, you would find it hard to apply yourself to anything; and yet that's my unhappy case. I was born into this unfinished contention with all its chances and changes, and it began to unsettle me before I quite knew the difference between a suit at law and a suit of clothes; and it has gone on unsettling me ever since; and here I am now, conscious sometimes that I am but a worthless fellow to love my confiding cousin Ada.' (p. 322)

Richard's words reveal that the heritage he has come into as one of the heirs to the disputed estate in Jarndyce and Jarndyce clearly bears the imprint of the Great Seal. Born into the 'unfinished contention', as if into original sin,[1] he is 'condemned' to be unsettled; is condemned, that is, as Mr. Jarndyce says, to 'a habit of putting off—and trusting to this, that, and the other chance, without knowing what chance' (p. 167); is condemned, like Jo, to move on. Richard moves on to some effect, abandoning Bayham Badger and medicine for Kenge and Carboy and the law, and them for the army and soldiering, and that for Vholes and Jarndyce and Jarndyce. His indecisiveness, his inability to take responsibility for the future course of his life, resembles nothing so much as a Chancery-begotten propensity to 'shirk and shark': 'It's not,' he says, 'as if I wanted a profession for life. These proceedings will come to a termination, and then I am provided for' (p. 323). Richard's last remark has the true parasitic stink, aligning him as it

---

[1] Mark Spilka argues the analogy in all earnestness in *Dickens and Kafka: A Mutual Interpretation* (London, 1963), pp. 215, 218.

does with Noodle and the politicians, with the lawyers and Vholes (that conscientious provider, with three daughters and a father in the Vale of Taunton), with Skimpole and with Mr. Turveydrop and with all the other characters in *Bleak House* who are analogously in search of a host. We are not surprised, therefore, that Esther's response to the communication of his modest aspiration is to wonder how he will end 'when so soon and so surely all his manly qualities' have been touched 'by the fatal blight' that ruins everything it rests on (p. 324).

Having been touched by the fatal blight, Richard succumbs, as in a moral pestilence, to the suspicion and distrust bred by Jarndyce and Jarndyce—the suspicion that Mr. Jarndyce has anticipated and attempted to fight against in applying to Chancery to have Richard and Ada live with him. Richard's distrust fixes itself, to start with, on Mr. Jarndyce. He comes to view Jarndyce's constant admonitions to him to have nothing to do with the suit as the tactics of self-interest, a design to keep him in indifferent ignorance of the proceedings (p. 524). Nor is he at a loss to account for so uncharitable an explanation of Jarndyce's motives:

> 'Come, sister, come,' said Richard, a little more gaily, 'you will be fair with me at all events. If I have the misfortune to be under that influence, so has he. If it has a little twisted me, it may have a little twisted him, too. I don't say that he is not an honourable man, out of all this complication and uncertainty; I am sure he is. But it taints everybody. You know it taints everybody. You have heard him say so fifty times. Then why should *he* escape?' (p. 525)

The distinctive tone of this, I think we are meant to recognize, is that of Harold Skimpole, it being noteworthy that Richard has just before been in Skimpole's company and confessed to a liking for him: 'He does me more good than anybody,' he tells Esther (p. 521). Richard's statement is characterized by the kind of specious logic we associate with Skimpole's description of his encounter with Bucket. Intent on making his point, moreover, Richard reveals a Skimpole-like indifference to the 'taint' he has admitted.

Mr. Jarndyce is magnanimous enough to acquit Richard of responsibility for his suspicions—he tells Esther that 'it is in the subtle poison of [abuses such as Chancery] to breed such diseases. His blood is infected, and objects lose their natural aspects in his sight. It is not *his* fault' (p. 492)—but Richard's corrupted blood, like that of Tom-all-Alone's, only spreads the infection. Fearing betrayal wherever he turns, he becomes suspicious, next, of Vholes, even drawing comfort from the failure of his military venture at the prospect of continued proximity to the lawyer: 'Why, if this bubble hadn't broken now . . .' he says, 'I must have been ordered abroad; but how could I have gone? How could I, with my experience of that thing, trust even Vholes unless I was at his back?' (p. 620). Even Ada, in the end, is involved in his presumption. Esther has previously suspected that he is 'postponing his best truth and earnestness' in his feeling for Ada 'until Jarndyce and Jarndyce should be off his mind' (p. 523); that there are grounds for her uneasiness is revealed when (at the time of his crisis in the army) she is the bearer of a letter to him from Ada in which his cousin offers him 'the little inheritance she is certain of so soon' in order that he may 'set [himself] right with it, and remain in the service'. He is deeply affected by the offer, but his distrust of Jarndyce is so great that, without his being aware of it, it contaminates even his love for Ada: 'And the dear girl,' he says, 'makes me this generous offer from under the same John Jarndyce's roof, and with the same John Jarndyce's gracious consent and connivance, I dare say, as a new means of buying me off' (pp. 620–1).

With his heart 'heavy with corroding care, suspense, distrust, and doubt', Richard is one day observed in the neighbourhood of Vholes's office by Mr. Guppy and Mr. Weevle. 'William,' says Weevle, as Richard passes, 'there's combustion going on there! It's not a case of Spontaneous, but it's smouldering combustion it is' (pp. 555–6). Just as Krook, in other words, is consumed by the corrupted humours of his own vicious body; just as the estate in Jarndyce and Jarndyce (together with all Richard's and all Ada's money) is consumed in costs; so does Richard consume himself with the care and suspense and distrust and doubt engendered by Chancery. As he obviously sickens, Woodcourt can diagnose 'no direct bodily illness' (p. 814); his illness is 'of the mind' (p. 864). On the day that Jarndyce and Jarndyce ends, his mouth fills with blood in the court, and, quite 'worn away' (p. 868), he is taken home to die. The blight of Chancery thus again falls on innocent victims, on his patient wife and on his unborn child, who —like Esther—is left to grow up without ever knowing a father.

V

That Esther's life is in this respect analogous to that of Richard's child suggests that there may perhaps be a connection between the fate of Richard and that of Lady Dedlock. Certainly the narrative method, we remember, implies some connection between Jarndyce and Jarndyce and Lady Dedlock's secret. The opening of the novel, moreover, firmly links the muddy, foggy world of Chancery and the wet world of fashion:

> It is but a glimpse of the world of fashion that we want on this same miry afternoon. It is not so unlike the Court of Chancery, but that we may pass from the one scene to the other, as the crow flies. Both the world of fashion and the Court of Chancery are things of precedent and usage; oversleeping Rip Van Winkles, who have played at strange games through a deal of thundery weather . . .
>
> It is not a large world. . . . There is much good in it . . . But the evil of it is, that it is a world wrapped up in too much jeweller's cotton and fine wool, and cannot hear the rushing of the larger worlds, and cannot see them as they circle round the sun. It is a deadened world, and its growth is sometimes unhealthy for want of air.
>
> . . . My Lady Dedlock has been down at what she calls, in familiar conversation, her 'place' in Lincolnshire. The waters are out in Lincolnshire. An arch of the bridge in the park has been sapped and sopped away. The adjacent low-lying ground, for half a mile in breadth, is a stagnant river, with melancholy trees for islands in it, and a surface punctured all over, all day long, with falling rain. . . . On Sundays, the little church in the park is mouldy; the oaken pulpit breaks out into a cold sweat; and there is a general smell and taste as of the ancient Dedlocks in their graves. . . . (p. 8–9)

What links the world of Chancery (where flakes of soot mourn the death of the sun) and the world of fashion, it is evident, is a common deadness. The description of the scene in Lincolnshire evokes a flooded world, a world in which everything stands stagnant, being slowly

181

'sapped and sopped away' like the arch of the bridge, suggestively evokes, in a word, the 'deadened world' that the world of fashion is explicitly said to be. This sense of deadness is associated with a number of characteristics of the world of fashion, and it is also related, as we slowly discover, to some aspects of Lady Dedlock's predicament. The deadness is associated, first, with a 'want of air', with a sense, that is, of unhealthy enclosure, with a narrow exclusiveness that takes no heed of 'larger worlds'; it seems to be the price paid for the suffocating embrace of soft jeweller's cotton and wool. Second, the deadness is associated with the influence of the past. Bound by 'precedent and usage', the world of fashion (an 'oversleeping Rip Van Winkle') is outmoded—and so denies itself, as it were. The dead past, moreover, like 'the ancient Dedlocks in their graves', infuses its 'general smell and taste' into the present.

This, then, is the world of fashion of which Lady Dedlock is the arbiter. 'Bored to death', she appears to be at one with her environment:

> My Lady Dedlock (who is childless), looking out in the early twilight from her boudoir at a keeper's lodge, and seeing the light of a fire upon the latticed panes, and smoke rising from the chimney, and a child, chased by a woman, running out into the rain to meet the shining figure of a wrapped-up man coming through the gate, has been put quite out of temper. My Lady Dedlock says she has been 'bored to death.'
> . . .
> Sir Leicester is twenty years, full measure, older than my Lady. . . . He is ceremonious, stately, most polite on every occasion to my Lady, and holds her personal attractions in the highest estimation. His gallantry to my Lady, which has never changed since he courted her, is the one little touch of romantic fancy in him.
> Indeed, he married her for love. A whisper still goes about, that she had not even family; howbeit, Sir Leicester had so much family that perhaps he had enough, and could dispense with any more. But she had beauty, pride, ambition, insolent resolve, and sense enough to portion out a legion of fine ladies. Wealth and station, added to these, soon floated her upward; and for years, now, my Lady Dedlock has been at the centre of the fashionable tree.
> How Alexander wept when he had no more worlds to conquer, everybody knows—or has some reason to know by this time, the

matter having been rather frequently mentioned. My Lady Dedlock, having conquered *her* world, fell, not into the melting, but
rather into the freezing mood. An exhausted composure, a worn-
out placidity, an equanimity of fatigue not to be ruffled by interest or satisfaction, are the trophies of her victory. She is perfectly well-bred. If she could be translated to Heaven to-morrow,
she might be expected to ascend without any rapture. (pp. 9–10)

The nature of Lady Dedlock's deadness is defined by that which
(disturbingly) bores her to death—the signs of animation she sees as
she gazes from her window at the keeper's lodge. In the cold, stagnant,
soggy scene the lodge (with its fire and movement and the 'shining'
figure of the man) is a place of warmth and life; the warmth and life
are associated, furthermore, with the love that seems to bind man,
woman and child together and that apparently communicates itself to
Lady Dedlock, ('who is childless'), and married to a man twenty years
her senior. Lady Dedlock's deadness, it is implied, is connected with the
sterility of her marriage, its emotional as well as physical sterility, for
if Sir Leicester has 'married her for love', she (in her ambition and
insolent resolve) has married 'wealth and station'. The coldness of her
choice, indeed (like that of Edith Dombey), is suggested by her 'freezing mood', the rigidity of which marks her posture in the 'deadened
world'. Her posture is also one of composure and placidity and equanimity, but if these are the visible 'trophies of her victory' over 'society',
they silently point (together with the affectation of exhaustion) to the
cost of victory over herself, to her ever-present, unrelaxed need of repressing feeling.

The feeling Lady Dedlock principally has to repress, of course, is
that connected with her past. Having chosen, like so many characters
in *Bleak House* to be provided for (to be a maggot in her own particular
kind of nut, as it were), she has, in defence of her position, to suppress
all suggestion of her illicit association with Hawdon and of the illegitimate birth of their daughter. To judge, moreover, by her response
when she catches sight of Hawdon's handwriting some twenty years
after she has broken with him, we may assume that she has had to
contend with a strong feeling for him, a feeling that remains as alive
as the child she thinks dead. Having denied Hawdon and betrayed his
love, Lady Dedlock, beneath her perfectly well-bred manner, has constantly to deny herself.

Though Lady Dedlock does not bequeath an estate to her daughter (companion to one of the parties to Jarndyce and Jarndyce), she leaves her to a future that promises to be as dark as any shadowed by the Court of Chancery. One of Esther's early memories is of her mother's sister exploiting the occasion of a birthday to say to her:

> 'Your mother, Esther, is your disgrace, and you were hers. . . . For yourself, unfortunate girl, orphaned and degraded from the first of these evil anniversaries, pray daily that the sins of others be not visited upon your head, according to what is written. Forget your mother, and leave all other people to forget her who will do her unhappy child that greatest kindness. . . .
>
> 'Submission, self-denial, diligent work, are the preparations for a life begun with such a shadow on it. You are different from other children, Esther, because you were not born, like them, in common sinfulness and wrath. You are set apart.' (pp. 17–18)

Miss Barbary's injunction to Esther is to pray that the sins of others be not visited on her head; her words make manifest how they are. The novel as a whole, however, suggests (with firm moral unconventionality) that Lady Dedlock's sin is not what her sister takes it to be;[1] the novel suggests, that is, that her 'sin' is not illicit love but a loveless marriage, not the bearing of an illegitimate child but the failure to live up to the love that brought the child into being. And the consequence of this failure is the blighting of the life of the child, the life that is 'begun with such a shadow on it', the child who from birth is 'set apart'; for Lady Dedlock is not exonerated by her ignorance of the child's fate—she knowingly abandoned its father and is responsible both for that betrayal and its effects.

It is, indeed, in the twice-enacted blighting of Esther's life that Lady Dedlock's past and Jarndyce and Jarndyce are most conspicuously connected. Her life blighted in infancy, the innocent victim of her mother's abandonment of her father, Esther survives to win happiness at Bleak House only to be struck down in young womanhood, the innocent victim of society's abandonment of Jo. In both cases, moreover, the complex of reasons that underlies the abandonment is not dissimilar. That we are meant to make this connection is confirmed, I think, by the way in which Dickens suggests that Jo's infection may

---

[1] Nor what a modern critic takes it to be either: Robert Garis considers Dickens's treatment of Lady Dedlock to be 'insufficient' and even 'rather offensive', but he regards her sin as that of 'the woman taken in adultery'. See *The Dickens Theatre: A Reassessment of the Novels* (Oxford, 1965), pp. 138–40.

be traced to two possible sources. It might well seem, as I have pre-viously indicated, that it is the corrupted blood of Tom-all-Alone's that infects Jo (and so infects Esther); it is made just as likely that he contracts the disease when he visits the churchyard in which Esther's father is buried: the churchyard is 'pestiferous and obscene', and com-municates 'malignant diseases . . . to the bodies of our dear brothers and sisters who have not departed'; when Hawdon is lowered down 'a foot or two', he is sown 'in corruption' only 'to be raised in corrup-tion'; the 'poisoned air deposits its witch-ointment slimy to the touch' on the iron gate of the churchyard (p. 151). When Jo takes the dis-guised Lady Dedlock to the churchyard, he excitedly watches the progress of a rat among the graves, while she 'shrinks . . . into a corner of [the] hideous archway, with its deadly stains contaminating her dress' (p. 225).[1] If Dickens is thus at some pains to make it an open question as to where Jo is infected, the uncertainty suggests it is the same blight, ultimately, of which Esther is the victim.

Esther, that is to say, is a victim of the corruption of both her mother and the society in which she lives; and with this kind of relation established, Lady Dedlock's fate—like that of Krook—is seen to have wider implications. Lady Dedlock, in the full maturity of experience, is forced to make a crucial choice when she discovers that Esther is her daughter, when she discovers, so to speak, that the world of fashion is more closely related than she has suspected to the larger worlds it habitually ignores. The alternatives she faces, it might seem, are either to accept the relation fully or to deny it. In the event, she temporizes and does neither. She reveals herself to Esther, but insists that the relation be kept secret, and that thenceforth they neither associate nor communicate (p. 510). She insists on the secrecy, she says, for the sake of both Sir Leicester and Esther herself, but this clearly is a rationalization; for Sir Leicester, it is later shown, needs no protecting, and Esther has no personal interest in keeping the secret. Lady Dedlock simply cannot face up to taking responsibility for the relation, cannot contemplate bearing the disgrace which she imagines the admission of her past conduct will entail. She parts from Esther to return, as she says, to 'the dark road' of her choice: 'The dark road I have trodden for so many years will end where it will. I follow it alone to the end,

[1] Mark Spilka takes the same view. He says Jo's illness 'might stem as much from the grave as from the slum'. *Dickens and Kafka*, p. 214. J. Hillis Miller seems to think there is no doubt that Jo contracts the disease in the churchyard, but allows for its origin in the slum. He talks of the disease 'which is bred in the "poisoned air" . . . of Tom-all-Alone's, and spreads from Nemo's graveyard to Jo the crossing sweeper . . .' *Charles Dickens*, p. 209.

whatever the end be. It may be near, it may be distant; while the road lasts, nothing turns me' (p. 511). The dark road is the road of continued evasion, of continued fencing with Tulkinghorn, the road of her final flight and the last evasive tactic of the exchange of clothes with the brickmaker's wife. But Lady Dedlock's choice of this road means, in the end, that she is driven to her death, for she is utterly worn out by her flight; and twist though it may, the road leads her back to the pestiferous churchyard in which Hawdon is buried, leads her back, that is, to an admission of the relation she has so long denied; leads her, if only in death, to a true identity, for Esther, seeing before her a woman dressed in Jenny's clothes, sees 'the mother of the dead child' (p. 811).

VI

How radical, then, is Dickens's attack on mid-Victorian England? Commenting on the symbolism of Krook's death, Edgar Johnson says 'the injustices of an unjust society' are no longer seen as 'subjects for local cure or even amputation': 'Nothing will do short of the complete annihilation that they will ultimately provide by blowing up of their own corruption';[1] while Monroe Engel (also in relation to Krook's '[dissolving] of spontaneous combustion') maintains that 'a kind of inevitable dissolution is the hope', though 'it is clear that Dickens has grave doubts that enough will happen by peaceful process'.[2] It seems to me, however, that at this stage of his career (and *Bleak House* should be regarded as his first major attempt to come to grips with the society in which he lived) Dickens was neither as radical nor as pessimistic as these pronouncements suggest. Though it is true that the novel presents an image of possible social collapse—presenting it not alone through the death of Krook but through the equally representative deaths of Richard and Lady Dedlock and through the pervasive disease imagery—the collapse is neither prescribed nor hoped for. It is presented as a warning, a prophetic warning of what will inevitably come to pass if a stiff-necked people refuses to change its ways. But the way to change, to peaceful recuperation, as it were, is throughout presented as both clear and accessible.

Since the two major factors in the diagnosis of what has caused the

[1] *Charles Dickens*, II, 782.
[2] *The Maturity of Dickens* (Cambridge, Massachusetts, 1959), p. 122.

corruption of Tom's blood are shown to be parasitism and the evasion of responsibility by properly constituted authority, it would seem to follow that all that is required in such a society is a readiness to make one's own way and to accept responsibility. Such, at any rate, is the cure apparently propounded in *Bleak House*. Anticipating Samuel Smiles, Dickens sets against the horde of parasites, as George H. Ford has pointed out,[1] some representative exemplars of self-help: the young Turveydrop, Rouncewell the ironmaster, Allan Woodcourt, and of course Esther Summerson. And against widespread dereliction he places the ubiquitous benevolence of Mr. Jarndyce. Since these characters epitomize qualities that Dickens may be taken to recommend, it is a drawback that they are not presented with greater imaginative vitality; Woodcourt, for instance, remaining pale for all his goodness, and the more robust presence of Mr. Jarndyce being a little too benign for ordinary flesh and blood. It is a further drawback that goodness should sometimes appear as the mask of the prig, as all too often in the case of Esther, or of smugness, as in the case of Rouncewell. Dickens, it seems, like so many artists, is more at home in the mud and mire and fog than in the pure empyrean. Nevertheless, the virtue of these characters, especially that of Mr. Jarndyce and Esther, has an important function in the novel.

Mr. Jarndyce is viewed as a kind of natural guardian (as other men are natural athletes), and he is called Guardian not alone by Esther but also by Ada (after Richard's death and at his insistence) and by Esther's children, who 'know him by no other name' (p. 877). He is viewed, that is, as performing functions on a personal level that are supposedly fulfilled by institutions (such as Chancery and Parliament) on a national level. Characteristically, he takes responsibility for all the weak and the needy with whom he comes in contact, though the typical object of his attentions (the symbolic object) is the orphan. Thus it is that he successively takes responsibility for Esther, for Ada and Richard, for Charley and Coavinses' other children, and for Jo. And he does so, of course, without in any way neglecting other responsibilities, being strongly differentiated from Mrs. Jellyby, whose assumption of responsibility in regard to the families of those who are to cultivate coffee and educate the natives of Borrioboola-Gha covers a multitude of evasions in regard to her own family; and from Mrs. Pardiggle, who arms herself with uplifting tracts and '[pounces] upon

---

[1] 'Self-Help and the Helpless in *Bleak House*', *From Jane Austen to Joseph Conrad*, ed. Robert C. Rathburn and Martin Steinmann (Minneapolis, 1958), pp. 97–100.

the poor . . . applying benevolence to them like a strait-waistcoat' (p. 423) while their children (as in the case of Jenny's baby) die round her; and he is equally differentiated from Harold Skimpole, who is only 'a mere child in the world'.

Mr. Jarndyce, moreover, typically helps those in need by enabling them to help themselves. 'Trust in nothing but in Providence and your own efforts,' he tells Richard (p. 180); and it is in this spirit that he providentially offers his services to others—as in the case of Esther, the representative instance. He is no sooner aware of the predicament of the unknown orphan than he willingly assumes responsibility for her, but with the 'expectation' that Conversation Kenge (inimitably) details:

> 'Mr. Jarndyce,' he pursued, 'being aware of the—I would say, desolate—position of our young friend, offers to place her at a first-rate establishment; where her education shall be completed, where her comfort shall be secured, where her reasonable wants shall be anticipated, where she shall be eminently qualified to discharge her duty in that station of life unto which it has pleased—shall I say Providence?—to call her.' . . .
>
> 'Mr. Jarndyce,' he went on, 'makes no condition, beyond expressing his expectation that our young friend will not at any time remove herself from the establishment in question without his knowledge and concurrence. That she will faithfully apply herself to the acquisition of those accomplishments, upon the exercise of which she will be ultimately dependent. That she will tread in the paths of virtue and honour, and—the—a—so forth.' (pp. 21–2)

What Mr. Jarndyce requires of Esther, we see, is quite simply that she keep faith with him, the expectation (and demonstration) of fidelity being as much a concomitant of the assumption of responsibility as betrayal is shown to be a consequence of its evasion. Having kept faith, Esther is rewarded not only by being given the chance to stand on her own feet but by being delegated her own area of responsibility: on becoming housekeeper at Bleak House, she stands looking at the basket of keys—the keys of office, as it were—with which she has been presented, 'quite lost in the magnitude of [her] trust' (p. 68).

Esther consolidates her position at Bleak House, becoming, as Skimpole puts it, 'the very touchstone of responsibility':

'Now when you mention responsibility,' he resumed, 'I am disposed to say, that I never had the happiness of knowing any one whom I should consider so refreshingly responsible as yourself. You appear to me to be the very touchstone of responsibility. When I see you, my dear Miss Summerson, intent upon the perfect working of the whole little orderly system of which you are the centre, I feel inclined to say to myself—in fact I do say to myself, very often—*that's* responsibility!' (p. 531)

Skimpole's evasive pleasantry should not be taken to invalidate the truth of his description of Esther's position. His account of her achievement, indeed, suggests how central (from yet another point of view) Esther's role in the novel is. If her success at Bleak House (a success which is capped, if not crowned, by Mr. Jarndyce's proposal of marriage to her) sets her as far apart as her social class from Jo, the abandoned orphan of the slums who is lower than a drover's dog; we cannot help reflecting that it is to Tom-all-Alone's—or thereabouts—that she would certainly have gone on the death of Miss Barbary if not for the grace of Mr. Jarndyce. Esther's success (with Mr. Jarndyce's aid), that is, is meant to be representative of what can be done through a combination of effort and due assumption of responsibility. Moreover, having achieved 'the perfect working of the whole little orderly system' of which she is the centre, and having achieved it through assuming responsibility in her turn, Esther also in effect demonstrates what is required for the efficient running of the 'great country' and the 'great system' of which Conversation Kenge boasts to Mr. Jarndyce, and of which Parliament and Chancery are the centres. Dickens, in other words, far from being a revolutionary, is calling in *Bleak House* for nothing more subversive than a change of housekeepers.

It is now clear, I think, why Dickens hesitated between a variant of Tom-all-Alone's and of Bleak House in choosing his title. Ruin and perfect system, disease and health—the question is which shall be bequeathed to the children of England. The choice of Bleak House as the title, the name of the house redeemed by Mr. Jarndyce from the ravages of Chancery, must be taken to point to the author's faith in the possibility of renovation, to his hope that a Jo, having made his way from Tom-all-Alone's to Bleak House, will find his permanent home there. Such a hope, of course, ignores the presence—even in a Bleak House—of a Skimpole. The Skimpoles remain impervious even to a Jarndyce; they are not willing to keep faith. It is only when Dickens perceives the limitations of Mr. Jarndyce's position, perceives the limits of his redemptive capacity, that he begins to think in terms of transformation rather than rehabilitation. In the closing pages of the novel we are given some idea of the kind of transformation he will steadily come to evisage: Esther reports that, despite the loss of her 'old looks', her husband thinks she is 'prettier' than she ever was (p. 880). If it is Mr. Jarndyce's benevolence that counteracts the blight of her childhood, it is Woodcourt's love, we see, that transforms the blight of Chancery.

6

LITTLE DORRIT

I

Dickens's comments on his own work (like those of Conrad after him) are, for the most part, not particularly interesting, being expressive, if anything, of the limitations of his critical intelligence when it is not a function of his creative imagination—as it so effectively is in the work itself. In the case of *Little Dorrit*, however, some remarks of Dickens concerning his intentions and procedure are immediately provocative. I quote the following three comments in the order in which they were made as he worked at the novel:

> I am in the first stage of a new book, which consists in going round and round the idea, as you see a bird in his cage go about and about his sugar before he touches it.[1]
>
> I had the general idea of the Society business before the Sadleir affair, but I shaped Mr. Merdle himself out of that precious rascality. Society, the Circumlocution Office, and Mr. Gowan, are of course three parts of one idea and design. . . .[2]
>
> I don't see the practicability of making the History of a Self-Tormentor, with which I took great pains, a written narrative. But I do see the possibility of making it a chapter by itself, which might enable me to dispense with the necessity of the turned commas. Do you think that would be better? I have no doubt that a great part of Fielding's reason for the introduced story,

[1] Letter to Captain Morgan, conjectured date November 1855, *Letters*, ed. Walter Dexter, II, 712. John Butt and Kathleen Tillotson date the letter March 1855 (*Dickens at Work*, p. 228). *Little Dorrit* was begun in May 1855, and published in monthly parts between December 1855 and June 1857.
[2] Letter to John Forster, conjectured date April 1856, *ibid.*, 766.

and Smollett's also, was, that it is sometimes really impossible to present, in a full book, the idea it contains (which yet it may be on all accounts desirable to present), without supposing the reader to be possessed of almost as much romantic allowance as would put him on a level with the writer. In Miss Wade I had an idea, which I thought a new one, of making the introduced story so fit into surroundings impossible of separation from the main story, as to make the blood of the book circulate through both. But I can only suppose, from what you say, that I have not exactly succeeded in this. . . .[1]

The image of the bird is not only evocative of the novelist's preliminary explorations of his subject but of his procedure in the actual writing of the novel, and it provides us with a conception of its structure. The 'one idea' of the novel, the heart of the matter, as it were, is to be seen as at the centre of a circular design; and 'the blood of the book' is pumped round and round the idea in a series of concentric circles. Correspondingly, at any point on the circumference of any of the circles there is a direct link with the centre. It is this, I think, that accounts for Dickens's talking—with such apparent oddity—of 'Society, the Circumlocution Office, and Mr. Gowan' in one breath; and it is this that also accounts for the centrality of Miss Wade, who, like Gowan, is a comparatively minor character. We are certainly challenged, at any rate, to incorporate both Gowan and Miss Wade in an analysis of the 'one idea and design' of *Little Dorrit*.[2]

We are also challenged to relate the pervasive use of the prison symbol to that idea and design, and to grant the symbol the kind of particularity it fails to receive in formulations such as this: 'The Marshalsea is more than a prison; it is a microcosm of the world. . . .

[1] Letter to John Forster, conjectured date 1856 (letter placed before June letters), *ibid.*, p. 776.

[2] There is an interesting link between Dickens's comments on the design of *Little Dorrit* and his view of the pattern of *Dombey and Son*. In the earlier novel, it will be recalled, Dickens implies that the structure of *Dombey and Son* is that of a 'round world of many circles within circles', and he elaborates the point with an image of weaving (see Ch. IV, p. 117 above); it is perhaps not without significance that the weaving image should be repeated in the opening paragraph of the Preface to the 1857 edition of *Little Dorrit*: 'I have been occupied with this story, during many working hours of two years. I must have been very ill employed, if I could not leave its merits and demerits as a whole, to express themselves on its being read as a whole. But, as it is not unreasonable to suppose that I may have held its threads with a more continuous attention than anyone else can have given them during its desultory publication, it is not unreasonable to ask that the weaving may be looked at in its completed state, and with the pattern finished.' The 1857 Preface is used in the Penguin English Library edition of the novel, ed. John Holloway.

We are shown the prison of poverty in Bleeding Heart Yard, the prison of administration in the Circumlocution Office, the prison of heredity and temperament in Mrs. Clennam and Miss Wade. . . .'[1] The kind of particularity with which symbolic meanings are established is perhaps nowhere better shown than in a description of London which is as central to the world of Little Dorrit as that of the city in fog and mud is to *Bleak House*:

It was a Sunday evening in London, gloomy, close and stale. Maddening church bells of all degrees of dissonance, sharp and flat, cracked and clear, fast and slow, made the brick-and-mortar echoes hideous. Melancholy streets in a penitential garb of soot, steeped the souls of the people who were condemned to look at them out of windows, in dire despondency. In every thoroughfare, up almost every alley, and down almost every turning, some doleful bell was throbbing, jerking, tolling, as if the Plague were in the city and the deadcarts were going round. Everything was bolted and barred that could by possibility furnish relief to an overworked people. No pictures, no unfamiliar animals, no rare plants or flowers, no natural or artificial wonders of the ancient world—all *taboo* with that enlightened strictness, that the ugly South Sea gods in the British Museum might have supposed themselves at home again. Nothing to see but streets, streets, streets. Nothing to breathe but streets, streets, streets. Nothing to change the brooding mind, or raise it up. Nothing for the spent toiler to do, but to compare the monotony of his seventh day with the monotony of his six days, think what a weary life he led, and make the best of it—or the worst, according to the probabilities.

. . . Fifty thousand lairs surrounded [Arthur Clennam] where people lived so unwholesomely, that fair water put into their crowded rooms on Saturday night, would be corrupt on Sunday morning; albeit my lord, their county member, was amazed that

---

[1] John Butt and Kathleen Tillotson, *Dickens at Work*, p. 233. The tendency in recent criticism has been to an increasing vagueness of interpretation, even as sensitive a critic as J. Hillis Miller making the prison symbol all things to all characters; he cites the following examples of 'forms of [spiritual] imprisonment' in the novel: '. . . Blandois' wicked imprisonment in his idea of himself as a gentleman "by right and by nature" (I, 30); John Chivery's constant anticipation of his own death . . .; Pancks' slavery to his master, Casby . . .; Mrs. Merdle's servitude to society; the sprightly Ferdinand Barnacle's willing acquiescence in the sham of the Circumlocution Office; Little Dorrit's brother's corruption by the prison atmosphere . . .' *Charles Dickens*, pp. 230–1.

they failed to sleep in company with their butcher's meat. Miles
of close wells and pits of houses, where the inhabitants gasped
for air, stretched far away towards every point of the compass
Through the heart of the town a deadly sewer ebbed and flowed,
in the place of a fine fresh river. What secular want could the
million or so of human beings whose daily labour, six days in the
week, lay among these Arcadian objects, from the sweet same-
ness of which they had no escape between the cradle and the
grave—what secular want could they possibly have upon their
seventh day? Clearly they could want nothing but a stringent
policeman. (pp. 28–9)

As J. Hillis Miller has pointed out,[1] the imagery of this passage makes
it clear that we are intended to view London itself as a huge prison
what require consideration are the symbolic overtones of this implied
metaphor. First, if sabbath restrictions are the immediate cause of the
'bolting and barring' of the city, the 'penitential garb of soot' that the
streets habitually wear reminds us that it is to life in an industrial
civilization, and not merely to a dull Sunday, that the inhabitants of
the city are 'condemned'. They are condemned, moreover, to a civilization that is undermined by its own taboos, for these impart a primitive
retrogressive quality to the life in which 'the ugly South Sea gods in
the British Museum' may suppose themselves 'at home again'. The
ugly gods, indeed, are the same kind of portent as the Megalosaurus of
Bleak House, and it is appropriate that Clennam, in the coffee-house
on Ludgate Hill, should be surrounded by fifty thousand 'lairs'
Second, the prison-like city is not unexpectedly a place of widespread
corruption: on the particular Sunday described, the bells seem to be
tolling the ravages of the Plague, and it is as if 'the deadcarts were
going round'; every evening and every day 'a deadly sewer' ebbs and
flows 'through the heart of the town', and water put into crowded
rooms would overnight be 'corrupt'. Like the prison in Marseilles
London, it seems, has a 'polluted atmosphere' (p. 3). Third, in this
city, which recalls the chartered streets of Blake's London, there is
'nothing to see but streets, streets, streets'; there is 'nothing to breathe
but streets, streets, streets'. In other words, in this city from which
there is 'no escape' life is not only an endless round; it is barred. The con
sequence of this arrested motion is stagnation. Life is subject to all that
is 'gloomy, close and stale', to all that is a denial of freshness and growth

[1] *Ibid.*, p. 227.

Mr. Arthur Clennam took up his hat and buttoned his coat, and walked out. In the country, the rain would have developed a thousand fresh scents, and every drop would have had its bright association with some beautiful form of growth or life. In the city, it developed only foul stale smells, and was a sickly, lukewarm, dirt-stained, wretched addition to the gutters. (pp. 30–1)

It is no coincidence that this note should also be sounded in the description of Marseilles with which the book begins, for this description is merely a prelude to that of life in its 'villainous prison': there is no wind, we are told, 'to make a ripple on the foul water within the harbour' of Marseilles; the harbour is an 'abominable pool' (p. 1). And this note is sounded insistently in descriptions of the two actual prisons with which the book deals:

A prison taint was on everything [in the Marseilles prison]. The imprisoned air, the imprisoned light, the imprisoned damps, the imprisoned men, were all deteriorated by confinement. As the captive men were faded and haggard, so the iron was rusty, the stone was slimy, the wood was rotten, the air was faint, the light was dim.... (p. 3)

Changeless and barren, looking ignorantly at all the seasons with its fixed, pinched face of poverty and care, the [Marshalsea] had not a touch of any of [the beauties of autumn] on it. Blossom what would, its bricks and bars bore uniformly the same dead crop. (p. 815)

I would suggest, then, that though the prison imagery of the novel accumulates a rich complexity of meaning, as I shall try to demonstrate, its primary significance is to make us realize that England itself is subject to a state of arrest, to a paralysing stagnation. This, in its simplest form, is the 'one idea' at the heart of the book. Certainly Dickens himself, in the period in which he described himself as going round and round his subject like a bird in its cage—the period of the Crimean War—repeatedly used an image of paralysis to convey his sense of England's affliction:

We know what a sight it would be to behold that miserable patient, Mr. Cabinet, specially calling his relations and friends together before Christmas, tottering on his emaciated legs in the last stage of paralysis, and feebly piping that if such and such powers were not entrusted to him for instant use, he would certainly go raving mad of defeated patriotism, and pluck his poor old wretched eyes out in despair . . .[1]

But you can no more help a people who do not help themselves, than you can help a man who does not help himself. And until the people can be got up from the lethargy which is an awful symptom of the advanced state of their disease, I know of nothing that can be done beyond keeping their wrongs continually before them.[2]

The bitter drug called Public Offices, formed the next subject of inquiry. . . . Analysis had detected in every [sample] from seventy-five to ninety-eight per cent of Noodledom. Noodledom was a deadly poison. . . . It was sometimes called Routine, sometimes Gentlemanly Business, sometimes The Best Intentions, and sometimes Amiable Incapacity . . . Thus, many of the samples before the Commission, positively contained nothing but Noodledom—enough, in short, to paralyze the whole country. . . .[3]

Some support for this explanation of the principal significance of the prison symbol is provided by the narrative itself, by our sense of its unusual movement. John Wain has called *Little Dorrit* Dickens's 'most stationary novel', pointing out that 'for all the scurry of event on its surface, it never for a moment suggests genuine movement'.[4] This is attributable to the fact that the movement is always from one prison to another. In Book I the narrative opens in the prison in Marseilles; it moves to the travellers, but they are '[shut] . . . up in quarantine' and Mr. Meagles refers to them as 'jail-birds' (pp. 15, 16); from Marseilles it moves to London, which (as we have seen) is described as a huge prison; in London, whenever it moves from the Marshalsea, we find ourselves in various metaphorical prisons. In Book II the narrative opens in the convent of the Great Saint Bernard, but to Little Dorrit it seems 'something like a prison' (p. 442); it moves to Italy,

[1] 'That Other Public', *Household Words*, II (3 February 1855), 3. The article is attributed to Dickens by Frederic G. Kitton, *The Minor Writings*, p. 125.

[2] Letter to Austen Henry Layard, 10. 4. 1855, *Letters*, ed. Walter Dexter, II, 652.

[3] 'Our Commission', *Household Words*, 12 (11 August 1855), 25–6. The article is attributed to Dickens by Kitton, p. 126.

[4] '*Little Dorrit*', *Dickens and the Twentieth Century*, ed. John Gross and Gabriel Pearson, p. 175.

the 'rugged mountain-chasm' widening and seeming to let the travellers out 'from a gloomy and dark imprisonment' (p. 464), but in Venice the Gowan residence is above a suite of rooms which has the appearance of 'a jail for criminal rats' (p. 491), while the 'waifs of seaweed' which cling to the walls of the Dorrit house in the same city seem to be weeping for 'their imprisoned relations' (p. 499); it moves from Italy back to the prison of London and then to Calais, where Clennam is strongly reminded of the Marshalsea (p. 654); it returns inexorably to the Marshalsea, and, in the end, the sun's rays are seen as the 'bars of the prison of this lower world' (p. 763). The overall impression of the development of the narrative, then, is of a movement that is constantly checked, of flight that is frustrated—in a word, of arrest.

That government business should have come to a stop, that there should be a state of arrest on a national scale, is directly attributed to the ministrations of the Circumlocution Office:

> The Circumlocution Office was (as everybody knows without being told) the most important Department under Government. No public business of any kind could possibly be done at any time, without the acquiescence of the Circumlocution Office. Its finger was in the largest public pie, and in the smallest public tart. It was equally impossible to do the plainest right and to undo the plainest wrong, without the express authority of the Circumlocution Office. . . .
>
> This glorious establishment had been early in the field, when the one sublime principle involving the difficult art of governing a country, was first distinctly revealed to statesmen. It had been foremost to study that bright revelation, and to carry its shining influence through the whole of the official proceedings. Whatever was required to be done, the Circumlocution Office was beforehand with all the public departments in the art of perceiving —HOW NOT TO DO IT.
>
> Through this delicate perception, through the tact with which it invariably seized it, and through the genius with which it always acted on it, the Circumlocution Office had risen to overtop all the public departments; and the public condition had risen to be—what it was. (p. 104)

The Circumlocution Office, it is clear, should not be viewed merely as 'the most important Department under Government', as the paradigm of all such departments, the thing itself; it is the representative institution of the society depicted in *Little Dorrit*. Its 'acquiescence' being required for all 'public business', its procedures (like those of the Court of Chancery in *Bleak House*) are representative of the functioning of a whole society. What needs to be insisted on first, then, is that the depiction of its procedures, of the application of the 'sublime principle' of How Not To Do It, is not as exaggerated as might casually be supposed. The Kafkaesque adventures of Clennam and Doyce in their dealings with the authorities are no doubt related in terms of broad satire, but given the administrative muddle and incompetence in matters connected with the prosecution of the Crimean War, Dickens's indictment of the office and all its works is, as Humphry House has said, 'substantially fair'.[1] It is also strikingly evocative of the 'public condition' to which the office is said to have given rise. The name of the office suggests not only the evasiveness of its techniques but the endless round to which its petitioners are condemned, like the unchanging streets in which Londoners are imprisoned; in its careful failure to do 'whatever [is] required to be done', it is the very model of paralysis. Indeed, it is characteristic of Dickens's imagination that a circumlocutionary incumbent should be envisaged as being physically 'stuck', as having lost the capacity for free movement and action: the eminent Mr. Tite Barnacle is confined to his home with a touch of the gout, and Clennam first sees him 'with his leg on a rest,' 'an express image and presentment of How not to do it' (p. 111). Conversely, effective purposiveness is suggested by the image of a man on his legs: Mr. Meagles assures Clennam that Doyce has 'fallen on his legs' out of England. 'Where they don't want things done and find a man to do 'em,' he says, 'that man's off his legs; but where they do want things done and find a man to do 'em, that man's on his legs' (p. 822).

---

[1] *The Dickens World*, p. 187. The judgement of a modern historian, though critical of Dickens, is in the end not dissimilar: 'In the winter of 1854–55 British administration contrived through sheer incompetence to let a magnificent army freeze and rot to death in the trenches before Sebastopol only nine miles from its base, and in 1856 in *Little Dorrit* Dickens wrote his bitter and brilliant chapter on the Circumlocution Office and the great family of the Tite Barnacles. Dickens was not being quite just, he only knew the office from the outside. It was not the aristocratic principle alone that had raised the Circumlocution Office in all its deadly perversity, it was partly the stringency of the rules of accounting imposed by the House of Commons for economy, and the general tendency of any large administrative system to strangle itself . . . If Dickens' attack was not sufficiently discriminating it would be difficult to say that his anger was not well deserved.' G. Kitson Clark, *The Making of Victorian England* (London, 1965; first published 1962), pp. 220–1.

Clennam is directed from the Circumlocution Office to Mr. Tite Barnacle's home by the latter's son, Barnacle Junior, and it soon becomes apparent that Britannia has been knocked off her feet by the sheer weight of Barnacles clinging to her. The Barnacles are a 'very high and very large family', and wherever there is 'a square yard of ground in British occupation under the sun or moon, with a public post upon it, sticking to that post [is] a Barnacle'. Barnacles have thus been sent 'all over the world' by the Circumlocution Office, 'despatch-boxing the compass' and sedulously snatching at 'anything to be pocketed' (p. 400). In other words, if in *Bleak House* politics is presented as the art of providing for Noodle, in *Little Dorrit* government is shown to be the science of preserving the Barnacles and their connections:

> It was agreed that the country (another word for the Barnacles and Stiltstalkings) wanted preserving, but how it came to want preserving was not so clear. It was only clear that the question was all about John Barnacle, Augustus Stiltstalking, William Barnacle and Tudor Stiltstalking, Tom, Dick, or Harry Barnacle or Stiltstalking, because there was nobody else but mob. (p. 314)

The parasitism and the evasion of responsibility by authority that are analysed in *Bleak House* are here shown to be the concomitant of a vast system of patronage.[1] And, shifting his ground somewhat, it is on the patronage that Dickens now concentrates. The patronage dispensed and graciously accepted by those 'more flush of blood than money' (p. 107) is seen to be the cause of the national inertia, it being the natural attribute of a Barnacle to stick, and no more. Spreading out from that sticky centre and deriving from it, bearing down on circle after circle of a whole society and inducing diverse manifestations of arrest, there go those made in the image of the Barnacles if not quite flesh of their flesh. It is the patrons, as we shall see, that fashion the prisons of *Little Dorrit*.

Patronage, moreover, is only one step from jobbery; and in this more delicate practice the circumlocutionary Barnacles are joined by

---

[1] Humphry House, citing John Morley, refers to a private memorandum found among Gladstone's papers which indicates that Dickens was not exaggerating the extent of the patronage in the society of his day. In this memorandum a 'leading reformer' asserted that *the old-established political families habitually batten on the public patronage*—their sons legitimate and illegitimate, their relatives and dependents of every degree, are provided for by the score'. *The Dickens World*, p. 188.

their parliamentary connections. The latter have long since introduced the 'sublime principle' of the Office into parliament. There is, for instance, the great Lord Decimus Tite Barnacle. Lord Decimus has 'risen to official heights' through the discovery of his 'Behoving Machine' which is 'the discovery of the political perpetual motion': he has discovered, that is, that it behoves a minister of a 'free country' not to interfere with the liberties of the subject; that it behoves him, that is, to do nothing but feather his own nest. He is supported by William Barnacle, who defends the House from being 'precipitated' into any course of action for which there is no 'precedent' (p. 405). The Barnacles, in other words, effectively bring about a parliamentary stoppage, the 'political perpetual motion' which gets nowhere being designed to bring any member trying to do something to a standstill, and the refusal to be precipitated ensuring immovability. Lord Decimus, however, is not averse to moving in the direction of Mr. Merdle. It having been intimated to that merchant by his wife that it is 'time to provide for Edmund Sparkler', Merdle enters into 'some delicate little negotiations' with Lord Decimus, a young Barnacle acting as intermediary. The result of these negotiations is that Merdle decides 'to cast the weight of his great probity and great riches into the Barnacle scale'. A further result is that Sparkler is made 'one of the Lords of the Circumlocution Office', it being proclaimed 'to all true believers' (with meticulous regard for appearances) that this 'admirable appointment' is to be 'hailed as a graceful and gracious mark of homage, rendered by the graceful and gracious Decimus, to that commercial interest which must ever in a great commercial country—and all the rest of it, with blast of trumpet' (pp. 557–8, 570).

The paralysis of the great commercial country, we see, is associated not only with a parasitic system of patronage but with jobbery and deception and false appearance. The paralysis is attributable, in a word, to an inner corruption. It is this cluster of ideas, I believe, that is at the centre of the design of the novel. But the novel, of course, is not concerned merely with the machinery of state. Dickens uses his analogical method to offer us a comprehensive analysis of the life of the country as it reveals itself not only in its government but in its social relations, in its high finance, in its religion, in its art, and in its love and sex. If *Little Dorrit* is inferior in power and liveliness to *Bleak House*, it is certainly a more ambitious undertaking. It is also inexorable in its analogical design. No matter where we move, we always encounter the same cluster of ideas and the same dominant image, though both are richly varied in their presentation. Pumped from that centre, the blood of the book indeed circulates through every part of it.

Even the plot, the much-maligned, melodramatic plot,[1] is tethered to that centre and (like that of *Bleak House*) has its own symbolic dimension. Its significance is best approached by way of yet another description of the city:

> As [Clennam] went along, upon a dreary night, the dim streets by which he went, seemed all depositories of oppressive secrets. The deserted counting-houses, with their secrets of books and papers locked up in chests and safes; the banking-houses, with their secrets of strong rooms and wells, the keys of which were in a very few secret pockets and a very few secret breasts; the secrets of all the dispersed grinders in the vast mill, among whom there were doubtless plunderers, forgers, and trust-betrayers of many sorts, whom the light of any day that dawned might reveal; he could have fancied that these things, in hiding, imparted a heaviness to the air. The shadow thickening and thickening as he approached its source, he thought of the secrets of the lonely church-vaults, where the people who had hoarded and secreted in iron coffers were in their turn similarly hoarded, not yet at rest from doing harm; and then of the secrets of the river, as it rolled its turbid tide between two frowning wildernesses of secrets, extending, thick and dense, for many miles, and warding off the free air and the free country swept by winds and wings of birds. (p. 542)

If the reference to the 'grinders in the vast mill' reminds us that this is the same city as that in which streets wear a garb of soot; and if the city's 'warding off' of 'the free air' and 'the free country' make it recognizably the same stagnant, prison-like place that Clennam broods over on that gloomy Sunday; its essential character is here given a different emphasis. It is above all a city of secrets, a general repository of secrets—a great lock-up, as it were. And secrets are precisely what the plot turns on, especially the two central secrets of Mr. Merdle and Mrs. Clennam. Those parts of the plot that are directly concerned with Mrs. Clennam's secret, particularly the climactic scenes in which

---

[1] John Wain, for instance, calls the plot 'tedious and artificial to a degree rarely found even in Dickens'. '*Little Dorrit*', *loc. cit.*, p. 175.

it is revealed, are no doubt crudely melodramatic, but the plot as a whole—that 'depository of oppressive secrets'—figures the deception and venality that have turned London into a prison.

II

Society (with a capital S) is in *Little Dorrit* a many-headed monster, but its main features are adequately suggested by those of three representative ladies: Mrs. Merdle, Mrs. Gowan and Mrs. General. Mrs. Merdle, indeed, is 'a Priestess of Society' (p. 394), and she jealously guards the portals of the Temple:

'There is very little to tell,' said Mrs. Merdle [to Little Dorrit], reviewing the breadth of bosom which seemed essential to her having room enough to be unfeeling in, 'but it is to your sister's credit. I pointed out to your sister the plain state of the case; the impossibility of the Society in which we moved recognising the Society in which she moved—though charming, I have no doubt; the immense disadvantage at which she would consequently place the family she had so high an opinion of, upon which we should find ourselves compelled to look down with contempt, and from which (socially speaking) we should feel obliged to recoil with abhorrence. In short, I made an appeal to that laudable pride in your sister.'

'Let my sister know, if you please, Mrs. Merdle,' Fanny pouted, with a toss of her gauzy bonnet, 'that I had already had the honour of telling your son that I wished to have nothing whatever to say to him.'

'Well, Miss Dorrit,' assented Mrs. Merdle, 'perhaps I might have mentioned that before. If I did not think of it, perhaps it was because my mind reverted to the apprehensions I had at the time, that he might persevere and you might have something to say to him. I also mentioned to your sister—I again address the non-professional Miss Dorrit—that my son would have nothing in the event of such a marriage, and would be an absolute beggar. (I mention that, merely as a fact which is part of the narrative, and not as supposing it to have influenced your sister, except in the prudent and legitimate way in which, constituted as our artificial system is, we must all be influenced by such considerations.) Finally, after some high words and high spirit on the part of your sister; we came to the complete understanding that there was no danger; and your sister was so obliging as to allow me to present her with a mark or two of my appreciation at my dressmaker's.'

Little Dorrit looked sorry, and glanced at Fanny with a troubled face.

'Also,' said Mrs. Merdle, 'as to promise to give me the present pleasure of a closing interview, and of parting with her on the best of terms. On which occasion,' added Mrs. Merdle, quitting her nest, and putting something in Fanny's hand, 'Miss Dorrit will permit me to say Farewell with best wishes, in my own dull manner.' (pp. 241–2)

We might be inclined, with numerous passages such as this, merely to record our admiration of their perfection of tone and to relax in their comedy, but we will usually find (as in the present instance) that they are thematically significant. Mrs. Merdle at once reveals, for example, that 'to move in Society' means to give up all freedom of movement: having been duly licensed herself ('Society was aware of Mr. and Mrs. Merdle. Society had said "Let us license them; let us know them"' (p. 246)), she is now 'compelled' to look down on such as the Dorrits and 'obliged' to recoil from them. In defence of her gentility, in other words, Mrs. Merdle is effectively brought to a stop by the barriers she raises to keep out those who do not belong. It is in pursuit of gentility, in pursuit, that is, of 'a gentlemanly residence' that is 'essential to the blood of the Barnacles', that Mr. Tite Barnacle, labouring under analogous compulsions, rents a 'fearful little' house, indeed a 'coop', at great expense because it is near Grosvenor Square (pp. 109–10). The absurdity of the formula to which Mrs. Merdle adheres in her dismissal of Fanny is exposed in the whirligig of time when the same lady is constrained to know (if not to 'recognise') the same Fanny, and ultimately to bless her as the choice of her shining son. The absurdity is imaged at the time by Mrs. Merdle's parrot, which is 'holding on by its beak' to 'the outside of a golden cage . . . with its scaly legs in the air, and putting itself into many strange upside-down postures. This peculiarity has been observed in birds of quite another feather, climbing upon golden wires' (p. 238). The image is effective not only because it vividly suggests the unbecoming position the social climber is reduced to taking up as he clings to his topsy-turvy world by his teeth, so to speak, but because it neatly implies his self-incarceration: when it could easily fly free, it is to the outside of its cage that the parrot so tenaciously clings.

While we grant, therefore, that Mrs. Merdle, 'in her nest of crimson and gold', may be taken for 'another splendid parrot of a larger species' (p. 390); we nevertheless note that she has an individual style. Characterising Fanny's submission to the 'influence' she has brought to bear on her as 'prudent and legitimate', Mrs. Merdle herself subscribes only to a doctrine of prudence—and so readily resorts to the kind of persuasion sanctioned by the 'artificial system' in which beggardom is a 'consideration' and 'appreciation' is shown at the dressmaker's. Moreover, she treats her visitors from the 'charming' though unknowable social reaches, 'the non-professional Miss Dorrit' equally with her dancing sister, with the kind of patronizing condescension that (among other things) fits her so eminently to be the spouse of 'the patron of patrons' (p. 710). Her patronage, indeed, seems to be infectious, for no sooner have the sisters left her than Fanny '[begins] to patronise' Amy, as she contrasts the latter's domesticity with her own excursions 'in Society' (p. 244).

Among the other things which fits Mrs. Merdle to be the spouse of Mr. Merdle is the 'breadth of bosom' which she is always 'reviewing', which seems essential 'to her having room enough to be unfeeling in', and which her husband bedecks with jewels. Mrs. Merdle *is* her bosom. Always moving in Society, always unmoved though flourished in demonstration of the capaciousness of her feeling, it is an emblem of the false front she continually presents to the world—and of the world which is Society.

An alternate emblem of that world is Mrs. Gowan's jobbed carriage:

> Among the friends of Mrs. Gowan (who piqued herself at once on being Society, and on maintaining intimate and easy relations with that Power), Mrs. Merdle occupied a front row. True, the Hampton Court Bohemians, without exception, turned up their noses at Merdle as an upstart; but they turned them down again, by falling flat on their faces to worship his wealth. In which compensating adjustment of their noses, they were pretty much like Treasury, Bar, and Bishop, and all the rest of them.

> To Mrs. Merdle, Mrs. Gowan repaired on a visit of self-

condolence, after having given the gracious consent aforesaid [i.e., to the marriage of her son to Pet Meagles]. She drove into town for the purpose, in a one-horse carriage, irreverently called at that period of English history, a pill-box. It belonged to a job-master in a small way, who drove it himself, and who jobbed it by the day, or hour, to most of the old ladies in Hampton Court Palace; but it was a point of ceremony, in that encampment, that the whole equipage should be tacitly regarded as the private property of the jobber for the time being, and that the job-master should betray personal knowledge of nobody but the jobber in possession. So, the Circumlocution Barnacles, who were the largest job-masters in the universe, always pretended to know of no other job but the job immediately in hand.

. . .

Now, Mrs. Merdle, who really knew her friend Society pretty well, and who knew what Society's mothers were, and what Society's daughters were, and what Society's matrimonial market was, and how prices ruled in it, and what scheming and counter-scheming took place for the high buyers, and what bargaining and huckstering went on, thought in the depths of her capacious bosom that [Pet Meagles] was a sufficiently good catch. Knowing, however, what was expected of her, and perceiving the exact nature of the fiction to be nursed, she took it delicately in her arms, and put her required contribution of gloss upon it.

. . .

And Mrs. Gowan, who of course saw through her own threadbare blind perfectly, and who knew that Mrs. Merdle saw through it perfectly, and who knew that Society would see through it perfectly, came out of this form, notwithstanding, as she had gone into it, with immense complacency and gravity. (pp. 390, 393, 394)

Imagery and pun function here to link realms in the world of the novel. If 'Society's matrimonial market' is an all too obvious counterpart of the market in which Mr. Merdle rather than his wife sets the tone, it is the 'worship' of Mr. Merdle's wealth that makes these realms kin. And Mrs. Gowan, who piques herself on 'being Society', the god incarnate to Mrs. Merdle's priestess, as it were, naturally venerates wealth. Not having as much of it as her friend, however, she is reduced (quite contentedly) to the Meagles's daughter for her son—and (not so contentedly) to the jobbed carriage for herself. Consequently she feels compelled to lament the one and disguise the other, for, like Mrs. Merdle, she knows Society 'pretty well' and knows what is 'expected' of her. Hence her 'visit of self-condolence' to Mrs. Merdle, her setting out—the very image of deception—in the carriage which is to be 'tacitly regarded' as her 'private property' in order to mourn the loss of her son. Deception being the life of Society, Mrs. Merdle (of the 'capacious bosom') in turn 'nurses the fiction', bringing it to greater warmth and delicacy than she ever displays to Edmund Sparkler. The jobbed carriage, in other words, is as apt an emblem of the deceptions by which Society lives as the Merdle bosom; and the Hampton Court job-master points to Mr. Merdle, the Stock Exchange job-master (and his deceptions) as well as to the Circumlocution Barnacles, 'the largest job-masters in the universe' (and their deceptions). Mrs. Gowan, moreover, is herself the recipient of a pension 'bestowed upon her by a grateful country (and a Barnacle)' (p. 389); and her ready acceptance of her country's bounty is matched by her easy patronage of her son's relations by marriage. Indeed, when the marriage has been safely consummated and her son provided for, she finds it 'impossible to know those people who [belong] to Henry's wife', and having broken with them, she gets into her jobbed carriage 'with distinguished serenity', and drives away (p. 525).

If Mrs. Merdle puts her 'required contribution of gloss' upon the fiction Mrs. Gowan wishes to be nursed, it is Mrs. General's 'province to varnish':

> Mrs. General had no opinions. Her way of forming a mind was to prevent it from forming opinions. She had a little circular set of mental grooves or rails on which she started little trains of other people's opinions, which never overtook one another, and never got anywhere. Even her propriety could not dispute that there was impropriety in the world; but Mrs. General's way of getting rid of it was to put it out of sight, and make believe that there was no such thing. This was another of her ways of forming a mind—to cram all articles of difficulty into cupboards, lock them up, and say they had no existence. It was the easiest way, and, beyond all comparison, the properest.
>
> Mrs. General was not to be told of anything shocking. Accidents, miseries, and offences, were never to be mentioned before

her. Passion was to go to sleep in the presence of Mrs. General, and blood was to change to milk and water. The little that was left in the world, when all these deductions were made, it was Mrs. General's province to varnish. In that formation process of hers, she dipped the smallest of brushes into the largest of pots, and varnished the surface of every object that came under consideration. The more cracked it was, the more Mrs. General varnished it. (pp. 450–1)

In the halls of Society Mrs. General appears at first simply as a mentor of the young, the instructor of unfamiliar novices in the intricacies of social ritual. The technique of her 'formation process', however, closely relates her to the distinguished Mrs. Merdle and Mrs. Gowan. The 'forming [of] a mind', under her capable, varnishing hands, becomes the formation of a surface, the acquisition of that polish with which Mrs. Merdle and Mrs. Gowan shine; and the varnishing of cracked objects becomes the sticking of a false front on to the whole universe. Mrs. General, indeed, in her capacity for glossing over the unpleasant is a precursor of the formidable Podsnap of *Our Mutual Friend*. In insisting that 'passion . . . go to sleep' in her presence, moreover, she prepares her charges for the matrimonial market that Mrs. Merdle and Mrs. Gowan manipulate so shrewdly—though she is not herself, in her own designs, above showing 'an air of as tender interest in Mr. Dorrit' as is 'consistent with rigid propriety'. (She improves the occasion by also showing 'much sweet patronage of manner towards Miss Dorrit' (p. 646).) Finally, it becomes clear that if Mrs. General has been engaged by the Dorrits (at her insistence) as 'a companion, protector, Mentor, and friend' (p. 449), she is in fact a Social jailer, it being her self-imposed task to 'lock up' and 'put out of sight' all that which might ruffle the smooth surface of Society. In preventing the minds under her care from 'forming opinions', furthermore, and in exposing them only to her own 'little circular set of mental grooves', on which she starts 'little trains of other people's opinions' which 'never [get] anywhere', she effectively assures their arrest.

To move, then, from Society to the Marshalsea is not to move very far. Indeed, in one of the early descriptions of life in the prison Dickens is at pains to suggest how small the move is:

And [Dorrit] grew to be proud of the title [i.e., the Father of the Marshalsea]. If any imposter had arisen to claim it, he would have shed tears in resentment of the attempt to deprive him of his rights. A disposition began to be perceived in him, to exaggerate the number of years he had been there; it was generally understood that you must deduct a few from his account; he was vain, the fleeting generations of debtors said.

All new-comers were presented to him. He was punctilious in the exaction of this ceremony. The wits would perform the office of introduction with overcharged pomp and politeness, but they could not easily overstep his sense of its gravity. He received them in his poor room (he disliked an introduction in the mere yard, as informal—a thing that might happen to anybody), with a kind of bowed-down beneficence. They were welcome to the Marshalsea, he would tell them. Yes, he was the Father of the place. So the world was kind enough to call him; and so he was, if more than twenty years of residence gave him a claim to the title. It looked small at first, but there was very good company there—among a mixture—necessarily a mixture—and very good air.

It became a not unusual circumstance for letters to be put under his door at night, enclosing half-a-crown, two half-crowns, now and then at long intervals even half-a-sovereign, for the Father of the Marshalsea. 'With the compliments of a collegian taking leave.' He received the gifts as tributes, from admirers, to a public character. Sometimes these correspondents assumed facetious names . . . but he considered this in bad taste, and was always a little hurt by it.

In the fulness of time, this correspondence showing signs of wearing out, and seeming to require an effort on the part of the correspondents to which in the hurried circumstances of departure many of them might not be equal, he established the custom of attending collegians of a certain standing, to the gate, and taking leave of them there. The collegian under treatment, after shaking hands, would occasionally stop to wrap up something in a bit of paper, and would come back again . . . (pp. 65–6)

The parody of the rituals of Society is effective in the precision of its phrasing and its range of tone: Dorrit's description of the Marshalsea is, in its effusive inanity, the very type of self-regarding, deprecatory

commendation beloved of hostesses, and it is perfectly modulated—
'It looked small at first, but there was very good company there—
among a mixture—necessarily a mixture—and very good air.' The
parody is not confined to manners and forms but extends to the kind
of preoccupation and calculation intimately known to Mrs. Merdle
and Mrs. Gowan: Mrs. Chivery, the wife of a turnkey, desires 'her
husband to take notice that if, on the one hand, their John [has]
means and a post of trust, on the other hand, Miss Dorrit [has] family';
and she accordingly desires him to note that 'their John's prospects of
the Lock would certainly be strengthened by an alliance with Miss
Dorrit' (pp. 212–13). The parody functions, in other words, as a
satirical *reductio ad absurdum*; but if Marshalsea pretensions are seen
to be patently absurd, they differ only in degree—not in kind—from
those of Society. In the end, it is Society, as well as the Dorrits and
Chiveries, that is subjected to comic deflation and ridicule. At the
same time, however, the parody firmly links the inmates of the Marshalsea and those who move in Society, and is thus another means of suggesting the plight of the latter. The link is sufficiently strong to make
quite unnecessary Dickens's heavy-handed attempt at tightening it in
the elaborate recital of other correspondences that begins: 'It appeared
on the whole, to Little Dorrit herself, that this same society in which
they lived [i.e., after Mr. Dorrit's release], greatly resembled a superior
sort of Marshalsea' (p. 511).

But William Dorrit, clearly, is not simply a figure of parody though
it is by means of parody that we are led to his place in the design—for
the Father of the Marshalsea is its Patron. It is a patron who puncti-
liously exacts the formal and ceremonious presentation to him of all
new-comers, receiving them (in recognition of his confined circumstances) with 'a kind of bowed-down beneficence'. It is a patron who
is 'so courtly, condescending, and benevolently conscious of a position'
that he can patronize even non-residents such as his brother Frederick,
who 'submissively . . . [accepts] his patronage' (p. 221). Above all,
it is the patron who reveals himself in his relationship with Mrs.
Plornish's father, Old Nandy, who lives in the workhouse. Dorrit is
in the habit of receiving Nandy 'as if the old man held of him in
vassalage under some feudal tenure' and of casually referring to him
as 'his old pensioner' (p. 365). After he has seen Little Dorrit coming
into the prison arm in arm with Nandy, he expresses his outrage in
the following terms:

'It is not that I have seen my good Amy attentive, and—ha—
condescending to my old pensioner—it is not *that* that hurts me.
It is, if I am to close the painful subject by being explicit, that
I have seen my child, my own child, my own daughter, coming
into this College out of the public streets—smiling! smiling!—
arm in arm with—O my God, a livery!' (p. 370)

On the same occasion he regains his composure and invites Nandy to
his room, begging him, as they walk together through the prison yard,
to 'be covered', to 'put [his] hat on' (p. 372). His 'magnanimous
protection' of Nandy is climaxed by his 'handsomely [regaling]' him
to tea, though the pensioner is given his on a newspaper on the
window-sill, apart from 'the good company' (p. 373); and by his parting beneficence: ' "We don't call this a shilling, Nandy, you know,"
he said, putting one in his hand. "We call it tobacco" ' (p. 374).

It is because he sees himself as Patron of the Marshalsea that Dorrit,
when departing collegians begin to slip their letters under his door at
night, receives their gifts 'as tributes, from admirers, to a public character'. He views the gifts, in other words, as no more than his due as
a gentleman, his gentility (like that of numerous Barnacles and the
Gowans, both mother and son) seeming to him to constitute sufficient
claim on the public support. Inevitably, in defence of his status, Dorrit
mounts a jobbed carriage of his own: the collegians begin to note 'a
disposition' in him 'to exaggerate the number of years' he has been at
the Marshalsea; the ready tears that any reference to 'his daughters'
earning their bread' elicits lead his family to maintain 'the genteel
fiction that they [are] all idle beggars together' (p. 74). And, inevitably,
the corruption which starts with his acceptance of the 'tributes' does
not end there: when the valedictory 'correspondence' begins to 'wear
out', the lordly dispenser of tobacco in the form of shillings passes
from a passive acceptance of homage to an active soliciting of it, and
applies the 'treatment' to those collegians whom he 'attends' to the
gate (though it is only collegians 'of a certain standing' that are so
honoured).

Like the 'deadly sewer' that flows through 'the heart of the town',
Dorrit's corruption steadily permeates his whole moral being. Dickens's
presentation of Dorrit is so subtle and marked by so profound an understanding that it alone should suffice to refute the popular belief that
he cannot create character, the belief that is allied to the criticism that
he cannot organize his material, the two beliefs being most succinctly

expressed together in George Orwell's 'rotten architecture, but wonderful gargoyles'.[1] This, for instance, is the way in which the extent of Dorrit's degradation is suggested:

> One afternoon he had been doing the honours of the place to a rather large party of collegians, who happened to be going out, when, as he was coming back, he encountered one from the poor side who had been taken in execution for a small sum a week before, had 'settled' in the course of that afternoon, and was going out too. The man was a mere Plasterer in his working dress; had his wife with him, and a bundle; and was in high spirits.
>
> 'God bless you, sir,' he said in passing.
>
> 'And you,' benignantly returned the Father of the Marshalsea.
>
> They were pretty far divided, going their several ways, when the Plasterer called out, 'I say!—sir!' and came back to him.
>
> 'It an't much,' said the Plasterer, putting a little pile of halfpence in his hand, 'but it's well meant.'
>
> The Father of the Marshalsea had never been offered tribute in copper yet. His children often had, and with his perfect acquiescence it had gone into the common purse, to buy meat that he had eaten, and drink that he had drunk; but fustian splashed with white lime, bestowing halfpence on him, front to front, was new.
>
> 'How dare you!' he said to the man, and feebly burst into tears.
>
> The Plasterer turned him towards the wall, that his face might not be seen; and the action was so delicate, and the man was so penetrated with repentance, and asked pardon so honestly, that he could make him no less acknowledgement than, 'I know you meant it kindly. Say no more.'
>
> 'Bless your soul, sir,' urged the Plasterer, 'I did indeed. I'd do more by you than the rest of 'em do, I fancy.'
>
> 'What would you do?' he asked.
>
> 'I'd come back to see you, after I was let out.'
>
> 'Give me the money again,' said the other, eagerly, 'and I'll

---

[1] 'Charles Dickens', *Critical Essays*, p. 49. Orwell recognizes the skill of the characterization in the case of Dorrit, but at the same time he dismisses the achievement: 'When [Dickens] produces a really subtle and damaging portrait, like John [sic] Dorrit or Harold Skimpole, it is generally of some rather middling, unimportant person' (p. 25).

keep it, and never spend it. Thank you for it, thank you! I shall
see you again?'

'If I live a week you shall.'

They shook hands and parted. The collegians, assembled in
Symposium in the Snuggery that night, marvelled what had
happened to their Father; he walked so late in the shadows of
the yard, and seemed so downcast. (pp. 66–7)

At first sight it seems that the offence of the 'mere Plasterer', the
'fustian splashed with white lime', is a boorish failure to realize just
how 'far divided' he is from the Father of the Marshalsea. Instead of
allowing Dorrit to keep his benignant distance, he thrusts his kindness
on him; unaware of the forms dear to him, he commits the solecism of a
'tribute in copper'. But the nature of Dorrit's response to the tribute,
both the anger and the tears, suggests a different kind of outrage. If
his knowing nothing about the copper his children receive while
acquiescing in its disbursement is simply part of the legerdemain that
goes with *his* jobbed carriage, his own view of himself in that convey-
ance is as cherished as the carriage itself. The Father of the Marshalsea,
in other words, is much given (unlike Mrs. Gowan) to self-deception;
and what the Plasterer innocently does is to make him see himself for
a moment as he is, as the beggar he has become. Hence the anger,
for illusion dies hard; and hence the feeble tears of self-pity when it
does. Hence, too, much later, the revealing denial when he breaks
down at Mrs. Merdle's dinner: 'In the acceptance of those—ha—
voluntary recognitions of my humble endeavours to—hum—to uphold a Tone here—a Tone—I beg it to be understood that I do not
consider myself compromised. Ha. Not compromised. Ha. Not a beggar. No: I repudiate the title!' (p. 648). And Dorrit also repudiates
the vision he has of himself in the yard. Helped by the Plasterer's
solicitude, reassured by his 'repentance' and begging of 'pardon', he
becomes something like the Father of the Marshalsea once more. It
is then that he reveals how utterly degraded he is. He is now incapable
of letting even copper slip from his hands, and so graciously (but
'eagerly'), as a mark of his condescension only (for he intends to keep
the money and never to spend it), the Patron allows the tribute after
all.

Dorrit has still further to fall, reaching the nadir of his descent in
his reproaches to his daughter, who has rejected the advances of young
John Chivery:

'I—hem!—I can't think, Amy, what has given Chivery offence. He is generally so—so very attentive and respectful. And to-night he was quite—quite short with me. Other people there too! Why, good Heaven! if I was to lose the support and recognition of Chivery and his brother officers, I might starve to death here.' While he spoke, he was opening and shutting his hands like valves; so conscious all the time of that touch of shame, that he shrunk before his own knowledge of his meaning.

'I—ha!—I can't think what it's owing to. I am sure I cannot imagine what the cause of it is. There was a certain Jackson here once, a turnkey of the name of Jackson (I don't think you can remember him, my dear, you were very young), and—hem! —and he had a—brother, and this—young brother paid his addresses to—at least, did not go so far as to pay his addresses to— but admired—respectfully admired—the—not the daughter, the sister—of one of us; a rather distinguished Collegian; I may say, very much so. His name was Captain Martin; and he consulted me on the question whether it was necessary that his daughter— sister—should hazard offending the turnkey brother by being too—ha!—too plain with the other brother. Captain Martin was a gentleman and a man of honour, and I put it to him first to give me his—his own opinion. Captain Martin (highly respected in the army) then unhesitatingly said, that it appeared to him that his—hem!—sister was not called upon to understand the young man too distinctly, and that she might lead him on—I am doubtful whether lead him on was Captain Martin's exact expression: indeed I think he said tolerate him—on her father's— I should say, brother's—account. I hardly know how I have strayed into this story. I suppose it has been through being unable to account for Chivery; but as to the connection between the two, I don't see—' (pp. 226–7)

Once again the characterization is superb. Dorrit's indestructible snobbery, the snobbery that is the man and that is disturbed by the turnkey's failure, in the presence of 'other people', to be 'attentive and respectful', is stamped even on the moral fable that he invents: the 'rather distinguished Collegian', who does duty for the Father in the fable, is, he can't help begging to say, 'very much so'; he is also described, in a parenthetic flight of the imagination, as being 'highly respected in the army'. Dickens's art here (both in what is said and what is left unsaid) is so delicate that it is difficult to accept, as we must, that he is capable in the very same novel of the grossest infelicities.[1] The art, in the passage under consideration, is not only delicate but profoundly ironic, for what the passage ultimately reveals is that Dorrit, the ineffectual debtor, absurdly and unjustly imprisoned for so long in the Marshalsea, has it in him to be more than a corrupter of words. The Father of the Marshalsea—and of Little Dorrit—can, indeed, go no further, for as he attempts to initiate her into the wiles of 'leading on', as he unknowingly anticipates Mrs. General's instruction in the craft of the false front, he sets out (hesitantly, but designedly trading on her love) to corrupt his own daughter.

III

When Dorrit is freed from the Marshalsea, his wealth gives him the entrée not only to Society (whose standards he has so strictly maintained in the prison) but to Mr. Merdle (whose wife's son marries his daughter). Mr. Merdle, being the wealthy husband of the bosom, is wedded to Society, and yet, being the man he is, an uneasy stranger in it. Accordingly, he is patronized by his own guests:

> Treasury hoped he might venture to congratulate one of England's world-famed capitalists and merchant-princes (he had turned that original sentiment in the house a few times, and it came easy to him) on a new achievement. To extend the triumphs of such men, was to extend the triumphs and resources of the nation; and Treasury felt—he gave Mr. Merdle to understand—patriotic on the subject.
>
> 'Thank you, my lord,' said Mr. Merdle; 'thank you. I accept your congratulations with pride, and I am glad you approve.'

---

[1] I am thinking particularly of some of his abuses of commentary. In the following instance, which I adduce as representative of this too frequently repeated weakness, the commentary is not only quite unnecessary in its obviousness but degenerates into the worst kind of sentimental cliché—Clennam has just intimated to Little Dorrit that he is too old for love:
'If he had known the sharpness of the pain he caused the patient heart, in speaking thus! While doing it, too, with the purpose of easing and serving her.
' "I found that the day when any such thing would have been graceful in me, or good in me, or hopeful or happy for me, or any one in connection with me, was gone, and would never shine again."
'O! If he had known, if he had known! If he could have seen the dagger in his hand, and the cruel wounds it struck in the faithful bleeding heart of his Little Dorrit!' (p. 381).

Little Dorrit

'Why, I don't unreservedly approve, my dear Mr. Merdle. Because,' smiling Treasury turned him by the arm towards the sideboard and spoke banteringly, 'it never can be worth your while to come among us and help us.'

. . .

Bar, with his little insinuating Jury droop, and fingering his persuasive double eye-glass, hoped he might be excused if he mentioned to one of the greatest converters of the root of all evil into the root of all good, who had for a long time reflected a shining lustre on the annals even of our commercial country— if he mentioned, disinterestedly, and as, what we lawyers called in our pedantic way, amicus curiae, a fact that had come by accident within his knowledge. He had been required to look over the title of a very considerable estate in one of the eastern counties—lying, in fact, for Mr. Merdle knew we lawyers loved to be particular, on the borders of two of the eastern counties. Now, the title was perfectly sound, and the estate was to be purchased by one who had the command of—Money (Jury droop and persuasive eye-glass), on remarkably advantageous terms. This had come to Bar's knowledge only that day, and it had occurred to him, 'I shall have the honour of dining with my esteemed friend Mr. Merdle this evening, and, strictly between ourselves, I will mention the opportunity.' . . . (pp. 250–1)

Mr. Merdle, who is not quite up to the tone of his guests—and how well Dickens's *oratio obliqua* catches their tone—is nevertheless (and despite the patronage) 'one of England's world-famed capitalists'. As such he has his own regality, bodying forth the age (in a 'commercial country') as a 'merchant-prince'. Merdle, in other words, is a representative man, *the* representative man in a commercial country, and his success is a measure of the state's, for (as Treasury assures him and all agree) to extend his triumphs is 'to extend the triumphs and resources of the nation'. Merdle, indeed, as Dorrit later puts it, is 'the man of this time. The name of Merdle is the name of the age' (p. 484). Merdle, consequently, inevitably, is a Patron, the very 'patron of patrons' (p. 710). Thus it is that Bar sees in him a natural supporter of enterprise, of his enterprise, and discreetly commends to him the virtues of the 'very considerable estate' that lies 'on the borders of two of the eastern counties'. Thus it is that Bishop, who comes 'undesignedly sidling in the direction of the sideboard' when Bar takes 'his persuasive eye-glass up the grand staircase', sees in Merdle a natural contributor to charity, and 'puts the case' of 'a mission or so to Africa' and of his 'Combined Additional Endowed Dignitaries Committee' (p. 252). And thus it is that Merdle is in fact the quiet patron of the Barnacles (in the interests of Edmund Sparkler); and thus it is that he is the obliging patron of those, such as Dorrit, whom he can relieve of their money, for though it is not easy (as he tells Dorrit) for 'a mere outsider' to come into any of his 'good things', he does 'generally retain in [his] own hands the power of exercising some preference' or, as people in general are pleased to call it, 'favour' (p. 617).

Merdle, the 'patron of patrons', is also an 'object of worship' to his time and age, despite the fact that the clay of which he is made is 'the commonest clay':

> All people knew (or thought they knew) that he had made himself immensely rich; and, for that reason alone, prostrated themselves before him, more degradedly and less excusably than the darkest savage creeps out of his hole in the ground to propitiate, in some log or reptile, the Deity of his benighted soul. (p. 556)

The deity of the commercial country, it is clear enough, is Mammon; and if the allusion to 'the darkest savage' suggests how retrograde (as well as degraded) this worship of Merdle is, the worship is of a piece with the civilization in which the ugly South Sea gods are at home. It is of a piece with the prison-like city of London, the centre of that civilization, in another respect, for the description of a whole society 'prostrated' before Merdle strikingly images a further manifestation of its arrest. Indeed Merdle, who is often late for his social engagements because he is 'detained' in the 'clutch of giant enterprises'; whose work, as Treasury pleasantly says, '[punishes] him a little' (p. 249); and whose favourite posture is to stand 'with his hands crossed under his uneasy coat-cuffs, clasping his wrists as if he were taking himself into custody' (p. 394), may be said constantly to arrest himself.

Mr. Merdle's characteristic stance is one of the external symptoms of that 'complaint' that troubles him and puzzles the 'famous physician' whom he attends. But Society and he are said to have 'so much to do with one another in all things else' that it is 'hard to imagine his complaint . . . being solely his own affair' (p. 254). As the air begins 'to resound more and more, with the name of Merdle' (after the great Decimus's homage to him), and as even the steady Mr. Baptist of

Bleeding Heart Yard begins to lay by his savings 'for investment in one of Mr. Merdle's certain enterprises', it is clear that what society has caught of Mr. Merdle is 'a moral infection':

> That is at least as difficult to stay a moral infection as a physical one; that such a disease will spread with the malignity and rapidity of the Plague; that the contagion, when it has once made head, will spare no pursuit or condition, but will lay hold on people in the soundest health, and become developed in the most unlikely constitutions; is a fact as firmly established by experience as that we human creatures breathe an atmosphere. (p. 571)

This obsessive image of Dickens's, analogous to the 'moral pestilence' of *Dombey and Son* and to 'Tom's corrupted blood' of *Bleak House*, is here given a limited and precise connotation. The moral infection caught off Merdle is a belief in speculation, in the making of easy money; and this belief, which is opposed to the kind of faith in steady application and industry that is represented by Doyce, which indeed undermines that faith, as in the case of Clennam, is seen to lead to an insidious corruption of the will. It leads ultimately, where Clennam is concerned, to imprisonment, Clennam's fate recalling (and symbolizing) that of the prostrated worshippers of Mammon; just as the reference to the malignant Plague in the quoted passage recalls the prisoners in the city where the bells throb and jerk and toll as if the Plague is there and the deadcarts are going round. It leads, too, to widespread ruin:

> Numbers of men in every profession and trade [are] blighted by [Merdle's] insolvency; old people who had been in easy circumstances all their lives [have] no place of repentance for their trust in him but the workhouse; legions of women and children [have] their whole future desolated by the hand of this mighty scoundrel. (p. 710)

The world of *Little Dorrit*, marked by its particular brand of parasitism, meets the world of *Bleak House* in the blight which spreads out over both.

Merdle's own complaint, his moral infection, is of course not only speculation but 'Forgery and Robbery', and in the end he commits himself to a lasting custody. If he is thus 'the greatest Forger and the greatest Thief that ever cheated the gallows' (p. 710), we are reminded by the young Ferdinand Barnacle that Merdle's vice (like Dorrit's view of his name) is the vice of his age; for the Circumlocution Ferdinand confesses to Clennam that 'we must have humbug, we all like humbug, we couldn't get on without humbug', and so admits to an admiration of Merdle, the 'master of humbug' (p. 738). Merdle, the criminal Master of Deception, is, as it were, the patron saint not only of the amateurs at the Circumlocution Office but also of a small-time practitioner of extortion such as the patriarchal Casby, a 'first-rate humbug' (p. 279), who contrives to dispose of 'an immense quantity of solid food with the benignity of a good soul who [is] feeding some one else' (p. 158). Casby has been 'town-agent' to Lord Decimus Tite Barnacle, a position for which he qualified by 'looking so supremely benignant that nobody could suppose the property screwed or jobbed under such a man' (p. 149); and, after leaving Lord Decimus, he continues, through the agency of Pancks and as the patron of Bleeding Heart Yard, to job in his own interest until Pancks publicly denounces him as 'a screwer by deputy' and 'a shabby deceiver' (p. 800). Merdle, moreover, may also be said to play the merchant-prince to Rigaud's 'Knight of Industry' (p. 768), for the latter's crude criminality is presented as a counterpart of the subtler corruptions of those, like Merdle, who affect gentility but live by their wits. Rigaud, like Hortense (the villain of *Bleak House*), is a melodramatic and unconvincing character, but his criminality is related to the themes of the novel in a way that hers is not. He too is a 'patron', if only that of John Baptist Cavalletto (pp. 131, 134); and from the outset, indeed in the jail at Marseilles, he takes up a position that leads straight to the Merdles and the Barnacles:

> 'Call me five-and-thirty years of age. I have seen the world. I have lived here, and lived there, and lived like a gentleman everywhere. I have been treated and respected as a gentleman universally. If you try to prejudice me, by making out that I have lived by my wits—how do your lawyers live—your politicians—your intriguers—your men of the Exchange?' (pp. 9–10)

IV

It is Mrs. Clennam who is the particular object of Rigaud's attentions.

In a book whose theme is the paralysis of a society, she is immediately recognizable as a symbolic figure: she never leaves her room, for, as she tells Clennam, 'what with [her] rheumatic affection, and what with its attendant debility or nervous weakness', she has 'lost the use of [her] limbs' (p. 34). It is clear, however, that her paralysis is more than a rheumatic disability. She goes on to say:

> 'All seasons are alike to me . . . I know nothing of summer and winter, shut up here. The Lord has been pleased to put me beyond all that.' With her cold grey eyes and her cold grey hair, and her immovable face, as stiff as the folds of her stony head-dress,—her being beyond the reach of the seasons, seemed but a fit sequence to her being beyond the reach of all changing emotions. (p. 34)

That Mrs. Clennam is 'beyond the reach of all changing emotions', that she is, indeed, beyond the reach of all change, for all seasons are alike to her, suggests that it is not only from a physical paralysis that she suffers. Her paralysis is symbolic, in the first place, of an inner arrest, of the freezing of her emotional being, its solidifying into cold stone. This emotional state is evoked by repeated images: her eyes are 'cold' and her hair is 'cold'; her face is 'immovable' and 'stiff'; she speaks 'in [a] frozen way' and she '[relapses] into stone' (p. 46); the 'rigid woman' builds an 'impious tower of stone' to 'scale Heaven' (p. 47); and, perhaps most effectively of all, her very head-dress, her 'stony head-dress', with its suggestion of a cold headstone, seems to posit the death in her of all emotion. Mrs. Clennam, in other words, is in this respect a female Mr. Dombey. But though she too is greatly concerned with her firm and with the business of money-making, her stony condition is not attributable to Dombey's monomania; it is 'the Lord' who 'has been pleased to put [her] beyond all that', beyond summer and winter:

> 'Reparation!' said she. 'Yes truly! It is easy for [Arthur] to talk of reparation, fresh from journeying and junketing in foreign lands, and living a life of vanity and pleasure. But let him look at me, in prison, and in bonds here. I endure without murmuring, because it is appointed that I shall so make reparation for my sins. Reparation! Is there none in this room? Has there been none here this fifteen years?'

Thus was she always balancing her bargain with the Majesty of heaven, posting up the entries to her credit, strictly keeping her set-off, and claiming her due. She was only remarkable in this, for the force and emphasis with which she did it. Thousands upon thousands do it, according to their varying manner, every day. (p. 50)

Though Mrs. Clennam invokes the Lord with grim satisfaction, we see clearly enough that it is she herself who has 'appointed' that she 'make reparation' for her sins through her paralysis. Her paralysis, as her dramatic release from it towards the end of the book indicates, is self-induced, a 'superficial hysterical paralysis',[1] her sense of guilt being so strong that she unconsciously feels compelled, like Merdle, to arrest herself, to place herself 'in prison and in bonds' in her own home.

Mrs. Clennam's paralysis should be viewed, furthermore, as symbolic of another kind of confinement. To confine religion to the auditing of a private profit and loss account with God, to reduce it, as Mrs. Clennam does, to a 'bargain with the Majesty of heaven', may be the means by which the 'thousands upon thousands' in a commercial country find a common ground between religion and commerce; but it is as much a sign of spiritual arrest as a benighted prostration before false gods. To adopt Mrs. Clennam's implacable Calvinistic creed, moreover, is to confine grace to the elect, like herself, for she takes it 'as a grace and favour to be elected to make the satisfaction' she is making in her suffering; it is also to restrict the wide earth to 'a scene of gloom, and hardship, and dark trial, for the creatures who are made out of its dust' (p. 357). It is to 'narrow' the world to the dimensions of her room (p. 33), to confine all virtue to it, and to limit all activity beyond it to 'journeying and junketing', to 'vanity and pleasure'. It is, as Clennam is made to realize on his first Sunday in London, to bolt and bar a whole city.

It is, also, to constitute oneself a divinely appointed scourger of sinners:

> 'I ask, what was the penitence, in works, that was demanded of [Arthur's mother]? "You have a child; I have none. You love that child. Give him to me. He shall believe himself to be my son, and he shall be believed by every one to be my son. To

---

[1] Edmund Bergler, ' "Little Dorrit" and Dickens' Intuitive Knowledge of Psychic Masochism', *The American Imago*, 14 (1957), 387.

save you from exposure, his father shall swear never to see or
communicate with you more; equally to save him from being
stripped by his uncle, and to save your child from being a beggar,
you shall swear never to see or communicate with either of them
more. That done, and your present means, derived from my
husband, renounced, I charge myself with your support. You
may, with your place of retreat unknown, then leave, if you
please, uncontradicted by me, the lie that when you passed out
of all knowledge but mine, you merited a good name." That was
all. She had to sacrifice her sinful and shameful affections; no
more. She was then free to bear her load of guilt in secret, and
to break her heart in secret; and through such present misery
(light enough for her, I think!) to purchase her redemption from
endless misery, if she could. If, in this, I punished her here, did
I not open to her a way hereafter? . . .

'They did *not* forget. It is appointed against such offences that
the offenders shall not be able to forget. If the presence of Arthur
was a daily reproach to his father, and if the absence of Arthur
was a daily agony to his mother, that was the just dispensation of
Jehovah. As well might it be charged upon me, that the stings of
an awakened conscience drove her mad, and that it was the will
of the Disposer of all things that she should live so, many years.
I devoted myself to reclaim the otherwise predestined and lost
boy; to give him the reputation of an honest origin; to bring him
up in fear and trembling, and in a life of practical contrition for
the sins that were heavy on his head before his entrance into this
condemned world. . . .' (pp. 776–7)

Mrs. Clennam, we see, is a very Dorrit in her self-deceptions. Ostensibly dispensing the justice of Jehovah, setting out to 'reclaim' the
'predestined and lost boy' and to give the fallen woman a chance 'to
purchase her redemption', she contrives both to secure herself, for,
the (financial) favour of the uncle being retained by keeping him in
ignorance, the sinful lovers are made to swear never to communicate
with each other; and to exact her own enduring revenge, for 'the
presence of Arthur' is to be 'a daily reproach to his father' and his
absence 'a daily agony to his mother'. Nor is that the only agony she
plans. Coldly, 'charging [herself] with [her] support', she seeks to
turn Arthur's mother into her Old Nandy, and sets herself up as her
patron. Her attitude to her is anticipatory of the way in which she

later shows an interest in Little Dorrit, 'in a hard way, and in an uncertain way that [fluctuates] between patronage and putting down' (p. 52). But, like so many patrons in the school for patrons of her society, she compromises herself in the very act of patronage. Her scheme, like any one of Merdle's more elaborate enterprises, rests on a deception: Clennam must 'be believed by every one to be [her] son'. In pretending to be Clennam's mother, she thus sets out on a course which leads ultimately to her criminal suppression of the codicil to the uncle's will. It leads, too, to her confinement to her room—and to her exposure to the Knight of Industry.

V

Another object of interest to the Knight of Industry is Gowan. Gowan is every inch his mother's son, treating Clennam, for instance, 'with his usual show of confidence, which [is] no confidence at all':

> 'You see, Clennam,' he happened to remark in the course of conversation one day, when they were walking near the Cottage within a week of the marriage, 'I am a disappointed man. That, you know already.'
> 'Upon my word,' said Clennam, a little embarrassed, 'I scarcely know how.'
> 'Why,' returned Gowan, 'I belong to a clan, or a clique, or a family, or a connection, or whatever you like to call it, that might have provided for me in any one of fifty ways, and that took it into its head not to do it at all. So here I am, a poor devil of an artist.'
> . . .
> Clennam thought (and as he thought it, again felt ashamed of himself), was this notion of being disappointed in life, an assertion of station which the bridegroom brought into the family as his property, having already carried it detrimentally into his pursuit? And was it a hopeful or a promising thing anywhere?
> 'Not bitterly disappointed, I think,' he said aloud.
> 'Hang it, no; not bitterly,' laughed Gowan. '. . . it's a dear good world, and I love it!'
> 'It lies fair before you now,' said Arthur.
> 'Fair as this summer river,' cried the other, with enthusiasm,

222

'and by Jove I glow with admiration of it, and with ardour to run a race in it. It's the best of old worlds! And my calling! The best of old callings, isn't it?'

'Full of interest and ambition, I conceive,' said Clennam.

'And imposition,' added Gowan, laughing; 'we won't leave out the imposition. . . . [I hope I shall be able] to help myself in my turn, as the man before me helps himself in his, and pass the bottle of smoke. To keep up the pretence as to labour, and study, and patience, and being devoted to my art, and giving up many solitary days to it, and abandoning many pleasures for it, and living in it, and all the rest of it—in short, to pass the bottle of smoke, according to rule.'

'But it is well for a man to respect his own vocation, whatever it is; and to think himself bound to uphold it, and to claim for it the respect it deserves; is it not?' Arthur reasoned. 'And your vocation, Gowan, may really demand this suit and service. I confess I should have thought that all Art did.'

. . .

'Clennam, I don't like to dispel your generous visions, and I would give any money (if I had any) to live in such a rose-coloured mist. But what I do in my trade, I do to sell. What all we fellows do, we do to sell. If we didn't want to sell it for the most we can get for it, we shouldn't do it. Being work, it has to be done; but it's easily enough done. All the rest is hocus-pocus. Now here's one of the advantages, or disadvantages, of knowing a disappointed man. You hear the truth.' (pp. 401–3)

If Merdle is the man of his time and age, Gowan, clearly, is its representative artist. What he does in his 'trade', he does (like all his 'fellows') to 'sell'; and 'all the rest' is 'hocus-pocus'. In a commercial country, in other words, even art is simply another commercial activity, like the buying and selling of Merdle's shares; and Gowan practises his art merely for what he can get out of it, just as his Circumlocution connections (the 'clan' or 'clique' or 'family' to which be belongs) practise the art of government. Indeed, Gowan has become 'a poor devil of an artist' only because his connections have failed to 'provide' for him in the first place. Art, that is, is not only a commercial activity but a refuge for gentlemen deprived of their rightful due, of the patronage of a grateful country. But Gowan's 'assertion of station', as Clennam realizes, is thoroughly 'detrimental' when 'carried

. . . into his pursuit', for 'all Art' does demand the kind of 'suit and service', the single-hearted dedication, that his sense of his own gentility makes him incapable of rendering—and makes him dismiss as professional pretence, 'the bottle of smoke' to be passed round 'according to rule'. Not surprisingly, therefore, though Gowan is filled with 'ardour' to 'run a race' in 'the best of old worlds', in the 'dear good world' that he loves so much, he does not get very far with his 'calling'; the race, indeed, is never run because he has 'a perceptible limp' in his 'devotion to art' (p. 205), because he '[saunters] into the Arts at a leisurely Pall-Mall pace' (p. 206), because he is in a 'halting state' (p. 488)—because, in a word, the way in which he practises his art ensures the arrest of his talent.

Having been denied official Barnacle patronage as a gentleman and a connection, Gowan not unreasonably seeks it as a painter. Lord Decimus is persuaded to '[buy] his picture', and is heard to say, 'with his own magnificent gravity', that there appears to him 'to be really immense merit' in the work; in addition, 'people of condition' take considerable pains 'to bring him into fashion'; but, 'somehow', it all fails and 'the prejudiced public' obstinately '[stands] out' against these recommendations (p. 206). Gowan is consequently reduced, as a 'journeyman' who 'must take jobs' when he can get them, to accepting the commissions of even such 'an upstart' as Mr. Dorrit, reduced because he '[resents] patronage almost as much as he [resents] the want of it'. By making a great show of rejecting 'the hocus-pocus' of 'the trade', however, and by refusing to 'fall on to order' for the 'mere sake of the sixpences', he succeeds in patronizing his patron and in skilfully placing himself 'on his usual ground in the new family' (pp. 507–8).

In his dealings with friends and sitters, in other words, Gowan likes to insist that the carriage *he* rides in *is* jobbed, likes, that is, as 'a disappointed man', always to tell 'the truth' and to expose pretension; but his 'show of confidence' to Dorrit as well as to Clennam is calculated to win belief that the carriage is his, after all. 'I am not a great impostor,' he tells Clennam. 'Buy one of my pictures, and I assure you, in confidence, it will not be worth the money' (p. 310). It is no doubt the case that, as an impostor, he is not as 'great' as Merdle or some of the Barnacles, but he is certainly a master of his own particular line of 'humbug'. He is also a master of a 'characteristic balancing . . . which [reduces] everything in the wide world to the same light weight' (p. 310) (a tendency which Dickens is reported to have disliked in

Thackeray, who, in this respect at least, may be said to have sat for Gowan).[1] Nor is it attributes only that Gowan balances so delicately, the state of the dear good world, for instance, and the state of being perpetually disappointed; he contrives, in the end, to balance disowning his father-in-law with taking his money:

> By this time, Mr. Henry Gowan had made up his mind that it would be agreeable to him not to know the Meagleses. He was so considerate as to lay no injunctions on his wife in that particular; but, he mentioned to Mr. Meagles that personally they did not appear to him to get on together, and that he thought it would be a good thing if—politely, and without any scene, or anything of that sort—they agreed that they were the best fellows in the world, but were best apart. . . . This arrangement involved the contingent advantage, which perhaps Henry Gowan had not foreseen, that both Mr. and Mrs. Meagles were more liberal than before to their daughter, when their communication was only with her and her young child: and that his high spirit found itself better provided with money, without being under the degrading necessity of knowing whence it came. (p. 806)

Gowan's crowning exercise in humbug, that is to say, is, in keeping with his 'high spirit', to make Meagles his Barnacle—and without the necessity of either owning to the connection or sticking to a post.

VI

If Miss Wade's history is clumsily introduced into the narrative—she hardly knows Clennam, to whom she presents the written account of her life, and yet she has written it and 'put [it] by' especially for his 'perusal' so that he may 'comprehend' what she means by hating (pp. 659–60)—it is nevertheless tied to the centre in such a way that the blood of the book does circulate through it:

> I went among young women next, and I found them no better. Fair words and fair pretences; but, I penetrated below

---

[1] See Edgar Johnson, who (citing Hesketh Pearson) says that Gowan 'is not a portrait of Thackeray, but he is a rendering of the attitude in Thackeray toward both life and the art the two men practised which Dickens found distasteful. . . .' *Charles Dickens*, II, 892.

those assertions of themselves and depreciations of me, and they were no better. Before I left them, I learned that I had no grandmother and no recognised relation. I carried the light of that information both into my past and into my future. It showed me many new occasions on which people triumphed over me, when they made a pretence of treating me with consideration, or doing me a service.

A man of business had a small property in trust for me. I was to be a governess. I became a governess; and went into the family of a poor nobleman, where there were two daughters—little children, but the parents wished them to grow up, if possible, under one instructress. The mother was young and pretty. From the first, she made a show of behaving to me with great delicacy. I kept my resentment to myself; but, I knew very well that it was her way of petting the knowledge that she was my Mistress, and might have behaved differently to her servant if it had been her fancy.

I say I did not resent it, nor did I; but I showed her, by not gratifying her, that I understood her. When she pressed me to take wine, I took water. If there happened to be anything choice at table, she always sent it to me: but I always declined it, and ate of the rejected dishes. These disappointments of her patronage were a sharp retort, and made me feel independent. (p. 665)

For Miss Wade, we see, one of the crucial experiences of her life is her realization that she is an illegitimate child, that she has 'no grandmother and no recognised relation'. She carries 'the light of that information' into her life to such good purpose that she believes she is illuminated by it wherever she goes, cherishing her status as social outcast, the sense of her inferiority. Hungry for love, but sensitive to the point of neurosis, '[refusing] to be lovable' in what Lionel Trilling calls 'the classic maneuver of the child who is unloved, or believes herself to be unloved',[1] she torments herself with the conviction that people are 'depreciating' her and 'triumphing' over her. Gradually, reducing the whole world to the dimensions of a jobbed carriage, she comes to believe that she is met everywhere by a false front, by 'fair words and fair pretences', by 'shows' of delicacy. Her life becomes so extreme an assertion of her independence, so dedicated to the 'disap-

[1] '*Little Dorrit*', *The Dickens Critics*, ed. George H. Ford and Lauriat Lane, p. 288. The essay was written as an introduction to a 1953 edition of the novel.

pointment' of all suspected 'patronage', that when she is 'pressed . . . to take wine', she takes water, and eats of the 'rejected dishes' when urged to something 'choice'. Miss Wade's view of the world, in other words, presents us with a mirror-image of the world we have become accustomed to see in *Little Dorrit*: wherever she looks, she sees (quite without justification, neurotically) deception and patronage—but she schools us in our view of the normal, apparently fair face of things. At the same time, her relationship with the wife of the poor nobleman reveals how inhibiting her attitude is, reveals, indeed, that (like Mrs. Clennam, though for different reasons) she is incapable, emotionally, of moving freely towards anyone, of responding to the advances of others without corrosive suspicion. And like Mrs. Clennam, she bears the telltale imprint of her confinement: her beauty has 'a certain worn expression' that gives it, 'though scarcely yet in its prime, a wasted look' (p. 25).

The result of Miss Wade's emotional arrest is her relationship with Tattycoram:

> In that company I found a girl, in various circumstances of whose position there was a singular likeness to my own, and in whose character I was interested and pleased to see much of the rising against swollen patronage and selfishness, calling themselves kindness, protection, benevolence, and other fine names, which I have described as inherent in my nature. I often heard it said, too, that she had 'an unhappy temper.' Well understanding what was meant by the convenient phrase, and wanting a companion with a knowledge of what I knew, I thought I would try to release the girl from her bondage and sense of injustice. I have no occasion to relate that I succeeded.
>
> We have been together ever since, sharing my small means. (p. 671)

Miss Wade believes that she is drawn to Tatty by a natural affinity, by a sympathy for one whose position bears 'a singular likeness' to her own, and with whom she has 'a common cause': 'What your broken plaything is as to birth,' she tells Meagles, 'I am. She has no name, I have no name. Her wrong is my wrong' (p. 330). We see, however, that she is drawn to Tatty as a kind of *alter ego*, narcissistically and defensively, for Tatty appears to be as vulnerable as she herself, to have a knowledge of what she knows, and consequently to pose no threat of an equally feared benevolence or disdain. She in unconsciously drawn to Tatty, in other words, because she believes she has at last found someone on whom she can safely bestow her pent-up feeling, whom she can even possess, without exposing herself to the dangers of being possessed. What she wants is not 'a companion', but a lover, and what she draws Tatty into, in the end, is a Lesbian relation—Mr. Meagles makes that quite clear:

> 'I don't know what you are, but you don't hide, can't hide, what a dark spirit you have within you. If it should happen that you are a woman, who, from whatever cause, has a perverted delight in making a sister-woman as wretched as she is (I am old enough to have heard of such), I warn her against you, and I warn you against yourself.' (pp. 329–30)

Miss Wade's reply to this outburst is to 'put her arm about [Tatty's] waist as if she took possession of her for evermore' (p. 330). She also, of course, takes her into a new servitude. If Miss Wade starts by being 'interested and pleased' to see Tatty's 'rising against swollen patronage and selfishness', and by deciding to 'try to release the girl from her bondage', she ends by setting herself up as her patron as well as her lover, sharing her 'small means' with her. Nor does she let Tatty forget the fact, as the girl complains to Clennam: '. . . she taunts me because she has made me her dependant. And I know I am so; and I know she is overjoyed when she can bring it to my mind.' Tatty, moreover, does not prove to be as amenable (and as vulnerable) as Miss Wade has anticipated. Clennam feels 'how each of the two natures must be constantly tearing the other to pieces', and he leaves them in their 'dull confined room', each condemned, by her own 'fixed determination', to '[torture] her own breast, and [torture] the other's' (pp. 661–2).

Tatty eventually flees from Miss Wade and returns, duly chastened, to the Meagleses. The extent, however, to which they have been chastened by her abandonment of them remains unclear. Mr. Meagles is a well-intentioned man, but he cannot help being patronizing, even to Doyce, let alone the girl whom he has named Tattycoram. Indeed, it is an ironic comment on the world of *Little Dorrit*, on the relationship of Clennam and Mrs. Clennam as well as on that of Tatty and the Meagleses and Tatty and Miss Wade, that its illegitimate children— the equivalents of the orphans of *Bleak House*—find *in loco parentis* not a guardian but a patron.

VII

The question insistently posed by the imagery of the novel is whether there is a way out from its manifold prisons, whether there is a possibility (as in the case of the long-imprisoned Dorrit) of winning release. One answer to this question is dramatized in the story of Clennam:

'And now, Mr. Clennam,' [said Mr. Meagles], 'perhaps I may ask you, whether you have yet come to a decision where to go next?'

'Indeed, no. I am such a waif and stray everywhere, that I am liable to be drifted where any current may set.'

'It's extraordinary to me—if you'll excuse my freedom in saying so—that you don't go straight to London,' said Mr. Meagles, in the tone of a confidential adviser.

'Perhaps I shall.'

'Ay! But I mean with a will.'

'I have no will. That is to say,' he coloured a little, 'next to none that I can put in action now. Trained by main force; broken, not bent; heavily ironed with an object on which I was never consulted and which was never mine; shipped away to the other end of the world before I was of age, and exiled there until my father's death there, a year ago; always grinding in a mill I always hated; what is to be expected from *me* in middle life? Will, purpose, hope? All those lights were extinguished before I could sound the words.'

'Light 'em up again!' said Mr. Meagles.

'Ah! Easily said. I am the son, Mr. Meagles, of a hard father and mother. I am the only child of parents who weighed, measured, and priced everything; for whom what could not be weighed, measured, and priced, had no existence. Strict people as the phrase is, professors of a stern religion, their very religion was a gloomy sacrifice of tastes and sympathies that were never their own, offered up as part of a bargain for the security of their possessions. Austere faces, inexorable discipline, penance in this world and terror in the next—nothing graceful or gentle anywhere, and the void in my cowed heart everywhere—this was

229

my childhood, if I may so misuse the word as to apply it to such a beginning of life.' (pp. 20-1)

What Clennam's account of his history makes clear is that it is not merely in quarantine that he is 'shut up' as he talks. Owning, in the prime of life, to having no will, feeling that he has been put out of action, as it were, he is seen to be as surely paralysed as Mrs. Clennam, to be suffering from as insidious an inner stagnation as that of Britannia herself under the Barnacles. It is not only an accident that he is 'locked in' the Marshalsea on his first visit to the Dorrits (p. 86); if, unlike Merdle, he is not for ever taking himself into custody, he is only too ready, on his return to England, to allow himself to be arrested. This is a state, indeed, to which he may be said to have been conditioned in childhood, in his 'heavily ironed' childhood, in the childhood of 'austere faces' and 'inexorable discipline' and 'penance'. More of 'a waif and stray' than he knows, lifelessly 'adrift' from the time of his depositing in Mrs. Clennam's haven, he returns to England with no enthusiasm for the 'mill' in which his fellow citizens are commercially grinding. But if he rejects the values in which he has been brought up, the weighing, measuring and pricing of everything, in business and religion alike; he has found nothing with which to replace these. With all guiding lights 'extinguished', he remains hopelessly in the dark—unmoving.

In so far as Clennam may be thought of as a victim of his circumstances, rather than a victimizer, such as Merdle; his condition may be said to be representative of the general condition under the Barnacles, and he the prototypic victim in the novel. On his return to England, the two possibilities open to him (and also representative of general options) are exemplified, appropriately, in action that takes place in the house in which he has been brought up. The first is the collapse of the house itself, which is prognosticated not only in the noises Affery hears but in the opening description of it:

> It was a double house, with long, narrow, heavily-framed windows. Many years ago, it had had it in its mind to slide down sideways; it had been propped up, however, and was leaning on some half-dozen gigantic crutches: which gymnasium for the neighbouring cats, weather-stained, smoke-blackened, and overgrown with weeds, appeared in these latter days to be no very sure reliance. (p. 31)

This house, whose 'crutches' call to mind the paralysed woman confined within it, itself symbolizes, in its 'propped up' condition (like the Barnacle with the gout) a state of arrest. As such, I take it that its collapse, its '[opening] asunder in fifty places' to the accompaniment of 'thundering sound' (p. 793), is meant to have the same kind of ominous force as the crashing down of houses, 'like the springing of a mine', in Tom-all-Alone's in *Bleak House*. Certainly Affery is said, in regard to the collapse, to be 'like greater people', always 'right in her facts, and always wrong in the theories she deduced from them' (p. 794). Revolutionary implications are, if anything, stronger in *Little Dorrit* than in *Bleak House*, as another house image suggests, though the same image simultaneously posits the possibility of a self-consuming, like Krook's spontaneous combustion in the earlier work: in Covent Garden Little Dorrit sees 'miserable children in rags' who are 'like young rats, [slinking] and [hiding], [feeding] on offal, [huddling] together for warmth, and . . . hunted about'; and then there follows this parenthetic apostrophe: '(look to the rats, young and old, all ye Barnacles, for before God they are eating away our foundations, and will bring the roofs on our heads!)' (p. 166.)[1]

As opposed to collapse, the other possibility open to Clennam is symbolized by Mrs. Clennam's dramatic recovery of the use of her limbs—is, in other words, the possibility of release from arrest. Unable to contemplate the possibility of Clennam's learning the truth about her while she sits passively in her chair, for she fears that will mean to die to him, she springs up and sets out for the Marshalsea in an effort to save herself by begging Little Dorrit to keep her secret:

> 'I would not, for any worldly recompense I can imagine, have [Clennam] in a moment, however blindly, throw me down from the station I have held before him all his life, and change me altogether, into something he would cast out of his respect, and think detected and exposed. Let him do it, if it must be done, when I am not here to see it. Let me never feel, while I am

---

[1] In Dickens's letters at this time there is certainly more than one reference to the possibility of revolution: 'There is nothing in the present time at once so galling and so alarming to me as the alienation of the people from their own public affairs. . . . And I believe the discontent to be so much the worse for smouldering, instead of blazing openly, that it is extremely like the general mind of France before the breaking out of the first Revolution, and is in danger of being turned by any one of a thousand accidents . . . into such a devil of a conflagration as never has been beheld since.' Letter to Austen Henry Layard, 10. 4. 1855, *Letters*, ed. Walter Dexter, II, 651–2. Cf. letter of 11. 5. 1855; *Letters from Charles Dickens to Angela Burdett-Coutts*, p. 298.

still alive, that I die before his face, and utterly perish away
from him, like one consumed by lightning and swallowed by an
earthquake.' (p. 791)

To 'die', for Mrs. Clennam, is not only to be detected by Clennam
but to be exposed to a particular kind of collapse, is to be 'thrown
down' from the station she has always held. Granted the hysterical
nature of her paralysis, we may say, therefore, that what brings her
release is a determination to be free, a vital renunciation of passivity,
of the passive abiding of collapse. It is this determination that saves
her from being caught in her house, a prisoner, like Rigaud, as it
disintegrates.[1]

It is an analogous determination that saves Clennam. Having 'dis-
embarrassed' himself of his former 'occupation', of continued par-
ticipation in the Clennam business (p. 198), but remaining uncertain
what to do with his life, remaining, that is, a 'waif and stray', passively
adrift; he takes the decisive step of becoming Doyce's partner. It is
this move that brings him release, that 'opens' to him 'an active and
promising career' (p. 266). The move, moreover, is not merely indicative of his discovery of a new sense of purpose, of his breaking out
of that paralysis of the will to which he confesses to Meagles; it represents his readiness to make himself partner, as it were, to the Doycean
virtues, to qualities which are opposed to those that have turned a
whole society into a huge prison. Doyce, like Mr. Jarndyce of *Bleak
House*, is above all a believer in self-help: 'a composed and unobtrusive
self-sustainment' is 'noticeable' in him (p. 191); Clennam describes
him as an 'honest, self-helpful, indefatigable old man, who has worked
his way all through his life' (p. 711). He is a plain and straightforward
man: when Clennam examines his 'way of managing his affairs', he

[1] In letters and articles Dickens repeatedly insisted on the need for 'the people' to help
themselves before they could be helped. See, for instance, the extract from the letter to
Austen Henry Layard, quoted on p. 196 above. Cf.: 'But the movement [for reform], to be
irresistible, must originate with themselves, the suffering many. Let *them* take the initiative,
and call the middle-class to unite with them: which they will do, heart and soul! Let the
working people, in the metropolis, in any one great town, but turn their intelligence, their
energy, their numbers, their power of union, their patience, their perseverance, in this
straight direction in earnest—and by Christmas, they shall find a government in Downing-
street and a House of Commons within hail of it, possessing not the faintest family resemblance to the Indifferents and Incapables last heard of in that slumberous neighbourhood.'
'To Working Men', *Household Words*, 10 (7 October 1854), 170. The article is not attributed to Dickens by Frederic G. Kitton, but the following statement made in it would seem
to proclaim that it is Dickens's: 'Long before this Journal came into existence, we syste-
matically tried to turn Fiction to the good account of showing the preventible wretchedness
and misery in which the mass of the people dwell . . .' (p. 169).

inds everything in 'its genuine working dress'; 'calculations and entries' re 'bluntly written' and 'always plain, and directed straight to the purpose' (pp. 265–6). As 'an ingenious man', Doyce has 'necessarily' to 'encounter every discouragement' that the Circumlocution Office can put in his way, but he works 'soberly' on, 'for the work's sake' (p. 514). He is strongly opposed to speculation: 'If I have a prejudice connected with money and money figures,' he tells Clennam, 'it is against speculating. I don't think I have any other. . . .' (p. 673.) Doyce, in other words, setting his face against patronage, deception and commercialism (whether of the bargain-balancing or speculative variety), is, in the society in which he lives, the prototype of a free man; and his liberating force is once again suggested when we see that it is he who arranges for Clennam's release from imprisonment in the Marshalsea. He also insists on Clennam's returning to his 'old place', and holds out the hope that 'a new and prosperous career' is 'opened' before them 'as partners' (p. 824).

Clennam, in the end, also becomes the partner of Little Dorrit, and his marriage to her should be viewed as another kind of liberation. In the first place, it joins him to a woman who herself exemplifies the typical Doycean qualities of industry, perseverance and disinterestedness: Clennam thinks of her as having '[toiled] on, for a good object's sake, without encouragement, without notice, against ignoble obstacles that would have turned an army of received heroes and heroines' (p. 720). It also joins him to a woman who has the gift of freedom, as it were, though it is regrettable that the uncontrolled note of idealization sounded in the reference to her battling with obstacles that would have turned an army is heard too often in the presentation of Little Dorrit—and particularly in regard to her possession of this gift. Her special position is suggested by the paradox of her circumstances: born in prison, having lived all her life in prison, she is free day by day to come and go as she pleases. It is as if this freedom is the talisman of an inner freedom, for, in an extraordinary manner, and quite unlike the other members of her family, she remains free from all taint of prison: she is 'inspired to be something which [is] not what the rest [are], and to be that something, different and laborious, for the sake of the rest' (p. 71); 'worldly wise in hard and poor necessities, she [is] innocent in all things else' (p. 78); when she states that it seems 'hard' to her that her father, on coming into his money, should have to pay all his debts before leaving the Marshalsea and so 'pay in life and money both', this is said to be the only 'speck' Clennam ever sees of

'the prison atmosphere' on her—'the prison, which [can] spoil so man:
things, [taints] Little Dorrit's mind no more than this', and he
'purity and goodness' are made 'the more beautiful' by 'the little spot
(p. 422).

Little Dorrit's love itself nurtures freedom. We are made to registe
its force when she visits Clennam in prison for the first time. He is 'i
and faint', sunk into a torpor:

> He roused himself, and cried out. And then he saw, in th
> loving, pitying, sorrowing, dear face, as in a mirror, how change
> he was; and she came towards him; and with her hands laid o:
> his breast to keep him in his chair, and with her knees upon th
> floor at his feet, and with her lips raised up to kiss him, and wit!
> her tears dropping on him as the rain from Heaven had droppe
> upon the flowers [i.e., which she has brought him], Little Dorrit
> a living presence, called him by his name.
>
> 'O, my best friend! Dear Mr. Clennam, don't let me see you
> weep! Unless you weep with pleasure to see me. I hope you do
> Your own poor child come back!' (p. 756)

The immediate effect of her entry, we see, is to 'rouse' him from hi:
torpor, to break through the deep lethargy produced by his confinement. But it is her love which has a profoundly liberating effect on
him. The nature of its effect is suggested by an image which at first
sight appears to be a sentimental cliché, but which is saved from being
so by the richness of its context, the image of her tears dropping on him
'as the rain from Heaven had dropped upon the flowers'. The image is
related to Clennam's thought, the night before, as he listens 'to the
fall of rain, on the yard pavement', of 'its softer fall upon the country
earth' (p. 755); it is related to the earlier association of rain in the
country with 'some beautiful form of growth or life' in contradistinction to the association of rain in London with the stagnation of the
city; and it is also related to the 'fountain of love and fidelity' which
Little Dorrit turns to her father, 'a captive with the jail-rot upon him'
(pp. 228–9). Little Dorrit's love, in other words, as it expresses itself
in the tears that fall on Clennam, has a sustaining quality that in its
power for life and growth brings release from all that is associated with
confinement. Similarly, it is suggested that their love, burning clean,
guards their freedom from the corruption that produces prisons: on

234

he morning of Clennam's release from the Marshalsea, Little Dorrit
[comes] into the prison with the sunshine' and requests him to burn
something' for her; he jokingly asks whether it is 'a charm', but
proceeds, as his last act before he leaves the prison, to burn the 'folded
paper' which, unknown to him, contains the record of Mrs. Clennam's
falsifications:

> 'Does the charm want any words to be said?' asked Arthur, as
> he held the paper over the flame. 'You can say (if you don't
> mind) "I love you!"' answered Little Dorrit. So he said it, and
> the paper burned away. (pp. 824–5)

On the day that Little Dorrit first visits Clennam, she wears her
'old, worn dress' (p. 756), as if in mute assertion that her feeling for
him has remained unchanged despite her new wealth; and Clennam
finally marries her after she has lost all her money. Their love, it is
thus intimated, is beyond the vicissitudes of wealth, and far removed
from that market in which the marriages of Fanny and Sparkler (if
not that of Gowan and Pet Meagles) is made. Like the love of John
Westlock and Ruth Pinch in *Martin Chuzzlewit* and of Florence
Dombey and Walter Gay in *Dombey and Son*, their love (in the world
which Merdle has prostrated before him) brings them, it is suggested,
the only riches that matter: Little Dorrit tells Clennam that she has
'nothing in the world' but that she is 'rich in being taken' by him (p.
817) The phrasing of Little Dorrit's declaration suggests, moreover,
that at the end of the novel Dickens is once again, as at the end of
Bleak House, envisaging the transforming power of love; but his treatment of the theme is again tentative, for he is content to assert no more
than Clennam's reciprocal experience of this power: on the day of
Little Dorrit's first visit to him in the Marshalsea, they sit side by side
'in the shadow of the wall', but the shadow is said to fall 'like light
upon him' (p. 758). At the end of *Little Dorrit*, however, Dickens
seems less hopeful than in *Bleak House*: the shadow of the Marshalsea
that falls on Clennam may be transformed by Little Dorrit's bright-
ness, but there is no suggestion that the shadow it casts on a whole
society will be transformed. There is even no closing assurance that
the society may be rehabilitated, as in *Bleak House*.[1] Having won his

---

[1] Dickens's pessimism is directly expressed in his correspondence: '. . . I do reluctantly
believe that the English people are habitually consenting parties to the miserable imbecility
into which we have fallen, *and never will help themselves out of it*. Who is to do it, if anybody

individual freedom, Clennam makes his way with Little Dorrit into
a world that is much the same as usual:

> They went quietly down into the roaring streets, inseparable and
> blessed; and as they passed along in sunshine and shade, the noisy
> and the eager, and the arrogant and the froward and the vain
> fretted, and chafed, and made their usual uproar. (p. 826)

---

is, God knows. But at present we are on the down-hill road to being conquered, and the
people WILL be content to bear it, sing "Rule Britannia", and WILL NOT be saved.

   'In No. 3 of my new book I have been blowing off a little of indignant steam which would
otherwise blow me up, and with God's leave I shall walk in the same all the days of my life,
but I have no present political faith or hope—not a grain.' Letter to W. C. Macready, 4. 10
1855, *Letters*, ed. Walter Dexter, II, 695.

7

GREAT EXPECTATIONS

I

Though its shorter length and more compact organization have prevented it from being classed with *Bleak House, Little Dorrit,* and *Our Mutual Friend, Great Expectations,*' says John H. Hagan, 'is really of a piece with that great social "trilogy" of Dickens's later years.'[1] This, it seems to me, is a mistaken judgement, but it is one that is implicit in much modern criticism of the novel. Time and again we are adjured to see in Pip 'the emblem of his age';[2] to realize that Pip's expectations are 'the great expectations of Victorian society';[3] and so to read the novel, at least in part, as 'a symbolic delineation of the criminal basis of wealth',[4] or as having a 'mythical side' which suggests that 'the wealth of society comes from tainted sources'.[5] Though the corrupting power of wealth, as I have argued, is Dickens's major theme, and though Pip is corrupted by his wealth, I do not think that the corruption of Victorian society is the theme of *Great*

---

[1] 'The Poor Labyrinth: The Theme of Social Injustice in Dickens's "Great Expectations" ', *Nineteenth-Century Fiction,* 9 (December 1954), 169.

[2] Jack Lindsay, *Charles Dickens* (London, 1950), p. 371.

[3] Edgar Johnson, *Charles Dickens,* II, 989. See too: T. A. Jackson, *Charles Dickens: The Progress of a Radical* (London, 1937), p. 197; Edmund Wilson, 'Dickens: The Two Scrooges', *The Wound and the Bow,* p. 54; Humphry House, 'G. B. S. on *Great Expectations'*, *All in Due Time* (London, 1955), pp. 203–4; Thomas E. Connolly, 'Technique in *Great Expectations'*, *Philological Quarterly,* 34 (January 1955), 48; Julian Moynahan, 'The Hero's Guilt: The Case of *Great Expectations'*, *Essays in Criticism,* 10 (January 1960), 67, 78.

[4] Barbara Hardy, 'The Change of Heart in Dickens' Novels', *Victorian Studies,* 5 (September 1961), 61.

[5] A. O. J. Cockshut, *The Imagination of Charles Dickens* (London, 1965; first published 1961), p. 162. See too G. Robert Stange, who says we are led 'to speculate on the connections between a gentleman and his money, on the dark origins of even the most respectable fortunes'. 'Expectations Well Lost: Dickens' Fable for His Time', *The Dickens Critics,* ed. George H. Ford and Lauriat Lane, pp. 303–4. The essay originally appeared in *College English,* 16 (1954–55).

Great Expectations

Expectations. So far as I can make out, there is nothing in the text
not a word or a phrase or an image, which indicates that Pip has th
sort of representative significance suggested; and in Dickens's matur
work, as we have seen, the representative is made plainly visible. No
does the plot support the more specific symbolic or mythical reading
quoted above. Magwitch may be a criminal and so tainted, but he i
given the chance to start life afresh in Australia; and the whol
point about the money that he makes there is that it is honestl
made.

The plot, indeed, as we might expect, is our best indication of wha
the novel is about; and what the plot does is insistently to link th
lives not only of Pip and Magwitch but also of Pip and Miss Havishan
and of Miss Havisham and Magwitch. Miss Havisham and Magwitch
it is true, never meet, but they are clear mirror-images in Pip's life
and Dickens goes out of his way to link them furthermore by providin
them with a mutual enemy, Compeyson being the destructive influenc
in both their lives, and by making Magwitch the father of Mis
Havisham's adopted daughter. In Dickens's late work plot connec
tions of this kind are indicative, as *Bleak House* demonstrates, of
thematic linking; and our awareness of the novelist's analogical metho
enables us to perceive that the stories of all three protagonists ar
variations on a theme.

Not only Pip but also Magwitch and Miss Havisham have 'grea
expectations', and all three characters allow their lives to be dominate
by their expectations.[1] Varied though their hopes are, moreover, ther
is a common pattern both in the origin of the expectations and in th
means by which these characters trust they will be realized. In eacl
case the expectations have their source in a desire for change, for th
transformation of an existing situation; and the expectations are sus
tained in each case by the belief that such a transformation may b
effected through the agency of another. Thus Pip's desire is for
change of status, for his transformation from a working-class boy int
a gentleman; and he hopes this change will be brought about by
patron. Magwitch's desire is also for a change of status, for a trans
formation from a social outcast into the 'maker' and 'owner' of

[1] I am glad to have found support for a long-held view of the novel in a short but weight
article by Arnold P. Drew, 'Structure in *Great Expectations*', *The Dickensian*, 52 (Jun
1956), 123–7. Drew makes the point that all three protagonists have expectations (p. 127)
and his view of the underlying significance of Magwitch's extension of patronage to Pip an
of Miss Havisham's adoption of Estella (pp. 125–6) is similar to that which I shall argue—
see p. 240 below.

entleman; and he relies on Pip to effect this change for him. Miss
Iavisham's desire is for a change of condition, for the transformation
f a condition of passive suffering into one in which she may inflict
uffering on others; and she trusts to Estella to work this change for
.er. This analogical pattern is suggestive of the theme that is dis-
ernible on the surface of the action: since the plot shows that none
f the expectations held by these characters is fulfilled—or, at any
ate, not in a way that is anticipated—the theme, at this level, would
:em to be the self-defeating folly of a reliance on such expectations.
t would certainly be possible to analyse *Great Expectations* along
hese lines, and such an analysis, I believe, would bring us closer to
he essential stuff of the novel than a consideration of the putative
ocial theme or an exclusive concern with Pip's moral progress once
.e is claimed by wealth; but a further feature of the plot adverts us to
. deeper level of meaning.

Perhaps the most striking aspect of the plot is the incidence of hidden
elationships. That several of these relationships are in no way con-
1ected with the two mysteries on which the plot is based (the identity
>f Pip's patron and the identity of Estella's parents) suggests that the
:xistence of such relationships is more than a natural dimension of the
nystery-plot. Pip's major relationships are a representative instance.
With Miss Havisham he believes that he has a hidden relationship,
`or he is sure that she is secretly his patron. He refrains from actively
:ourting Estella out of a delicate sense of a hidden relationship with
.er, for he believes that Miss Havisham has secretly selected him as
Estella's husband and that the girl has no choice in the matter. Living
he life of a gentleman in London, Pip is unaware of his hidden re-
ationship with Magwitch, his secret benefactor. As a gentleman it is
>ne of Pip's prime concerns to keep his relationship with Joe Gargery
1idden. And in his relationship with Herbert Pocket, Pip, playing
Magwitch, secretly becomes Herbert's patron and closely guards his
;ecret. Pip's hidden relationships have a number of analogues in the
1ovel: Estella is quite unaware of her relationship to Jaggers's housekeeper, her mother, and to Magwitch, her father; Jaggers keeps the
;ecret of his relationship with his housekeeper, and is in turn unaware
>f the relationship between his client, Magwitch, and the girl he has
led another client, Miss Havisham, to adopt; Orlick has a mysteriously
hidden relationship with Compeyson, and a secret relationship with
Mrs. Joe; Herbert remains for a long time secretly engaged to Clara,
and her relationship with her bedridden father is hidden from the eyes (if

not the ears) of her lover; finally, Wemmick, in Little Britain, zealously hides his relationships with the Aged P. and Miss Skiffins.

The plot, therefore, is productive of two main analogues, and, given the nature of Dickens's art, we might expect to find a connection between the two. It is only, I suggest, when we relate the motive of hidden relationship to that of the expectations of the protagonists that we get to the heart of the novel. The avowed expectations of Pip and Magwitch and Miss Havisham, we then see, hide deeper, more fundamental urges on the part of each than is at first apparent. In the course of this discussion I shall try to substantiate my argument by close analysis of relevant passages in the text; for the moment, however, I would simply advance the proposition that the protagonists' profounder hopes are for the transformation of relationships whose true significance is for long hidden even from themselves. Thus Pip so readily embraces the idea of a patron because his secret desire is for a parent, for the kind of relation that he, the orphan, has never known. Thus Magwitch does not so much want to own a gentleman as win a son, and so make up for the child he has lost. And thus Miss Havisham does not so much want to use Estella as an instrument of revenge as bind her to herself as a daughter, and so make up (like Magwitch) for the child she cannot have. If it is granted that the plot pattern justifies such a formulation, then it would appear that the theme of the novel is the need for love, and that the novel, at its deepest level of meaning, is concerned with various manifestations of a search for love—not with a search for money.

To view *Great Expectations* in this way enables us to understand its place in Dickens's development as a novelist. This novel is not of a piece with *Bleak House*, *Little Dorrit* and *Our Mutual Friend*; but coming after the first two works in the 'trilogy', it was for Dickens necessary prior undertaking to the writing of his last completed novel. In *Bleak House* and *Little Dorrit* the force of love is opposed (among other things) to the evils of parasitism and patronage that are shown to be consuming and paralysing the societies portrayed; but, as I have pointed out, the love relationships in these novels are not fully realized and carry nothing like the weight of the social indictment. In *Great Expectations* there is a significant shift of emphasis. The theme of parasitism and patronage, though greatly reduced in scope, are carried over from the earlier novels into the account of Pip's relations with Miss Havisham and Magwitch; but they are treated with little of the imaginative intensity and vigour that attend the transformation of these relations into relationships of love. It is notable, moreover, that Pip's relationship with Estella, despite the amount of passion that Pip invests in it, is no more substantial as a relationship, a vital exchange, than that of Esther Summerson and Woodcourt or that of Clennam and Little Dorrit. It is as if Dickens were free to express reciprocally powerful emotion, at this stage of his development, only within the framework of parent-child relationships; as if he had first to get his own personal craving for parental love out of his system before he could go on to deal effectively with sexual love; as if, therefore, his treatment of parent-child relationships in *Great Expectations* served as a clearing ground for his profound presentation of love between adult men and women in *Our Mutual Friend*. At all events, the writing of *Great Expectations* certainly enabled him to explore and establish the nature of meaningful love as he came to understand it, to define a mutual selflessness and understanding as the necessary condition of love; and it also preceded the achievement of a new equilibrium in *Our Mutual Friend*, in which his most comprehensive social criticism is balanced by his most complex portrayal of sexual relations.

Great Expectations is one of Dickens's most personal novels, as personal, perhaps, even as *David Copperfield*; and consequently it bears the marks of his own cravings to an unusual degree. It has generally been held that Pip's passion for Estella, the most strongly expressed passion in the novels to this point, is a reflection of Dickens's feelings for Ellen Ternan; we may add that his relationship with the young actress is furthermore reflected in the emphasis in the novel on hidden relationship. But I would suggest that it was Dickens's decision to use Pip as a first-person narrator that determined the emotional centre of the novel, which is not the relationship of Pip and Estella. For Dickens this decision meant that his new novel would inevitably challenge comparison with *David Copperfield*, the only other work from which he had debarred himself as omniscient author; and to ensure that he did not repeat himself, he read the earlier novel again some six weeks before the first instalment of the new novel appeared: 'To be quite sure I had fallen into no unconscious repetitions, I read *David Copperfield* again the other day, and was affected by it to a degree you would hardly believe.'[1] It seems at least likely that the use of the first-person method and the reading of *David Copperfield* reactivated Dickens's sense of his early traumatic experiences, particularly the

[1] Letter to John Forster, October 1860, *Charles Dickens*, III, 329.

sense of being abandoned by both his parents when he was sent to work at the blacking warehouse; and in the incalculable ways of the imagination this led to his unconsciously shaping the plot he had devised into a vehicle for the vicarious satisfaction of his own deepest need as a child. Certainly the matrix of the plot is the abandonment and rejection of children: Pip, the orphan, who has never seen his father and mother and is brought up by hand, has the continued sense as a child of being always treated as if he 'had insisted on being born in opposition to the dictates of reason, religion, and morality, and against the dissuading arguments of [his] best friends' (p. 20); this is how Magwitch recounts his earliest memory: 'I first become aware of myself, down in Essex, a thieving turnips for my living. Summun had run away from me—a man—a tinker—and he'd took the fire with him, and left me wery cold' (p. 328); and Estella, as a child, is handed over to Jaggers by her mother, to be done with as he sees fit. We may add that Miss Havisham, though not a child, is abandoned by her lover on her wedding day.

To locate the centre of the novel in Pip's need for love and in his relations with Magwitch and Miss Havisham furthermore enables us, I believe, to account for the unsatisfactory figure of Orlick. In a most skilfully and carefully plotted work Orlick stands out as an apparently gratuitous embodiment of violence. Julian Moynahan has persuasively argued that Orlick is bound to Pip 'by ties of analogy as double, *alter ego* and dark mirror-image', that in the novel 'criminality is displaced from the hero on to a melodramatic villain', that this villain, however, is 'part of a complex unity' which might be called 'Pip-Orlick', and that through Pip-Orlick Dickens makes a 'profound analysis of the immoral and criminal elements in his hero's (and the century's) favourite dream'.[1] This is a fascinating explanation of Orlick's role, but it seems to me to be open to two objections. First, as I have already remarked, there is nothing in the text to support the extended, 'social' significance of the relationship. Second, as Moynahan himself admits, 'the only clue to [the Pip-Orlick] unity which is given at the surface level of the narrative is Pip's obsession of criminal guilt'; and he adds that 'we do not find the objective correlative of that conviction until we recognise in the insensate and compunctionless Orlick a shadow image of the tender-minded and yet monstrously ambitious young hero' (p. 70). To this I think we must object that an interpretation of a literary text, no matter how deep it may probe, must be founded on

[1] 'The Hero's Guilt', *loc. cit.*, pp. 69–70.

the surface of the action, and that if the only clue at this level to the Pip-Orlick unity is Pip's obsession of guilt, then this is simply insufficient evidence. As far as I can see, on every occasion that Pip feels guilty an adequate explanation of his feeling is provided in the text; and nowhere does the text clearly support an identification of Pip and Orlick. Orlick's criminality, therefore, cannot be an 'objective correlative' of Pip's guilt. It may well be that Moynahan has expertly analysed a split in Dickens himself, and that feelings in Dickens which were not allowed expression in the portrayal of Pip were compulsively projected on to Orlick. This may help to account for the unsatisfactoriness of Orlick, but it is not relevant to an understanding of Pip.

Orlick should rather be seen as a counterpart of Pip in an altogether simpler sense. This is how he is first presented:

> Dolge Orlick was at work and present, next day, when I reminded Joe of my half-holiday. He said nothing at the moment, for he and Joe had just got a piece of hot iron between them, and I was at the bellows; but by-and-by he said, leaning on his hammer:
>
> 'Now, master! Sure you're not a going to favour only one of us? If Young Pip has a half-holiday, do as much for Old Orlick.' I suppose he was about five-and-twenty, but he usually spoke of himself as an ancient person.
>
> 'Why, what'll you do with a half-holiday, if you get it?' said Joe.
>
> 'What'll *I* do with it? What'll *he* do with it? I'll do as much with it as *him*,' said Orlick.
>
> 'As to Pip, he's going up-town,' said Joe.
>
> 'Well, then, as to Old Orlick, *he's* a going up-town,' retorted that worthy. 'Two can go up-town. Tain't only one wot can go up-town.'
>
> 'Don't lose your temper,' said Joe.
>
> 'Shall if I like,' growled Orlick. 'Some and their up-towning! Now, master! Come. No favouring in this shop. Be a man!' (p. 106)

Orlick, we see, may be a man of twenty-five and insist on calling himself Old Orlick, but in this scene he behaves like a child. He behaves, indeed, like a rival sibling, incensed at the 'favour' shown Pip; and it is with a compulsive nastiness and violence, akin to that charac-

teristically manifested by a rejected child, that he thereafter proceeds
to draw out a red-hot bar from the furnace, makes at Pip with it 'as if
he were going to run it through [his] body', and hammers it out on
the anvil as if, Pip thinks, it were he, 'and the sparks were [his] spirting
blood' (p. 106). The actual violence in which Orlick engages, moreover, his murderous attacks on Mrs. Joe and on Pip, are motivated by
the same feelings of rejection and jealousy, as he himself admits. Prior
to his attempt to kill Pip, he tells him that it was he who attacked
Mrs. Joe and 'left her for dead', and he adds: 'But it warn't Old
Orlick as did it; it was you. You was favoured, and he was bullied
and beat. Old Orlick bullied and beat, eh? Now you pays for it. You
done it; now you pays for it' (pp. 404–5). This, I believe, is the only
place in the text that might be held to lend support to Moynahan's view
of Orlick as Pip's *alter ego*, but then Orlick's words here are at least
equally susceptible of a perfectly straightforward explanation; they also
emphatically reveal the kind of feeling in which his violence is rooted.
This feeling is expressed in a different manner when, as he taunts Pip, he
sits 'hugging himself' (p. 402). If Orlick is to be seen as a counterpart
of Pip, then it is as a man who retains an abiding sense of being unloved, and unlike Pip, is denied the chance to palliate it, his one
attempt to seek love being repulsed by Biddy. Orlick, in other words,
is necessary to the design of the novel though he is not successfully
incorporated in it, and despite what may be an element of compulsion
in his creation; for, where Pip wins new life through love, Orlick
demonstrates that to be deprived of love is to breed violence and hate
and death. The relationship of Pip and Orlick should be viewed, I
think, as a preliminary exploration of a theme that is triumphantly
handled in the far more subtle and powerful relationship of Eugene
Wrayburn and Bradley Headstone in *Our Mutual Friend*.

II

The pattern of Pip's progress to man's estate is revealed to us through the
mist-marsh symbolism, which dominates the novel. As a boy Pip likes
to wander on the marshes, which adjoin the village in which he lives:

> I remember that at a later period of my 'time,' I used to stand
> about the churchyard on Sunday evenings, when night was fall-
> ing, comparing my own perspective with the windy marsh view,

and making out some likeness between them by thinking how
flat and low both were, and how on both there came an unknown
way and a dark mist and then the sea. . . . (p. 100)

This passage does more than equate the low, flat marshes with the
bleak, dismal emptiness of Pip's life and prospects as he sees them;
the marshes, leading by 'an unknown way' and through 'a dark mist'
to 'the sea', image the course of life itself, leading from a point in the
present through an unknown future to death;[1] and it is indicated that
Pip too is destined to make his way through the dark mist. What
awaits him when that happens has been previously intimated in the
scene in which he sets out to take the stolen food to the convict:

> On every rail and gate, wet lay clammy, and the marsh-mist
> was so thick, that the wooden finger on the post directing people
> to our village . . . was invisible to me until I was quite close under
> it. Then, as I looked up at it, while it dripped, it seemed to my
> oppressed conscience like a phantom devoting me to the Hulks.
>
> The mist was heavier yet when I got out upon the marshes,
> so that instead of my running at everything, everything seemed
> to run at me. This was very disagreeable to a guilty mind. The
> gates and dykes and banks came bursting at me through the mist,
> as if they cried as plainly as could be, 'A boy with Somebody-
> else's pork pie! Stop him!' The cattle came upon me with like
> suddenness, staring out of their eyes, and steaming out of their
> nostrils, 'Halloa, young thief!' . . .
>
> All this time I was getting on towards the river; but however
> fast I went, I couldn't warm my feet, to which the damp cold
> seemed riveted, as the iron was riveted to the leg of the man I
> was running to meet. I knew my way to the Battery, pretty
> straight, for I had been down there on a Sunday with Joe . . .
> However, in the confusion of the mist, I found myself at last too
> far to the right, and consequently had to try back along the river-
> side, on the bank of loose stones above the mud and the stakes
> that staked the tide out. . . . (pp. 14–15)

The mist here has a strange effect on the marsh scene: it not only blots
out the usual aspect of familiar things but transforms those things which

---

[1] Dickens repeatedly views the sea in this light—see, for instance, the references in *Dombey
and Son* (Ch. IV, pp. 137, 138 above) and in *Our Mutual Friend* (Ch. VIII, p. 279 below).

are apprehended through it, for the fixed gates and dykes and banks now seem to 'run at' Pip, 'bursting' at him 'through the mist'. The mist, moreover, as we might guess from its having obscured the village finger-post, has a not unexpected effect on Pip himself: though he knows his way to the Battery 'pretty straight', it confuses him and makes him lose his way. The mist, that is to say, which both transforms and confuses the scene on the marshes, which, we remember, image the course of life, is analogous to something which may transform and confuse the progress of a man's life—is analogous, in a word, to 'great expectations'. The analogy, indeed, is made quite explicit towards the end of the novel: 'But whether Joe knew how poor I was, and how my great expectations had all dissolved, like our own marsh mists before the sun, I could not understand' (p. 445). The mist, an apt symbol of the insubstantiality of Pip's expectations, is neatly used to mark stages in his progress. When he leaves his village for London, following Jaggers's momentous communication, he notices with satisfaction that 'the mists had all solemnly risen now, and the world lay spread before [him]' (p. 152); Pip's feeling here is a measure of his delusion, for it is into a confusing, fallen world that he makes his way— as the Miltonic echo ironically suggests. When Pip begins to see what his expectations are doing to him, the moment is appropriately marked by a lifting of the mist in which he is enveloped: 'Once more, the mists were rising as I walked away [i.e., from the village, after Mrs. Joe's funeral]. If they disclosed to me as I suspect they did, that I should *not* come back, and that Biddy was quite right, all I can say is— they were quite right too' (p. 271). Finally, in the last sentence of the novel, the evening mists rise as Pip, having given up his expectations, is reunited with Estella.

The mist-marsh symbolism, therefore, prompts us to regard Pip's story as a *Bildungsroman* in which the hero's development is viewed as a process that involves a loss of direction and culminates in his finding of the way. The novel furthermore prompts the reflection that the achievement of maturity is not necessarily a concomitant of adulthood, and that, if Miss Havisham and Magwitch find their way only at the end of their lives, the story of their development is analogous to that of Pip. It is only in the case of Pip that the line of development is divided into three equal and clearly marked 'stages',[1] but the develop-

---

[1] The novel is divided into three 'books': 'The First Stage of Pip's Expectations', Chs. I–XIX; 'The Second Stage of Pip's Expectations', Chs. XX–XXXIX; 'The Third Stage of Pip's Expectations', Chs. XL–LIX.

ment of all three protagonists conforms to a pattern, which may be described as follows: Stage One reveals how an inner desolation generates the desire for a transformation of circumstance and for 'expectations', and how this desire is associated with an immature dependence on another; Stage Two makes clear that a reliance on expectations represents an obscuring of real issues that results in a loss of direction, a side-tracking movement away from true development; Stage Three indicates how an abandonment of the cherished expectations leads to a finding of the way, a recognition of the paramount need for love which is presented as the mark of an achieved maturity.

III

The sort of world in which Pip finds himself is vividly described in the opening scene of the novel:

> Ours was the marsh country, down by the river, within, as the river wound, twenty miles of the sea. My first most vivid and broad impression of the identity of things, seems to me to have been gained on a memorable raw afternoon towards evening. At such a time I found out for certain, that this bleak place overgrown with nettles was the churchyard; and that Philip Pirrip, late of this parish, and also Georgiana wife of the above, were dead and buried; and that Alexander, Bartholomew, Abraham, Tobias, and Roger, infant children of the aforesaid, were also dead and buried; and that the dark flat wilderness beyond the churchyard, intersected with dykes and mounds and gates, with scattered cattle feeding on it, was the marshes; and that the low leaden line beyond was the river; and that the distant savage lair from which the wind was rushing, was the sea; and that the small bundle of shivers growing afraid of it all and beginning to cry, was Pip.
>
> 'Hold your noise!' cried a terrible voice, as a man started up from among the graves at the side of the church porch. 'Keep still, you little devil, or I'll cut your throat!' (pp. 1–2)

If on this raw afternoon Pip gains his first 'impression of the identity of things', it is clear that what he experiences in a new way is a sense of what Stephen Dedalus, following Aquinas, calls '*quidditas*, the *what-*

ness of a thing'. Thus what Pip 'finds out' is the reverse of that which is suggested by the syntax of this passage; that is to say, he finds out not that 'this bleak place' is 'the churchyard', which presumably he knows already, but that the churchyard is a bleak place. Similarly, he finds out that the marshes are a 'dark flat wilderness', that the river is a 'low leaden line', and that the sea is a 'savage lair'. Pip, that is, experiences a sudden sense of the inner meaning of things, experiences, in a word, a series of Joycean epiphanies. And clearly the central epiphany he experiences on this memorable occasion is that connected with the family graves: it is not the fact that his father and mother and brothers are 'dead and buried' that he discovers but the meaning of death. He has a vivid apprehension of what it means to be dead and buried, and that dead and buried is what his family is.

The scene that Pip surveys, the bleak churchyard 'overgrown with nettles' giving way to the wilderness of the marshes which lead to the savage lair of the sea, is apparently both barren and threatening; yet we realize that it is his perceiving consciousness which makes it so. It is his sense of himself as a small, frightened, tearful 'bundle of shivers', his sense of his own helplessness and defencelessness, that colours the scene, that makes the sea, for instance, into a savage lair. The menace and barrenness that Pip registers in the scene around him, in other words, are a projection of his own inner fear and desolation; and his feelings of fear and desolation are directly attributable to the epiphany of the graves, to the sense that is borne in on him in the churchyard of his own aloneness in the world.

Pip, indeed, is so much on his own that in effect he even names himself, as we are told in the opening sentences of the novel: 'My father's family name being Pirrip, and my christian name Philip, my infant tongue could make of both names nothing longer or more explicit than Pip. So I called myself Pip, and came to be called Pip.' Certainly the one remaining member of his family, in whose house he lives, does little to make him feel at home. The failure of his sister, Mrs. Joe, to provide him with the maternal succour he needs is figured not alone in her having brought him up 'by hand' ('a hard and heavy hand') but by the coarse apron she 'almost always' wears which has 'a square impregnable bib in front, that [is] stuck full of pins and needles' (p. 6); and Mrs. Joe is not slow to express the resentment she feels at the role that has been forced on her: 'I may truly say I've never had this apron of mine off,' she tells Pip, 'since born you were. It's bad enough to be a blacksmith's wife (and him a Gargery), without being your mother' (p. 7). She also repeatedly reminds Pip of 'all the times' she has wished him 'in [his] grave', and that he has 'contumaciously refused to go there' (p. 24). It is true that the boy is loved by Joe, but 'in those early days' Pip loves his brother-in-law 'perhaps for no better reason . . . than because the dear fellow [lets him] love him' (p. 37); and it is clear that he can in no way think of him *in loco parentis*: 'I always treated him,' Pip tells us, 'as a larger species of child, and as no more than my equal' (p. 7).

It should be apparent, then, that the real need of 'the small bundle of shivers growing afraid of it all and beginning to cry' is for warmth and security, in a word, for parental love. This is Pip's fundamental need though it comes (in a manner familiar to Freudians) to be displaced by the spurious need for wealth and station that is epitomized by his expectations. We are given an oblique indication of the two needs that are posed against each other in the novel in a parenthetic remark of the narrator as Pip gazes at the graves of his brothers—(in passing it might be noted that Dickens effortlessly and consistently succeeds in simultaneously evoking both the world of the young boy and that of the adult who is telling his story): the 'five little brothers' are said to have given up 'trying to get a living exceedingly early in that universal struggle' (p. 1); and if it is thus intimated that the universal struggle to get a living may be interpreted (as Pip comes to interpret it) as a need to get on financially, the dead brothers make us think here of a deeper need—the need to live, to find that which may support and nourish life. If the reference to a universal struggle, moreover, adverts us to what might be regarded as a 'mythical' element in the narrative, then—*pace* A. O. J. Cockshut—the animating myth of *Great Expectations* is surely that of the search for the father: the point is underlined for us when, in a local newspaper, the officious Pumblechook is referred to in relation to Pip as 'the Mentor of our young Telemachus' (p. 218).[1]

The two needs in Pip's life that are juxtaposed here point to an interesting development in Dickens's treatment of the victim theme that runs through the novels. Pip is characteristically a victim, cast from birth, as it were, for the role. In his childhood and youth he is the inevitable victim of his sister's rampages, of Pumblechook's ministra-

[1] G. Robert Stange lists the search for a father as one of the characteristic features of the development-novel': 'The recurrent themes of the genre are all there [i.e., in *Great Expectations*]: city is posed against country, experience against innocence; there is a search for the true father; there is the exposure to crime and the acceptance of guilt and expiation.' 'Expectations Well Lost', *loc. cit.*, p. 296.

tions, and of Wopsle's theatrical proclivities, not to mention of Trabb's boy's deflations. As he grows older, he may be seen as the victim of Magwitch's secret plans for him, of Miss Havisham's deception of him, and of Orlick's murderous rage. But, above all, Pip is really his own victim, the victim of his own conflicting needs. And in this respect, as in so many others, there is an analogy between Pip's case and that of Magwitch and Miss Havisham: they are both victims of Compeyson, but far more radically, I shall argue, of themselves.

If Pip's real need is for parental love, then the scene in the churchyard presents a striking prefigurement of how he will eventually come to find it. It is at the moment that Pip begins to cry, it will be remembered, that Magwitch starts up 'from among the graves'. At the moment when Pip feels most alone, that is, we are shown that he is in fact not alone; it is as if Magwitch, indeed, comes into Pip's life in place of his dead parents. It is many years, of course, before Pip comes to accept the consequences of his compassion for the convict; on the contrary, about to leave his village in pursuance of his expectations, he is glad to think that his encounter with him is a thing of the past:

> If I had often thought before, with something allied to shame, of my companionship with the fugitive whom I had once seen limping among those graves, what were my thoughts on this Sunday, when the place recalled the wretch, ragged and shivering, with his felon iron and badge! My comfort was, that it happened a long time ago, and that he had doubtless been transported a long way off, and that he was dead to me, and might be veritably dead into the bargain. (p. 139)

Far from being 'dead' to Pip, Magwitch, we see, has become part of Pip's life, as his strong and vivid memory of him and his frequent thoughts of his 'companionship' with him reveal. And from the time of his meeting with the convict, the plot functions in such a way that Pip's sense of relationship with Magwitch is regularly and continually kept alive: there is Magwitch's first gift to Pip of the 'two fat sweltering one-pound notes' (p. 73); there is the attack on Mrs. Joe with Magwitch's leg-iron (pp. 113–14); there is Pip's coach journey in the enforced company of the convict whom Magwitch had asked to give him the two pounds (pp. 214–17); there is Pip's visit to Newgate, which makes him recall his encounters with both Magwitch and his messenger (p. 249); and finally—shortly before Magwitch's return to England (p. 299)—Pip is assailed in Jaggers's office by a sudden memory of the way Magwitch had put him on a tombstone (p. 272). As a boy, moreover, though Pip is often tempted to tell Joe about his experience with the convict, he finally recognizes that he cannot bring himself to do so: '. . . the secret was such an old one now, had so grown into me and become a part of myself, that I could not tear it away' (p. 114). The language of this passage suggests that Pip's secret relationship with Magwitch has become so much a part of him that it is flesh of his flesh.

What Pip takes to be his secret relationship with Miss Havisham begins when she asks Pumblechook whether he knows of a boy who could come and play at her house. Pumblechook and Mrs. Joe seize designingly on Pip for the purpose: 'For you do not know,' Mrs. Joe triumphantly tells her husband, 'that Uncle Pumblechook, being sensible that for anything we can tell, this boy's fortune may be made by his going to Miss Havisham's, has offered to take him into town to-night in his own chaise-cart, and to keep him to-night, and to take him with his own hands to Miss Havisham's to-morrow morning' (p. 47). Pip's expectations of fortune, it is clear, are bred by his elders: they have no doubt that Miss Havisham will 'do something' for him (p. 64); Pumblechook falls into the habit of coming 'over of a night' for the express purpose of discussing Pip's 'prospects' with Mrs. Joe (p. 90). Pip's expectations, that is, are grounded in the values of his elders, in a prevailing barrenness of value that is the spiritual equivalent of the marsh 'wilderness' in which he grows up. If we would descry a 'social' significance in the novel, then it may be asserted in relation to the fact that the right to have one's fortune made for one is presented as an almost unchallenged assumption in the society portrayed. Biddy and Joe have their reservations, but they are lone voices where Pumblechook sets the tone; and in London, too, Pip's associates, Herbert and Jaggers and Wemmick, never question his right to his expectations. The world of *Bleak House* is not far off when Miss Havisham assigns her relations 'stations' at the table where they may 'come to feast' upon her when she is dead (pp. 81–2); but the Pockets are minor characters in this novel, and the distinctive concern of *Great Expectations*, revealed in the genesis of Pip's expectations, is not with parasitism.

Pip himself begins to hope that Miss Havisham will do something for him when he first meets Estella:

'Call Estella,' [Miss Havisham] repeated, flashing a look at me. 'You can do that. Call Estella. At the door.'

To stand in the dark in a mysterious passage of an unknown house, bawling Estella to a scornful young lady neither visible nor responsive, and feeling it a dreadful liberty so to roar out her name, was almost as bad as playing to order. But, she answered at last, and her light came along the dark passage like a star.

Miss Havisham beckoned her to come close, and took up a jewel from the table, and tried its effect upon her fair young bosom and against her pretty brown hair. 'Your own, one day, my dear, and you will use it well. Let me see you play cards with this boy.'

'With this boy! Why, he is a common labouring-boy!'

I thought I overheard Miss Havisham answer—only it seemed so unlikely—'Well? You can break his heart.'

'What do you play, boy?' asked Estella of myself, with the greatest disdain.

'Nothing but beggar my neighbour, Miss.'

'Beggar him,' said Miss Havisham to Estella. So we sat down to cards. . . .

'He calls the knaves, Jacks, this boy!' said Estella with disdain, before our first game was out. 'And what coarse hands he has! And what thick boots!'

I had never thought of being ashamed of my hands before; but I began to consider them a very indifferent pair. Her contempt for me was so strong, that it became infectious, and I caught it.

She won the game, and I dealt. I misdealt, as was only natural, when I knew she was lying in wait for me to do wrong; and she denounced me for a stupid, clumsy labouring-boy. (pp. 54–5)

The emotional insecurity that Pip is heir to is figured yet once again as he stands in the dark in the passage, alone, uncertain, afraid. Suddenly, into that darkness there comes Estella, bringing light, 'like a star'; and it is apparent that from this moment Pip's hunger for love is directed to her. Given the distance that separates the 'common labouring-boy' from the 'scornful young lady', however, Pip's hunger is that of a Tantalus; and it is in these circumstances that his own expectations, first conceived by Pumblechook and Mrs. Joe, are born. Aspiring to Estella and accepting her standards, for he is at once ashamed of his 'coarse hands' and 'thick boots', Pip can only hope to be transformed from a labouring-boy into a gentleman, and is emotionally and spiritually ready to seize at the chance of a patron miraculously effecting such a transformation for him. In the end Magwitch's patronage changes the course of his life for him, but then Pip's life (shrouded in mist) takes the turn he wants it to take. Pip, in other words, is corrupted first by his own expectations, and only later by those which Magwitch provides for him. His corruption is implicit here in his being 'infected' by Estella's contempt for him; and his capitulation to her values of class and money heralds his later transformation not only into a gentleman but into an insufferable snob, the sign of whose errant career is the extent to which he loses touch with both Joe and Biddy. Pip's snobbery, however, is only a superficial instance of his moral corruption—it is shown to be only skin-deep— but what really undermines him is his confusion of love and wealth. The two become linked for him when Miss Havisham tries out the jewel on Estella, and Pip speedily comes to believe that the one is inseparable from the other. In this respect the game of cards that he plays with Estella is premonitory of what happens to him. Estella does 'beggar him', as Miss Havisham directs, for, an emotional beggar to start with, avid of love, he is soon reduced to soliciting material aid in his desire to win her: after he has been going to Miss Havisham's for some time, he takes the opportunity of 'enlarging' to her upon his 'knowing nothing and wanting to know everything, in the hope that she might offer some help towards that desirable end' (p. 88); when Jaggers informs him that he has Great Expectations, his response is: 'My dream was out; my wild fancy was surpassed by sober reality; Miss Havisham was going to make my fortune on a grand scale' (p. 130); and when he comes of age and hopefully repairs to Jaggers's office, the lawyer relentlessly forces him to make the inquiry: 'Have— I—anything to receive, sir?' (p. 273).

The game of cards, which Pip and Estella play at Miss Havisham's command and which Pip loses, is also a prefigurement of the game Miss Havisham plays with them, a game in which he is the ordained loser—as he was shown to be in the original, and surely preferable, ending of the novel.[1] Given the facts of Estella's upbringing, the game

---

[1] As is well known, Dickens changed the end of the novel at Bulwer-Lytton's suggestion, putting in 'a very pretty piece of writing' and bringing Pip and Estella together again (see letter to John Forster, 1. 7. 1861, *Letters*, ed. Walter Dexter, III, 226). Dickens had no doubt the story would 'be more acceptable through the alteration', but it sadly contradicts all that has gone before; it is dramatically right that Pip should lose Estella, as I trust the following analysis will indicate.

for Pip, indeed, is not worth the candle, as he himself realizes time and again: 'I asked myself the question whether I did not surely know that if Estella were beside me at the moment instead of Biddy, she would make me miserable? I was obliged to admit that I did know it for a certainty, and I said to myself, "Pip, what a fool you are!"' (p. 123); 'Once for all; I knew to my sorrow, often and often, if not always, that I loved her against reason, against promise, against peace, against hope, against happiness, against all discouragement that could be' (p. 219); 'I thought that with her I could have been happy there [i.e., in the frowzy room of an inn] for life. (I was not at all happy there at the time, observe, and I knew it well.)' (p. 252); 'And still I stood looking at the house, thinking how happy I should be if I lived there with her, and knowing that I never was happy with her, but always miserable' (p. 256); 'I never had one hour's happiness in her society, and yet my mind all round the four-and-twenty hours was harping on the happiness of having her with me unto death' (p. 287). Pip's love for Estella, that is to say, is patently sentimental, in the sense that his feeling for her is inappropriate; and the question that arises is why he persists in it 'against trust and against hope' and despite the fact that it constantly causes him 'pain' (p. 254). One answer, as I have suggested, is that his love for Estella is inextricably bound up with his expectations, and as long as he persists in them, he is incapable of making his heart follow his head. Ross H. Dabney has pointed out that 'he intends to take Estella as a gift from Miss Havisham, part of his expectations, a being who has no choice but to follow her guardian's money';[1] and we may add that, though he is sufficiently generous in this respect not to force his attentions on Estella, he is as much prepared to live on unearned income in his emotional life as in his life as a gentleman.

But the fact that Pip finally declares his love for Estella not only in the face of his knowledge of her but after he has discovered that it is not Miss Havisham who is his patron, and that his expectations, therefore, have all 'dissolved', suggests that he is impelled to her by more profound forces in his nature. 'I have loved you,' he tells her, 'ever since I first saw you in this house' (p. 343):

> '. . . You are part of my existence, part of myself. You have been in every line I have ever read, since I first came here, the rough common boy whose poor heart you wounded even then.

[1] *Love and Property in the Novels of Dickens*, pp. 127–8

You have been in every prospect I have ever seen since—on the river, on the sails of the ships, on the marshes, in the clouds, in the light, in the darkness, in the wind, in the woods, in the sea, in the streets. You have been the embodiment of every graceful fancy that my mind has ever become acquainted with. The stones of which the strongest London buildings are made, are not more real, or more impossible to be displaced by your hands, than your presence and influence have been to me, there and everywhere, and will be. Estella, to the last hour of my life, you cannot choose but remain part of my character, part of the little good in me, part of the evil. . . .' (p. 345)

Pip's love for Estella, dating from the time he first saw her at Miss Havisham's, has been, as it were, a calling in the dark, an attempt to assuage the longings of the 'poor heart' to which he revealingly refers with such self-pity here. His love, accordingly, as Edgar Johnson has well said, and as the quoted passage strikingly exemplifies, has been 'all self-absorbed need . . . not at all the desire to give, only the desire to receive'.[1] In his love for Estella, Pip is as much the victim of self-deception as he is in his expectations of Miss Havisham. There is more to love than need—as is shown in the development of Pip's relations with both Magwitch and Miss Havisham.

The opening scene in the churchyard suggests that Magwitch's need is as great as Pip's:

> 'Now,' he pursued, 'you remember what you've undertook, and you remember that young man, and you get home!'
> 'Goo—good night, sir,' I faltered.
> 'Much of that!' said he, glancing about him over the cold wet flat. 'I wish I was a frog. Or a eel!'
> At the same time, he hugged his shuddering body in both his arms—clasping himself, as if to hold himself together—and limped towards the low church wall. As I saw him go, picking his way among the nettles, and among the brambles that bound the green mounds, he looked in my young eyes as if he were eluding the hands of the dead people, stretching up cautiously out of their graves, to get a twist upon his ankle and pull him in.

[1] *Charles Dickens*, II, 992.

When he came to the low church wall, he got over it, like a
man whose legs were numbed and stiff, and then turned round
to look for me. When I saw him turning, I set my face towards
home, and made the best use of my legs. But presently I looked
over my shoulder, and saw him going on again towards the river,
still hugging himself in both arms, and picking his way with his
sore feet among the great stones dropped into the marshes here
and there, for stepping-places when the rains were heavy, or the
tide was in. (p. 4)

Shackled and starving, exposed to 'the cold wet flat', Magwitch, in his
utter desolation, is a representative figure in this novel; and he characteristically expresses a wish for a transformation—though of a bitterly
ironical kind. His experiences, indeed, have in fact turned him into a
dog, if not into a frog or an eel: when Pip later brings him food, he
notices 'a decided similarity between [a] dog's way of eating, and the
man's' (p. 16); and when Magwitch is recaptured and rowed out to
'the black Hulk lying out a little way from the mud of the shore, like
a wicked Noah's ark', somebody in the boat growls 'as if to dogs,
"Give way, you!"' (p. 36). Reduced to living like an animal and
'hunted [to] near death and dunghill' (p. 16), Magwitch, it is clear,
is a pariah. It is only later that we find out what his history has been,
but it is imaged in his movements in the churchyard and on the marshes,
the marshes that seem to Pip 'a long black horizontal line' (p. 4) and
that thus evoke, once again, the line of a dark life: 'picking his way'
among nettles and brambles, 'eluding the hands of the dead people'
that seem to want to 'pull him in' to their graves, Magwitch acts out,
as it were, the fruitless picking among nettles and brambles, the barren
struggle merely to stay alive that his whole life has been. And as he
'[hugs] his shuddering body in both his arms—clasping himself, as if
to hold himself together', it is furthermore suggested that, if this is the
only embrace he now knows, it is human warmth and love that he (like
Orlick) is most in need of, that it is this that might hold him together.

When the terrified Pip brings the convict his food, he cannot help
'pitying his desolation', and, watching him eat, he makes 'bold to say,
"I am glad you enjoy it"' (p. 16). It is a moment of genuine compassion, and it proves to be one of the decisive moments of Pip's life. It
is soon followed by another when he is the unwilling witness of the
recapturing of Magwitch:

As one of the soldiers, who carried a basket in lieu of a gun, went down on his knee to open it, my convict looked round him for the first time, and saw me. I had alighted from Joe's back on the brink of the ditch when we came up, and had not moved since. I looked at him eagerly when he looked at me, and slightly moved my hands and shook my head. I had been waiting for him to see me, that I might try to assure him of my innocence. It was not at all expressed to me that he even comprehended my intention, for he gave me a look that I did not understand, and it all passed in a moment. But if he had looked at me for an hour or for a day, I could not have remembered his face ever afterwards, as having been more attentive. . . .

My convict never looked at me, except that once. . . . Suddenly, he turned to the sergeant, and remarked:

'I wish to say something respecting this escape. It may prevent some persons laying under suspicion alonger me.'

'You can say what you like,' returned the sergeant . . . 'but you have no call to say it here. You'll have opportunity enough to say about it, and hear about it, before it's done with, you know.'

'I know, but this is another pint, a separate matter. A man can't starve; at least *I* can't. I took some wittles, up at the willage over yonder—where the church stands a'most out on the marshes.'

'You mean stole,' said the sergeant.

'And I'll tell you where from. From the blacksmith's.' (pp. 34–5)

Magwitch's 'attentive' look, we see, registers far more than his comprehension of the meaning of Pip's gesture; it expresses his touched recognition of the fact that Pip has not only not betrayed him but has sufficient regard for him as a man to want him to know it. And, in making his 'confession', Magwitch expresses his gratitude to Pip in the only way open to him. It is significant that Magwitch tries to protect Pip here, for when he later becomes the boy's secret benefactor, his gratitude takes the same protective form: his money, it seems, is designed to smooth Pip's way through the nettles and brambles that have for so long torn at the convict: 'Yes, Pip, dear boy,' he later says, 'I've made a gentleman on you. . . . I swore that time, sure as ever I earned a guinea, that guinea should go to you. . . . I lived rough, that you should live smooth; I worked hard that you should be above work'

(p. 304). But then Magwitch is clearly animated by further considerations in becoming Pip's patron. The encounter with the boy reminds him of his own lost daughter, as Herbert, who has heard his story, tells Pip: '. . . you brought into his mind the little girl so tragically lost, who would have been about your age' (p. 386). In becoming Pip's patron, that is, Magwitch in effect adopts Pip, and he does so because he wants to bind the boy to him, to ensure a continuation of the kind of human communion that at the Battery and at the brink of the ditch redeems his pariah-like existence: 'Look'ee here, Pip,' he says to the horrified young gentleman. 'I'm your second father You're my son—more to me nor any son' (p. 304).

In his relationship with Pip, Magwitch thus initially wants to give as well as to receive, but in time he loses sight, like a man in a mist, of the path he is pursuing:

> 'And then, dear boy, it was a recompense to me, look'ee here, to know in secret that I was making a gentleman. The blood horses of them colonists might fling up the dust over me as I was walking; what do I say? I says to myself, "I'm making a better gentleman nor ever *you'll* be!" When one of 'em says to one another, "He was a convict, a few years ago, and is a ignorant common fellow now, for all he's lucky," what do I say? I says to myself, "If I ain't a gentleman, nor yet ain't got no learning, I'm the owner of such. All on you owns stock and land; which on you owns a brought-up London gentleman?" This way I kep myself a going. And this way I held steady afore my mind that I would for certain come one day and see my boy, and make myself known to him, on his own ground.' (p. 306)

Pip's love for Estella, we remember, becomes falsely bound up with a desire for wealth; this passage reveals how Magwitch's love for Pip is corrupted by his desire for station. If his initial attitude to Pip is both generous and selfless, over the years it becomes thoroughly self-centred. His 'making a gentleman' becomes for him a personal 'recompense', a devious means not only of keeping himself going but of transforming his condition: 'I tell [you what I've done for you],' he says to Pip, 'fur you to know as that there hunted dunghill dog wot you kep life in, got his head so high that he could make a gentleman' (p. 304). Preoccupied with getting his own head high, Magwitch becomes blind to the fact that he is insensibly turning Pip into an object, a mere instrument for his own purposes: it is 'with an air of admiring proprietorship' (p. 315) that he surveys the 'brought-up London gentleman' whom he has made and 'owns'. To use a person as a thing is a mark, as Dickens showed as early as *Martin Chuzzlewit*, of the loss of true value, and so Magwitch ironically devalues what he would prize. Yet the worth of his feeling for Pip is indicated with the same artlessness that reveals its erosion: if Pip's utility as a gentleman has kept Magwitch going in Australia, it is a desire to see his 'boy' that brings him to England—at the risk of his life. In the end it is Pip who helps to reclaim the convict's feeling, just as he helps to free the self-convicted Miss Havisham.

Miss Havisham has for long been shut up in Satis House, confining herself to her dressing-room and to the room, arranged for her wedding-feast, into which she sends Pip on one of his early visits:

> I crossed the staircase landing, and entered the room she in-
> dicated. From that room, too, the daylight was completely ex-
> cluded, and it had an airless smell that was oppressive. A fire
> had been lately kindled in the damp old-fashioned grate, and it
> was more disposed to go out than to burn up, and the reluctant
> smoke which hung in the room seemed colder than the clearer
> air—like our own marsh mist. Certain wintry branches of
> candles on the high chimney-piece faintly lighted the chamber;
> or, it would be more expressive to say, faintly troubled its dark-
> ness. It was spacious, and I dare say had once been handsome,
> but every discernible thing in it was covered with dust and mould,
> and dropping to pieces. The most prominent object was a long
> table with a table-cloth spread on it, as if a feast had been in
> preparation when the house and the clocks all stopped together.
> An épergne or centre-piece of some kind was in the middle of
> this cloth; it was so heavily overhung with cobwebs that its
> form was quite undistinguishable; and, as I looked along the
> yellow expanse out of which I remember its seeming to grow,
> like a black fungus, I saw speckle-legged spiders with blotchy
> bodies running home to it, and running out from it, as if some
> circumstance of the greatest public importance had just transpired
> in the spider community. (p. 78)

The fact that the smoke which hangs in the room is said to be 'like . . .

marsh mist' at once relates this scene to those crucial marsh scenes in which both Pip and Magwitch are first presented to us. The room, moreover, in its barren desolation, is like an interior marshland, and with everything in it 'covered with dust and mould, and dropping to pieces', it suggests the kind of decay that is located in the marsh churchyard. Since it is Miss Havisham herself who has deliberately 'laid the whole place waste', as Herbert later tells Pip (p. 172), it is clear that the room is a projection of her own desolation (as the marsh is that of Pip and Magwitch), and that it images her sense that life, as well as 'the house and the clocks', has 'stopped' for her, that there is nothing left her after her desertion by Compeyson but decay. Indeed, the name of the house in which she lives, though 'it meant, when it was given,' Estella tells Pip, 'that whoever had this house, could want nothing else' (p. 51), seems in her tenancy to convey ironically that she, who in her bridal dress is 'withered like the dress', whose figure has 'shrunk to skin and bone', and who reminds Pip both of a 'wax-work and skeleton' that he has seen (p. 53), has had more than enough of life. At the same time Satis House, which is notable for the 'arrest of everything' (p. 55), has 'a great many iron bars to it', some of its windows have been 'walled up' and 'of those that remained', all the lower are 'rustily barred', the courtyard is barred too, and 'the great front entrance' has 'two chains across it outside' (pp. 50, 52). Waiting for death in her prison, Miss Havisham is like Mrs. Clennam in *Little Dorrit*; and it becomes clear that she too has subjected herself to arrest because she wants to punish herself.

Why Miss Havisham wants to punish herself is suggested later in the novel:

> As Estella looked back over her shoulder before going out at the door, Miss Havisham kissed [her] hand to her, with a ravenous intensity that was of its kind quite dreadful.
>
> Then, Estella being gone and we two left alone, she turned to me and said in a whisper:
>
> 'Is she beautiful, graceful, well-grown? Do you admire her?'
>
> 'Everybody must who sees her, Miss Havisham.'
>
> She drew an arm round my neck, and drew my head close down to hers as she sat in the chair. 'Love her, love her, love her! How does she use you?'
>
> Before I could answer . . . she repeated, 'Love her, love her, love her! If she favours you, love her. If she wounds you, love

her. If she tears your heart to pieces—and as it gets older and stronger it will tear deeper—love her, love her!'

Never had I seen such passionate eagerness as was joined to her utterance of these words. I could feel the muscles of the thin arm round my neck, swell with the vehemence that possessed her.

'Hear me, Pip! I adopted her to be loved. I bred her and educated her, to be loved. I developed her into what she is, that she might be loved. Love her!'

She said the word often enough, and there could be no doubt that she meant to say it; but if the often repeated word had been hate instead of love—despair—revenge—dire death—it could not have sounded from her lips more like a curse.

'I'll tell you,' said she, in the same hurried passionate whisper, 'what real love is. It is blind devotion, unquestioning self-humiliation, utter submission, trust and belief against yourself and against the whole world, giving up your whole heart and soul to the smiter—as I did!' (pp. 226–7)

In the sudden baring of her soul Miss Havisham is a melodramatic figure, but she reveals a great deal in what she says. Her definition of 'real love' is striking: love, as she sees it, would seem to be characterized by its unquestioning blindness and utter abandonment; and, given the fact of her self-imprisonment which dates from the day of her desertion, it is suggested that, having really loved and been betrayed, she is now punishing herself for her own vulnerability, for having exposed herself to 'the smiter'. At the same time, in having bred and educated Estella 'to be loved', and so to smite and wound and tear in her turn, it seems that Miss Havisham has been motivated not so much by a desire to enjoy a vicarious revenge on the male sex as by a need to justify herself through repeated re-enactments of her own story. Wandering in the room which is filled with smoke, like mist, wanting both to punish and to justify herself, Miss Havisham, we see, is subject (like Pip and Magwitch) to the confusions attendant on irreconcilable desires. Nor, the scene suggests, is it revenge or punishment or justification that she is really seeking: it is 'with a ravenous intensity' that she kisses her hand to Estella, just as later she looks at the girl 'as though she were devouring the beautiful creature she [has] reared' (p. 288). It is a ravenous hunger for love that Miss Havisham is seeking to satisfy, and she reveals more than she intends when she says, elliptically: 'I adopted her to be loved'. It is the final irony of her position, however, that, in bringing Estella up 'to be loved' by others and to smite them, in perversely and self-centredly ensuring that her heart will be impervious to her victims, she fails to give Estella the love she needs and so unfits her for her adopted role: 'And if you ask me to give you what you never gave me,' Estella says to Miss Havisham, 'my gratitude and duty cannot do impossibilities' (p. 290).

IV

Wandering confused and lost, Pip, Miss Havisham and Magwitch all help one another to find their way. In the midst of his 'agony' when he declares his love for Estella and finds her 'perfectly unmoved', Pip cannot help noticing that Miss Havisham puts 'her hand to her heart' as she witnesses the scene between them, that there is 'a ghastly look' upon her face, and that she seems 'all resolved into a ghastly stare of pity and remorse' (pp. 343, 344, 346). Pip's agony, it is clear, so strongly and unexpectedly recalls her own—she later tells him that on this occasion she sees in him 'a looking-glass' which shows her what she 'once felt' herself (p. 378)—that it nullifies her triumph and confronts her with her shocked realization of her pity for him. The 'ghastly stare' into which she is 'resolved', moreover, is compounded of remorse as well as pity, and this resolution is productive of 'a new expression' when she next meets Pip:

> As I brought another of the ragged chairs to the hearth, and sat down, I remarked a new expression on her face, as if she were afraid of me.
>
> 'I want,' she said, 'to pursue that subject you mentioned to me when you were last here, and to show you that I am not all stone. But perhaps you can never believe, now, that there is anything human in my heart?'
>
> When I said some reassuring words, she stretched out her tremulous right hand, as though she was going to touch me; but she recalled it again before I understood the action, or knew how to receive it.
>
> 'You said, speaking for your friend, that you could tell me how to do something useful and good. Something that you would like done, is it not?'

'Something that I would like done very much.'

'What is it?'

I began explaining to her that secret history of the partner-
ship. I had not got far into it, when I judged from her looks that
she was thinking in a discursive way of me, rather than of what
I said. It seemed to be so, for, when I stopped speaking, many
moments passed before she showed that she was conscious of the
fact.

. . .

'Are you very unhappy now?'

She asked this question, still without looking at me, but in an
unwonted tone of sympathy. I could not reply at the moment,
for my voice failed me. She put her left arm across the head of her
stick, and softly laid her forehead on it.

'I am far from happy, Miss Havisham; but I have other
causes of disquiet than any you know of. They are the secrets I
have mentioned.'

After a little while she raised her head, and looked at the fire
again.

' 'Tis noble in you to tell me that you have other causes of
unhappiness. Is it true?'

'Too true.'

'Can I only serve you, Pip, by serving your friend? Regarding
that as done, is there nothing I can do for you yourself?'

'Nothing. I thank you for the question. I thank you even more
for the tone of the question. But, there is nothing.'

. . .

She read me what she had written, and it was direct and clear,
and evidently intended to absolve me from any suspicion of
profiting by the receipt of the money. I took the tablets from her
hand, and it trembled again, and it trembled more as she took
off the chain to which the pencil was attached, and put it in
mine. All this she did without looking at me.

'My name is on the first leaf. If you can ever write under my
name, "I forgive her," though ever so long after my broken
heart is dust—pray do it!'

'O Miss Havisham,' said I, 'I can do it now. There have been
sore mistakes; and my life has been a blind and thankless one;
and I want forgiveness and direction far too much, to be bitter
with you.'

She turned her face to me for the first time since she had averted it, and to my amazement, I may even add to my terror, dropped on her knees at my feet; with her folded hands raised to me in the manner in which, when her poor heart was young and fresh and whole, they must often have been raised to Heaven from her mother's side.

To see her with her white hair and her worn face, kneeling at my feet, gave me a shock through all my frame. I entreated her to rise, and got my arms about her to help her up; but she only pressed that hand of mine which was nearest to her grasp, and hung her head over it and wept. I had never seen her shed a tear before, and in the hope that the relief might do her good, I bent over her without speaking. She was not kneeling now, but was down upon the ground. (pp. 375–7)

This passage, like so many others in Dickens, defeats criticism, for, if it has some gross sentimental touches, it also has a genuinely moving quality. What can be analysed, however, is the way in which it convincingly resolves the relationship between Pip and Miss Havisham. The 'new expression' on Miss Havisham's face, we note, is one of fear, a fear, the rest of the scene implies, that Pip must now hate her for what she has done to him. The new expression, therefore, suggests a new realization that what matters is not revenge but love, a realization that is given expression in the hesitant and tremulous stretching out of her hand to Pip. What Miss Havisham now wants is human contact;[1] and it is significant that, though Pip senses 'a new desolation in the desolate house' now that Estella has left it (p. 377), Miss Havisham's response to being left alone once again is to seek love, not to impose her desolation on all around her. It is with 'an earnest

---

[1] Attention has been drawn to a related hand symbolism in the relationship of Pip and Magwitch. J. Hillis Miller points out that 'Magwitch's handclasp, originally a symbolic appropriation of Pip as his creation and possession, [at the end of the novel] becomes the symbol of their mutual love' (*Charles Dickens*, pp. 275–6); and Christopher Ricks says: 'Pip's love for Magwitch is not a matter of confessing or verbalizing—it is as simple and faithful as a smile and shake of the hand. . . . The joined hands of Pip and Magwitch have their loving dignity enhanced by their contrast with the absurdly sycophantic shakes of the hand from Pumblechook ("May I?"), and with the one-sided relationship when Magwitch first returns: "I reluctantly gave him my hands. . . . Once more he took me by both hands and surveyed me with an air of admiring proprietorship" ' (*'Great Expectations'*, *Dickens and the Twentieth Century*, ed. John Gross and Gabriel Pearson, pp. 208–9). An earlier incident between Pip and Wemmick is suggestive in this respect:

I put out my hand, and Wemmick at first looked at it as if he thought I wanted something. Then he looked at me, and said, correcting himself,

'To be sure! Yes. You're in the habit of shaking hands?' (p. 163)

womanly compassion for [Pip] in her new affection' that, at the end
of this scene, she twice calls him 'my Dear' (p. 378). In seeking to
show, moreover, that she is 'not all stone', Miss Havisham demonstrates
a new comprehension of the meaning of love, an understanding that
love is a giving not a devouring, since it is for Pip that she wants 'to
do something useful and good'. The realization is liberating, for, when
her stoniness at last gives way to tears, she not only feels genuine
grief in place of her long-lived 'vanity of sorrow' (p. 378) but breaks
out of the state of emotional arrest in which she has been held for
years: kneeling before Pip and weeping, she is at last moved beyond a
fixity of self. Her tears should also be related to Pip's earlier comment
on his own tears when he first parts from Joe: he declares then that
tears 'are rain upon the blinding dust of earth, overlying our hard
hearts' (p. 151); the comment suggests that, having softened her heart,
Miss Havisham can now see the way clear before her.

If Pip's life too has been 'blind', if he too needs 'forgiveness and
direction', as he admits to Miss Havisham, his eyes are now also
opened. Hitherto as self-absorbed in his relationship with her as with
Estella, he now exhibits a new sense of self and a new selflessness.
Though Miss Havisham, in her desire to make up to him for what
she has done, is now (ironically) ready to 'do something' for him, his
quiet refusal of any help for himself is indicative of the lesson he has
learnt. Indeed, his new determination to stand on his own feet appears
to be the more secure in that it is productive of the strength to accept
aid from her for Herbert. And the selflessness with which he pursues
Herbert's interests at this nadir of his own fortunes is further manifested
in his attitude to Miss Havisham. It is with a generous nobility, as
she perceives, that he tells her he has 'other causes of disquiet' for his
unhappiness; and in responding to her misery with compassionate forgiveness, he evinces a kind of fellow-feeling that is akin to love. It is
a fellow-feeling that is soon put to the test when he returns to her
room and finds that her clothes have caught fire. In going to her aid,
in exposing himself to the 'great flaming light' and dragging 'the great
cloth from the table' in order to fight the flames, Pip not only shows
that his compassion extends to a readiness to risk his life for her but
sweeps away 'the heap of rottenness' that has been the concomitant
of their relationship (p. 380). Miss Havisham, in the end, does not
recover from her injuries, but when Pip leaves her, he leans over her
and touches her lips with his (p. 382). A seal of final forgiveness and
reconciliation, the kiss is also a kiss of love.

Magwitch risks his life in coming back to England to see Pip. 'I was sent for life,' he tells Pip. 'It's death to come back. There's been over-much coming back of late years, and I should of a certainty be hanged if took':

> Nothing was needed but this; the wretched man, after load-ing me with his wretched gold and silver chains for years, had risked his life to come to me, and I held it there in my keeping! If I had loved him instead of abhorring him; if I had been at-tracted to him by the strongest admiration and affection, instead of shrinking from him with the strongest repugnance; it could have been no worse. On the contrary, it would have been better, for his preservation would then have naturally and tenderly ad-dressed my heart.
>
> My first care was to close the shutters, so that no light might be seen from without, and then to close and make fast the doors While I did so, he stood at the table drinking rum and eating biscuit; and when I saw him thus engaged, I saw my convict on the marshes at his meal again. It almost seemed to me as if he must stoop down presently, to file at his leg. (p. 307)

Pip, whose memory of the shackled convict is so vivid that he half expects him 'to file at his leg', suddenly sees here that his acceptance of his expectations has loaded him with 'gold and silver chains', that for years he has been no more than a slave to Magwitch—and to Miss Havisham. Accordingly, his 'shrinking . . . with the strongest re-pugnance' from the stranger signifies more than a gentlemanly dis-taste for him. His shrinking from his unsavoury patron makes it im-possible for him to take his money, and leads in the end to a shrinking from the unsavouriness of patronage, from taking anyone's money. At the same time it is clear that his gold and silver chains have also bound him to Magwitch. Pip sees his convict at his meal again, but we see the boy who took pity on him; for his 'first care' is to close the shutters and doors, and he does so as 'naturally' as if he 'loved him instead of abhorring him'. And, indeed, from this point on in his relationship with Magwitch, Pip is wholly concerned with his 'preservation'—with safeguarding his life and not his money. Having been protected by him, Pip now becomes Magwitch's protector and is surprised to find how 'heavy and anxious' his 'heart' is in respect of his welfare (p. 359). So dedicated is Pip to his welfare, so 'wholly set on [his] safety' (p. 412), that when, for instance, he receives the anonymous message concerning him, he does not hesitate to hasten to the marshes (though, in the event, this nearly costs him his life): 'in case any harm should befall him through my not going,' he reasons, 'how could I ever forgive myself!' (p. 398). Nor is Magwitch slow to respond to Pip's concern: both Pip and Herbert soon find that he is 'softened' and 'improved' (p. 384)— is transformed, as it were.

It is when Magwitch is recaptured and faces a sentence of death, when he is once more chained, that Pip's chains finally fall from him:

> We remained at the public-house until the tide turned, and then Magwitch was carried down to the galley and put on board. . . . when I took my place by Magwitch's side, I felt that was my place henceforth while he lived.
>
> For now my repugnance to him had all melted away, and in the hunted wounded shackled creature who held my hand in his, I only saw a man who had meant to be my benefactor, and who had felt affectionately, gratefully, and generously, towards me with great constancy through a series of years. I only saw in him a much better man than I had been to Joe. . . .
>
> As we returned towards the setting sun we had yesterday left behind us, and as the stream of our hopes seemed all running back, I told him how grieved I was to think he had come home for my sake.
>
> 'Dear boy,' he answered, 'I'm quite content to take my chance. I've seen my boy, and he can be a gentleman without me.'
>
> No. I had thought about that while we had been there side by side. No. Apart from any inclinations of my own, I understood Wemmick's hint now. I foresaw that, being convicted, his possessions would be forfeited to the Crown.
>
> 'Lookee here, dear boy,' said he. 'It's best as a gentleman should not be knowed to belong to me now. Only come to see me as if you come by chance alonger Wemmick. Sit where I can see you when I am swore to, for the last o' many times, and I don't ask no more.'
>
> 'I will never stir from your side,' said I, 'when I am suffered to be near you. Please God, I will be as true to you as you have been to me!'
>
> I felt his hand tremble as it held mine, and he turned his face away as he lay in the bottom of the boat, and I heard that old

sound in his throat—softened now, like all the rest of him. It was a good thing that he had touched this point, for it put into my mind what I might otherwise not have thought of until too late: that he need never know how his hopes of enriching me had perished. (pp. 423–4)

The action has come full circle, we see, as the references to 'the hunted wounded shackled creature', who makes the 'old sound in his throat', evoke the opening scenes on the marshes and so support the presentation of the decisive change in Pip. The fact that Pip's 'repugnance' for Magwitch is said to have 'melted away' indicates how superficial his abhorrence has been, an expression of the snobbery with which his better nature has become overlaid; when it melts away, a younger Pip is free to come to the surface again and respond to Magwitch as naturally as he did as a child. As Pip's benefactor, Magwitch, we remember, has stipulated that the boy should 'always bear the name of Pip' (p. 130): if the stipulation seems designed to ensure that a new and fortunate Pip should not forget his origins, what Magwitch does here is to help Pip rediscover his old, forgotten self, to find himself, as it were. He does so, in his concern for Pip, through a selfless renunciation of the gentleman he has made and owned, of the gentleman he feels 'should not be knowed to belong' to him any longer. But in being ready to lose his gentleman, Magwitch finds in Pip one who wishes to be closer to him than that, one who 'will never stir' from his side. It is a humbled Pip who takes his place by his side, seeing in Magwitch 'a much better man' than himself, and it is a Pip who makes his renunciation too, finally giving up his expectations: 'I had no claim [to Magwitch's property], and I finally resolved, and ever afterwards abided by the resolution, that my heart should never be sickened with the hopeless task of attempting to establish one' (p. 425). Pip, moreover, is now big enough, mature enough, to want to give, not only to receive; and it is with a compassion which recalls his attitude to Miss Havisham that he decides Magwitch 'need never know how his hopes of enriching' him have 'perished'.

Pip's compassion sweetens into undisguised love as Magwitch dies:

'Dear Magwitch, I must tell you, now at last. You understand what I say?'

A gentle pressure on my hand.

'You had a child once, whom you loved and lost.'

A stronger pressuer on my hand.

'She lived and found powerful friends. She is living now. She is a lady and very beautiful. And I love her!'

With a last faint effort, which would have been powerless but for my yielding to it, and assisting it, he raised my hand to his lips. Then he gently let it sink upon his breast again, with his own hands lying on it. The placid look at the white ceiling came back, and passed away, and his head dropped quietly on his breast. (p. 436)

Pip has earlier indicated his understanding of what true need is when he reassures Herbert, who expresses regret at having to leave his friend at a time of need: 'Herbert, I shall always need you, because I shall always love you; but my need is no greater now, than at another time' (p. 426). At Magwitch's bedside, thinking only of the dying man, Pip exemplifies this understanding. Obliquely, for Estella is married, but emphatically, for he goes out of his way to make his declaration, Pip here avows his sense of loving kinship with Magwitch, for he conveys to him that he would have wished him to be what he himself wanted to be, his 'second father'. The scene is a striking affirmation of Pip's moral regeneration, a development which is symbolized by his recovery from the critical illness to which he thereafter succumbs.[1] He is nursed back to life by the loving Joe and fancies that he is 'little Pip again': 'For the tenderness of Joe was so beautifully proportioned to my need, that I was like a child in his hands' (p. 442). It is clearly love, though of a non-sexual kind, that works Pip's regeneration; it is the regenerative power of sexual love that is the subject of Dickens's next and greatest novel.

---

[1] Cf. G. Robert Strange: 'It is not too fanciful to regard this illness as a symbolic death; Pip rises from it regenerate and percipient.' 'Expectations Well Lost', *loc. cit.*, p. 295.

8

OUR MUTUAL FRIEND

I

Chapter VI, Book IV of *Our Mutual Friend* opens with a description that sets the scene for Eugene Wrayburn's climactic meeting with Lizzie Hexam and for Bradley Headstone's attack on him. It is a simple and straightforward description, evoking, it would seem, merely the placidity of the setting, but it also provides us with a view of both the form and the theme of the novel:

> The Paper Mill had stopped work for the night, and the paths and roads in its neighbourhood were sprinkled with clusters of people going home from their day's labour in it. . . . Into the sheet of water reflecting the flushed sky in the foreground of the living picture, a knot of urchins were casting stones, and watching the expansion of the rippling circles. So, in the rosy evening, one might watch the ever-widening beauty of the landscape— beyond the newly-released workers wending home—beyond the silver river—beyond the deep green fields of corn, so prospering, that the loiterers in their narrow threads of pathway seemed to float immersed breast-high—beyond the hedgerows and the clumps of trees—beyond the windmills on the ridge—away to where the sky appeared to meet the earth, as if there were no immensity of space between mankind and Heaven. (p. 689)

We are struck, first, by the analogy between the game played by the knot of urchins and the way in which the novelist handles his plot. The stone that he casts is the body which Gaffer Hexam finds in the river at the beginning of the novel; what we watch is the expansion of an action that links the body with the doings of an increasing number of characters. The expansion, moreover, is similar to that of the rippling circles in the river in that the characters who become involved in the action are differentiated in terms of social class, and (moving, as it were, in distinct and representative social circles) are presented to us in successive groups. The plot, in other words, is developed in a way that provides us with a cross-section of England of the eighteen-sixties —as yet another river image more directly suggests:

> Thus, like the tides on which it had been borne to the knowledge of men, the Harmon Murder—as it came to be popularly called—went up and down, and ebbed and flowed, now in the town, now in the country, now among palaces, now among hovels, now among lords and ladies and gentlefolks, now among labourers and hammerers and ballast-heavers, until at last, after a long interval of slack water, it got out to sea and drifted away. (p. 31)

The stone and the circles are evocative not only of the pattern of incident that forms the plot but also of a pattern of imagery that gives the novel its distinctive poetic texture. *Our Mutual Friend* is the most poetic of all Dickens's novels, and—like *Wuthering Heights*—its affiliations are with poetic drama. It is suggestive to note, in this respect, that Jack Lindsay, having called *Our Mutual Friend* 'one of the greatest works of prose ever written', goes on to say that it 'vindicates Dickens's right to stand, as no other English writer can stand, at the side of Shakespeare'.[1] That it is not inappropriate to invoke Shakespeare is borne out, I think, not alone by the quality of the novel, by its imaginative range and complexity and control, but by the way in which Dickens puts language to work and by the way in which he imaginatively orders his material. For, superimposed on the ordering of the action by means of plot, there is a subtler ordering by means of image. On this level, the way in which the stones are thrown into the river is analogous to the manner in which Dickens deploys his images. The function of these images is to evoke the imaginative background against which the drama is enacted, against which the major relationships of Eugene and Lizzie and of Harmon and Bella are worked out. These images occur together in a centrally important description of London, to which I shall presently refer; and they move out from this

[1] *Charles Dickens*, p. 380.

centre in ever-widening circles of application, changing line and form as they grow, and encompassing ever-increasing areas of meaning. It is this expanding movement that distinguishes the structure of *Our Mutual Friend* from that of *Little Dorrit*, which, as we have seen, can also be viewed as a series of concentric circles. The circles of *Little Dorrit* are themselves emblematic of confinement, of that arrest of which the book treats; with each successive circle we are brought to a stop, so to speak, and returned to the centre. In *Our Mutual Friend* the stone at the centre, though never forgotten, drops from sight, and one circle gives way to another as we move freely ahead, ever outward in a widening perspective. The narrative principle of the novel may thus be said to be expansive, a simultaneous movement, on the two levels of plot and image pattern, from fixed centres to the furthermost reaches of the narrative—a movement analogous to that in 'the living picture' at the river, a movement from the stones and the circles in the water to the circles of landscape, and to the ultimate circle of the horizon, 'away to where the sky [appears] to meet the earth'.

The living picture provides us, furthermore, with a broad outline of the theme of the novel, for the sky appears to meet the earth, we are told, 'as if there were no immensity of space between mankind and Heaven'. What the novel is concerned with is precisely the immensity of the gap between the citizens of nineteenth-century commercial England and heaven. Indeed, it is the function of the central cluster of images to evoke what may be called, in relation to the sky that is also 'Heaven', the damnations of a materialist hell. *Our Mutual Friend* is not only the greatest of Dickens's novels and his most poetic; it is also his most religious work, and religious in a way that is far removed from the recital of the Lord's Prayer at Jo's deathbed in *Bleak House*. Dickens is here profoundly concerned with spiritual experience, specifically with the experience of spiritual rebirth; and the stories of the protagonists dramatize his belief in the possibility of individual regeneration in the society he excoriates. In two cases, moreover, the regeneration is associated with an immersion in the waters of that very river from whose banks the immensity of space between mankind and heaven seems to be denied.

The description of London in which the major images cluster together occurs about midway through the novel. Unlike the descriptions of the London of fog and mud in *Bleak House* and of a London bolted and barred in *Little Dorrit*, this is an unobtrusive description of the city, casually introduced into the narrative; but, like them, it is of central significance. It is astonishing how much of what Dickens has to say in the late novels is concentrated in the images by which London is variously evoked:

> A grey dusty withered evening in London city has not a hopeful aspect. The closed warehouses and offices have an air of death about them, and the national dread of colour has an air of mourning. The towers and steeples of the many house-encompassed churches, dark and dingy as the sky that seems descending on them, are no relief to the general gloom; a sundial on a church-wall has the look, in its useless black shade, of having failed in its business enterprise and stopped payment for ever; melancholy waifs and strays of housekeepers and porters sweep melancholy waifs and strays of papers and pins into the kennels, and other more melancholy waifs and strays explore them, searching and stooping and poking for anything to sell. The set of humanity outward from the City is as a set of prisoners departing from gaol, and dismal Newgate seems quite as fit a stronghold for the mighty Lord Mayor as his own state-dwelling. (p. 393)

Perhaps the most striking image in this passage is that of the sundial which, in its 'useless black shade', looks as if it has 'failed in its business enterprise and stopped payment for ever'. The image at once evokes the distinctive aura of *this* London, a city in which everything, even the operation of a sundial, is reduced to terms of money; and at the same time it neatly implies the bankruptcy of such a reduction. This is a city in which most citizens, like Fledgeby (to whom the following passage directly refers), see 'nothing written on the face of the earth and sky but the three letters L. S. D.—not Luxury, Sensuality, Dissoluteness, which they often stand for, but the three dry letters' (p. 272). This is a city whose 'gritty streets' are the price paid for the grinding of its 'money-mills' (p. 603), and whose 'City grit', on the dusty evening in question, 'gets into the hair and eyes and skin' (p. 393). This is a city in which 'melancholy waifs and strays' sift even the rubbish in the gutters, looking among the 'melancholy waifs and strays of papers and pins' for something that can be turned into cash. Their 'searching and stooping and poking for anything to sell', moreover, is analogous to the activity which has produced the Harmon fortune, the 'old hard jailer of Harmony Jail' having 'coined every

s   273

waif and stray' in his mounds 'into money' (p. 779); and it suggests that the city has itself become a vast dust-heap.

In the light of this implied metaphor we begin to understand better what is meant by the 'grey dusty withered evening' not having 'a hopeful aspect', for the life lived in the dust-heap is not only grey and dismal but seems itself to have withered. The withering, it is clear, applies to more than 'the fallen leaves of the few unhappy City trees' (p. 393) since the whole city, like the closed warehouses and offices, seems to have 'an air of death' about it. London, steeped in a 'general gloom' and in an 'air of mourning', is, so to speak, a city of death. Certainly on 'a foggy day' when 'the whole metropolis' is 'a heap of vapour', London is 'a sooty spectre'; the sun shows 'as if it [has] gone out, and [is] collapsing flat and cold'; and buildings struggle 'to get their heads above the foggy sea', the dome of St. Paul's especially seeming 'to die hard' (p. 420).

These metaphors, then—London as a dust-heap and a city of death —are the stones which set rippling circles in motion; and the images function as central analogues in the novel. In the same descriptive passage there is another image which is of importance in the direct working out of the action though it does not figure prominently in the pattern of imagery that creates the background to the action. The view of animate London as a 'set of humanity' suggests that in the city of the failed sundial man has lost his individual identity and become part of an amorphous mass. Dickens's people move out of the city in much the same way that T. S. Eliot's crowd flows into it over London Bridge, alike undone by death. The victims in Dickens's last completed novel are not hapless individuals, as in his early work, but all the denizens of the dusty city. The 'set of humanity', moreover, is like 'a set of prisoners departing from gaol', but though the use of the simile in this passage arouses expectations of significance, the prison image—a carry-over from *Little Dorrit*—is not extensively exploited.

Since Dickens orders his material by means both of plot and image, our awareness of the central images enables us to do justice to the aptness of the plot. It is an act of justice that needs to be done, for the plot of *Our Mutual Friend* has come in for its share of undeserved condemnation. A recent critic, for instance, referring to one of the main lines of the plot, talks of 'the complicated and improbable solution' to the Harmon murder mystery, and goes on to say: 'This is a silly and trivial mystery, but fortunately Dickens could feel that he had thus done his duty in providing the obligatory "mystery" element for this novel.'[1] It seems to me misguided to speak, at any rate in relation to the late novels, of an 'obligatory "mystery" element'. The mystery-plot of *Our Mutual Friend* is not a trapping, added in response to the supposed demand of a market, but a frame that both supports the whole and bears its imprint. This imprint is stamped, for example, on the incident that sets the plot in motion, Gaffer Hexam's finding of the body in the river; for this event dramatizes some of the significances gradually conveyed by the central images. It is, to start with, a case of mistaken identity; and arising from it, Harmon (who, at the Veneerings', is described successively as 'the man from Jamaica', 'the man from Somewhere' and 'the man from Nowhere (pp. 11–12)) adopts the identities of Handford, Rokesmith and 'the oakum-headed, oakum-whiskered man' (p. 365) who persuades Riderhood to retract his accusation against Hexam. Nor is this the only instance of assumed identity. Bradley Headstone disguises himself as Rogue Riderhood when he sets out to murder Eugene; Sloppy appears as the foreman in charge of the disposal of the mounds at Boffin's Bower; Boffin himself assumes the identity of a miser; and Fledgeby hides behind the identity he has foisted on Riah. What this aspect of the plot dramatizes, in other words, is the absence of true identity, a lack more widely apparent in the set of humanity that streams out of London; and what the clarification of the mistaken identities suggests is the need (among the dust-mounds) for the discovery of a true identity, one that will sustain life in the city of death.

Second, Gaffer's finding of the body presents us, in the opening pages of the novel, with a physical impression of the death that is present throughout, of the death that is the city of London's investment. The presence of the body, moreover, is not only striking as an opening to the novel but in its relation (like that of the stone to the circles in the water) to the death-in-life theme it projects. We eventually discover, for one thing, that the dead man has not only been salvaged for his money but killed for it as well. And the first question asked about the corpse is Mortimer's: 'Were any means taken, do you know, boy, to ascertain if it was possible to restore life?' (pp. 18–19)—a question that could well stand as an epigraph to the novel as a whole. The finding of the body poses another question, one related to the mystery of the numerous Harmon wills and to the machinations of Wegg: who will inherit the Harmon fortune; who, in the end, will take over the estate after the dust-mounds have been removed? The

[1] Philip Collins, *Dickens and Crime*, p. 284.

answer provided by the plot is John Harmon, the man who, like Radfoot, is thrown in the river for dead but is restored to life.

II

The image of London as a dust-heap that occurs midway through the novel derives its force from the vivid presentment of the actual Harmon dust-mounds. The mounds, from the moment we first hear of them (in Book I, Chapter 2) at the Veneering dinner, are kept constantly before our eyes:

> 'The man,' Mortimer goes on, addressing Eugene, 'whose name is Harmon, was the only son of a tremendous old rascal who made his money by Dust.'
>
> 'Red velveteens and a bell?' the gloomy Eugene inquires.
>
> 'And a ladder and basket if you like. By which means, or by others, he grew rich as a Dust Contractor, and lived in a hollow in a hilly country entirely composed of Dust. On his own small estate the growling old vagabond threw up his own mountain range, like an old volcano, and its geological formation was Dust. Coal-dust, vegetable-dust, bone-dust, crockery-dust, rough dust, and sifted dust—all manner of Dust. . . .
>
> 'The moral being—I believe that's the right expression—of this exemplary person, derived its highest gratification from anathematising his nearest relations and turning them out of doors. Having begun (as was natural) by rendering these attentions to the wife of his bosom, he next found himself at leisure to bestow a similar recognition on the claims of his daughter. He chose a husband for her, entirely to his own satisfaction and not in the least to hers, and proceeded to settle upon her, as her marriage portion, I don't know how much Dust, but something immense. At this stage of the affair the poor girl respectfully intimated that she was secretly engaged to that popular character whom the novelists and versifiers call Another, and that such a marriage would make Dust of her heart and Dust of her life— in short, would set her up, on a very extensive scale, in her father's business. Immediately, the venerable parent—on a cold winter's night, it is said—anathematised and turned her out.' (pp. 13–14)

Our enjoyment of the witty ease of this passage and of its mastery of tone should not prevent us from examining it closely. We need to take note, for instance, of the 'geological formation' of the mounds, for if Mortimer says that they comprise 'all manner of Dust', Humphry House has told us that 'the term "dust" was often used as a euphemism for decaying human excrement'; and that 'one of the main jobs of a dust-contractor in Early Victorian London was to collect the contents of the privies and the piles of mixed dung and ashes which were made in the poorer streets'.[1] We also need to note, in relation to Mortimer's description of the portion of dust which Harmon proceeds to settle on his daughter as 'something immense', that Victorian dust-contractors did in fact realize large sums of money from the sale of the contents of their mounds; Edgar Johnson refers to a mound which was sold (about a hundred years ago) for £40,000.[2] If in a world of dust-mounds dust thus means money (and it is part of the richness of Dickens's conception that the word 'dust' has since the seventeenth century had a slang connotation of money or cash), if dust, in terms of the symbolic equation established by the source of the Harmon fortune, *is* money; then, by the same token, money is dust, and varied associations of the word rub off on to it. First and foremost, money is associated, by way of the euphemism and in a foreshadowing of Freud, with something that is putrescent, with the process of putrefaction; the making of money, that is, is linked (through the dust-mounds) not only with dirt that is inherently foul but also with a process of corruption. It is linked, too, by way of the same process and also by way of the dust and ashes of which the mounds are in part composed, with the idea of death. Finally, money is equated, simply and directly, with rubbish, that is, with a false scale of values.

The dust-mounds are thus a richly evocative symbol, and as the chief symbol of the novel they are similar in importance to the Court of Chancery of *Bleak House* and to the Circumlocution Office of *Little Dorrit*. The comparison at once suggests how Dickens has changed his ground in the last of the three large 'social' novels. *Our Mutual Friend* digs deeper than the other two novels, and is concerned not with parasitism or patronage but with the ravening after money that is anterior to both; consequently the symbol best suited to Dickens's purpose is not an institution at the top typifying a particualr vice but the very dust on which the society is built, making for a general weak-

[1] *The Dickens World*, p. 167.
[2] *Charles Dickens*, II, 1030.

ness and rottenness. *Dust*, indeed, was one of the projected titles of the novel,[1] and it is a pity that Dickens decided not to use it.

Some of the consequences of an obsession with dust are indicated in Mortimer's story of the Dust Contractor. In the first place, what Harmon does to his children is, so to speak, to consign them to his mounds, anathematizing them both and turning them 'out of doors'. He also in fact makes dust of his daughter's heart and 'Dust of her life', as her early demise in 'sorrow and anxiety' (p. 14) confirms. Second, amassing dust, he throws up on his estate 'his own mountain range, like an old volcano', the simile implying that such an un-natural activity invites violent eruption—and pointing not only to the murder with which the book begins but to the continued violence of the action. Third, living (like Mr. Venus) amid the trophies of his art, he lives 'in a hollow in a hilly country entirely composed of Dust'; the effect of his money-making, that is, is to turn all about him into a kind of desert or waste land.

Both Edgar Johnson[2] and Lionel Trilling[3] have drawn attention to the links between *Our Mutual Friend* and *The Waste Land*. It is per-haps worth stressing that the waste land imagery in the novel derives directly from that of the dust-mounds—it is one of its expanded dimen-sions—and that it has parallels in Dickens's earlier work. The first instance I have come across is Dickens's description of London as 'this great wilderness' in a speech in 1844.[4] This is followed by a passage in *David Copperfield* (1850) in which the image is developed, and in which, interestingly enough, it is related to an image of hollow men:

> Or perhaps this *is* the Desert of Sahara! For, though Julia has a stately house, and mighty company, and sumptuous dinners every day, I see no green growth near her; nothing that can ever come to fruit or flower. What Julia calls 'society,' I see . . . But when society is the name for such hollow gentlemen and ladies, Julia, and when its breeding is professed indifference to everything that can advance or can retard mankind, I think we must have lost ourselves in that same Desert of Sahara, and had better find the way out. (pp. 875–6)

---

[1] It appears in a list headed 'Available Names' in Dickens's Memorandum Book. Another projected title among the nineteen listed is *The Cinder Heap. Letters*, ed. Walter Dexter, III, 794.
[2] *Charles Dickens*, II, 1043–4.
[3] 'The Dickens of Our Day', *A Gathering of Fugitives* (Boston, 1956), pp. 42–3.
[4] *The Speeches of Charles Dickens*, ed. K. J. Fielding (Oxford, 1960), p. 68.

There is a further parallel in *A Tale of Two Cities* (1859):

> When [Carton] got out of the house, the air was cold and sad,
> the dull sky overcast, the river dark and dim, the whole scene like
> a lifeless desert. And wreaths of dust were spinning round and
> round before the morning blast, as if the desert-sand had risen
> far away, and the first spray of it in its advance had begun to
> overwhelm the city.
>
> Waste forces within him, and a desert all around, this man stood
> still on his way across a silent terrace, and saw for a moment,
> lying in the wilderness before him, a mirage of honourable
> ambition, self-denial, and perseverance. . . . (pp. 84–5)

The most powerful waste land image in *Our Mutual Friend* is
associated, ironically, with the movement of water:

> The chaining of the door behind her, as she went forth, dis-
> enchanted Lizzie Hexam of that first relief she had felt. The
> night was black and shrill, the river-side wilderness was melan-
> choly, and there was a sound of casting-out, in the rattling of the
> iron links, and the grating of the bolts and staples under Miss
> Abbey's hand. . . . And as the great black river with its dreary
> shores was soon lost to her view in the gloom, so, she stood on
> the river's brink unable to see into the vast blank misery of a
> life suspected, and fallen away from by good and bad, but know-
> ing that it lay there dim before her, stretching away to the great
> ocean, Death. (pp. 70–1)

The movement of the river, making inexorably for 'the great ocean,
Death', clearly images the passage of life; but, in the dust-heap, life
itself has become a journey through a desert, past 'dreary shores' and
through 'the river-side wilderness'. In another image the desert is
directly linked to contractors' dust. To get home from the drug-
house of Chicksey, Veneering, and Stobbles, Mr. Wilfer has to skirt
'the border of [a] desert': 'Between Battle Bridge and that part of the
Holloway district in which he dwelt, was a tract of suburban Sahara,
where tiles and bricks were burnt, bones were boiled, carpets were
beat, rubbish was shot, dogs were fought, and dust was heaped by
contractors' (p. 33). And the representative inhabitant of the desert,
the man who is ready to sell his soul (not to mention his literary ac-

complishments) for money, is Silas Wegg, whose stall is 'the hardest little stall of all the sterile little stalls in London'; who is himself, like his stall and his stock, 'as dry as the Desert'; and who is 'so wooden a man that he [seems] to have taken his wooden leg naturally' (pp. 45–6).

The image of the dust-mounds also expands into an image of what we might call dust-heaps in public life:

> The train of carts and horses came and went all day from dawn to nightfall, making little or no daily impression on the heap of ashes, though, as the days passed on, the heap was seen to be slowly melting. My lords and gentlemen and honourable boards, when you in the course of your dust-shovelling and cinder-raking have piled up a mountain of pretentious failure, you must off with your honourable coats for the removal of it, and fall to the work with the power of all the queen's horses and all the queen's men, or it will come rushing down and bury us alive.
>
> Yes, verily, my lords and gentlemen and honourable boards, adapting your Catechism to the occasion, and by God's help so you must. For when we have got things to the pass that with an enormous treasure at disposal to relieve the poor, the best of the poor detest our mercies, hide their heads from us, and shame us by starving to death in the midst of us, it is a pass impossible of prosperity, impossible of continuance. . . . We must mend it, lords and gentlemen and honourable boards, or in its own evil hour it will mar every one of us. (p. 503)

Dickens's address to the 'lords and gentlemen and honourable boards', which conveys the feeling that he directly expresses in his denunciation of the Poor Law in his Postscript, may violate the canons of impersonal narration, but it shows the coherence of his imaginative vision in this novel. The reference to the 'dust-shovelling and cinder-raking' of the same gentlemen suggests that they treat the poor, whom it is their duty 'to relieve', as so much social refuse. And, indeed, in a society in which money is the measure of all things, the poor may easily be viewed as its waste (and disposable) product—as is more explicitly indicated in another passage: at the beginning of the novel Charley Hexam leads Mortimer and Eugene to his father's, taking them down to where 'accumulated scum of humanity seemed to be washed from higher grounds, like so much moral sewage, and to be pausing until its own weight forced it over the bank and sunk it in the river' (p. 21). The intimation of the likely consequences of this social injustice, of the collection in public life of heaps of rottenness, sounds the kind of ominous note that is heard too in *Bleak House* and *Little Dorrit*, for there would seem to be a direct connection between the collapsing houses in those novels and the assertion that the 'mountain of pretentious failure' may come 'rushing down and bury us alive'. There certainly is a connection between this image and the mountain range that old Harmon has thrown up, the mountain range that is like a volcano. Social injustice, however, may result in an insidious corruption, rather than violent destruction, for the putrescence will 'mar' even if it does not bury alive, will exact the kind of revenge that is taken by Tom's corrupted blood in *Bleak House*.

The dust-mound is so rich an image that it lends itself readily to yet another kind of variation. Professional, as opposed to public, gentlemen are neatly encompassed by it when Boffin refers to the Temple as 'a spot where lawyer's dust is contracted for' (p. 91). This recalls an earlier use of the image in *Hard Times*, to which Edgar Johnson has drawn attention:[1]

> [Mr. Gradgrind] then returned with promptitude to the national cinder-heap, and resumed his sifting for the odds and ends he wanted, and his throwing of the dust about into the eyes of other people who wanted other odds and ends—in fact resumed his parliamentary duties. (p. 206)

This passage from *Hard Times* (1854) is an elaboration of the image in an 1850 letter (its use in the letter revealing how long the image was present in Dickens's imagination before he fully exploited it in *Our Mutual Friend*): 'I am in a very despondent state of mind over Peel's death. He was a man of merit who could be ill spared from the Great Dust Heap down at Westminster.'[2]

In other images connected with the dust-mounds Dickens develops the fundamental money-dust equation. First, there is a highly metaphorical elaboration of the image of 'waifs and strays of papers and pins':

> It was not summer yet, but spring; and it was not gentle spring ethereally mild, as in Thomson's *Seasons*, but nipping

[1] *Charles Dickens*, II, 1030.
[2] Letter to Hon. Richard Watson, 3. 7. 1850, *Letters*, ed. Walter Dexter, II, 220–21.

spring with an easterly wind, as in Johnson's, Jackson's, Dickson's, Smith's, and Jones's Seasons. The grating wind sawed rather than blew; and as it sawed, the sawdust whirled about the sawpit. Every street was a sawpit, and there were no top-sawyers; every passenger was an under-sawyer, with the sawdust blinding him and choking him.

That mysterious paper currency which circulates in London when the wind blows, gyrated here and there and everywhere. Whence can it come, whither can it go? It hangs on every bush, flutters in every tree, is caught flying by the electric wires, haunts every enclosure, drinks at every pump, cowers at every grating, shudders upon every plot of grass, seeks rest in vain behind the legions of iron rails. . . .

The wind sawed, and the sawdust whirled. The shrubs wrung their many hands, bemoaning that they had been over-persuaded by the sun to bud; the young leaves pined; the sparrows repented of their early marriages, like men and women; the colours of the rainbow were discernible, not in floral spring, but in the faces of the people whom it nibbled and pinched. And ever the wind sawed, and the sawdust whirled. (p. 144)

This passage not only brilliantly reinforces the presentation of the city itself as a huge receptacle of rubbish, for every bush, every tree, every enclosure, every pump, every grating and every plot of grass is adorned with the scraps of paper that are blown about in the wind, but also extends the connection between money and dust and makes it quite explicit: all the litter 'circulating' in London (and not only the rubbish profitably collected in mounds) is now seen as a 'mysterious paper currency'. And the consequence of the extensive circulation of this currency, of turning London into a vast counting house, so to speak, is that even in spring (and the spring scene is in this respect powerfully and ironically related to the autumn and winter scenes previously referred to) there is a smothering of life. Covered in sawdust, the shrubs wring their hands and the young leaves pine; it is as if a blight has fallen on nature. It is a vision of the city which recalls that in *Bleak House*; and we may assume that it is not only dust and dirt that the 'easterly wind', moving through the East End, blows into the more fashionable quarters of London.

Second, there is the scene in which Gaffer washes the money taken from the pockets of the body that he has found in the river:

It was not until now that the upper half of the man came back into the boat. His arms were wet and dirty, and he washed them over the side. In his right hand he held something, and he washed that in the river too. It was money. He chinked it once, and he blew upon it once, and he spat upon it once,—'for luck,' he hoarsely said—before he put it in his pocket.

'Lizzie!'

The girl turned her face towards him with a start, and rowed in silence. Her face was very pale. He was a hook-nosed man, and with that and his bright eyes and his ruffled head, bore a certain likeness to a roused bird of prey. (pp. 2–3)

If Gaffer's washing of the money in the opening pages of the novel is a simple and effective means of dramatizing the connection between money and dirt that the book as a whole elaborates, his action has several implications. It can be seen as a symbolic disavowal of the dirt that taints his money-making. It thus points, in one direction, to Fledgeby, who leaves Riah to do his dirty work for him; and, in another, to Venus, who confesses to Boffin that in the first stages of the plot against the dustman, 'in the beginning of this dirt,' as he puts it, '[his] hands were not, for a few hours, quite as clean as [he] could wish' (p. 786). The washing of the dirty money is also a means of linking the dust-mounds and another major symbol, the river, it being expressive of the complex ambiguity of the river symbolism (which remains to be considered); for, if the money has been dirtied in the river, it is also the river that washes it clean.

It is worth noting that the most striking feature of Gaffer's occupation, his plundering of corpses whenever he gets a chance, is not the fruit of Dickens's fertile imagination but as much rooted in the daily fact of Victorian England as Harmon's dust contracting. Harland S. Nelson quotes Henry Mayhew on 'the well-known fact' that 'no body recovered by a dredgerman [the dredgermen being the men "who find almost all the bodies of persons drowned"] ever happens to have any money about it, when brought to shore'.[1] It is Gaffer's readiness to ensure that the bodies he finds should be similarly unencumbered, quite as much as his being 'a hook-nosed man' and having 'bright eyes' and a 'ruffled head', that makes the comparison between him and a 'bird of prey' so apt, for Gaffer, like the bird, feeds on death. In the

[1] 'Dickens's *Our Mutual Friend* and Henry Mayhew's *London Labour and the London Poor*', *Nineteenth-Century Fiction*, 20 (December 1965), 217.

opening chapters the comparison is insistent: Riderhood accuses Gaffer of being 'like the wulturs' in the way he scents out bodies (p. 4); when Gaffer turns from the fire to greet Mortimer, he '[looks] like a bird of prey' (p. 21), and on the same occasion he is said to have 'the special peculiarity of some birds of prey, that when he [knits] his brow, his ruffled crest [stands] highest' (p. 23); when Gaffer goes to sleep, he is a 'bird of prey' going 'to roost' (p. 30). The comparison is insistent because it is important, not least because there is an implied analogy between Gaffer's feeding on death and old Harmon's making a living out of dust and ashes.[1] The analogy is fundamental to our understanding of the novel, for it suggests that the money-maker in the dust-heap—whether solid citizen or social outlaw—is a scavenger. The parasite of *Bleak House* and the barnacle of *Little Dorrit* give way in this novel to a more predatory image, an image effectively exploited by Ben Jonson in the persons of Voltore, Corbaccio and Corvino. In *Our Mutual Friend*, it may be noted, it is an image that, like a circle in the rippling water, grows out of the two main images of the dust-heap and the city of death, mediating between them.

An interesting combination of the bird of prey image and of images from *Bleak House* and *Little Dorrit* is to be found in a passage in which Dickens's indignation, as in the address to the honourable boards, is allowed direct expression:

The mature young lady is a lady of property. The mature young gentleman is a gentleman of property. He invests his property. He goes, in a condescending amateurish way, into the City, attends meetings of Directors, and has to do with traffic in Shares. As is well known to the wise in their generation, traffic in Shares is the one thing to have to do with in this world. Have no antecedents, no established character, no cultivation, no ideas, no manners; have Shares. Have Shares enough to be on Boards of Direction in capital letters, oscillate on mysterious business between London and Paris, and be great. Where does he come from? Shares. Where is he going to? Shares. What are his tastes? Shares. Has he any principles? Shares. What squeezes him

[1] Arnold Kettle, though from a different point of view, also sees a parallel between the two: 'It is the filth of London, itself one vast fog-infested dust-heap, that pollutes the river and turns it from a pleasing and refreshing stream into a flowing sewer of filth and refuse. There is indeed a grim and significant parallel between the image of old Harmon (and Silas Wegg) fishing his wealth out of the dust of commercial London and Gaffer Hexam fishing his sordid living out of the polluted waters of the chartered Thames.' '*Our Mutual Friend*', *Dickens and the Twentieth Century*, ed. John Gross and Gabriel Pearson, pp. 221–2.

into Parliament? Shares. Perhaps he never of himself achieved success in anything, never originated anything, never produced anything! Sufficient answer to all; Shares. O mighty Shares! To set those blaring images so high, and to cause us smaller vermin, as under the influence of henbane or opium, to cry out night and day, 'Relieve us of our money, scatter it for us, buy us and sell us, ruin us, only we beseech ye take rank among the powers of the earth, and fatten on us!' (p. 114)

The Mammon of *Little Dorrit*, before whom a whole society lies prostrate, ramifies into the 'blaring images' of this passage; and in 'this world' speculation is both the opium and the religion of the masses, of the 'smaller vermin', who, as in *Bleak House*, parasitically seek to be provided for through it. What marks this world as the world of *Our Mutual Friend*, however, is, first, the irony that supreme value in it is attributed to scraps of paper that are destined for the sawpit; and, second, that the speculators of distinction, who (like Mr. Veneering) have 'no antecedents, no established character, no cultivation, no ideas, no manners' but who do have shares, are viewed as birds of prey that devour the smaller vermin and 'fatten' on them. It is characteristic of the ironies of *Our Mutual Friend*, moreover, that the 'lady of property' and the 'gentleman of property' referred to in this passage, that is, the Lammles, should themselves turn out to be birds of prey, each of whom has seen a juicy victim in the other. When they discover their mutual deception, when they find out, as Mr. Lammle says, that they have 'both been biting, and . . . have both been bitten' (p. 125), it is again characteristic that they should set up in business together, as it were, fixing first on Georgiana Podsnap and Fledgeby as their prey, and then, when Podsnap (unknowingly aided by Mrs. Lammle) frustrates a kill, on the Boffins.

When the Boffins come into their dust, it is in the nature of the dust-heap that they should be 'a prey to prosperity' (p. 178). Long before the Lammles come on the scene, there is Wegg, for instance, who, in triumphantly negotiating the sale of his services to Boffin, balances himself on his wooden leg and '[flutters] over his prey with extended hand' (p. 188). Wegg, appropriately, heads for the dust-mounds and takes up his abode there, obsessed with the idea of finding treasure in them, and becoming, if not a 'fish of the shark tribe' (p. 213), a devourer in waiting. With Boffin surrounded by tradesmen whose 'books hunger' and whose 'mouths water' for his dust, and who 'offer hypothetical corruption' to his servants to secure an order from him (p. 210); and approached by 'corporate beggars', 'individual beggars', 'inspired beggars' and 'nobly independent beggars' (pp. 211–12); this line of imagery culminates in the presentation of Boffin as so much carrion—the dustman himself transformed into dust for scavengers:

> And now, in the blooming summer days, behold Mr. and Mrs. Boffin established in the eminently aristocratic family mansion, and behold all manner of crawling, creeping, fluttering, and buzzing creatures, attracted by the gold dust of the Golden Dustman! (p. 209)

The range of the bird of prey imagery is deftly and humourously extended:

> Veneering was more than ready to do it, for he had prospered exceedingly upon the Harmon Murder, and had turned the social distinction it conferred upon him to the account of making several dozen of bran-new bosom-friends. Indeed, such another lucky hit would almost have set him up in that way to his satisfaction. So, addressing himself to the most desirable of his neighbours, while Mrs. Veneering secured the next most desirable, he plunged into the case, and emerged from it twenty minutes afterwards with a Bank Director in his arms. In the meantime, Mrs. Veneering had dived into the same waters for a wealthy Ship-Broker, and had brought him up, safe and sound, by the hair. Then Mrs. Veneering had to relate, to a larger circle, how she had been to see the girl, and how she was really pretty, and (considering her station) presentable. And this she did with such a successful display of her eight aquiline fingers and their encircling jewels, that she happily laid hold of a drifting General Officer, his wife and daughter, and not only restored their animation which had become suspended, but made them lively friends within an hour. (p. 134)

The Veneerings, we are clearly meant to see, as they fish in the waters round the dinner table, make their way in a manner which is analogous to that of Gaffer Hexam; they are, that is to say, social birds of prey, greedily clutching at anyone who can help sustain their social position. Mrs. Veneering, indeed, with her 'eight aquiline fingers and their encircling jewels', is suitably equipped for her plunges. But as the Veneerings busily give their expensive dinners, the irony of their position, recalling that of the biting Lammles who are bitten, is that they are fed on by a multitude of disparaging guests. So disparaging are their guests that they even fashion a drably conventional plumage for these very special birds of prey: 'nobody seems to think much more of the Veneerings than if they were a tolerable landlord and landlady doing the thing in the way of business at so much a head' (p. 120); and the guests 'almost carry themselves like customers' in the general sense they have of the landlord and landlady making 'a pretty good profit' out of the dinners (p. 121). It is a final irony of the Veneerings' social manoeuvres that their plunges and dives, on the occasion referred to, are sanctioned (for his own purposes) by one even more adept in the enterprise of entertaining: Podsnap, their host on that evening, tolerates discussion of 'Bodies in rivers' because he feels he has 'a share' in the affair which makes him 'a part proprietor. As its returns [are] immediate, too, in the way of restraining the company from speechless contemplation of the wine-coolers, it [pays], and he [is] satisfied' (p. 134).

The death imagery of the novel is as subtly developed and expanded as that of the dust-mounds. It is fundamentally related, as I have already suggested, to the money-making activities that reduce everything to dust; and the connection between money-making and death is pointed to time and again. At dawn on the waterside, for instance, 'the staring black and white letters upon wharves and warehouses' seem to Eugene 'like inscriptions over the graves of dead businesses' (p. 171). If this is recognizably the world of the failed sundial, it is also a world of dead men, as the discovery almost at once of Gaffer's body indicates, though Gaffer himself has vehemently maintained that the dead belong to another world in an earlier altercation with Riderhood:

> 'Has a dead man any use for money? Is it possible for a dead man to have money? What world does a dead man belong to? T'other world. What world does money belong to? This world. How can money be a corpse's? Can a corpse own it, want it, spend it, claim it, miss it? Don't try to go confounding the rights and wrongs of things in that way. . . .' (pp. 4–5)

Gaffer's own fate—and the riverside bird of prey is a representative, almost archetypal, figure—makes clear that the worlds of death and of money are as confounded as the rights and wrongs of Riderhood, and that while money may belong to this world and so cannot be a corpse's, it is his wanting money that has made a corpse of him. The world of money, it is more and more strongly suggested, is in fact a world of corpses.

Gaffer's death is representative in another way:

> 'You must be frozen,' [said Lizzie to Gaffer].
> 'Well, Lizzie, I ain't of a glow; that's certain. And my hands seemed nailed through to the sculls. See how dead they are!' Something suggestive in their colour, and perhaps in her face, struck him as he held them up; he turned his shoulder and held them down to the fire. (p. 74)

If Gaffer's 'dead' hands, taken in conjunction with his sense of them being 'nailed through to the sculls', vividly suggest that he is crucified by his occupation, the bold image just hints at the possibility of something beyond this quotidian death. The image comes to mind when Mr. Inspector reconstructs the circumstances of Gaffer's actual death, for one of the explanations he offers for his having overbalanced and fallen overboard is that his boat was caught 'in the cross-swell of two steamers'; he also points out that Gaffer has died with the silver he gave his life for still grasped in his 'tightly clenched right hand' (p. 175), a mid-Victorian Nostromo. And once again there is a suggestion that death is perhaps not the end: Gaffer is said to be 'baptized unto Death' (p. 174). The image of death, we note, has generated an image of rebirth, though Gaffer belongs irretrievably to 't'other world'.

So, too, do Mr. Venus's bones and skulls:

> 'Oh dear me, dear me!' sighs Mr. Venus, heavily, snuffing the candle, 'the world that appeared so flowery has ceased to blow! You're casting your eye round the shop, Mr. Wegg. Let me show you a light. My working bench. My young man's bench. A Wice. Tools. Bones, warious. Skulls, warious. Preserved Indian baby. African ditto. Bottled preparations, warious. Everything within reach of your hand, in good preservation. The mouldy ones a-top. What's in those hampers over them again, I don't quite remember. Say, human warious. Cats. Articulated English baby. Dogs. Ducks. Glass eyes, warious. Mum-

mied bird. Dried cuticle, warious. Oh dear me! That's the general panoramic view.'...

'Where am I?' asks Mr. Wegg.

'You're somewhere in the back shop across the yard, sir; and speaking quite candidly, I wish I'd never bought you of the Hospital Porter.' (pp. 81–2)

Like Gaffer's, Venus's occupation, as his answer to Wegg's question indicates, is in a world of golden dust a representative occupation; it is typical, that is to say, of a world in which everything is bought and sold—even human flesh. Accordingly, such a world offers numerous analogues to Venus's purchase of Wegg from the Hospital Porter, even though Wegg stoutly maintains that 'you can't buy human flesh and blood in this country, sir; not alive, you can't' (p. 297). There is, first of all, the case of Bella, who is willed to Harmon by his father; Harmon sees clearly enough that 'to come into possession' of his father's money will be 'to buy a beautiful creature' (p. 372). There is Georgiana Podsnap, for whom Fledgeby, as Lammle bullyingly tells him, has given 'his dirty note of hand for a wretched sum payable on the occurrence of a certain event' (p. 273); and whom her father believes can be 'exactly put away like the plate, brought out like the plate, polished like the plate, counted, weighed, and valued like the plate' (p. 143). There is 'the uniform principle' of 'bargain and sale' that Mr. and Mrs. Milvey encounter when they try to find a suitable orphan for the Boffins to adopt, for as soon as it becomes known that an orphan is wanted, there is always 'some affectionate relative' to 'put a price upon the orphan's head' (pp. 195–6). There is also Twemlow, whom Veneering regards as 'a remunerative article' (p. 10).

Venus, morever, showing Wegg a light, illuminates more than the interior of his interesting shop, for the shop, we see, is a miniature replica of Society. Certainly 'the general panoramic view' it yields is not unlike that at a Veneering gathering; almost wherever we look, we are met by 'human warious', by the stuffed illusion of life or by the skeleton beneath the skin. Lady Tippins is a representative example in this respect:

Whereabout in the bonnet and drapery announced by her name, any fragment of the real woman may be concealed, is perhaps known to her maid; but you could easily buy all you see of her, in Bond Street: or you might scalp her, and peel her, and scrape her, and make two Lady Tippinses out of her, and yet not penetrate to the genuine article. . . (pp. 118–19)

The Veneerings are ready to buy all they see of Lady Tippins, but the lady they do not see, a lady you might scalp and peel and scrape, differs from one of Venus's skeletons only in being articulated for the social occasion. Eugene sees through her, of course, and whispers to Mortimer that the corpse they have just viewed in the police mortuary is 'not *much* worse than Lady Tippins' (p. 24).

Then there is the 'dead-weight of Podsnappery' (p. 129) that presses heavily on the celebrants of Georgiana's eighteenth birthday. 'Sixteen disciples of Podsnappery' dance, that is, go through the figures of '1, Getting up at eight and shaving close at a quarter-past—2, Breakfasting at nine—3, Going to the City at ten—4, Coming home at half-past five—5, Dining at seven, and the grand chain'. The grand chain, however, is eventually 'riveted to the last link', and the procession slowly circles, 'like a revolving funeral' (pp. 137–8). The disciples, in a word, are as lively as the General Officer and his family, whom Mrs. Veneering lays hold of and whose 'animation' is 'suspended' (p. 134); or as 'Boots and Brewer, and two other stuffed Buffers' who are always 'interposed between the rest of the company and possible accidents' at the Veneerings' (p. 11).

Finally, it might be noted that Venus, mourning 'the world that appeared so flowery' but that 'has ceased to blow', comically faces a dilemma that is central in the novel. He is called on to choose between the dusty money of his business and love; for Pleasant Riderhood, the object of his affections, takes exception to his business even though she 'knows the profits of it': 'I do not wish,' she writes to him, 'to regard myself, nor yet to be regarded, in that bony light' (p. 84). In the comic mode, his dilemma is resolved and the lady won when he agrees to liven up the general panoramic view by confining himself to 'the articulation of men, children, and the lower animals', this effectively relieving her apprehensions of being regarded—as a lady—'in a bony light' (pp. 782–3).

Bradley Headstone fashions a grand chain of his own, seeing to it that everything in his teaching is riveted to the last link:

> He had acquired mechanically a great store of teacher's knowledge. He could do mental arithmetic mechanically, sing at sight

mechanically, blow various wind instruments mechanically, even play the great church organ mechanically. From his early childhood up, his mind had been a place of mechanical stowage. The arrangement of his wholesale warehouse, so that it might be always ready to meet the demands of retail dealers—history here, geography there, astronomy to the right, political economy to the left—natural history, the physical sciences, figures, music, the lower mathematics, and what not, all in their several places—this care had imparted to his countenance a look of care; while the habit of questioning and being questioned had given him a suspicious manner, or a manner that would be better described as one of lying in wait. There was a kind of settled trouble in the face. It was the face belonging to a naturally slow or inattentive intellect that had toiled hard to get what it had won, and that had to hold it now that it was gotten. He always seemed to be uneasy lest anything should be missing from his mental warehouse, and taking stock to assure himself. (p. 217)

Commenting on the arrangement of Bradley's 'wholesale warehouse', Arnold Kettle says that 'in a single sentence' Dickens has produced 'a profound humanist critique of the modern British educational system', a 'socio-intellectual system' that is 'revealed as inhuman not only in its underlying values—commercial and mechanical—but in its division of knowledge and experience into isolated compartments'.[1] This is well said, and it merely remains to add that if Bradley is a victim of this system, he may also be seen (and his surname is suggestive in this respect) as representative of yet another aspect of the deadness of nineteenth-century England, the deadness that results from the substitution of the mechanical for the organic principle. The vision, indeed, as in *Dombey and Son*, is quite Lawrencean, and Bradley is father to Mr. Brunt, Ursula Brangwen's colleague at the Brinsley Street school in *The Rainbow*, the man who teaches 'like a machine'. He is also cousin-german to Podsnap, for the disposition of his 'mental warehouse'—with 'history here, geography there, astronomy to the right, political economy to the left'—is suggestive of nothing so much as getting up at eight and shaving close at a quarter-past, breakfasting at nine, and so on; is suggestive, in a word, of the dead-weight of an intellectual Podsnappery. Middle-class commercialism, we might say, meets a working-class aspiration to the bourgeois in the image of the

---

[1] *'Our Mutual Friend', loc. cit.*, p. 217.

warehouse. It is appropriate, therefore, that Bradley, who is always taking stock of his goods, and whose 'habit of questioning and being questioned' has given him a manner that can be described as one of 'lying in wait', should be presented as a species of scavenger, ready to pounce on the children he teaches. Certainly his pupils, like those 'all over the country', are rendered sufficiently lifeless to fit the bill—as another passage implies:

> The schools—for they were twofold, as the sexes—were down in that district of the flat country tending to the Thames, where Kent and Surrey meet, and where the railways still bestride the market-gardens that will soon die under them. The schools were newly built, and there were so many like them all over the country, that one might have thought the whole were but one restless edifice with the locomotive gift of Aladdin's palace. . . .
>
> But even among school-buildings, school-teachers, and school-pupils, all according to pattern and all engendered in the light of the latest Gospel according to Monotony, the older pattern into which so many fortunes have been shaped for good and evil, comes out. It came out in Miss Peecher the schoolmistress, watering her flowers, as Mr. Bradley Headstone walked forth. It came out in Miss Peecher the schoolmistress, watering the flowers in the little dusty bit of garden attached to her small official residence, with little windows like the eyes in needles, and little doors like the covers of schoolbooks. (pp. 218–19)

Just as the market-gardens 'will soon die' under the railways that bestride them, so the brilliant pun of the schools with 'the locomotive gift' suggests how the spontaneous life of the children will wither under the mechanical instilling of knowledge that is their schooling. The representative product of these schools, we remember, is Charley Hexam, who 'walks forth' with Bradley that evening, casting a shadow over 'the older pattern' that comes out in Miss Peecher. In such a landscape Miss Peecher is pathetic, for, watering the flowers in her 'little dusty bit of garden' and watching the schoolmaster, she not only cherishes life but loves.

In this respect she is like Betty Higden:

> 'Now lookee here,' [said Betty to Rokesmith]. ' 'Tis a poor living

and a hard as is to be got out of this work that I am a-doing now, and but for Sloppy I don't know as I should have held to it this long. But it did just keep us on, the two together. Now that I'm alone—with even Johnny gone—I'd far sooner be upon my feet and tiring of myself out, than a-sitting folding and folding by the fire. And I'll tell you why. There's a deadness steals over me at times, that the kind of life favours and I don't like. Now, I seem to have Johnny in my arms—now, his mother—now, his mother's mother—now, I seem to be a child myself, a-lying once again in the arms of my own mother—then I get numbed, thought and senses, till I start out of my seat, afeerd that I'm a-growing like the poor old people that they brick up in the Unions, as you may sometimes see when they let 'em out of the four walls to have a warm in the sun, crawling quite scared about the streets. . . . I'd far better be a-walking than a-getting numbed and dreary. I'm a good fair knitter, and can make many little things to sell. The loan from your lady and gentleman of twenty shillings to fit out a basket with would be a fortune for me. Trudging round the country and tiring of myself out, I shall keep the deadness off, and get my own bread by my own labour. And what more can I want?' (p. 383)

The 'deadness' that steals over Betty and that her 'kind of life' favours is yet another analogue of the life that is lived in the city of death as well as in Brentford. It is an image of the life that is forced upon the poor in a 'commercial country', for it is but 'a poor living' that they get at best, an image of the soul-destroying labour of a life that is spent 'a-sitting folding and folding'. It is significant that it is only when Johnny's death leaves Betty 'alone' that she becomes aware of the deadness; it is as if the deadness is staved off till then by love, by a loving concern for others, as if love is a regenerative force—a proposition that is fully demonstrated elsewhere in the novel. It is concern for Sloppy that leads to her decision to try to 'keep the deadness off' by taking to the road. Unable to continue her work without his help, unwilling to stand in his way with the Boffins, for he refuses to give her up, she rejects the only two alternatives to 'trudging round the country' that seem to offer themselves. The one is to accept the relief that is provided by the honourable boards (the dust-shovellers and cinder-rakers) and go into the workhouse; but this would simply be to court the death she is trying to escape, to be 'bricked up', like other 'poor old people', in a communal tomb.[1] The other alternative (the one so often resorted to in *Bleak House* and *Little Dorrit*, which are called to mind by the phrasing here) is to allow the Boffins to 'set [her] up' (p. 383), to 'provide for her' (p. 384), to become her patrons; but Betty is determined to 'get [her] own bread by [her] own labour', and rejecting all charity, trudges away 'from paralysis and pauperism' (p. 391). If the road she chooses leads ultimately to her death, her choice of it not only epitomizes her determination to stand on her own feet to the end but, paradoxically, her true vitality.

The death imagery is related to the main action of the novel in two symbolic incidents, Rogue Riderhood's near-drowning, and Fledgeby's encounter with Jenny Wren on the roof of Pubsey and Co. Out on the river in his boat, Riderhood is run down by a steamer; and he is brought into the Six Jolly Fellowship-Porters apparently dead, the 'outer husk and shell' of himself, a 'dank carcase' (p. 443). Efforts are made, however, to 'reanimate' him:

> See! A token of life! An indubitable token of life! The spark may smoulder and go out, or it may glow and expand, but see! The four rough fellows seeing, shed tears. Neither Riderhood in this world, nor Riderhood in the other, could draw tears from them; but a striving human soul between the two can do it easily.
>
> He is struggling to come back. Now he is almost here, now he is far away again. Now he is struggling harder to get back. And yet—like us all, when we swoon—like us all, every day of our lives when we wake—he is instinctively unwilling to be restored to the consciousness of this existence, and would be left dormant, if he could. (pp. 444–5)

The parenthetic aside that relates Riderhood's struggle to return to consciousness from death to our daily return to a waking consciousness from sleep may well be felt to be chilling by those of us who find it hard to get up in the morning, but it effectively universalizes Riderhood's experience. What Dickens insists on is that we all instinctively

[1] The metaphor is not far-fetched. Humphry House refers to Charlotte Crippin, who died of starvation in a workhouse in 1862, 'while Dickens was first planning *Our Mutual Friend*'. At the inquest the Coroner said: 'It was clear that the deceased and her family, being in extreme starvation, presented herself at the union-house. . . . They were placed in a room and there had to undergo such dreadful starvation that deceased died of the effects, and they would have all perished had not their groans attracted the attention of the neighbours.' *The Dickens World*, p. 105.

cling to the passivity of death, to the sleep that is a little death, unwilling to wake to the responsibilities of life. We realize, moreover, that this view is extended still further in the novel. The waking life—and not merely the sleep—of most of those who live in the city of death is, as we have seen, a kind of death; they too are so many dank carcases and outer husks, and they too, like Riderhood, resist a restoration to life. At the same time, the doctor and the men who help him try to save Riderhood, though they are not concerned with him as an individual, since none of them has 'the least regard' for him as a man and 'with them all, he has been an object of avoidance, suspicion, and aversion', are animated by a veneration of life itself; for they are concerned with the 'spark of life' that is 'curiously separable' from him, 'probably because it *is* life, and they are living and must die' (p. 443). If, with one part of him, man clings to death, we are also made to see that, with another, he instinctively cherishes life. What Riderhood's recovery dramatizes, therefore, is the possibility of regeneration—despite an appearance of death and despite a resistance to life; the spark, apparently quenched in the river, is in the end made to 'glow and expand'.

The incident is thus a development of hints that are conveyed to us, as we have seen, in the account of the life and death of Gaffer Hexam. It should also be related to the view taken of the diurnal cycle and of the river. On the night of Gaffer's death, when Riderhood reports his discovery of Gaffer's empty boat to the waiting party on the shore, they all think of Lizzie and look at the light of the fire that is shining through her window:

> It was fainter and duller. Perhaps fire, like the higher animal and vegetable life it helps to sustain, has its greatest tendency towards death, when the night is dying and the day is not yet born. (p. 170)

Night and dawn tend naturally enough to be associated with death and birth, but what is striking about this passage, especially in the context of Gaffer's being 'baptized unto Death', is the suggestion of a death that is followed, in the daily cycle, by a birth, of a reborn day that emerges from a dead night. And this suggestion of a death and a life that are bound together in the same cycle, flowing into and out of each other, is in turn related to the view taken of the river as both the destroyer and preserver of life. The river is felt as destroyer in respect of all the drownings that take place in it; this sense of it is specifically communicated on the night that Riderhood takes his party to Gaffer's boat:

> Not a sluice-gate, or a painted scale upon a post or wall, showing the depth of water, but seemed to hint, like the dreadfully facetious Wolf in bed in Grandmamma's cottage, 'That's to drown *you* in, my dears!' Not a lumbering black barge, with its cracked and blistered side impending over them, but seemed to suck at the river with a thirst for sucking them under. And everything so vaunted the spoiling influences of water—discoloured copper, rotten wood, honey-combed stone, green dank deposit—that the after-consequences of being crushed, sucked under, and drawn down, looked as ugly to the imagination as the main event. (p. 172)

Yet from this river, which spoils and destroys and whose only prospect is death, life can be said to emerge, for Gaffer maintains that the river has been Lizzie's 'living' and her 'meat and drink':

> 'How can you be so thankless to your best friend, Lizzie? The very fire that warmed you when you were a baby, was picked out of the river alongside the coal barges. The very basket that you slept in, the tide washed ashore. The very rockers that I put it upon to make a cradle of it, I cut out of a piece of wood that drifted from some ship or another.' (p. 3)

And the river which brings death is also presented, we remember, as an image of life, for it is the river that 'stretches away to the great ocean, Death'.

The incident of Riderhood's near-drowning is not only used to dramatize this kind of relation between life and death; it is also used to suggest that the life that emerges from death may be transformed. As Pleasant watches her father struggle for life, she has a 'vague idea' that 'the old devil is drowned out of him, and that if he should happily come back to resume his occupation of the empty form that lies upon the bed, his spirit will be altered' (p. 445). Restored to life, Riderhood at once demonstrates how unfounded his daughter's expectations are:

> 'Well, Riderhood,' says the doctor, 'how do you feel?'

He replies gruffly, 'Nothing to boast on.' Having, in fact, re turned to life in an uncommonly sulky state. . . .

Mr. Riderhood next demands his shirt; and draws it on over his head . . .

'Warn't it a steamer?' he pauses to ask [Pleasant].

'Yes, father.'

'I'll have the law on her, bust her! and make her pay for it.' . . .

'Where's my fur cap?' he asks in a surly voice, when he has shuffled his clothes on.

'In the river,' somebody rejoins.

'And warn't there no honest man to pick it up? O' course there was though, and to cut off with it arterwards. You are a rare lot, all on you.' (pp. 447–8)

It is a mark of Dickens's subtlety that Riderhood's unregenerate state should be revealed not alone by his uncommon sulkiness and surliness but by his concern to make the steamer 'pay for it' and to recover his cap—by a preoccupation with money and property. 'I mean to be paid,' he later says, 'for the life as the steamer took' (p. 550), thereby indicating the deathly nature of his tenure in the dust-heap to which he returns. But this is not the main significance of the twist which Dickens gives to the incident, a significance which I think escapes both A. O. J. Cockshut, who says 'the scene helps to prevent the regenerative power of the river in other cases from seeming too like a facile convenience. It reminds us that a gift can be refused';[1] and Arnold Kettle, who says that 'Dickens goes out of his way to laugh at any such idea as the restorative power of drowning'.[2] It seems to me that Cockshut overlooks the fact that the river by itself can have no 'regenerative power',[3] that its power as a poetic and symbolic setting for a transformation should be distinguished from its power actually to work that transformation, and that the only 'gifts' it gives are those of the kind that Gaffer fishes out of it. At the same time, I believe that Kettle, in his impatience with 'mythic' and 'ritual' interpretations, is led to ignore significances that the scene manifestly has; if 'drowning' clearly can have no 'restorative power', Dickens as clearly

---

[1] *The Imagination of Charles Dickens*, p. 178.

[2] '*Our Mutual Friend*', loc. cit., p. 222.

[3] It cannot, other than in terms of electricity, be 'a generative power' either, and does not 'generate' the 'meat and drink' that Gaffer tells Lizzie it has been to her. Monroe Engel refers to Gaffer's words in support of his view that 'the river is seen as a generative power'. *The Maturity of Dickens*, p. 139.

goes out of his way to show that in a case of near-drowning, of apparent death, life can be restored. And it is here that the twist he gives to the incident has its significance in relation to the two other cases of near-drowning that are of major importance in the novel, those of Harmon and Eugene. What Riderhood's recovery demonstrates is that, whereas life can be physically restored by others, a spiritual transformation can come only from within; it demonstrates that to be spiritually reborn one must first die to an old self.

What one has to die to in a world of dust-heaps is vividly suggested in the scene on the roof of Pubsey and Co. Fledgeby is taken out to the 'little garden' on the roof by Riah, and there he meets Jenny and Lizzie. Satisfied that Jenny has been buying the firm's waste, Fledgeby asks Lizzie whether she has been buying or selling anything:

> Looking askew at the questioner, Jenny stole her hand up to her friend's, and drew her friend down, so that she bent beside her on her knee.
>
> 'We are thankful to come here for rest, sir,' said Jenny. 'You see, you don't know what the rest of this place is to us; does he, Lizzie? It's the quiet, and the air.'
>
> 'The quiet!' repeated Fledgeby, with a contemptuous turn of his head towards the City's roar. 'And the air!' with a 'Poof!' at the smoke.
>
> 'Ah!' said Jenny. 'But it's so high. And you see the clouds rushing on above the narrow streets, not minding them, and you see the golden arrows pointing at the mountains in the sky from which the wind comes, and you feel as if you were dead.'
>
> The little creature looked above her, holding up her slight transparent hand.
>
> 'How do you feel when you are dead?' asked Fledgeby, much perplexed.
>
> 'Oh, so tranquil!' cried the little creature, smiling. 'Oh, so peaceful and so thankful! And you hear the people who are alive, crying, and working, and calling to one another down in the close dark streets, and you seem to pity them so! And such a chain has fallen from you, and such a strange good sorrowful happiness comes upon you!'
>
> Her eyes fell on the old man, who, with his hands folded, quietly looked on.
>
> 'Why, it was only just now,' said the little creature, pointing

at him, 'that I fancies I saw him come out of his grave! He toiled
out at that low door so bent and worn, and then he took his
breath and stood upright, and looked all round him at the sky,
and the wind blew upon him, and his life down in the dark was
over!—Till he was called back to life,' she added, looking round
at Fledgeby with that lower look of sharpness. 'Why did you
call him back?'

'He was long enough coming, anyhow,' grumbled Fledgeby.

'But *you* are not dead, you know,' said Jenny Wren. 'Get
down to life!' (pp. 280–1)

What it means to be 'called back to life' by Fledgeby, the embodiment
of the kind of vital force that even a dustman might envy, is precisely
defined on another occasion:

'And I take it for granted,' pursued Fledgeby, 'that to get
the most of your materials for nothing would be well worth your
while, Miss Jenny?'

'You may take it for granted,' returned the dressmaker with
many knowing nods, 'that it's always well worth my while to
make money.'

'Now,' said Fledgeby approvingly, 'you're answering to a
sensible purpose. Now, you're coming out and looking alive! . . .'
(p. 717)

To 'look alive', then, is to have an eye to the main chance; it is 'to
make money', to do what pays (p. 716), to get one's 'money's worth'
(p. 566). Viewed from the roof of Pubsey and Co., however, to look
alive is to suffer the fate of those who are 'alive' below, 'crying and
working'; it is, like them, to be 'chained', to be bound to the money-
mills; it is to live 'down in the dark', in the 'close dark streets', like so
many blind mouths; it is to be buried alive in a mass 'grave'. Coming
up to the roof, consequently, to 'the rest of [the] place', to 'the quiet,
and the air', is a respite from looking alive; and it is like being dead,
as Jenny says, because it is like a sleep, a sleep that is both a restorative
and a lull in the business of living, a sleep that is analogous to the condition from which Rogue Riderhood emerges. It is also, therefore, to
die to the world down below. What dying to the world means is
effectively defined by the scene itself: it means to rise above it, to
look down on and despise the values of the dust-heap. It means to

behave in a way that is beyond the comprehension of Fledgeby, who comes on to the roof talking only of buying and selling, and who, as Jenny tells him, is 'not dead'. To die to the world, moreover, is to 'come out of [the] grave', is to be delivered from the life that is death, is, in a word, to be reborn.[1] To die to the world, we see, is to win life in the city of death and the dust-heap—and it is this struggle for life that is dramatized in the stories of Eugene and Lizzie and Bella and Harmon.

III

In a delightful scene Mr. Podsnap, invited for the first time to the home of Mr. Veneering, effusively greets an astonished Twemlow as his host. Twemlow himself has just before this been introduced by the host to 'his two friends, Mr. Boots and Mr. Brewer', it being clear that Veneering has 'no distinct idea which is which' (p. 8). It is a scene which might be calculated to appeal to Eugene Wrayburn's sense of the absurd, but it is also expressive of the loss of identity with which the 'set of humanity' is afflicted, and, indeed, of Eugene's own predicament:

> 'You must take your friend,' [he said to Mortimer,] 'as he is. You know what I am, my dear Mortimer. You know how dreadfully susceptible I am to boredom. You know that when I became enough of a man to find myself an embodied conundrum, I bored myself to the last degree by trying to find out what I meant. You know that at length I gave it up, and declined to guess any more. Then how can I possibly give you the answer that I have not discovered? The old nursery form runs, "Riddle-me-riddle-me-ree, p'raps you can't tell me what this may be?" My reply runs, "No. Upon my life, I can't." ' (p. 286)

Eugene, we see, has no more succeeded in establishing a meaningful

[1] I am indebted to J. Hillis Miller, who stresses the importance of the scene on the roof. He maintains that what is symbolized in the case of Fledgeby is an inability to 'die to the quotidian world', but his repeated use of the word 'somehow' seems to me to evade the issue of what is involved in 'being dead': 'Riah's life in the dark streets below, we feel, is somehow made significant and good, as are Jenny's and Lizzie's, by the fact that, unlike Fledgeby, they can "be dead." Their lives are constantly in contact with the alien and inhuman, present in the sky, the water, the mountains, and the wind, and, though this means that they are in touch with what from the human point of view is death, such contact somehow gives an authenticity to their lives which is wholly lacking to those remaining within the human world.' *Charles Dickens*, p. 315.

identity than Veneering and other stuffed Buffers, though he is 'enough of a man' to know that he is 'an embodied conundrum'. He may assert, moreover, that he has given up 'trying to find out what [he means]', but his final words suggest that the riddle may not be as lightly dismissed as he believes. In a way not realized by him, his life does depend on his finding an answer to it, for, as I have previously pointed out, the plot functions to suggest that life in the city of death is sustained (among other things) by the discovery of identity. Eugene's acceptance of his meaninglessness is an acceptance of his own vital inanition.

His failure to solve the riddle is also productive of an uncertainty about his position in the society in which he lives. On the one hand, he rejects its ethic of work and money-making, as he indicates to Boffin when referred by the dustman to the industrious habits of bees:

> 'Ye-es,' returned Eugene, disparagingly, 'they work; but don't you think they overdo it? They work so much more than they need—they make so much more than they can eat—they are so incessantly boring and buzzing at their one idea till Death comes upon them—that don't you think they overdo it? And are human labourers to have no holidays, because of the bees? And am I never to have change of air, because the bees don't? Mr. Boffin, I think honey excellent at breakfast; but regarded in the light of my conventional schoolmaster and moralist, I protest against the tyrannical humbug of your friend the bee. With the highest respect for you.' (p. 94)

This, unmistakably, is the voice of Skimpole, whose 'discourse about Bees' in *Bleak House* it recalls; but it is not, as in the case of Skimpole, a 'Drone philosophy'. Eugene simply refuses, in the idiom of *Our Mutual Friend*, to be either a bird or beast of prey:

> 'Then idiots talk,' said Eugene . . . 'of Energy. If there is a word in the dictionary under any letter from A to Z that I abominate, it is energy. . . . What the deuce! Am I to rush out into the street, collar the first man of a wealthy appearance that I meet, shake him, and say, "Go to law upon the spot, you dog, and retain me, or I'll be the death of you?" Yet that would be energy.' (p. 20)

And he also disdains to operate in the 'marriage market' (the haunt of those birds of a feather, the Lammles), refusing to consider the proposition ('with some money, of course') provided by his 'respected father' (pp. 146–7). On the other hand, if he is decided in his rejections, he has not discovered the positive values by which he can direct his life. He starts out, that is to say, from a position that is similar to that of Clennam at the opening of *Little Dorrit*. Eugene is furthermore burdened by his acceptance of conventional class distinctions, though he displays as little sense of direction in his social relations as in his life at large. He is contemptuous of the people with whom he mixes, the Podsnaps and Veneerings and Tippinses, but he allows himself to drift along in their company nevertheless, a dependable diner. It is because his life has no direction, because everything consequently seems so weary, stale, flat and unprofitable, that he is so 'dreadfully susceptible . . . to boredom'. Boredom, that bountiful product of the waste land, is a clue to the conundrum.

Eugene's inner uncertainty is masked by an outer self-possession that is imperturbable. Just how imperturbable he is, Bradley Headstone and Charley Hexam discover when they call on him in order to warn him off Lizzie:

> Passing [Charley] with his eyes as if there were nothing where he stood, Eugene looked on to Bradley Headstone. With consummate indolence, he turned to Mortimer, inquiring: 'And who may this other person be?'
>
> 'I am Charles Hexam's friend,' said Bradley; 'I am Charles Hexam's schoolmaster.'
>
> 'My good sir, you should teach your pupils better manners,' returned Eugene.
>
> Composedly smoking, he leaned an elbow on the chimney-piece, at the side of the fire, and looked at the schoolmaster. It was a cruel look, in its cold disdain of him, as a creature of no worth. The schoolmaster looked at him, and that, too, was a cruel look, though of the different kind, that it had a raging jealousy and fiery wrath in it. . . .
>
> 'In some high respects, Mr. Eugene Wrayburn,' said Bradley, answering him with pale and quivering lips, 'the natural feelings of my pupils are stronger than my teaching.'
>
> 'In most respects, I dare say,' replied Eugene, enjoying his cigar, 'though whether high or low is of no importance. You have my name very correctly. Pray what is yours?'

'It cannot concern you much to know, but—'

'True,' interposed Eugene, striking sharply and cutting him short at his mistake, 'it does not concern me at all to know. I can say Schoolmaster, which is a most respectable title. You are right, Schoolmaster.' (p. 288)

If Eugene's wit here is quick and deadly, striking sharp and cutting deep in a way the slower Bradley cannot hope to match, his attitude is intolerable. His 'consummate indolence' is the physical expression of a consummate insolence, and the insolence is evoked, in the first instance, by a sense of the social inferiority of his interlocutors. Bradley is dismissed as 'a creature of no worth' because he is a schoolmaster; and he is given his due, not to mention his 'most respectable title', as the teacher of such as Charley, over whom Eugene's eyes pass 'as if there were nothing' where he stands. Nor is Eugene's disparagement of his social inferiors confined to those whom he personally resents, as in this instance, for he knows well enough what the visit of Bradley and Lizzie's brother portends. His treatment of them is equivalent in its 'cold disdain' to the treatment he metes out, for example, to Jenny's father when that 'most disgraceful shadow of a man' calls on him. Eugene has no idea of his name, and simply refers to him as 'Mr. Dolls', the 'first appellation that his associations [suggest]' (p. 537); he also deems it 'expedient to fumigate' him:

> He took the shovel from the grate, sprinkled a few live ashes on it, and from a box on the chimney-piece took a few pastilles, which he set upon them; then, with great composure, began placidly waving the shovel in front of Mr. Dolls, to cut him off from his company. (p. 538)

At the end of the visit Eugene picks up the drunkard's 'worn-out hat with the tongs, [claps] it on his head, and, taking him by the collar—all this at arm's length—[conducts] him down-stairs and out of the precincts into Fleet Street' (p. 540). Mortimer laughs at Eugene's behaviour—'Lord bless my soul, Eugene!' he says, 'what a mad fellow you are!' (p. 538)—but we cannot help feeling that Eugene's expression of contempt for Jenny's father, which differs in degree but not in kind from the contempt he displays to Bradley Headstone and Charley Hexam, is itself disgraceful. Nor are Eugene's discriminations only a matter of class, as appears when he wishes to get rid of Riah, in whose company he one night finds Lizzie:

> With an air of perfect patience the old man, remaining mute and keeping his eyes cast down, stood, retaining Lizzie's arm, as though, in his habit of passive endurance, it would be all one to him if he had stood there motionless all night.
>
> 'If Mr. Aaron,' said Eugene, who soon found this fatiguing, 'will be good enough to relinquish his charge to me, he will be quite free for any engagement he may have at the Synagogue. Mr. Aaron, will you have the kindness?'
>
> But the old man stood stock still.
>
> 'Good evening, Mr. Aaron,' said Eugene, politely; 'we need not detain you.' Then turning to Lizzie, 'Is our friend Mr. Aaron a little deaf?'
>
> 'My hearing is very good, Christian gentleman,' replied the old man, calmly; 'but I will hear only one voice to-night desiring me to leave this damsel before I have conveyed her to her home. If she requests it, I will do it. I will do it for no one else.' (pp. 405–6)

While Eugene's invention of a name as a ready means of scorn recalls his reception of Jenny's father, his attitude to Riah is distinguished by his nonchalant anti-Semitism (the tone of which Dickens catches perfectly), which Riah ineffectually tries to counter with his 'Christian gentleman'. His attitude to Riah, moreover, aligns him, alone of all the characters in the novel, with the wholly unsympathetic Fledgeby, whose anti-Semitism is pursued with greater energy. It is surprising, indeed, how unsympathetic Eugene himself is made to appear in scenes like those just referred to. Capable of an inhumanity that is compounded of the witty irresponsibility of a Skimpole and the snobbery and cynicism of a Gowan, he is Dickens's most complex 'hero'; and his development may serve as a further refutation of the charge that Dickens's art is one of caricature.

The agent of Eugene's development, of course, is Lizzie. What her entry into his life means is defined on the night on which Gaffer's body is found. Eugene and Mortimer leave the Fellowship-Porters to join Mr. Inspector and Riderhood, Eugene acting out his supposed interest in the lime trade in a final exchange with Bob:

'Eugene,' Mortimer apostrophized him, laughing quite heartily when they were alone again, 'how *can* you be so ridiculous?'

'I am in a ridiculous humour,' quoth Eugene; 'I am a ridiculous fellow. Everything is ridiculous. Come along!'

It passed into Mortimer Lightwood's mind that a change of some sort, best expressed perhaps as an intensification of all that was wildest and most negligent and reckless in his friend, had come upon him in the last half-hour or so. Thoroughly used to him as he was, he found something new and strained in him that was for the moment perplexing. This passed into his mind, and passed out again; but he remembered it afterwards.

'There's where she sits, you see,' said Eugene, when they were standing under the bank, roared and riven at by the wind. 'There's the light of her fire.'

'I'll take a peep through the window,' said Mortimer.

'No, don't!' Eugene caught him by the arm. 'Best not make a show of her. Come to our honest friend.' (pp. 165–6)

The change that Mortimer senses in his friend is more complex than he supposes. It is not only 'an intensification of all that [is] wildest and most negligent and reckless' in him, though we realize that with one part of him Eugene is strongly urged to start on a devil-may-care adventure with Lizzie. There is something more than an unwonted energy in him, something more than the 'unusual heat' (p. 170) with which he soon afterwards turns on Riderhood for suggesting that Lizzie should be taken into custody in the absence of her father, since the something that is 'new' in him is also 'strained'. The nature of that strain is suggested in his response to Mortimer's announced intention to 'take a peep' at Lizzie. If Lizzie has attracted him in an uncomplicated way as an object of passion, we see that in a world in which 'everything is ridiculous' she has also come to represent something of value, something which he is not prepared lightly to mock or 'make a show of'. From the start of his relationship with her, therefore, Eugene is torn between love and seduction, between a full acceptance of the value he discerns in her and the view that A. O. J. Cockshut says is 'natural to a man of his class and indolent habits', the view that Lizzie 'can only be his prey'.[1] But the devouring of prey is 'natural' only to a bird or beast of prey, and the ethos of *Our Mutual Friend* makes the

---

[1] *The Imagination of Charles Dickens*, p. 175.

choice with which Eugene is faced a momentous one. It is between a preying on the dust-heap—there are dust-heaps, we remember, on which social refuse is piled—between, that is, an adherence to the dust-heap, which is death; and an affirmation of love, of that which, as in the case of Betty Higden, keeps off death, of a love which is life. In the case of Eugene, however, it is an affirmation that implies a conception of value which challenges that of the society he lives in, a society in which money is the supreme attribute and class a stamp of status. It is an affirmation, therefore, that is dependent on his active repudiation of the values of that society, of what are in part at least his own values; and, like Riderhood after he is run down by the steamer, like us all when we wake every day, Eugene clings to passivity, content to drift along. It is an affirmation, furthermore, that is dependent on a solution to the conundrum, as he begins to perceive when Mortimer questions him about Lizzie after the visit of Bradley and Charley:

> 'Are you in communication with this girl, Eugene, and is what these people say true?'
> 'I concede both admissions to my honourable and learned friend.'
> 'Then what is to come of it? What are you doing? Where are you going?' . . .
> 'And, my dear Mortimer,' returned Eugene . . . 'believe me, I would answer [your questions] instantly if I could. But to enable me to do so, I must first have found out the troublesome conundrum long abandoned. Here it is. Eugene Wrayburn.' Tapping his forehead and breast. 'Riddle-me, riddle-me-ree, perhaps you can't tell me what this may be?—No, upon my life I can't. I give it up!' (p. 295)

Lizzie, for her part, accepts that her poverty and her class separate her ineluctably from Eugene, but she has no doubt about her love for him or about its value—though she is able to speak about it only in terms of the feelings of an imaginary 'lady':

> 'What does [the lady] say about [Mr. Wrayburn]?' asked Miss Jenny, in a low voice: watchful, through an intervening silence, of the face looking down at the fire.
> 'She is glad, glad to be rich, that he may have the money.

306

She is glad, glad to be beautiful, that he may be proud of her. Her poor heart—'

'Eh? Her poor heart?' said Miss Wren.

'Her heart—is given him, with all its love and truth. She would joyfully die with him, or, better than that, die for him. She knows he has failings, but she thinks they have grown up through his being like one cast away, for the want of something to trust in, and care for, and think well of. And she says, that lady rich and beautiful that I can never come near, "Only put me in that empty place, only try how little I mind myself, only prove what a world of things I will do and bear for you, and I hope that you might even come to be much better than you are, through me who am so much worse, and hardly worth the thinking of beside you." ' (p. 349)

When we read this passage, and other passages like it, we are struck by apparent inconsistencies that obtrude themselves in the presentation of Lizzie. First, we are told early on that Lizzie, the daughter of the illiterate Gaffer, is herself illiterate (p. 30); and yet her language throughout, as in this passage, is distinguished by a surprising purity and soundness of syntax. Randolph Quirk is probably right when he says that, in the case of Oliver Twist as well as that of Lizzie, Dickens is 'not striving after a simple or slavish linguistic realism but after a linguistic congruence with fundamental intention',[1] that, in other words, the purity of Lizzie's language is intended to be symbolic of the purity of her character, but I do not think that this satisfactorily settles the issue. Though *Our Mutual Friend* has a strongly poetic and symbolic texture, its narrative mode is realistic, and Lizzie's speech offends against its own canons of verisimilitude, the more especially since Dickens makes ineffectual efforts to account for it:

'I suppose—your sister—' [said Bradley] with a curious break both before and after the words, 'has received hardly any teaching, Hexam?'

'Hardly any, sir.'

'Sacrificed, no doubt, to her father's objections. I remember them in your case. Yet—your sister—scarcely looks or speaks like an ignorant person.'

[1] 'Some Observations on the Language of Dickens', *A Review of English Literature*, 2 (July 1961), 22.

'Lizzie has as much thought as the best, Mr. Headstone. Too much, perhaps, without teaching. I used to call the fire at home her books, for she was always full of fancies—sometimes quite wise fancies, considering—when she sat looking at it.' (p. 231)

This offence against verisimilitude is more than a minor defect because it represents a shirking on Dickens's part, a shirking of the full implications of a relationship between a man of Eugene's background and a woman of Lizzie's upbringing; that she is so well-spoken makes his final decision to marry her the easier. Eugene, moreover, is no Professor Higgins, and we remain uneasily aware that his relationship with Lizzie might not have developed at all had she spoken like her father or Rogue Riderhood.

Second, the very purity of character that is apparent in Lizzie's words in the quoted passage, and that her language is generally intended to reflect, is itself open to a similar kind of questioning. How is it, we may well ask, that Lizzie is so delicate and refined and virtuous when her father is a bird of prey and her brother 'a curious mixture . . . of uncompleted savagery, and uncompleted civilisation', whose voice is 'hoarse and coarse', whose face is 'coarse', whose 'stunted figure' is 'coarse' (p. 18), and who, we might add, is a selfish prig? Dickens himself, reporting on a visit to a slum dwelling, provides us with an interesting comment in this regard:

> In the midst of the kitchen . . . sits a young, modest, gentle-looking creature, with a beautiful child in her lap. She seems to belong to the company, but is so strangely unlike it. She has such a pretty, quiet face and voice, and is so proud to hear the child admired . . . Is she as bad as the rest, I wonder? Inspectorial experience does not engender a belief contrariwise, but prompts the answer, not a ha'porth of difference![1]

To this, and to our own questionings, I think we must reply that the experience of a great imaginative novelist is likely to be more profound than that of an inspector of police or our own; and that Lizzie's remarkable goodness, though perhaps unexpected in one of her circumstances, is not in itself unconvincing. There are occasions when we feel it is overdone—when she says to her brother, for instance: '. . . if

---

[1] 'On Duty with Inspector Field', *Household Words*, 3 (14 June 1851), 268. The article is attributed to Dickens by Frederic G. Kitton, *The Minor Writings*, p. 125.

I could make [father] believe that learning was a good thing, and that we might lead better lives, I should be a'most content to die' (pp. 27–8)—but the goodness is Dickens's *donnée*, and, as in the case of Dostoevsky's Prince Myshkin, what matters is what the novelist does with it.

Lizzie's remarks in the quoted passage might also be thought open to a charge of sentimentality. It seems to me, however, that though Lizzie is a little coy about her 'lady', she is not sentimental about Eugene; indeed, her relationship with him is notably free of the touches of sentimentality that cling to the relationship of Clennam and Little Dorrit, for example. It is not only that the expression of her love is sincere, an appropriate revelation of the nature of her feeling; it is redeemed from sentimental cliché by resonances of earned significance. Her willingness to 'die for him', for instance, expresses in simple and direct terms what her relationship with him slowly and painfully establishes, the necessity (which Pip also discovers) for a selflessness in love, for a readiness to 'mind' oneself but 'little'. And her hope that he 'might even come to be much better' than he is 'through [her] who [is] so much worse' implies a view of love as a transforming power that is steadily enlarged by the action as a whole. Her understanding of the effect on Eugene of a lack of love, of a 'want of something to trust in, and care for, and think well of', is penetratingly expressed in a homely image that links up with the major images of the novel. For the want of love, she sees, Eugene is 'like one cast away', is like one, that is, without value in his own eyes and cast, like so much spiritual refuse, on the dust-heap—or out on the river that heads inexorably for the great ocean. We are thus made to see that it is love that is an anchorage, binding to life; it is love which can reclaim that which is thrown away and give it a value that is not dust. We are made to see, that is, that it is love—not a river—that is a regenerative power, that it is love that can revive one bound upon a wheel of fire and take him out of the grave.

Eugene, however, is unable to commit himself to Lizzie though he remains drawn to her. When she leaves London, he tracks her down—and is disconcerted by her distress:

'In the name of all that's good—and that is not conjuring you in my own name—for Heaven knows I am not good'—said Eugene, 'don't be distressed!'

'What else can I be, when I know the distance and the

difference between us? What else can I be, when to tell me why you came here is to put me to shame!' said Lizzie, covering her face.

He looked at her with a real sentiment of remorseful tenderness and pity. It was not strong enough to impel him to sacrifice himself and spare her, but it was a strong emotion.

'Lizzie! I never thought before, that there was a woman in the world who could affect me so much by saying so little. But don't be hard in your construction of me. You don't know what my state of mind towards you is. You don't know how you haunt me and bewilder me. You don't know how the cursed carelessness that is over-officious in helping me at every other turning of my life, won't help me here. You have struck it dead, I think, and I sometimes almost wish you had struck me dead along with it.' (p. 692)

This is a crucial moment in their relationship because the 'strong emotion' that Eugene feels in response to her tears signifies his inability to regard her any longer merely as a sexual object, as his prey: it is 'a real sentiment of remorseful tenderness and pity', the kind of awareness of her as an individual that takes no account of 'the distance and the difference' between them. It is a response, moreover, that marks the breakdown in him of what he calls his 'carelessness', of what we have seen is his cynical imperviousness to others, to the Schoolmasters and the Dolls and the Aarons of his disdain. It is significant that he should think of this habitual carelessness as having been 'struck . . . dead' in him by Lizzie, for this suggests the kind of death, the dying to an old self, that is a necessary prelude to spiritual rebirth; and it establishes Lizzie as a regenerative agent. At the same time—for Dickens handles the process of change with great delicacy—Eugene's sense of self remains stronger than his awareness of Lizzie: his feeling is 'not strong enough to impel him to sacrifice himself and spare her'. To be 'reborn', it is implied, Eugene must first die to self, as well as to an old self, must be prepared, as it were, to lose himself before he can find himself. He must be ready, as he himself unwittingly phrases it, to have himself struck dead along with his carelessness.

It is at this point that he is very nearly struck dead in actuality by Bradley:

The rippling of the river seemed to cause a correspondent

stir in his uneasy reflections. He would have laid them asleep if he could, but they were in movement, like the stream, and all tending one way with a strong current. As the ripple under the moon broke unexpectedly now and then, and palely flashed in a new shape and with a new sound, so parts of his thoughts started, unbidden, from the rest, and revealed their wickedness. 'Out of the question to marry her,' said Eugene, 'and out of the question to leave her. The crisis!'

He had sauntered far enough. Before turning to retrace his steps, he stopped upon the margin, to look down at the reflected night. In an instant, with a dreadful crash, the reflected night turned crooked, flames shot jaggedly across the air, and the moon and stars came bursting from the sky.

Was he struck by lightning? With some incoherent half-formed thought to that effect, he turned under the blows that were blinding him and mashing his life, and closed with a murderer, whom he caught by a red neckerchief—unless the raining down of his own blood gave it that hue. (p. 698)

The meaning for Eugene, the cast-away, of his refusal to contemplate marriage to Lizzie is symbolized by the direction his thoughts are said to take as he comes to that conclusion: like the river, they tend 'one way with a strong current', tend, that is, to 'the great ocean, Death'. It is indeed a crisis for him, and the murderer's blows function, ironically, to save him from himself. That is not to say, as Angus Wilson maintains, that his 'salvation is really immensely arbitrary'.[1] Eugene, as we have seen, has begun to change before the attack, even if the change is not sufficiently far-reaching to obviate the crisis that follows; what the attack does is to force him to complete the change, to accept to the full the change of values that his relationship with Lizzie has slowly been bringing about. The attack forces him to realize that he owes all to Lizzie, who saves him from drowning, to realize that she has given him no less than life, and that she means more to him than 'the distance and the difference' between them. The blows that '[blind] him and [mash] his life', that is to say, are the means by which his eyes are opened (for, like Gloucester, he stumbled when he saw) and his life re-formed. At the same time, his near-drowning and rescue by Lizzie symbolize the spiritual experience

[1] 'The Heroes and Heroines of Dickens', *A Review of English Literature*, 2 (July 1961), 17.

through which he passes, the experience of dying to self and to the world and of being reborn, for his being 'raised from death' implies more than a physical recovery:

> Now, merciful Heaven be thanked for that old time, [thought Lizzie,] enabling me, without a wasted moment, to have got the boat afloat again, and to row back against the stream! And grant, O Blessed Lord God, that through poor me he may be raised from death, and preserved to some one else to whom he may be dear one day, though never dearer than to me! (p. 701)

If it is 'that old time' that gives Lizzie the skill to get the boat afloat and row back against the stream, it is her love for Eugene that gives her the power to do so. It is a love, we note, that is utterly selfless since she renounces him while affirming both in her thoughts and by her deeds that there is no one who loves him more. The scene suggests, then, that it is selfless love that is a saving force; it is through the operation of this force in Lizzie that Eugene is 'raised from death'.

It is through the operation of a like force in himself, called into being by her, that his regeneration is completed. Though he believes he is dying, he marries her; the ceremony is concluded as the sun rises, and is followed by this moving scene:

> 'Lizzie,' said Eugene, after a silence: 'when you see me wandering away from this refuge that I have so ill deserved, speak to me by my name, and I think I shall come back.'
>
> 'Yes, dear Eugene.'
>
> 'There!' he exclaimed, smiling. 'I should have gone then but for that!'
>
> A little while afterwards, when he appeared to be sinking into insensibility, she said, in a calm loving voice: 'Eugene, my dear husband!' He immediately answered: 'There again! You see how you can recall me!' and afterwards, when he could not speak, he still answered by a slight movement of his head upon her bosom.
>
> The sun was high in the sky when she gently disengaged herself to give him the stimulants and nourishment he required. The utter helplessness of the wreck of him that lay cast ashore there now alarmed her, but he himself appeared a little more hopeful.

'Ah, my beloved Lizzie!' he said, faintly. 'How shall I ever pay all I owe you, if I recover!'

'Don't be ashamed of me,' she replied, 'and you will have more than paid all.'

'It would require a life, Lizzie, to pay all; more than a life.'

'Live for that, then; live for me, Eugene; live to see how hard I will try to improve myself, and never to discredit you.'

'My darling girl,' he replied, rallying more of his old manner than he had ever yet got together. 'On the contrary, I have been thinking whether it is not the best thing I can do, to die.'

'The best thing you can do, to leave me with a broken heart?'

'I don't mean that, my dear girl. I was not thinking of that. What I was thinking of was this. Out of your compassion for me, in this maimed and broken state, you make so much of me—you think so well of me—you love me so dearly!'

'Heaven knows I love you dearly!'

'And Heaven knows I prize it! Well. If I live, you'll find me out.'

'I shall find out that my husband has a mine of purpose and energy, and will turn it to the best account?'

'I hope so, dearest Lizzie,' said Eugene wistfully, and yet somewhat whimsically. 'I hope so. But I can't summon the vanity to think so. How can I think so, looking back on such a trifling, wasted youth as mine! I humbly hope it; but I daren't believe it. There is a sharp misgiving in my conscience that if I were to live, I should disappoint your good opinion and my own —and that I ought to die, my dear!' (pp. 753–4)

The man who was 'like one cast away' for want of love is here 'cast ashore' at last. The shore that is his 'refuge' is marriage; and it is love that binds him to life, for he is 'recalled' from 'insensibility' by Lizzie's call of 'Eugene, my dear husband', by a consciousness of her love for him and of his own love for her, by his sense of himself as her husband. He is recalled to life, in other words, because he finally knows who he is. Lizzie's loving words are the answer to the conundrum. If Eugene can therefore be said to have found himself in marriage to Lizzie, the marriage itself shows a new selflessness on his part, a readiness to lose himself. Believing that he is going to die, Eugene, it is clear, asks nothing for himself in the marriage, but, in Mortimer's words, seeks only to follow 'the right course of a true man' and make his 'reparation' to Lizzie 'complete' (pp. 741–2). After the attack, indeed, his concern is always only for Lizzie, never for himself, for he also makes Mortimer promise to see that Bradley is not brought to justice: 'Don't think of avenging me,' he says; 'think only of hushing the story and protecting her' (p. 738). Eugene's attitude to Lizzie, like the unwonted humility of his self-criticism, points to his growth into a new self.

The marriage also represents Eugene's attempt to 'pay' Lizzie all that he 'owes' her, and to show her how much he 'prizes' her love. It is, that is to say, a tender of love; and it implies (with far greater force than analogous hints in *Martin Chuzzlewit*, *Dombey and Son*, *Bleak House* and *Little Dorrit*) that love is the only wealth that is not dust. Lizzie is acute enough to realize, however, that a love such as theirs can be held only in the teeth of the world, and so the payment she asks of him is that he should not be ashamed of her. Her demand is far-reaching in its implications—as Eugene finally comes to see:

'. . . I have had an idea, Mortimer,' [said Eugene,] 'of taking myself and my wife to one of the colonies, and working at my vocation there.'

'I should be lost without you, Eugene; but you may be right.'

'No,' said Eugene, emphatically. 'Not right. Wrong!'

He said it with such a lively—almost angry—flash, that Mortimer showed himself greatly surprised.

'You think this thumped head of mine is excited?' Eugene went on, with a high look; 'not so, believe me. I can say to you of the healthful music of my pulse what Hamlet said of his. My blood is up, but wholesomely up, when I think of it! Tell me! Shall I turn coward to Lizzie, and sneak away with her, as if I were ashamed of her! Where would your friend's part in this world be, Mortimer, if she had turned coward to him, and on immeasurably better occasion?'

'Honourable and staunch,' said Lightwood. 'And yet, Eugene—'

'And yet what, Mortimer?'

'And yet, are you sure that you might not feel (for her sake, I say for her sake) any slight coldness towards her on the part of—Society?'

'Oh! You and I may well stumble at the word,' returned Eugene, laughing. 'Do we mean our Tippins?'

'Perhaps we do,' said Mortimer, laughing also.

'Faith, we DO!' returned Eugene, with great animation. 'We may hide behind the bush and beat about it, but we DO. Now my wife is something nearer to my heart, Mortimer, than Tippins is, and I owe her a little more than I owe to Tippins, and I am rather prouder of her than I ever was of Tippins. Therefore, I will fight it out to the last gasp, with her and for her, here in the open field. When I hide her, or strike for her, faint-heartedly, in a hole or a corner, do you, whom I love next best upon earth, tell me what I shall most righteously deserve to be told:—that she would have done well to have turned me over with her foot that night when I lay bleeding to death, and to have spat in my dastard face.'

The glow that shone upon him as he spoke the words so irradiated his features, that he looked, for the time, as though he had never been mutilated. . . . (pp. 812–13)

This passage makes clear, with an explicitness that is appropriate to the discussion of the friends, just what Eugene's marriage to Lizzie means. It is not merely, we see, that in marrying her he has put her before the world, that he has mounted, as it were, to the roof of his own Pubsey and Co., of his own worldliness, and risen above it; his decision to stay in England and 'fight it out . . . with her and for her' constitutes an active repudiation of the values of Society, a direct challenging of them. The man who abominated the word 'energy' in its association with money-making speaks here with a vigour that suggests he does have 'a mine of purpose and energy', as Lizzie believes, and that he is ready to turn it 'to the best account'. We are to infer that, having found himself, Eugene has also found a purpose in life. It is even suggested that his purposiveness itself endows him with vital force, and is itself a factor in his regeneration: he speaks with a 'lively' flash; he has 'a high look'; he says his 'blood is up'; he answers Mortimer 'with great animation'; and his features are 'irradiated' by a 'glow' that 'shines' upon him. He even looks 'as though he [has] never been mutilated'—as though he has indeed been transformed.

The significance of Eugene's regeneration is heightened by the contrasted death of Bradley Headstone, his rival for Lizzie. Bradley, like Eugene, is tested by his relationship with Lizzie; and, as in the case of Eugene, his fate is decided by his attitude to her. His attitude is most clearly revealed when he proposes marriage to her:

She yielded to the entreaty—how could she do otherwise?—
and they paced the stones in silence. One by one the lights
leaped up, making the cold grey church tower more remote, and
they were alone again. He said no more until they had regained
the spot where he had broken off; there, he again stood still, and
again grasped the stone. In saying what he said then, he never
looked at her; but looked at it and wrenched at it.

'You know what I am going to say. I love you. What other
men may mean when they use that expression, I cannot tell;
what *I* mean is, that I am under the influence of some tremendous attraction which I have resisted in vain, and which over-
masters me. You could draw me to fire, you could draw me to
water, you could draw me to the gallows, you could draw me
to any death, you could draw me to anything I have most avoided,
you could draw me to any exposure and disgrace. This and the
confusion of my thoughts, so that I am fit for nothing, is what
I mean by your being the ruin of me. But if you would return
a favourable answer to my offer of myself in marriage, you could
draw me to any good—every good—with equal force. My circumstances are quite easy, and you would want for nothing. My
reputation stands quite high, and would be a shield for yours. If
you saw me at my work, able to do it well and respected in it,
you might even come to take a sort of pride in me:—I would
try hard that you should. Whatever considerations I may have
thought of against this offer, I have conquered, and I make it
with all my heart. Your brother favours me to the utmost, and
it is likely that we might live and work together; anyhow, it is
certain that he would have my best influence and support. I
don't know that I could say more if I tried. I might only weaken
what is ill enough said as it is. I only add that if it is any claim
on you to be in earnest, I am in thorough earnest, dreadful
earnest.' (p. 397)

Though Bradley is at once ready to commit himself to Lizzie, while
Eugene is not, his proposal smacks as much of self-centredness as
Eugene's hesitations. The self-centredness is revealed in the very
wording of his proposal, in '[his] offer of [himself] in marriage'; and
it is suggested too by his posture as he proposes: 'he never [looks] at
her', but only at the stone at which he wrenches, concerned, it would
appear, only with the violence of his own feelings. He is also smugly

316

condescending to her (a very Podsnap of patronage) when he assures her that his 'reputation' will be 'a shield' for hers, and that he has 'conquered' the 'considerations' that might well have prevented him from making the offer. Seeking thus to imbue her with a sense of his superiority to worldly considerations (and of the sacrifice he is making in being superior to them), he is sufficiently worldly to assume that Lizzie will not be indifferent to similar matters, that she will be as ready to look alive as any Fledgeby, and that she will thus see that marriage to him will secure his 'best influence and support' for her brother. It will also provide easy circumstances for herself; and, as he tells Charley though not her, it will 'place' her in his 'station', if not 'raise' her to it, for he scrupulously refrains from attributing that meaning to what he has in fact intimated (p. 388).

Bradley's attitude to Lizzie, in other words, is hardly admirable; but, when all is said and done, he is no more culpable, morally, than Eugene, no more worldly and self-centred than he in the first stage of his relationship with Lizzie. It is thus in the contrasted fates of these men that what Dickens has to say is emphasized with particular force. They are counterparts, and their stories dramatize alternate possibilities of life in the dust-heap, of the life that can be redeemed, Dickens seems to say, only by love. Eugene is granted love and saved; Bradley (impervious to Miss Peecher) is denied it and damned. Bradley, indeed, unwittingly formulates the alternatives in his proposal: given Lizzie's love, he believes he can be drawn 'to any good', even drawn out, as he tells her just before, from 'a strong prison' if he were shut up in it (p. 396); refused her love, he intuitively knows that he can be drawn 'to any exposure and disgrace', even to 'the gallows' and 'any death'. Refused it, he is 'cast out' (p. 399), and is like one who has been cast away.

Bradley's decline is convincingly related not only to Lizzie's rejection of him but to the demands that his profession has made on him. In the process of mechanically stocking his warehouse and dealing out its goods, he has had rigorously to school himself: as he is provoked into telling Eugene, he has had to '[watch] and [repress]' himself both in 'forming' himself for his 'duties' and in seeking 'to discharge them well' (p. 291). But it is the very repression that his attempt to make his way in the world has forced on him, the repression of all in him that is vital and natural, that undoes him; for it bursts out in his violent passion for Lizzie: 'It seemed to him as if all that he could suppress in himself he had suppressed, as if all that he could restrain in himself he had restrained, and the time had come—in a rush, in a moment—when the power of self-command had departed from him' (p. 341). 'Over-mastered', as he tells Lizzie when he proposes, by the 'tremendous attraction' that he cannot resist, the master thus becomes a prey to his own passions. When Lizzie rejects him, the violence of his feeling is deflected destructively on to the man he is sure has supplanted him. No sooner does Lizzie tell him that he has no chance than he brings his hand down on the stone 'with a force that [lays] the knuckles raw and bleeding' and declares: 'then I hope that I may never kill him!' (p. 398). From that moment Bradley is transformed, as it were, into a beast of prey. Or a waterside rat—as the disguise he adopts when he sets out to murder Eugene suggests. The disguise also epitomizes his loss of identity, for though he slides into that of Rogue Riderhood, he continues mechanically to lead his life as a teacher. In the end, Bradley is himself a conundrum: 'And whereas, in his own schoolmaster clothes, he usually looked as if they were the clothes of some other man, he now looked [i.e., disguised as Riderhood], in the clothes of some other man, or men, as if they were his own' (p. 631).

The conclusion of Bradley's story provides a grimly ironic contrast to that of Eugene. Having rid himself of his disguise after the attempted murder of Eugene, he is said to have 'risen, as it were, out of the ashes of the Bargeman' (p. 791). He is not left, however, to take up his life anew; for Riderhood, who knows his secret and is determined to make what he can out of it, remorselessly drags him back to the ashes, back to the death that he has vainly tried to escape:

> Not one other word did Bradley utter all that night. Not once did he change his attitude, or loosen his hold upon his wrist. Rigid before the fire, as if it were a charmed flame that was turning him old, he sat, with the dark lines deepening in his face, its stare becoming more and more haggard, its surface turning whiter and whiter as if it were being overspread with ashes, and the very texture and colour of his hair degenerating.
>
> Not until the late daylight made the window transparent did this decaying statue move. . . . (p. 800)

What Bradley sees in the fire as he physically degenerates before the eyes of Riderhood is that, having failed to dispose successfully of the evidence of his crime, he now has no alternative but to dispose of his blackmailer or of himself. His degeneration is complete. He now needs no disguise to be like Riderhood—he *is* the waterside rat, so to speak, and in destroying him he destroys himself.

IV

In a world of bankrupt sundials and mounting dust-heaps, Bella Wilfer's 'case' is not only 'hard', as she puts it, but representative:

> 'It's a shame! There never was such a hard case! I shouldn't care so much if it wasn't so ridiculous. It was ridiculous enough to have a stranger coming over to marry me, whether he liked it or not. It was ridiculous enough to know what an embarrassing meeting it would be, and how we never could pretend to have an inclination of our own, either of us. It was ridiculous enough to know I shouldn't like him—how *could* I like him, left to him in a will, like a dozen of spoons, with everything cut and dried beforehand, like orange chips? Talk of orange flowers indeed! I declare again it's a shame! Those ridiculous points would have been smoothed away by the money, for I love money, and want money—want it dreadfully. I hate to be poor, and we are degradingly poor, offensively poor, miserably poor, beastly poor. But here I am, left with all the ridiculous parts of the situation remaining, and added to them all, this ridiculous dress! . . . I declare it's a very hard case indeed, and I am a most unfortunate girl. The idea of being a kind of widow, and never having been married! And the idea of being as poor as ever after all, and going into black, besides, for a man I never saw, and should have hated—as far as *he* was concerned—if I had seen!' (pp. 37–8)

Bella's views, we see, resemble those of Eugene in at least one respect—she too finds everything 'ridiculous', as her repeated references to the ridiculous aspects of her position emphasize. Whereas Eugene is inclined, however, to be unimpressed by the honey-making capacity of bees and to find value only in the sterling qualities of Lizzie, Bella believes that the one thing that is not ridiculous is money, that money, indeed, can even '[smoothe] away' the 'ridiculous points' of her 'situation'. What she does not seem to realize is that it is her desire for money, not the Harmon will or the supposed death of John Harmon, that has made her world ridiculous. It is her desire for money that has made her acquiesce, in the first place, in what amounts to her own dehumanization, for though she clearly resents having been 'left to [Harmon] in a will, like a dozen of spoons', she as clearly has never even considered the possibility of refusing to marry him. It is Harmon, not she, who is required to comply with the terms of the will on pain of penalties. It is her attitude, not her poverty, that is 'degrading', though Dickens makes us see, amid the dust-heaps, that poverty, as well as wealth, can be corrupting, that Bella is (as she is later described) a 'doubly spoilt girl: spoilt first by poverty, and then by wealth' (p. 308). It is her attitude that has placed her in an unreal world in which she is 'a kind of widow' though 'never having been married', in which her 'going into black' and wearing the 'ridiculous dress' signifies her loss of identity. It is an unreal world, moreover, like the 'hilly country entirely composed of Dust' that old Harmon turns his estate into, in which money is set against love, in which money drives out love: while Bella says that she '[loves] money', she not only admits that neither she nor Harmon could ever have pretended 'to have an inclination' for each other but that she 'should have hated' him.

Bella continues to oppose money to love even after she is taken up by the Boffins, as she insists on making clear to her father:

> 'I have made up my mind that I must have money, Pa. I feel that I can't beg it, borrow it, or steal it; and so I have resolved that I must marry it.'
>
> R. W. cast up his eyes towards her, as well as he could under the operating circumstances, and said in a tone of remonstrance, 'My de-ar Bella.'
>
> 'Have resolved, I say, Pa, that to get money I must marry money. In consequence of which, I am always looking out for money to captivate.'
>
> 'My de-a-r Bella!'
>
> 'Yes, Pa, that is the state of the case. If ever there was a mercenary plotter whose thoughts and designs were always in her mean occupation, I am the amiable creature. But I don't care. I hate and detest being poor, and I won't be poor if I can marry money. Now you are deliciously fluffy, Pa, and in a state to astonish the waiter and pay the bill.'
>
> 'But, my dear Bella, this is quite alarming at your age.'

'I told you so, Pa, but you wouldn't believe it,' returned Bella, with a pleasant childish gravity. 'Isn't it shocking?'

'It would be quite so, if you fully knew what you said, my dear, or meant it.'

'Well, Pa, I can only tell you that I mean nothing else. Talk to me of love!' said Bella, contemptuously: though her face and figure certainly rendered the subject no incongruous one. 'Talk to me of fiery dragons! But talk to me of poverty and wealth, and there indeed we touch upon realities.' (pp. 320–1)

Once again Bella does not realize the implications of her own attitude. Though she says that it is 'shocking', she is unaware that her resolve to 'marry money' (which is the logical development of her readiness to be married to money under the Harmon will) is ironically juxtaposed with the begging, borrowing and stealing at which she draws the line. Her resolve turns her into a fortune-hunter, and like all other money-makers in the novel, it is implied that she, who is 'always looking out for money to captivate', has also become a bird of prey. She is an unusual predator, however, in that she is concerned about her own rapaciousness, even though she declares that she does not 'care'. The very fact that she is so self-critical, that she can refer to herself as 'a mercenary plotter' pursuing a 'mean occupation', shows that she does care. It also suggests that, in the interests of her 'occupation', she has—like Bradley—deliberately repressed a part of herself. That she is sometimes surprised into acting in a warmly spontaneous and uncalculating manner is revealed, for instance, just prior to the discussion with her father, when she presses money on him (p. 316), and forces him to attain 'the modest object of his ambition: which [is], to wear a complete new suit of clothes, hat and boots included, at one time' (p. 32); or, soon after the discussion, when her 'behaviour' to the sick Johnny is 'very tender and very natural', and she kneels 'on the brick floor to clasp the child' (p. 327). Bella, in other words, as Boffin at once sees (and as Mrs. Boffin reports him as saying) may be 'a leetle spoilt . . . on the surface' but is 'true golden gold at heart' (p. 772). To ensure that the gold does not turn to dust, therefore, what is required of Bella is not, like Eugene, that she should die to an old self, but that she should bring a buried self to life. There is little hope of this development, however, as long as Bella continues to believe that 'poverty and wealth' are the only 'realities', and that she has outgrown love as she has the 'fiery dragons' of fairy tale and romance; for it is implied that love alone can warm a buried self into life. This is what Bella has to learn; her 'gravity', as she points out how 'shocking' her beliefs are, may be 'pleasant', but it is also said to be 'childish'. The rest of her story is the tale of her education.

Bella is exposed to the influence of two teachers, as it were—Boffin and Lizzie. Her encounter with Lizzie (on the occasion of Betty Higden's funeral) is short, but it leaves her feeling afterwards 'as if much [has] happened—to [herself]' (p. 530):

> 'No. I don't want to wear . . . out [my feeling for Eugene],' was [Lizzie's] flushed reply, 'nor do I want to believe, nor do I believe, that he is not worthy of it. What should I gain by that, and how much should I lose!'

Bella's expressive little eyebrows remonstrated with the fire for some short time before she rejoined:

'Don't think that I press you, Lizzie; but wouldn't you gain in peace, and hope, and even in freedom? Wouldn't it be better not to live a secret life in hiding, and not to be shut out from your natural and wholesome prospects? Forgive my asking you, would that be no gain?'

'Does a woman's heart that—that has that weakness in it which you have spoken of,' returned Lizzie, 'seek to gain anything?'
. . .

'[If I wore it out], I should leave off prizing the remembrance that he has done me nothing but good since I have known him, and that he has made a change within me, like—like the change in the grain of these hands, which were coarse, and cracked, and hard, and brown when I rowed on the river with father, and are softened and made supple by this new work as you see them now.'

They trembled, but with no weakness, as she showed them.

'Understand me, my dear;' thus she went on. 'I have never dreamed of the possibility of his being anything to me on this earth but the kind of picture that I know I could not make you understand, if the understanding was not in your own breast already. I have no more dreamed of the possibility of *my* being his wife, than he ever has—and words could not be stronger than that. And yet I love him. I love him so much and so dearly, that when I sometimes think my life may be but a weary one, I am proud of it and glad of it. I am proud and glad to suffer something for him, even though it is of no service to him, and he will never know of it or care for it.'

Bella sat enchained by the deep, unselfish passion of this girl or woman of her own age, courageously revealing itself in the confidence of her sympathetic perception of its truth. And yet she had never experienced anything like it, or thought of the existence of anything like it. (pp. 526–8)

The lesson that Bella is given here is one in 'understanding', but it is an understanding that Lizzie assumes is 'in [her] own breast already'. Lizzie, in other words, serves as a mirror, revealing to Bella what she really is, what lies hidden and obscured in her; and she also presents an image of what she may become. Bella is made to realize, if not that she may gain the whole world and lose her soul, that a woman may be enriched by her love even if she loses her beloved; that by not '[seeking] to gain anything', one may gain everything, that one may be made 'proud' and 'glad' of one's life. Bella is also made to see, and Lizzie drives the lesson home by pointing to 'the change in the grain of [her] hands', which were 'coarse and cracked, and hard, and brown' and which are now 'softened and . . . supple', that one can be trans-formed by love, refined and changed within—just as we have been made to see by the image of Gaffer's hands 'nailed through to the sculls' (which Lizzie's reference to her rowing on the river with her father recalls) that one can be martyred by a desire for the only kind of 'gain' Bella has hitherto admitted. If Bella sits 'enchained by the deep, unselfish passion' of Lizzie, enthralled by her simple sincerity, it is thereafter her own grasping hands that are 'enchained' by her 'perception' of the 'truth' of what Lizzie has said and shown.

The lesson that Boffin teaches Bella is complementary to that taught by Lizzie:

'I am very fond of you, my dear,' [Boffin said to Bella,] 'and I am entirely of your mind, and you and I will take care that you shall be rich. These good looks of yours (which you have some right to be vain of, my dear, though you are not, you know) are worth money, and you shall make money of 'em. The money you will have, will be worth money, and you shall make money of that too. There's a golden ball at your feet. Good night, my dear.'

Somehow, Bella was not so well pleased with this assurance

and this prospect as she might have been. Somehow, when she put her arms round Mrs. Boffin's neck and said Good night, she derived a sense of unworthiness from the still anxious face of that good woman and her obvious wish to excuse her husband. 'Why, what need to excuse him?' thought Bella, sitting down in her own room. 'What he said was very sensible, I am sure, and very true, I am sure. It is only what I often say to myself. Don't I like it then? No, I don't like it, and, though he is my liberal benefactor, I disparage him for it. Then pray,' said Bella, sternly putting the question to herself in the looking-glass as usual, 'what do you mean by this, you inconsistent little Beast?'

The looking-glass preserving a discreet ministerial silence when thus called upon for explanation, Bella went to bed with a weariness upon her spirit which was more than the weariness of want of sleep. And again in the morning, she looked for the cloud, and for the deepening of the cloud, upon the Golden Dustman's face. (pp. 465–6)

The fact that it is 'to herself in the looking-glass' that Bella puts her question as to what she means by her inconsistency suggests that she will only know the answer when she is able to see herself as she is, when, like Eugene Wrayburn, she finds the answer to her own conundrum and knows what she herself means. For Bella has continued at the Boffins' to wear her widow's dress, as it were, presenting herself as what she is not, a supporter of the doctrine that her 'good looks' (along with other 'human warious') are 'worthy money', while she instinctively inclines to 'disparage' the man who enunciates it. It is by insisting on the enunciation in as indelicate a manner as possible that Boffin proves to be a better mirror than her glass: he later reproves Rokesmith in her presence, for instance, for failing to appreciate that she was 'lying in wait . . . for money' and 'looking about the market for a good bid', and that she was therefore not 'to be snapped up by fellows that had no money to lay out; nothing to buy with' (p. 590). If, in other words, Lizzie teaches Bella what she is by showing her what she may become; Boffin teaches her what she is by showing her what she has become, by reflecting what she takes to be her own values in a form that appalls her. And if Lizzie's passion chains Bella's hands, Boffin's miserliness and acquisitiveness make her feel that her feet are shackled, so to speak; the 'weariness upon her spirit', which is not due to a 'want of sleep', would seem perhaps to be attributable to the 'golden ball' which he has placed at her feet. It is the kind of golden ball that is being chased by the 'set of humanity' in the streets beneath the roof of Pubsey and Co., the set of humanity, we remember, that, in leaving the city, is like 'a set of prisoners departing from gaol'. It is the kind of chase that leads to 'Old Harmon living solitary' in 'Harmony Jail' (p. 54).

Bella's chase comes to an end when Boffin stages a scene of 'righting' her against Rokesmith, whom he accuses of having 'pestered' her with his 'impudent addresses' (p. 590), and whom he 'discharges' from his service (p. 592). Before leaving, Rokesmith once again declares his love for Bella, opposing a view of love as true wealth to Boffin's belief in the love of money as a master passion: Rokesmith maintains that simply to have been near Bella has been for him a daily 'recompense', and that he is 'incapable' of 'a mercenary project, or a mercenary thought' in connection with her because 'any prize' that he could fancy 'would sink into insignificance beside her' (pp. 593–4). It is a view that Eugene, in his tender of love to Lizzie, also comes to, as we have seen; and it is the view that is repeatedly put before us in the development of the relationship between Bella and Harmon-Rokesmith: after they are married, but before Harmon has revealed his true identity to her, he tells her that he knows he is 'rich beyond all wealth' in having her (p. 680); and we are later told that he cares for his wife as 'a most precious and sweet commodity' that is never 'worth less than all the gold in the world' (p. 683).

The scene between Rokesmith and Boffin has the effect on Bella that the dustman has calculated. She first 'shrinks' from Boffin, and bursts into a 'passion of tears' (p. 596), a development that heralds the release of what she has been repressing; and then tries to right herself with, not against, Rokesmith:

> 'The only fault you can be truly charged with, in having spoken to me as you did that night . . . is that you laid yourself open to be slighted by a worldly shallow girl whose head was turned, and who was quite unable to rise to the worth of what you offered her. Mr. Rokesmith, that girl has often seen herself in a pitiful and poor light since, but never in as pitiful and poor a light as now, when the mean tone in which she answered you—sordid and vain girl that she was—has been echoed in her ears by Mr. Boffin.' (p. 598)

This speech effectively brings together those factors which we have been led to expect will combine to bring about a change in Bella. Boffin's behaviour leads her to repudiate not only him but also herself, for she has seen herself, in 'as pitiful and poor a light' as she can bear to contemplate, in him. In seeing herself, moreover, as 'a worldly shallow girl', who was 'quite unable to rise to the worth' of what was offered her, she now rises above her own worldliness in a manner that suggests she has ceased to be concerned with 'looking alive', that she is now prepared, like Jenny on the roof of Pubsey and Co., to be 'dead'. What has 'died' in her is her 'shallow' self, the worldly shallowness she has imposed on herself, and her true self is now free to come to the surface. And what has brought this self to life, of course, is her love for Rokesmith, the love which she cannot yet bring herself to admit to him but which she proudly declares to the Boffins after he has left (p. 600).

Having repudiated Boffin, Bella refuses to accept his patronage any longer, and announcing to him that she 'must go home for good', remains proof against his final temptation:

> 'You mustn't expect,' Mr. Boffin pursued, 'that I'm a-going to settle money on you, if you leave us like this, because I am not. No, Bella! Be careful! Not one brass farthing.'
> 'Expect!' said Bella, haughtily. 'Do you think that any power on earth could make me take it, if you did, sir?' (p. 600)

The wheel, we see, has come full circle. No longer a slave to a testator, Bella is now free to marry the very man to whom she was willed but whom she thought she had lost. If, however, the portrayal of her liberation is convincing, though lacking the power of that of Eugene, Dickens falters badly in his representation of the married bliss to which she attains. This, it is intimated, consists not only in her love for Harmon but in 'her desire to be in all things his companion'; and this desire leads her 'for a regular period every day' to attempt 'the mastering of the newspaper, so that she [may] be close up with John on general topics when John [comes] home' (p. 682). It also consists in the birth of a child, but the way in which Bella communicates the news of her pregnancy to her husband suggests that she is woefully unprepared for it. It suggests, furthermore, that, to the end, Dickens was capable of a sentimentality that it is simply impossible to reconcile with the profundities of his work:

As he bent his face to hers, she raised hers to meet it, and laid her little right hand on his eyes, and kept it there.

'Do you remember, John, on the day we were married, Pa's speaking of the ships that might be sailing towards us from the unknown seas?'

'Perfectly, my darling!'

'I think.....among them.....there is a ship upon the ocean..... bringing.....to you and me.....a little baby, John.' (p. 688)

The story of Bella's regeneration lacks the power of that of Eugene for another reason—a false note is sounded at its climax:

'I hate you!' cried Bella, turning suddenly upon [Boffin], with a stamp of her little foot—'at least, I can't hate you, but I don't like you!'

'HUL-LO!' exclaimed Mr. Boffin in an amazed under-tone.

'You're a scolding, unjust, abusive, aggravating, bad old creature!' cried Bella. 'I am angry with my ungrateful self for calling you names; but you are, you are: you know you are!'

Mr. Boffin stared here, and stared there, as misdoubting that he must be in some sort of fit.

'I have heard you with shame,' said Bella. 'With shame for myself, and with shame for you. You ought to be above the base tale-bearing of a time-serving woman; but you are above nothing now.'

Mr. Boffin, seeming to become convinced that this was a fit, rolled his eyes and loosened his neckcloth.

'When I came here, I respected you and honoured you, and I soon loved you,' cried Bella. 'And now I can't bear the sight of you. At least, I don't know that I ought to go so far as that—only you're a—you're a Monster!' Having shot this bolt out with a great expenditure of force, Bella hysterically laughed and cried together.

'The best wish I can wish you is,' said Bella, returning to the charge, 'that you had not one single farthing in the world. If any true friend and well-wisher could make you a bankrupt you would be a Duck; but as a man of property you are a Demon!' (p. 597)

The false note that sounds here is the note of whimsey, and it is introduced by the soft pedal of reservation. The reservation is apparent throughout: the foot that Bella stamps is a 'little' foot; her passionate cry of hatred is amended ('at least, I can't hate you') to one of dislike, just as her avowal that she cannot bear the sight of Boffin is retracted ('at least, I don't know that I ought to go so far as that'); and her denunciation of the 'bad old creature' becomes a 'calling [of] names' which culminates in her saying that he is a—'a Monster'. There follows a statement that should have been climactic and triumphant (for if we have been shown the transforming power of love, Bella has been made to see that money can work its own transformations—and that is the point of her denunciation) but which succeeds only in being bathetic and whimsical: '[as] a bankrupt you would be a Duck; but as a man of property you are a Demon.' A scene, in other words, that should have the weight and seriousness of the scene which follows Eugene's marriage to Lizzie, is marred by a damaging holding back; and it is marred because Dickens, in cheating his readers, in the end cheats himself. He has cheated us, of course, in withholding from us the information that Boffin is only playing a part; he robs himself of a desired effect because, knowing that he still has to reinstate Boffin, he does not want to risk a total loss of sympathy on our part and so holds back. The result is that, in a scene in which everyone except Bella is playing a part, she is the only one who appears theatrical.

Dickens's handling of Boffin, indeed, is the major blemish of *Our Mutual Friend*. It is not merely that it leads to the kind of unsatisfactoriness just referred to; the revelation of the deception diminishes the importance of what he is saying and blunts the sharpness of his attack on the passion for money. What Dickens is concerned with, as the dust-mounds vividly suggest, is the corrupting influence of wealth; and it is perhaps a measure of Boffin's thematic centrality that the only time this theme is allowed an explicit formulation is in relation to him: 'As though he began each new day in his healthy natural character, and some waking hours were necessary to his relapse into the corrupting influences of his wealth, the face and the demeanour of the Golden Dustman were generally unclouded at [breakfast]' (p. 588). If we are meant to see that wealth corrupts, then we are surely also meant to see that it is no respecter of persons, that—like 'Tom's corrupted blood' in *Bleak House*—it strikes down good and bad alike. The corruption of a good, simple man like Boffin, in other words, is necessary to the design of the novel. From a structural point of view, the corruption of Boffin is as necessary a counterpart to the redemption of Bella (and of Harmon, which remains to be discussed) as the degeneration of Bradley is to the regeneration of Eugene. When it emerges that Boffin has not been corrupted after all, it is as if a hole has been blown through one part of the design.

Arnold Kettle attempts to justify his claim that Boffin's 'apparent corruption' is 'one of Dickens's happiest inspirations' by saying: 'Bella is tested and changed by her experiences . . . and at the same time the possibilities of corruption inherent in the Boffin-situation are triumphantly revealed. Dickens gets it both ways: the alternative possibilities before Boffin are both dramatized and the degrading horror of the one throws into relief the humane excellence of the other.'[1] It seems to me, however, that neither the 'possibilities of corruption' nor the 'degrading horror' can be said to be revealed when we are told, in the end, that they are not there after all. Dickens does not have it both ways—one never can—for, having taken seriously what we are afterwards asked to dismiss, we not only feel let down but react, I think, in one of two ways: either we consider that what we have taken seriously does not have the consequence we have attributed to it; or we remain convinced that it does and that the novelist is falsifying. It is a doubtful tribute to the happy inspiration that we can only continue to respect the novelist's seriousness at the cost of impugning his integrity as an artist; and yet this is the position, I feel, that we must take. It is as if Dickens suffered a failure of nerve in his treatment of Boffin, as if all that was pious and sentimental in him forced him to discount what his imagination had seized on as truth. The proof of the imaginative truth, like that of the pudding in the eating, lies in our reaction to the writing: is there a reader of the novel who is *not* taken in by Boffin? It is, on the contrary, the assumption that Boffin has had the subtlety to play the part so successfully that is hard to swallow; just as it is difficult to accept that Mrs. Boffin's evident dismay at the change in her husband, which is convincingly registered, is due (as he later says) to her thinking 'so high' of him that she cannot 'abear to see and hear' him 'coming out as a regular brown one' (p. 776). A final, telling indication of the imaginative truth of Boffin's corruption is that it fits naturally not only into the structural pattern of the novel but also into its pattern of imagery. In the chapter, entitled 'A Dismal Swamp', which details the various 'crawling, creeping, fluttering, and buzzing creatures' that are attracted by 'the gold dust of the Golden Dustman', the jobbers 'who job in all the jobberies jobbed' are referred

---

[1] '*Our Mutual Friend*', loc. cit., p. 215.

to as 'the Alligators of the Dismal Swamp . . . always lying by to drag the Golden Dustman under' (p. 213). Later in the novel, Venus instructs Boffin to hide from Wegg in the following terms:

> 'Hush! here's Wegg!' said Venus. 'Get behind the young alligator in the corner, Mr. Boffin, and judge him for yourself. I won't light a candle till he's gone: there'll only be the glow of the fire: Wegg's well acquainted with the alligator, and he won't take particular notice of him. Draw your legs in, Mr. Boffin; at present I see a pair of shoes at the end of his tail. Get your head well behind his smile, Mr. Boffin, and you'll lie comfortable there; you'll find plenty of room behind his smile. He's a little dusty, but he's very like you in tone. Are you right, sir?' (p. 580)

The symbolism is clear: among the birds and beasts of prey, Boffin seems destined, as he disappears behind the alligator (which is not only 'very like' him 'in tone' but a little 'dusty' and well known to Wegg) to become the biggest man-eater of them all.

Boffin's transformation is also a necessary counterpart, as I have suggested, to that of Harmon. Harmon is presented, at the beginning of his story, as a divided man, the split in him being occasioned by his inheriting his father's wealth, by his coming into his dust-mounds, that is. On the one hand, he is 'attracted' by the accounts he hears of his 'fine inheritance', and comes back to England (with which he has 'none but most miserable associations') in order to claim it; on the other hand, he 'shrinks' both from his 'father's money' and from his 'father's memory', and is 'mistrustful' of 'being forced on a mercenary wife'. He thus comes back to England 'divided in [his] mind' (p. 366). On a rainy night, in the company of Radfoot, he changes his wet clothes for those of his companion; and is given some coffee, which is drugged. His impressions, thereafter, are 'sick and deranged', but he becomes aware of 'a violent wrestling of men' in the room in which he has previously been attacked; then he is 'trodden upon and fallen over':

> 'I heard a noise of blows, and thought it was a wood-cutter cutting down a tree. I could not have said that my name was John Harmon—I could not have thought it—I didn't know it— but when I heard the blows, I thought of the wood-cutter and his axe, and had some dead idea that I was lying in a forest.

'This is still correct? Still correct, with the exception that I cannot possibly express it to myself without using the word I. But it was not I. There was no such thing as I, within my knowledge.

'It was only after a downward slide through something like a tube, and then a great noise and a sparkling and a crackling as of fires, that the consciousness came upon me, "This is John Harmon drowning! John Harmon, struggle for your life. John Harmon, call on Heaven and save yourself!" I think I cried it out aloud in a great agony, and then a heavy horrid unintelligible something vanished, and it was I who was struggling there alone in the water.

'I was very weak and faint, frightfully oppressed with drowsiness, and driving fast with the tide. . . . When . . . I at last caught at a boat moored, one of a tier of boats at a causeway, I was sucked under her, and came up, only just alive, on the other side. . . .' (pp. 369–70)

Before Harmon is thrown into the river, we see, he imaginatively experiences his own death. His impressions are no doubt 'sick and deranged', but he takes the noise of blows to be that of 'a wood-cutter cutting down a tree', and associates it with the 'dead idea' that he is 'lying in a forest', presumably like a felled tree. At the same time, this experience is associated with an overwhelming sense of a loss of identity: he 'could not have said' that his name is John Harmon, and he does not 'know it'; there is 'no such thing as I' within his knowledge. His sense of a loss of identity can be accounted for, of course, in terms of his drugged befuddlement, but it also must be taken to express a more fundamental bewilderment, a bewilderment that is the result of his own inner self-division. Torn between adopting his father's values (and lending himself to a mercenary marriage) and following his own shrinkings, Harmon is no longer himself—as his wearing of another man's clothes at the time symbolizes. It is in this condition, then, that Harmon is thrown into the river, but after 'a downward slide through something like a tube', the consciousness that 'this is John Harmon drowning' comes upon him. In trying to save himself, he registers that it is he, the 'I' he thought he had lost, that is struggling in the water. Again, we can account quite simply for what happens by saying that it is the plunge into the cold water that brings him back to himself, but this formulation is itself suggestive. Harmon is brought back to himself in the sense that he discovers his lost identity, in the sense that, drowning, he discovers a self that clings wholeheartedly to life; and he lets go, as it were, of a divided self whose will to live has been sapped, of a self ready to acquiesce in the wood-cutter's axe.

That Harmon's imaginative apprehension of death and his actual near-drowning are the means by which he undergoes a profound spiritual experience is confirmed by his changed attitude to Bella. Before the attack on him, he has had the desire 'to see and form some judgment' of his 'allotted wife' before she can know him for himself; and to that end he has planned to dress in 'common sailor's, garb and to see what comes of throwing himself in her way: 'If nothing came of it, I should be no worse off, and there would merely be a short delay in my presenting myself to Lightwood' (p. 367). It seems clear that, at this stage, Harmon is motivated merely by curiosity. His plan amounts to his having arranged for himself a private viewing of the goods which are for sale, and it is evident that he has decided to buy, whatever he finds. To cling wholeheartedly to life, however, means to reject the dust-heap and all its ways; and it is while Harmon is assimilating his near-experience of death that he changes his attitude to Bella:

> 'I have checked the calculation often, and it must have been two nights that I lay recovering in that public-house. Let me see. Yes. I am sure it was while I lay in that bed there, that the thought entered my head of turning the danger I had passed through, to the account of being for some time supposed to have disappeared mysteriously, and of proving Bella. The dread of our being forced on one another, and perpetuating the fate that seemed to have fallen on my father's riches—the fate that they should lead to nothing but evil—was strong upon the moral timidity that dates from my childhood with my poor sister.' (p. 370)

Harmon 'turns the danger' he has passed through not only to the account of being supposed to have disappeared but also to that of refusing any longer blindly to risk his well-being for the sake of money; and he now decides not only to see Bella but to 'prove' her. Nor does this merely imply a testing of Bella; he decides at this point to forfeit the fortune not only if she should prove to be unworthy but if she should prove to be 'unhappy in the prospect of [the] marriage (through her heart inclining to another man or for any other cause)' (p. 379).

Harmon's disappearance into Rokesmith (when the dead Radfoot is taken for him) not only makes Bella a kind of widow but complicates his position by establishing the Boffins in the Harmon fortune:

> When he saw [the Boffins] and knew them, and even from his vantage-ground of inspection could find no flaw in them, he asked himself, 'And shall I come to life to dispossess such people as these?' There was no good to set against the putting of them to that hard proof. He had heard from Bella's own lips when he stood tapping at the door on that night of his taking the lodgings, that the marriage would have been on her part thoroughly mercenary. He had since tried her, in his unknown person and supposed station, and she not only rejected his advances but resented them. Was it for him to have the shame of buying her, or the meanness of punishing her? Yet, by coming to life and accepting the condition of the inheritance, he must do the former; and by coming to life and rejecting it, he must do the latter. . . .
>
> Thus John Rokesmith in the morning, and it buried John Harmon still many fathoms deeper than he had been buried in the night. (pp. 379–80)

The decision that Harmon now takes to renounce the money is indicative of the consolidation of his newly accepted values. What concerns him now is not money but people, and what he sets against the claiming of the inheritance is the 'good' of renouncing it, the continued well-being of both the Boffins and Bella. Nor is Harmon actuated merely by a considerate selflessness; in his true concern and love for Bella he rises above himself, rises, that is, not only above 'the shame of buying her' but above the temptation of pandering to his pride, above 'the meanness of punishing her' by 'coming to life' and rejecting her and the inheritance. In his readiness to be 'dead', indeed, he is—like Jenny Wren—most truly alive, just as his 'burying' of 'John Harmon' signifies that he has died to his old self, that the prior condition of spiritual rebirth has been fulfilled.

Harmon's regeneration is fully evident in his renunciation of the fortune; it is symbolized by his apparent return from the grave, by his reappearance as 'John Harmon':

'Harkee to me, deary,' pursued Mrs. Boffin, taking Bella's

hands between her own . . . 'It was after a night when John had made an offer to a certain young lady, and the certain young lady had refused it. It was after a particular night, when he felt himself cast-away-like, and had made up his mind to go seek his fortune. It was the very next night. . . . I tapped at his door, and he didn't hear me. I looked in, and saw him a-sitting lonely by the fire, brooding over it. He chanced to look up with a pleased kind of smile in my company when he saw me, and then in a single moment every grain of the gunpowder, that had been lying sprinkled thick about him ever since I first set eyes upon him as a man at the Bower, took fire! Too many a time had I seen him sitting lonely, when he was a poor child, to be pitied, heart and hand! Too many a time had I seen him in need of being brightened up with a comforting word! Too many and too many a time to be mistaken, when that glimps of him come at last! No! no! I just makes out to cry, "I know you now! You're John!" And he catches me as I drops. . . .' (p. 770)

Despite his having come up on shore alive, and despite his having firmly taken up his life again, Harmon, we see, is (like Eugene) 'cast-away-like' because he is denied love, because 'the certain young lady' has refused his 'offer'. What stops him from drifting off to 'seek his fortune', what, indeed, brings 'John Harmon' back to life, is love, though of a non-sexual kind; for it is the love and compassion that Mrs. Boffin has felt in times past for the 'poor child' whom she was accustomed to see 'sitting lonely', as Harmon is 'a-sitting lonely' at that moment, that revives in her and that, focussing on the adult, leads to his identification. It is Boffin, moreover, who gives his return from the dead an official stamp, as it were, by getting him to take possession of his father's fortune, even though Old Harmon, in his last will, has in fact left the fortune to Boffin. Boffin agrees to part with 'the secret of the Dutch bottle' (which contains the last will) only on condition that Harmon 'take the fortune' and he 'his Mound and no more'. Harmon tells Wegg that, though there are 'no words' that can satisfactorily express his sense of the quality of the Boffins, he owes everything he possesses 'solely to [their] disinterestedness, uprightness, tenderness, goodness' (p. 788)—in a word, to their love.

Similarly, Harmon is brought back to life for Bella by her love. Though he constantly delays revealing his true identity to her, protesting to the Boffins (in what must be the most delightful stroke of irony in the novel) that he so relishes her as she is that he 'can't afford to be rich yet'; he allows Mrs. Boffin to tell her after Bella has proved her love for him beyond all question, after she has proved completely 'trusting' and 'true' even when he is under suspicion of murder (p. 774).

It remains for the Harmons to take possession of their new house, and they do so on an auspicious occasion:

> Mr. and Mrs. John Harmon had so timed their taking possession of their rightful name and their London house, that the event befell on the very day when the last waggonload of the last Mound was driven out at the gates of Boffin's Bower. (p. 779)

Having learnt that money is dust, having disposed, as it were, of the dust-mounds in their own lives as well as of those at the Bower, the Harmons are ready for their wealth. The change in them is projected in a change in the atmosphere of the house itself. As it first presents itself to Wegg, the house is like a great extinguisher of life:

> It was a great dingy house with a quantity of dim side window and blank back premises, and it cost his mind a world of trouble so to lay it out as to account for everything in its external appearance. But, this once done, was quite satisfactory, and he rested persuaded that he knew his way about the house blindfold: from the barred garrets in the high roof, to the two iron extinguishers before the main door—which seemed to request all lively visitors to have the kindness to put themselves out, before entering. (p. 45)

When the Harmons take possession of the house it is said to be 'a dainty house' and 'a tastefully beautiful'. Its nursery is 'garnished as with rainbows', and when the Harmon child is 'heard screaming among the rainbows' and Bella quietens her, 'smiling Peace [associates] herself with that young olive branch'. The house, in other words, now seems to promote the life it formerly appeared to extinguish, just as to Mrs. Boffin, watching Bella and her child, it now 'looks' as if Old Harmon's money has 'turned bright again, after a long, long rust in the dark, and [is] at last beginning to sparkle in the sunlight' (p. 778).

Our Mutual Friend, as a whole, may be regarded as a sustained plea for life, for the kind of life that Bella and Harmon and Eugene and Lizzie win through to, for the kind of life that is earned by a dying. It is the kind of life, of course, that is smothered by the 'deadweight of Podsnappery', and it is to Podsnap that Dickens very nearly gives the last word in the novel. The fact that Podsnappery bulks so large in the final pages places the stories of individual regeneration in perspective. It suggests, too, that what is required is nothing less than the death and rebirth of a whole society. *Our Mutual Friend* is not only one of the greatest English novels of the nineteenth century; it is also one of the most subversive.

INDEX

Characters are indexed under the names by which they are commonly referred to.

Ada (Clare) (in *Bleak House*), 172, 179, 180, 187

Affery (Mrs. Flintwinch) (in *Little Dorrit*), 230, 231

Alice (Brown, Marwood) (in *Dombey and Son*), 118, 120, 130–1, 136

American Notes, 111, 113

analogy, 13–14
  in *Pickwick Papers*, 43–8
  in *Oliver Twist*, 50, 54, 55, 67, 75–6
  in *Martin Chuzzlewit*, 86–91, 99–102, 107
  in *Dombey and Son*, 118, 121, 129–33
  in *Bleak House*, 158–9, 160, 163, 167, 178–80, 181, 183, 184–5
  in *Little Dorrit*, 200–1, 203, 206, 207, 209, 210, 216, 218, 220, 221, 222, 223, 224, 225, 227, 230, 232
  in *Great Expectations*, 238–40, 243–4, 246–7, 250, 260, 261
  in *Our Mutual Friend*, 274, 278–80, 280–1, 283, 286–7, 288–94, 295, 299, 306, 315, 317, 321, 326, 332, 333

Anglo-Bengalee, The (Disinterested Loan and Life Assurance Company) (in *Martin Chuzzlewit*) 83, 87, 96, 97–9, 113

Anthony Chuzzlewit and Son (in *Martin Chuzzlewit*), 92–5, 97, 99, 123

Aquinas, Thomas, 247

Arabella (Allen) (in *Pickwick Papers*), 37, 43

Auerbach, Erich, 40 n

Austen, Jane, 33, 42
  Mansfield Park, 37

Badger, Bayham (in *Bleak House*), 178

Bagstock, Major (in *Dombey and Son*), 129–30

Bailey Junior (in *Martin Chuzzlewit*), 96, 98

Bar (in *Little Dorrit*), 215

Barbary, Miss (in *Bleak House*), 159 n, 184, 189

Bardell, Mrs. (in *Pickwick Papers*), 20, 27, 28, 29, 36, 37, 43, 44, 47

Barnaby Rudge, 175

Barnacle, Ferdinand (in *Little Dorrit*), 218

Barnacle Junior (in *Little Dorrit*), 199

Barnacle, Lord Decimus Tite (in *Little Dorrit*), 200, 216, 218, 224

Barnacle, Mr. Tite (in *Little Dorrit*), 198, 203

Bates, Charley (in *Oliver Twist*), 70, 77

Bayley, John, 74–5

Beardsley, Monroe C., 79 n

Beaumont and Fletcher, *The Maid's Tragedy*, 144–5, 147

Bella (Wilfer) (in *Our Mutual Friend*), 39, 142, 143, 271, 289, 300, *319–26*, 327, 328, 329, 332, 333, 334, 335, 336

Benjamin, Edwin B., 80 n, 91

Bergler, Edmund, 220 n

Betty (Higden) (in *Our Mutual Friend*), 292–4, 306, 322

Bevan, Mr. (in *Martin Chuzzlewit*), 113

Biddy (in *Great Expectations*), 244, 251, 253

Bishop (in *Little Dorrit*), 215–16

Blake, 194

BLEAK HOUSE, 13, 38, 39, 42, 47, 48, 60, 64, 65, 103, 118, 123, 134, *156–90*, 193, 194, 198, 199, 200, 201, 217, 218, 228, 231, 232, 235, 238, 240, 251, 272, 277, 281, 282, 284, 285, 294, 301, 314, 328

Bleak House, 157, 158, 184, 188, 189

Bleeding Heart Yard (in *Little Dorrit*), 217, 218

Blimber, Doctor (in *Dombey and Son*), 131–2, 133

Blotton, Mr. (in *Pickwick Papers*), 30

Boffin, Mr. (in *Our Mutual Friend*), 108, 275, 281, 283, 285, 286, 289, 293, 294, 301, 320, 321, 322, 323, 324, 325, 326, *328–30*, 333, 334

Boffin, Mrs. (in *Our Mutual Friend*), 285, 289, 293, 294, 320, 321, 324, 329, 333, 334, 335

Boldwig, Captain (in *Pickwick Papers*), 45, 46

Bradley (Headstone) (in *Our Mutual Friend*), 244, 270, 275, *290–2*, 302, 303, 306, 310, 314, *315–19*, 321, 329

Brick, Jefferson (in *Martin Chuzzlewit*), 114

Brontë, Charlotte, 42

Brontë, Emily, 42
  Wuthering Heights, 271; Cathy and Heathcliff, 52

Brown, Mrs. (in *Dombey and Son*), 118, 130, 134

Brownlow, Mr. (in *Oliver Twist*), 49, 53, 54, 66, 69, 70, 74, 77, 78

Bucket, Mr. (in *Bleak House*), 156, 161, 162, 166, 179

Bulder, Colonel (in *Pickwick Papers*), 45

Butt, John, 17 n, 166 n, 191 n, 193 n

Buzfuz, Serjeant (in *Pickwick Papers*), 28

Byron, 136

Carker, Harriet (in *Dombey and Son*), 141

Carker, James (in *Dombey and Son*), 117, 121, 126, 129, *139–41*, 142, 143, 144, 145, 146, 147

Casby, Christopher (in *Little Dorrit*), 218

Cavaletto, John Baptist (in *Little Dorrit*), 216–17, 218

Index

Cervantes, 21, 22, 25
 Don Quixote, Don Quixote, 19, 21, 23, 26, 34; Sancho Panza, 26
Chancery, Court of, 47, 60, 157, 159, 161, 165, 166, 167, 169, 170, 172, 175, 177, 178, 179, 180, 181, 184, 189, 198, 277
Chancery Prisoner (in *Pickwick Papers*), 35, 38
characterization,
 in *Pickwick Papers*, 33
 in *Oliver Twist*, 72
 in *Dombey and Son*, 124–5
 in *Little Dorrit*, 210–14
 in *Our Mutual Friend*, 301–4
Charley (Hexam) (in *Our Mutual Friend*), 280, 292, 302, 303, 306, 308, 317
Charley (Neckett) (in *Bleak House*), 159 n, 175, 187
Cherry (Charity Pecksniff) (in *Martin Chuzzlewit*), 87–8, 89, 92, 101
Chesterton, G. K., 38
Chick, Mrs. (in *Dombey and Son*), 125, 135, 148
Chicken, the (in *Dombey and Son*), 125
Chicksey, Veneering, and Stobbles (in *Our Mutual Friend*), 279
Chivery, John (in *Little Dorrit*), 212
Chivery, Mrs. (in *Little Dorrit*), 209
Choke, General (in *Martin Chuzzlewit*), 113
Chollop, Mr. (in *Martin Chuzzlewit*), 114
Chuffey, Mr. (in *Martin Chuzzlewit*), 88, 97
Churchill, R. C., 80 n
Chuzzlewit, Anthony (in *Martin Chuzzlewit*), 88, 94, 95, 97
Chuzzlewit, George (in *Martin Chuzzlewit*), 100

Circumlocution Office, 60, 197–9, 200, 218, 233, 277
Clara (Barley) (in *Great Expectations*), 239
Clark, G. Kitson, 198 n
Claypole, Noah (Mr. Bolter) (in *Oliver Twist*), 67, 77
Clennam, Arthur (in *Little Dorrit*), 194, 197, 198, 201, 214 n, 217, 218, 219, 220, 222, 223, 224, 225, 228, *229–36*, 241, 302, 309
Clennam, Mrs. (in *Little Dorrit*), 201, *218–22*, 227, 228, 230, 231, 232, 235, 260
'Coavinses' (in *Bleak House*), 159 n, 187
Cockshut, A. O. J., 237 n, 249, 297, 305
Collins, Philip, 72 n, 275 n
Compeyson (in *Great Expectations*), 238, 239, 250, 260
Connolly, Thomas E., 237 n
Conrad, 191
 Nostromo, Nostromo, 288
Crackit, Toby (in *Oliver Twist*), 71, 77
Crippin, Charlotte, 294 n
Crompton, Louis, 165
Cuttle, Captain (in *Dombey and Son*), 146, *149–50*, 152, 154

Dabney, Ross H., 14 n, 84 n, 96, 108, 254
David (Copperfield) (in *David Copperfield*), 22 n
David Copperfield, 22 n, 145, 241, 278
Dedlock, Lady (in *Bleak House*), 39, 156, 157, 158, 159, 164, 181, *182–6*
Diver, Colonel (in *Martin Chuzzlewit*), 114

Dodger, the Artful (in *Oliver Twist*), 52, 57, 67–8, 70, 77

Dodson and Fogg (in *Pickwick Papers*), 28–9, 32, 35, 36, 37, 38, 47, 98

'Dolls, Mr.' (in *Our Mutual Friend*), 303, 304

DOMBEY AND SON, 13, 94, 104, *116–55*, 158, 175, 192 n, 217, 235, 245 n, 291, 314

Dombey and Son, 95, 118, 121, 123, 132, 139, 140, 141, 155

Dombey, Mr. (in *Dombey and Son*), 116, 117, 118, 119, 120, 121, *122–9*, 131, 132, 133, 135, 136, 138, 139, 140, 141, 142, 143, 144, 145, 146, 147, 148, 150, 151, 152, 153, 154, 155, 219

Dorrit, Frederick (in *Little Dorrit*), 209

Dorrit, Mr. William (in *Little Dorrit*), 197, 207, *208–14*, 215, 216, 218, 221, 224, 229

Dostoevski,
  Crime and Punishment, Raskolnikov, 81
  The Idiot, Prince Myshkin, 26, 309

Dotheboys Hall (in *Nicholas Nickleby*), 60, 167

Dowler, Mr. and Mrs. (in *Pickwick Papers*), 45

Doyce, Daniel (in *Little Dorrit*), 198, 217, 218, 232–3

Drew, Arnold P., 238 n

Edith (Dombey) (in *Dombey and Son*), 39, 117, 118, 126, 129, 130, 131, 136, *141–7*, 148, 152, 153, 183

Eliot, George, 42
  Middlemarch, Dorothea Brook and Lydgate, 157

Eliot, T. S., 274
  The Waste Land, 278

Elliotson, Dr. John, 177 n

Engel, Monroe, 186, 297 n

Estella (in *Great Expectations*), 238, 239, 240, 241, 242, 251, 252, 253, 254, 255, 260, 261, 262, 264, 265, 269

Esther (Summerson) (in *Bleak House*), 156, 157, 158, 159, 160, 161, 162, 163, 169, 173, 175, 179, 180, 184, 185, 186, 187, 188–9, 241

Eugene (Wrayburn) (in *Our Mutual Friend*), 244, 270, 271, 275, 280, 287, 290, 298, *300–6*, 308, 309, 310, 311, 312, 313, 314, 315, 316, 317, 318, 319, 321, 324, 325, 326, 327, 328, 329, 334, 336

Fagin (in *Oliver Twist*), 49, 51, 52, 56, 68, 69, 70, 71, 72, 74, 76, 77, 78, 99, 141

Fairclough, Peter, 72 n

Fang, Mr. (in *Oliver Twist*), 62

Fanny (Dorrit) (in *Little Dorrit*), 203, 204, 235

Feenix, Cousin (in *Dombey and Son*), 118

Fielding, Henry, 22–3, 25, 26, 27, 29, 43
  Joseph Andrews, Parson Adams, 22–7; Fanny, 22, 24, 26, 27; Lady Booby, 23–4; Beau Didapper, 22–3; Mrs. Slipslop, 22–3; Joseph, 24
  Tom Jones, 22 n

Fladdock, General (in *Martin Chuzzlewit*), 114

Fledgeby, Mr. (in *Our Mutual Friend*), 163, 273, 275, 283,

Index

Fledgeby—cont.
285, 289, 294, 298, 299, 300, 304, 317

Fleet, the (in *Pickwick Papers*), 31–6

Flite, Miss (in *Bleak House*), 158, 176

Florence (Dombey) (in *Dombey and Son*), 117, 122, 125, 127, 128, 129, 136, 139, 141, 142, 146, 148, 149, 150, 151, 152, 153, 154, 235

Ford, George H., 38 n, 40, 56 n, 85 n, 166 n, 187, 226 n, 237 n

Forster, E. M., *Howards End*, 85

Forster, John, 21, 41, 65, 66, 79, 87, 102, 111, 116 n, 136, 137 n, 144 n, 145, 170, 191 n, 192 n, 241 n, 253 n

Freud, 277

Gaffer (Hexam) (in *Our Mutual Friend*), 270, 275, 282–3, 284, 286, 287, 288, 289, 295, 296, 297, 304, 307, 308, 323

Gamfield, Mr. (in *Oliver Twist*), 60

Gamp, Mrs. (in *Martin Chuzzlewit*), 81–2, 90, 98

Gargery, Mrs. Joe (in *Great Expectations*), 239, 244, 248, 250, 251, 252

Garis, Robert, 184 n

General, Mrs. (in *Little Dorrit*), 202, 206–7, 214

George (Rouncewell) (in *Bleak House*), 163, 164, 166, 173

Georgiana (Podsnap) (in *Our Mutual Friend*), 285, 289, 290

Giles (in *Oliver Twist*), 72, 77

Gills, Solomon (in *Dombey and Son*), 117, 119, 146, 149

Gladstone, William Ewart, 199 n

Gowan, Henry (in *Little Dorrit*), 39, 192, 197, 210, *222–5*, 235, 304

Gowan, Mrs. (in *Little Dorrit*), 202, *204–6*, 207, 209, 210, 212

Gordon Riots, 175–6

Gradgrind, Mr. (in *Hard Times*), 131

GREAT EXPECTATIONS, 13, 14, 160, *237–69*

Great White Horse Inn (in *Pickwick Papers*), 17–20, 22

Gridley, Mr. (in *Bleak House*), 159 n, 166

Gross, John, 75 n, 82 n, 147 n, 157 n, 196 n, 264 n, 284 n

Grummer, Mr. (in *Pickwick Papers*), 29

Guppy, Mr. (in *Bleak House*), 158, 180

Gusher, Mr. (in *Bleak House*), 164

Hagan, John H., 237

Haight, Gordon S., 177 n

Haines, Thomas, 62

Hard Times, 131–2, 281

Hardy, Barbara, 82, 113, 114 n, 237 n

Hardy, Thomas, 42

Harmon, John (Rokesmith) (in *Our Mutual Friend*), 271, 274, 275, 276, 289, 298, 300, 320, 324, 325, 326, 329, *330–5*, 336

Harris, Mrs. (in *Martin Chuzzlewit*), 98

Harvey, W. J., 157 n, 160

Havisham, Miss (in *Great Expectations*), 238, 239, 240, 242, 246, 250, 251, 253, 254, 255, *259–62*, *262–5*, 266, 268

Hawdon, Captain (in *Bleak House*), 159 n, 164, 171, 172 n, 183, 185, 186

Herbert (Pocket) (in *Great Expectations*), 239, 251, 258, 260, 265, 267, 269

Index

Hogarth, Mary, 138
Holloway, John, 192 n
Hortense, Mademoiselle (in *Bleak House*), 159, 218
House, Humphry, 54 n, 133, 134 n, 198, 199 n, 237 n, 277, 294 n
Household Words, 58 n, 59 n, 196 n, 308 n
Hunt, Leigh, 160
Hunter, Mrs. Leo (in *Pickwick Papers*), 31, 32, 44, 45, 46

Inspector, Mr. (in *Our Mutual Friend*), 288, 304
institutions,
  in *Oliver Twist*, 59–60
  in *Bleak House*, 165–7
  in *Little Dorrit*, 197–200

Jackson, T. A., 237 n
Jacob's Island (in *Oliver Twist*), 63–5, 67
Jaggers, Mr. (in *Great Expectations*), 239, 242, 246, 251, 253
James, Henry, 42, 118, 156
Jarndyce and Jarndyce (in *Bleak House*), 157, 158, 159, 161, 165, 166, 169, 170, 172, 178, 179, 180, 181, 184
Jarndyce, Mr. (in *Bleak House*), 164, 169, 170, 171, 178, 179, 180, *187–9*, 190, 232
Jarndyce, Tom (in *Bleak House*), 159 n
Jeffrey, Francis, Lord Jeffrey, 116, 136, 145
Jellyby, Mrs. (in *Bleak House*), 39, 158, 187
Jenny (in *Bleak House*), 186, 188
'Jenny Wren' (in *Our Mutual Friend*), 294, 298, 299, 300, 326, 333

Jingle (in *Pickwick Papers*), 20, 31, 32, 33, 37, 39, 42, 43, 44, 45, 46
Jo (in *Bleak House*), 159 n, 161, 162, 166, 167, *170–4*, 175, 176, 178, 184, 185, 187, 189, 272
Job (Trotter) (in *Pickwick Papers*), 37
Joe (Gargery) (in *Great Expectations*), 239, 249, 251, 253, 265, 269
Johnny (in *Our Mutual Friend*), 293, 321
Johnson, Edgar, 14, 22 n, 79 n, 114 n, 121, 123, 136 n, 138, 157 n, 166, 166 n, 186, 225 n, 237 n, 255, 277, 278, 281
Jonas (Chuzzlewit) (in *Martin Chuzzlewit*), 81, 82, 83, 85, 87, 88–9, 90, 91, 92, 93, 95, 96, 97, 98, 99, 100, 103, 104, 105, 106, 112
Jonson, Ben, 284
Joyce, James, 247–8
  A Portrait of the Artist as a Young Man, Stephen Dedalus, 247

Kafka, 42
Kenge and Carboy (in *Bleak House*), 178
Kenge, Mr. (in *Bleak House*), 167, 188, 189
Kettle, Arnold, 55–7, 67, 284 n, 291, 297, 329
Kitton, Frederic G., 59 n, 196 n, 308 n
Krook, Mr. (in *Bleak House*), 158, 159 n, 163, 176–7, 180, 185, 186, 231

Laing (Hatton Garden magistrate), 61–2

Lammle, Mr. (*in Our Mutual Friend*), 285, 287, 289, 302
Lammle, Mrs. (in *Our Mutual Friend*), 285, 287, 302
Lane, Lauriat, 38 n, 56 n, 76, 85 n, 226 n, 237 n
Lawrence, D. H., 128, 291
Lady Chatterley's Lover, Clifford Chatterley, 125, 127; Mellors, 125
The Rainbow, Mr. Brunt, 291
Layard, Austen Henry, 196 n, 231 n
Leavis, F. R., 126, 145
Leicester, Sir (Dedlock) (in *Bleak House*), 164, 166, 167, 183, 185
Lemon, Mark, 136
Letters (ed. Walter Dexter), 177 n, 191 n, 192 n, 196 n, 231 n, 236 n, 253 n, 278 n, 281 n
Letters (ed. Madeline House and Graham Storey), 62 n
Letters to Angela Burdett-Coutts (ed. Edgar Johnson), 133 n, 231 n
Lewes, George Henry, 177
Lindsay, Jack, 237 n, 271
LITTLE DORRIT, 13, 38, 46, 48, 60, 99, 103, 118, 164, 166 n, *191–230*, 240, 260, 272, 274, 277, 281, 284, 285, 294, 302, 314
Little Dorrit (Amy) (in *Little Dorrit*), 196, 204, 209, 214, 222, 231, *233–6*, 241, 309
Lizzie (Hexam) (in *Our Mutual Friend*), 270, 271, 295, 296, 297 n, 298, 300, 302, 304, 305, *306–9*, 310, 311, 312, 313, 314, 315, 316, 317, 318, 319, 322, 323, 324, 325, 328, 336
London, 65, 93, 101, 167, 193–4, 196, 197, 216, 220, 234, 239, 246, 251, 271, 272–3, 274, 275, 276, 278, 282

love, 14
    in *Martin Chuzzlewit*, 103–4
    in *Dombey and Son*, 120–1, 135, 148, 153–5
    in *Bleak House*, 190
    in *Little Dorrit*, 234–6
    in *Great Expectations*, 240–1, 242, 244, 247, 249, 250, 252, 253, 254–5, 256, 258, 261–2, 264–5, 268–9
    in *Our Mutual Friend*, 293, 305–6, 309, 312–15, 317, 320, 321–2, 323, 325, 326, 333, 334–5
Lupin, Mrs. (in *Martin Chuzzlewit*), 86, 89, 101
Lytton, Edward Bulwer-, 50, 253 n
    Paul Clifford, 50

Mack, Maynard, 27, 33
Macready, W. C., 236 n
Magnus, Peter (in *Pickwick Papers*), 19–20, 44
Magwitch, Abel (in *Great Expectations*), 238, 239, 240, 242, 246, 250, 251, 253, *255–9*, 260, 261, 262, 264 n, 266–7, 268, 269
Man from Shropshire (in *Bleak House*), 47
Marbé, Alan, 112 n
Marcus, Steven, 13, 40, 43–4, 48, 67, 81–2, 114 n, 126, 144
Marshalsea Prison (in *Little Dorrit*), 196, 197, 207–14, 230, 231, 233, 234, 235
MARTIN CHUZZLEWIT, 13, 14, 78, *79–115*, 116, 117, 119, 121, 141, 153, 158, 235, 259, 314
Mary (in *Pickwick Papers*), 37
Mary (Graham) (in *Martin Chuzzlewit*), 83, 87, 88, 97, 106, 108

Mayhew, Henry, 283
Maylie, Harry (in *Oliver Twist*), 53, 54
Maylie, Mrs. (in *Oliver Twist*), 53, 55, 75, 78
Meagles, Mr. (in *Little Dorrit*), 196, 198, 206, 225, 227, 228, 232
Meagles, Pet (in *Little Dorrit*), 235
melodrama, 82
  in *Oliver Twist*, 66–7
  in *Dombey and Son*, 145, 154
  in *Bleak House*, 159
  in *Little Dorrit*, 202, 218
  in *Great Expectations*, 261
Mendilow, A. A., 22 n
Merdle, Mr. (in *Little Dorrit*), 99, 200, 201, 203, 204, 205, 206, *214–18*, 220, 222, 223, 224, 230, 235
Merdle, Mrs. (in *Little Dorrit*), *202–4*, 205, 206, 207, 209, 212
Merry (Mercy Pecksniff) (in *Martin Chuzzlewit*), 83, 87–8, 89, 97, 101
Middleton, Thomas, *The Change-ling*, 145
Miller, J. Hillis, 30 n, 36, 43, 59, 69, 80, 84 n, 157 n, 185 n, 193 n, 194, 264 n, 300 n
Milton, 53, 246
Milvey, Mr. and Mrs. (in *Our Mutual Friend*), 289
Moddle, Augustus (in *Martin Chuzzlewit*), 92
Molly (in *Great Expectations*), 239
money, 14
  in *Pickwick Papers*, 37
  in *Martin Chuzzlewit*, 83–6, 91, 93–4, 112
  in *Dombey and Son*, 118–21, 140, 143
  in *Bleak House*, 158, 169, 183

  in *Little Dorrit*, 215–17, 219, 220, 223, 230, 233, 235
  in *Great Expectations*, 237–8, 239, 240, 249, 253, 266
  in *Our Mutual Friend*, 273–4, 275, 277–8, 279–80, 281–3, 284, 287–8, 289, 297, 301, 306, 314, 320, 328, 330, 332, 333, 335
Monks (in *Oliver Twist*), 52, 66, 69, 70
Morfin, Mr. (in *Dombey and Son*), 141
Morgan, Captain, 191 n
Morley, John, 199 n
Mortimer (Lightwood) (in *Our Mutual Friend*), 275, 277, 278, 280, 284, 290, 303, 304, 305, 306, 313, 314, 315
Mould, Mr. (in *Martin Chuzzlewit*), 80–1, 94, 119
Moynahan, Julian, 147, 148, 151, 154, 237 n, 242, 243, 244

Nancy (in *Oliver Twist*), 49, 52, *72–6*, 77
Ned, Mrs. (in *Martin Chuzzlewit*), 101
Nelson, Harland S., 283
Newgate Novel, 50
Nicholas Nickleby, 60, 167
Nisbet, Ada, 21 n
Nupkins, Mr. (in *Pickwick Papers*), 20, 27, 29, 46
Nupkins, Mrs. (in *Pickwick Papers*), 44

Old Curiosity Shop, The, 163
Old Martin (Chuzzlewit) (in *Martin Chuzzlewit*), 82, 83, 86, 87, 88, 89, 91, 95, 96, 97, 99, 100, 101, 103, 104, 105, 107, 108, 109

Old Nandy (in *Little Dorrit*), 209, 210, 221

OLIVER TWIST, 13, 38, 41, *49–78*, 88, 98, 104, 133, 167

Oliver (Twist) (in *Oliver Twist*), 52, 53, 54, 55, 56, 57, 59, 60, 61, 62, 63, 65, 66, 67, 68, 69, 70, 71, 72, 74, 75, 76, 77, 78, 110, 307

'On Duty with Inspector Field', 308 n

Orlick, Dolge (in *Great Expectations*), 239, *242–4*, 250, 256

Orwell, George, 29, 211

'Our Commission', 196 n

OUR MUTUAL FRIEND, 13, 14, 38, 48, 84, 95, 100, 103, 108, 118, 119, 142, 143, 163, 207, 240, 241, 244, 245 n, *270–336*

Pancks, Mr. (in *Little Dorrit*), 218

parasitism,
  in *Bleak House*, 162, 163, 164, 165, 167, 171, 172, 173, 178, 187
  in *Little Dorrit*, 217
  in *Great Expectations*, 240, 251

Pardiggle, Mrs. (in *Bleak House*), 164, 165, 187

patronage,
  in *Little Dorrit*, 199, 200, 204, 206, 207, 215, 218, 221–2, 224, 227, 228, 233
  in *Great Expectations*, 239, 240, 253, 266
  in *Our Mutual Friend*, 236

Paul (Dombey) (in *Dombey and Son*), 117, 118, 119, 120, 123, 126, 127, 128, 129, 131, 133, *135–9*, 143, 151, 153

Paulson, Ronald, 27 n

Pawkins, Major (in *Martin Chuzzlewit*), 112

Pearson, Gabriel, 75 n, 82 n, 147 n, 157 n, 196 n, 264 n, 284 n

Pecksniff, Mr. (in *Martin Chuzzlewit*), 78, 79, 81–2, 83, *84–7*, 89, 90, 91, 92, 93, 96, 97, 98, 99, *100–2*, 103, 104, 106, 107, 108, 109, 112

Peecher, Miss (in *Our Mutual Friend*), 292, 317

Perker, Mr. (in *Pickwick Papers*), 32, 36, 37, 45

Phil (Squod) (in *Bleak House*), 163, 164

Pickwick, Mr. (in *Pickwick Papers*), 17–21, 24–5, 26, 27–8, 29, 30–2, 33, 34, 35–6, 37, 38, 39, 41, 42, 43, 45, 46

Pickwick Club (in *Pickwick Papers*), 30, 31, 32, 42, 45

PICKWICK PAPERS, 13, *17–48*, 55, 99, 133

Pip (in *Great Expectations*), 237, 238, 239, 240, 241, 242, 243, 244, 245, 246, *247–55*, 256, 257, 258, 259, 260, 261, 262, 264, 265, 266, 268, 269, 309

Pipchin, Mrs. (in *Dombey and Son*), 131, 133

Pleasant (Riderhood) (in *Our Mutual Friend*), 290, 296

Plornish, Mr. (in *Little Dorrit*), 212

Plornish, Mrs. (in *Little Dorrit*), 209

plot,
  in *Pickwick Papers*, 43
  in *Oliver Twist*, 49, 66–7, 72, 75
  in *Martin Chuzzlewit*, 82–3, 107–9, 111
  in *Dombey and Son*, 117–18, 131
  in *Bleak House*, 159, 165
  in *Little Dorrit*, 201–2
  in *Great Expectations*, 238–40, 242, 250–1

plot—cont.

in *Our Mutual Friend*, 270–2, 274–6, 301

Podsnap, Mr. (in *Our Mutual Friend*), 207, 285, 287, 289, 291, 300, 302, 317, 336

Pogram, Mr. (in *Martin Chuzzlewit*), 114

point of view,

in *Pickwick Papers*, 42

in *Bleak House*, 156–9

in *Great Expectations*, 241, 249

Polly ('Toodle, Richards) (in *Dombey and Son*), 121, 123, 125, 126, 127, 128, 135, 136, 137, 138, 147, 148, 150

Poor Law (1834), 58, 280

Pott, Mr. (in *Pickwick Papers*), 45, 46

Pott, Mrs. (in *Pickwick Papers*), 44, 45

Prig, Betsey (in *Martin Chuzzlewit*), 90, 98

Pubsey and Co. (in *Our Mutual Friend*), 294, 298, 299, 315, 325, 326

Pumblechook, Mr. (in *Great Expectations*), 249, 250, 251, 252

Quale, Mr. (in *Bleak House*), 164

Quirk, Randolph, 307

Rachael (Miss Wardle) (in *Pickwick Papers*), 39, 46

Raddle, Mrs. (in *Pickwick Papers*), 44

Radfoot (in *Our Mutual Friend*), 276, 330, 333

Ramsey (in *Pickwick Papers*), 28–9, 47

Rathbun, Robert C., 187 n

Reichstein, Lillian, 159 n

Riah, Mr. (in *Our Mutual Friend*), 163, 275, 283, 298, 304

Richard (Carstone) (in *Bleak House*), 157 n, 159 n, 161, 162, 165, 172, 175, *178–80*, 181, 186, 187, 188

Richards, I. A., 138

Ricks, Christopher, 264 n

Riderhood, 'Rogue' (in *Our Mutual Friend*), 275, 284, 287, 288, *294–8*, 299, 304, 305, 306, 308, 318, 319

Rigaud (Blandois) (in *Little Dorrit*), 218, 222, 232

Roker (in *Pickwick Papers*), 35

Rose (Maylie) (in *Oliver Twist*), 49, 53, 54, 55, 72, 73, 74, 75, 78

Rouncewell, Mr. (in *Bleak House*), 187

Ruth (Pinch) (in *Martin Chuzzlewit*), 95, 103, 153, 235

Sam (Weller) (in *Pickwick Papers*), 25, 26, 27, 29, 33, 34, 35, 36, 37, 42, 44, 46

Satis House (in *Great Expectations*), 259–60

Sawyer, Bob (in *Pickwick Papers*), 44

Scadder, Mr. (in *Martin Chuzzlewit*), 113

sentimentality,

in *Oliver Twist*, 72

in *Dombey and Son*, 117, 137–9

in *Bleak House*, 174

in *Great Expectations*, 264

in *Our Mutual Friend*, 326–7, 329

Shakespeare, 271

Henry IV, Falstaff, 162

King Lear, 154; Gloucester, 311

The Winter's Tale, Hermione, 147

Shaw, Bernard, *Pygmalion*, Higgins, 308

Shelley, 105

Sikes, Bill (in *Oliver Twist*), 52, 56, 66, 71, 72, 74, 76, 77

Skettles, Sir Barnet and Lady (in *Dombey and Son*), 118

Skewton, Mrs. (in *Dombey and Son*), 118, 120, 129, 130, 152

Skiffins, Miss (in *Great Expectations*), 240

Skimpole, Harold (in *Bleak House*), 158, *160–3*, 164, 166, 179, 188, 189, 301, 304

Slammer, Dr. (in *Pickwick Papers*), 44

Sloppy (in *Our Mutual Friend*), 275, 293

Smallweed, Grandfather (in *Bleak House*), 158, 163–4, 166

Smiles, Samuel, 187

Smith, Grahame, 14 n

Snagsby, Mr. (in *Bleak House*), 158, 159 n, 166, 171, 173

social criticism,
    in *Pickwick Papers*, 26–7, 29, 33–6
    in *Oliver Twist*, 49, 57–9, 60–5, 77–8
    in *Martin Chuzzlewit*, 102–3
    in *Dombey and Son*, 132–5
    in *Bleak House*, 165–77, 186, 189–90
    in *Little Dorrit*, 197–202, 203–7, 209, 216–18, 232, 235
    in *Great Expectations*, 237–8, 239, 242, 251
    in *Our Mutual Friend*, 241, 272, 273–4, 280–1, 284–5, 291–4

Sparkler, Edmund (in *Little Dorrit*), 200, 206, 216, 235

Speeches, The (ed. K. J. Fielding), 278 n

Spilka, Mark, 178 n, 185 n

Stables, Honourable Bob (in *Bleak House*), 164

Stange, G. Robert, 237 n, 249 n, 269 n

Steinmann, Martin, 187 n

Stephen, Fitzjames, 166 n

Stephen, Leslie, 166 n

Stevenson, Lionel, 21 n

Stiggins (The Rev. Mr.) (in *Pickwick Papers*), 39, 46

Stumps, Bill (in *Pickwick Papers*), 19, 21, 34

Surtees, Robert Smith, 39–41
    Jorrocks's Jaunts and Jollities, Jorrocks, 39–40

Susan (Nipper) (in *Dombey and Son*), 121, 127, 136

Sweedlepipe, Poll (in *Martin Chuzzlewit*), 98

symbolism,
    in *Oliver Twist*, 60–1, 68–70
    in *Bleak House*, 158, 159, 165, 167, 175, 177, 187
    in *Little Dorrit*, 192–7, 201–2, 219, 220, 231
    in *Great Expectations*, 244–7
    in *Our Mutual Friend*, 277–8, 283, 294–300, 311–12, 330, 331

Tale of Two Cities, A, 279

Tapley, Mark (in *Martin Chuzzlewit*), 106, 113, 114

Tattycoram (in *Little Dorrit*), 227–8

Ternan, Ellen, 241

Thackeray, 42, 136, 225

'That Other Public', 196 n

Tigg, Montague (Montague, Tigg) (in *Martin Chuzzlewit*), 81, 82, 83, 87, 89, 90, 93, 95, 96, 97, 98, 99, 100, 101, 103, 104, 105, 106, 112, 113

Tillotson, Kathleen, 10, 17, 54, 64, 66, 117 n, 140, 166 n, 191 n, 193 n

Tippins, Lady (in *Our Mutual Friend*), 289–90, 302

Todgers, Mrs. (in *Martin Chuzzlewit*), 99, 102, 103

Todgers's (Commercial Boarding House) (in *Martin Chuzzlewit*), 86, 92, 94, 96

Tolstoy, 13

Tom (Pinch) (in *Martin Chuzzlewit*), 86, 91, 95, 96, 97, 108

Tom-all-Alone's (in *Bleak House*), 65, 167, *170–2*, 174, 175, 176, 177, 180, 185, 189, 231

Toodle (in *Dombey and Son*), 125, 126, 148

Toots (in *Dombey and Son*), 125, 154

Tox, Miss (in *Dombey and Son*), 120, 131, 135, 148

Trabb's Boy (in *Great Expectations*), 250

Trask, Willard, 40 n

Treasury (in *Little Dorrit*), 215, 216

Trevelyan, George Macaulay, 58

Trilling, Lionel, 226, 278

Tulkinghorn, Mr. (in *Bleak House*), 159, 163, 165, 166, 186

Tupman (in *Pickwick Papers*), 30–2, 45

Turveydrop, Mr. (in *Bleak House*), 158, 164, 165, 179

Turveydrop, Prince (in *Bleak House*), 187

Twemlow, Mr. (in *Our Mutual Friend*), 289, 300

Van Ghent, Dorothy, 85, 92, 94–5

Veneering, Mr. (in *Our Mutual Friend*), 275, 276, 285, 286–7, 289, 290, 300, 301, 302

Veneering, Mrs. (in *Our Mutual Friend*), 275, 286–7, 290, 302

Venus, Mr. (in *Our Mutual Friend*), 278, 283, *288–90*, 330

Vholes, Mr. (in *Bleak House*), 157 n, 162, 165, 178, 179, 180

victims and victimization,
in *Pickwick Papers*, 41–2, 46–8
in *Oliver Twist*, 55, 66, 75
in *Martin Chuzzlewit*, 97
in *Dombey and Son*, 136, 141
in *Bleak House*, 175, 184–5
in *Little Dorrit*, 230
in *Great Expectations*, 249–50, 255
in *Our Mutual Friend*, 274, 291

Volumnia, Miss (in *Bleak House*), 164

Wade, Miss (in *Little Dorrit*), 192, *225–8*

Wain, John, 196, 201 n

'Walk in a Workhouse, A', 58–9

Walter (Gay) (in *Dombey and Son*), 117, 137, 138, 153, 154, 235

Wardle, Mr. (in *Pickwick Papers*), 45

Wardle, Mrs. (in *Pickwick Papers*), 44

Watson, Hon. Richard, 281 n

Weevle, Mr. (Tony Jobling) (in *Bleak House*), 180

Wegg, Silas (in *Our Mutual Friend*), 275, 279–80, 285, 289, 330, 334, 335

Weller, Mr. (Tony) (in *Pickwick Papers*), 39, 42, 46

Weller, Mrs. (in *Pickwick Papers*), 44

Welsh, Alexander, 21, 35

Wemmick, Mr. (in *Great Expectations*), 240, 251, 264 n

Wemmick, Mr. (the Aged P.) (in *Great Expectations*), 240

Westlock, John (in *Martin Chuzzlewit*), 85, 86, 100, 103, 121, 153, 235

Wilfer, Mr. (in *Our Mutual Friend*), 279, 320, 321

Williamson, Colin, 70

Wilson, Angus, 72 n, 311

Wilson, Edmund, 14, 41–2, 47, 77, 176, 237 n

Wimsatt, W. K., 79

Winkle, Mr. (in *Pickwick Papers*), 37, 43, 44, 45

Witherfield, Miss (in *Pickwick Papers*), 17, 19, 25, 27, 44

Withers (in *Dombey and Son*), 130

Woodcourt, Allan (in *Bleak House*), 173, 180, 187, 190, 241

Wopsle, Mr. (in *Great Expectations*), 250

Wordsworth, 136

Young Martin (Chuzzlewit) (in *Martin Chuzzlewit*), 80, 82, 83, 84, 87, 88, 89, 97, 101, 106, 107, *109–11*, 114

Zabel, Morton Dauwen, 157 n